Duxbury

Student S

for the

International Student Edition of

Statistics for Management and Economics

Seventh Edition

Gerald Keller
Wilfrid Laurier University

THOMSON
BROOKS/COLE

Australia • Canada • Mexico • Singapore • Spain • United Kingdom • United States

Printed in Canada
1 2 3 4 5 6 7 09 08 07 06 05

Printer: Webcom Limited

0-495-01340-4

For more information about our products, contact us at:
Thomson Learning Academic Resource Center
1-800-423-0563

For permission to use material from this text or product, submit a request online at **http://www.thomsonrights.com.**
Any additional questions about permissions can be submitted by email to **thomsonrights@thomson.com.**

Thomson Higher Education
10 Davis Drive
Belmont, CA 94002-3098
USA

Asia (including India)
Thomson Learning
5 Shenton Way
#01-01 UIC Building
Singapore 068808

Australia/New Zealand
Thomson Learning Australia
102 Dodds Street
Southbank, Victoria 3006
Australia

Canada
Thomson Nelson
1120 Birchmount Road
Toronto, Ontario M1K 5G4
Canada

UK/Europe/Middle East/Africa
Thomson Learning
High Holborn House
50–51 Bedford Road
London WC1R 4LR
United Kingdom

Latin America
Thomson Learning
Seneca, 53
Colonia Polanco
11560 Mexico
D.F. Mexico

Spain (including Portugal)
Thomson Paraninfo
Calle Magallanes, 25
28015 Madrid, Spain

TABLE OF CONTENTS

How the Solutions Were Produced	1
Chapter 1: What is Statistics?	3
Chapter 2: Graphical Descriptive and Tabular Techniques	5
Chapter 3: Art and Science of Graphical Presentations	39
Chapter 4: Numerical Descriptive Techniques	49
Chapter 5: Data Collection and Sampling	71
Chapter 6: Probability	73
Chapter 7: Random Variables and Discrete Probability Distributions	87
Chapter 8: Continuous Probability Distributions	101
Chapter 9: Sampling Distributions	109
Chapter 10: Introduction to Estimation	115
Chapter 11: Introduction to Hypothesis Testing	119
Chapter 12: Inference about One Population	131
Chapter 13: Inference about Two Populations	147
Chapter 14: Review of Chapters 12 and 13	171
Chapter 15: Analysis of Variance	187
Chapter 16: Chi-Squared Tests	211
Chapter 17 Simple Linear Regression	229
Chapter 18: Multiple Regression	255
Chapter 19: Model Building	277
Chapter 20 Time-Series Analysis and Forecasting	299
Chapter 21: Nonparametric Statistical Techniques	309
Chapter 22 Statistical Process Control	333
Chapter 23: Decision Analysis	351
Chapter 24: Statistical Inference: Conclusion	365

How the Solutions Were Produced

All answers have been-double-checked for accuracy. However, we cannot be absolutely certain that there are no errors. When and if we discover mistakes we will post corrected answers on our web page. (See page 8 in the textbook for the address.) If you find any errors, please email the author (address on web page). We will be happy to acknowledge you with the discovery.

Chapter 2

Excel was employed to draw the histograms, bar charts, pie charts, line charts, and scatter diagrams.

Chapter 4

Excel was used to draw box plots and compute the descriptive statistics for exercises with data sets.

Chapters 6 through 9

Probabilities were computed manually. Probability trees were used where possible.

Chapters 10 through 19 and 21

Calculations for exercises that provided statistics either in the exercise itself or in Appendix A were completed manually. The solutions to exercises requiring the use of a computer were produced using Excel. Confidence interval estimates used critical values obtained from the tables in Appendix B. In some cases we were required to use approximations. As a consequence some confidence interval estimates will differ slightly from those produced by computer. In tests of hypothesis where the sampling distribution is normal, p-values were computed manually using Table 3. Excel was employed to calculate the p-value for all other tests.

Chapters 13, 14, and 24

We employed the F-test of two variances at the 5% significance level to decide which one of the equal-variances or unequal-variances t-test and estimator of the difference between two means to use to solve the problem. Additionally, for exercises that compare two populations and are accompanied by data files, our answers were derived by defining the sample from population 1 as the data stored in the first column (often column A in Excel and column 1 in Minitab). The data stored in the second column represent the sample from population 2. Paired differences were defined as the difference between the variable in the first column minus the variable in the second column.

Chapters 21 and 24

In the exercises whose datasets contained interval data we used a nonparametric technique after examining the relevant histograms and subjectively judging the variable to be "extremely nonnormal."

Chapters 18 and 19

Excel produced all the solutions to these exercises.

Chapter 20

Most solutions were produced manually. Excel solved the more time-consuming exercises.

Chapter 22

All control charts were produced by Excel.

Chapter 23

Solutions to these exercises were completed manually.

Chapter 1

1.2 Descriptive statistics summarizes a set of data. Inferential statistics makes inferences about populations from samples.

1.4a The complete production run

b 600 chips

c Proportion of the production run that is defective

d Proportion of sample chips that are defective (3.5%)

e Parameter

f Statistic

g Because the sample proportion is less than 5%, we can conclude that the claim is true.

1.6a Flip the coin 100 times and count the number of heads and tails

b Outcomes of flips

c Outcomes of the 100 flips

d Proportion of heads

e Proportion of heads in the 100 flips

1.8a The population consists of the fuel mileage of all the taxis in the fleet.

b The owner would like to know the mean mileage.

c The sample consists of the 50 observations.

d The statistic the owner would use is the mean of the 50 observations.

e The statistic would be used to estimate the parameter from which the owner can calculate total costs. We computed the sample mean to be 19.8 mpg.

Chapter 2

2.2 a Interval

b Nominal

c. Nominal

d Interval

e Interval

f Ordinal

2.4 a Interval

b Nominal

c Nominal

2.6 a Interval

b Interval

c Nominal

d Ordinal

2.8 a Interval

b Nominal

c Nominal

d Interval

e Ordinal

2.10 a Interval

b Interval

c Nominal

d Ordinal

e Interval

2.12a

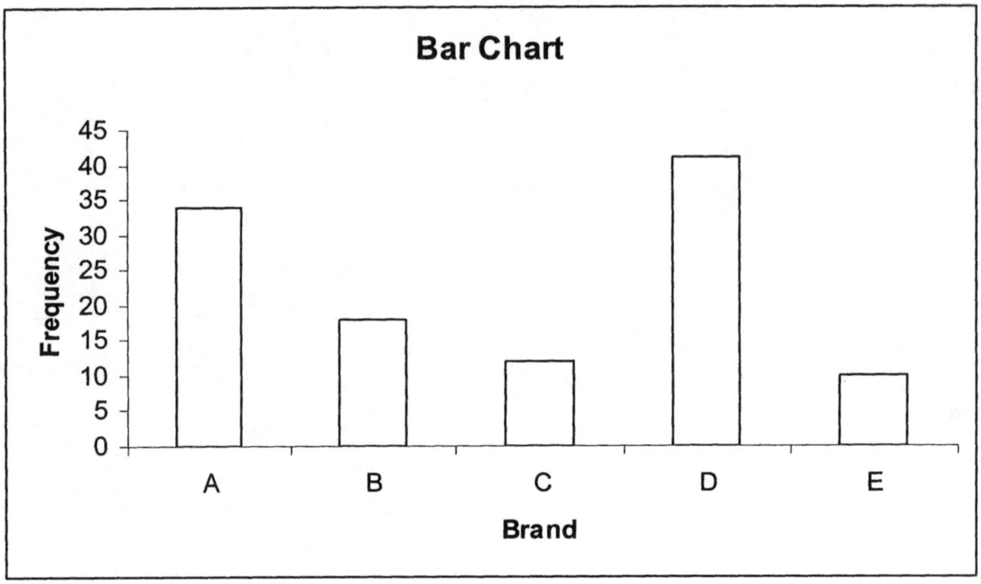

b

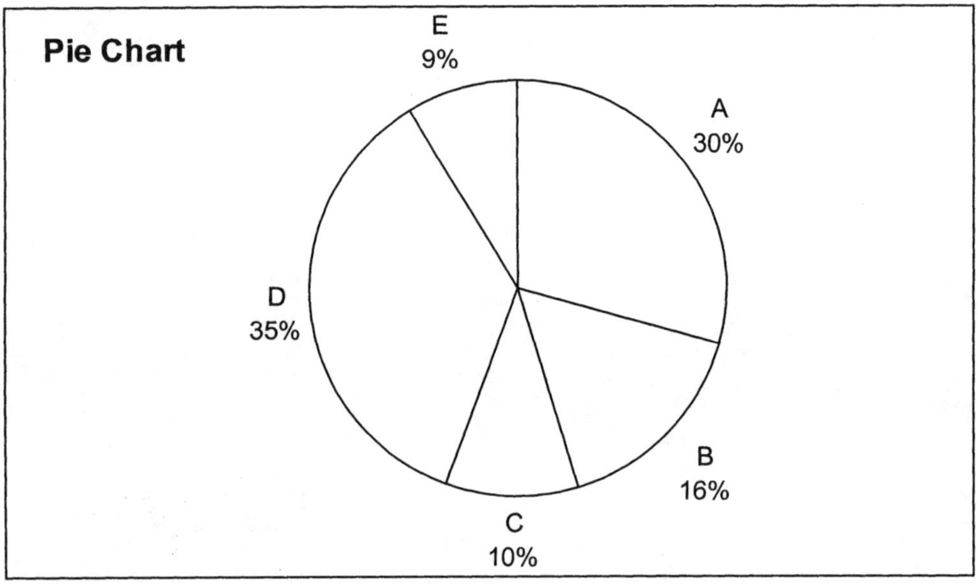

c Brands A and D are most popular, but no one brand dominates the market.

2.14

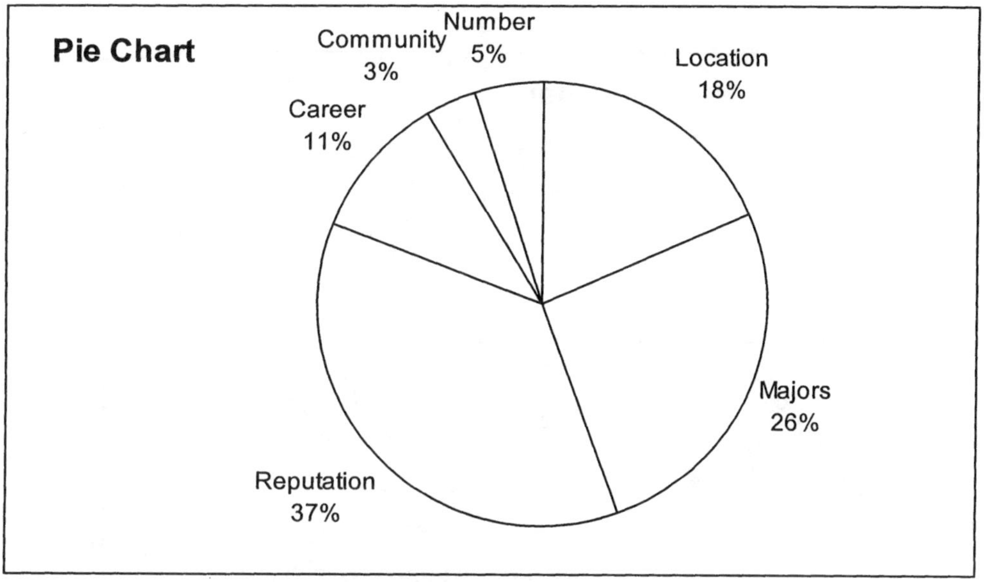

Reputation and choice of majors dominate the responses.

2.16

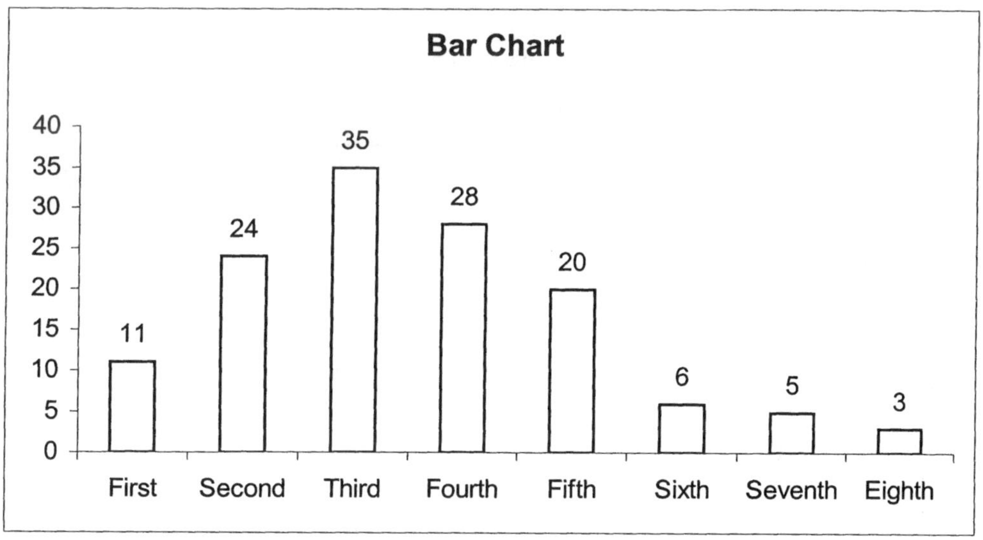

The horse has had a satisfactory career, but not outstanding one.

2.18a A bar chart is suitable for these results. A pie chart is incorrect.

b

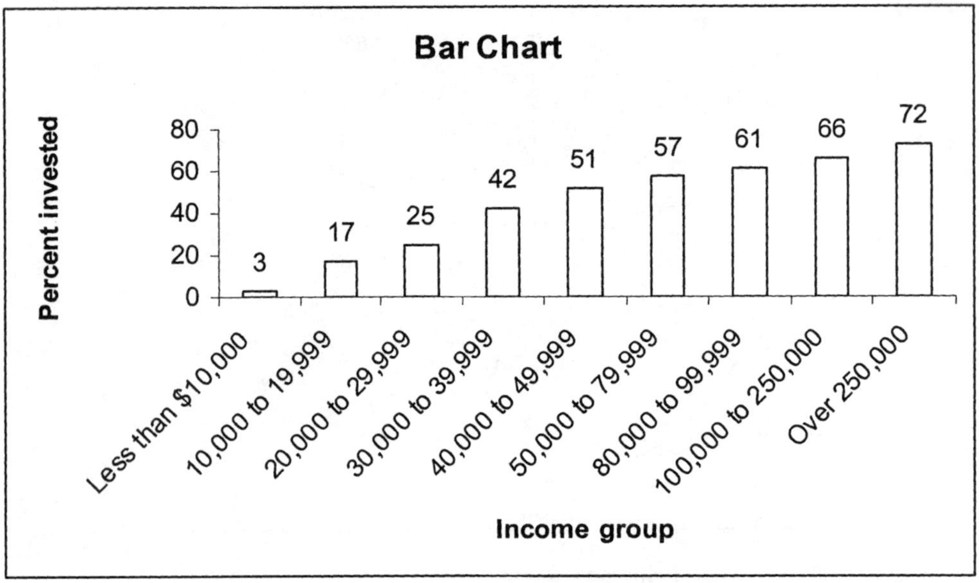

As income increases so does ownership of retirement savings plans.

2.20

We use a pie chart to depict the proportion of all firms with health insurance categorized by the size of the firm. Thus, 40% of all firms with health insurance have fewer than 10 employees.

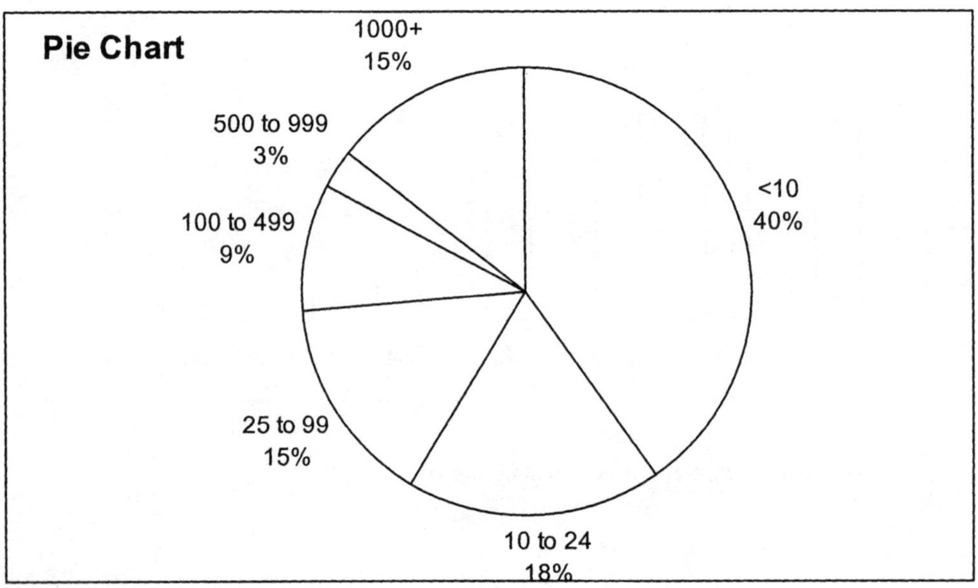

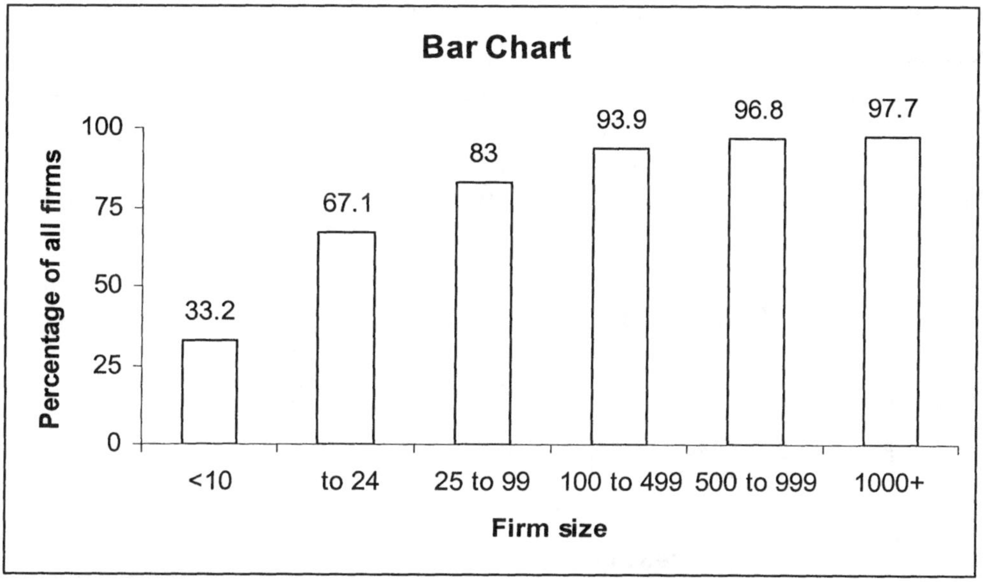

We use a bar chart to depict the proportion of firms in each size category that has health insurance. For example, 97.7% of firms with 1,000 or more employees have health insurance.

2.22

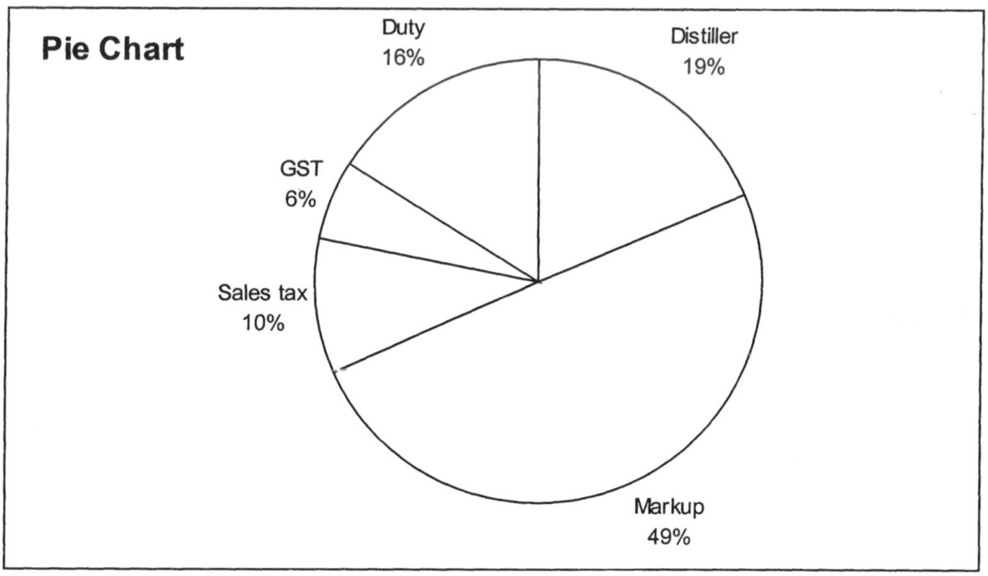

Canadians pay too much tax.

2.24 a

Reason	Frequency	Relative Frequency
Sickness	69	.66
Death in family	6	.06
Team	22	.21
Forgot	8	.08

b

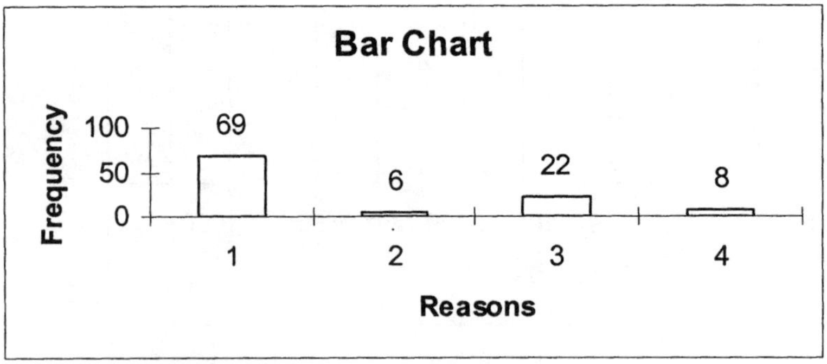

2.26

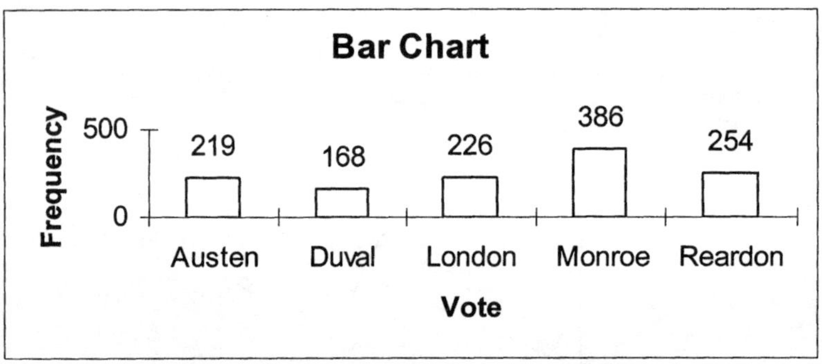

Monroe is the predicted winner in a tight race.

2.28 a

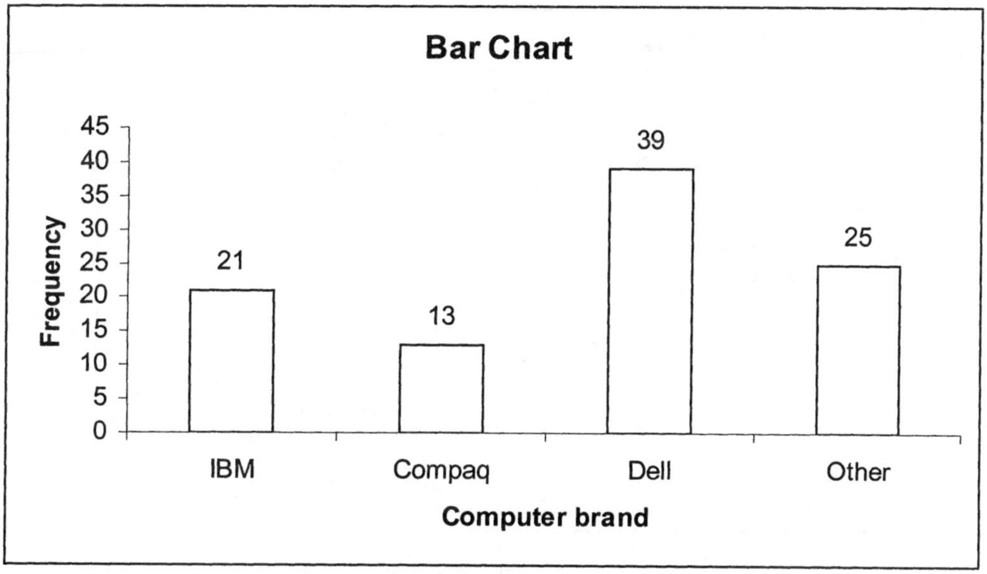

b

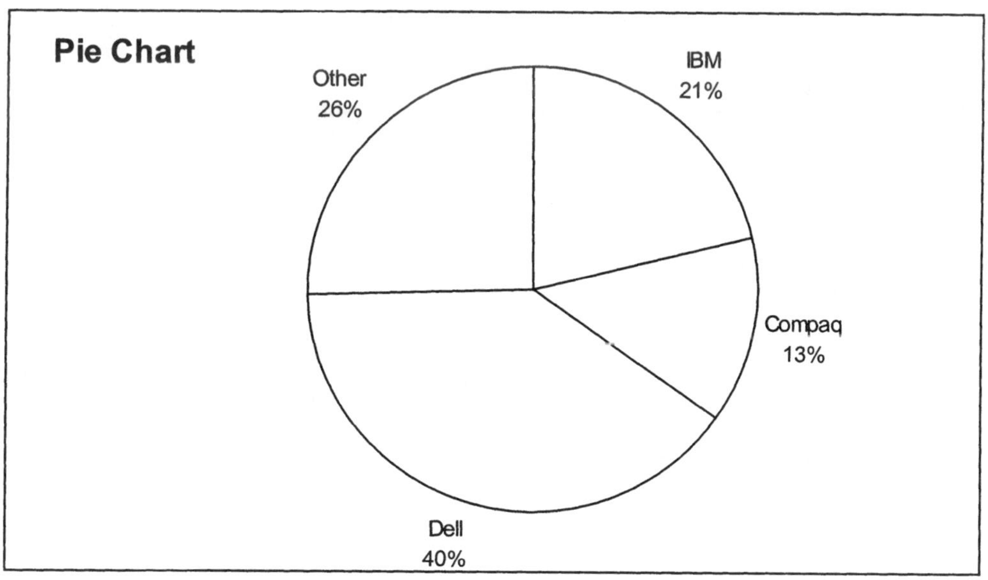

c Dell is most popular with 40% proportion, followed by other, 26%, IBM, 21% and Compaq, 13%.

2.30

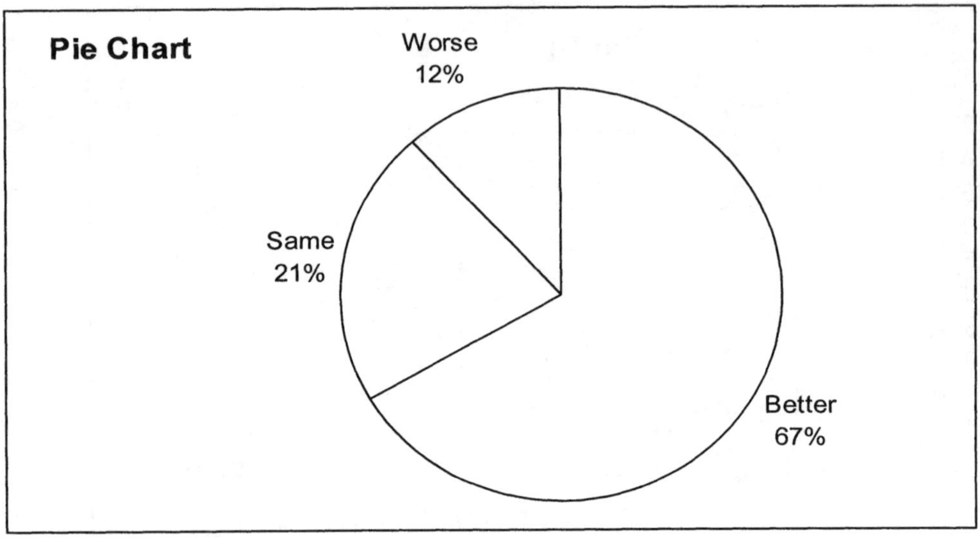

67% said the economy would get better, 21% said the same, and the rest stated that the economy would worsen.

2.32 5, 6, or 7

2.34 a 7 to 9

b Interval width $\approx \frac{560-240}{8} = 40$; upper limits: 280, 320, 360, 400, 440, 480, 520, 560

2.36 a

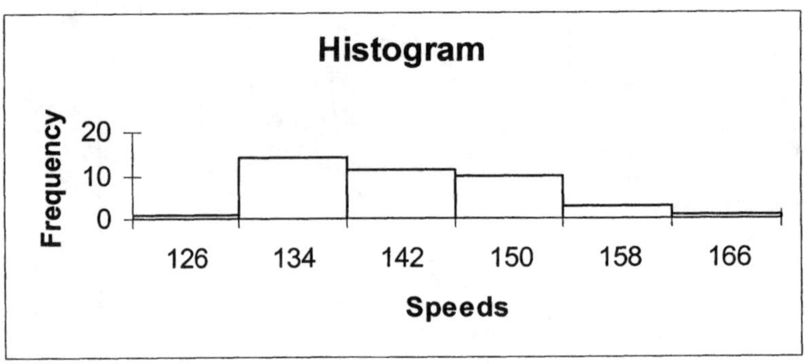

b The histogram is positively skewed.

2.38 a

	A	B	C
1	**Stem & Leaf Display**		
2			
3	**Stems**	**Leaves**	
4	19	->18	
5	20		
6	21	->178	
7	22	->1125	
8	23	->277	
9	24	->78	
10	25	->033557	
11	26	->0123333568	
12	27	->01222788	
13	28	->25578	
14	29	->3	
15	30	->12357	
16	31		
17	32		
18	33	->2	

b

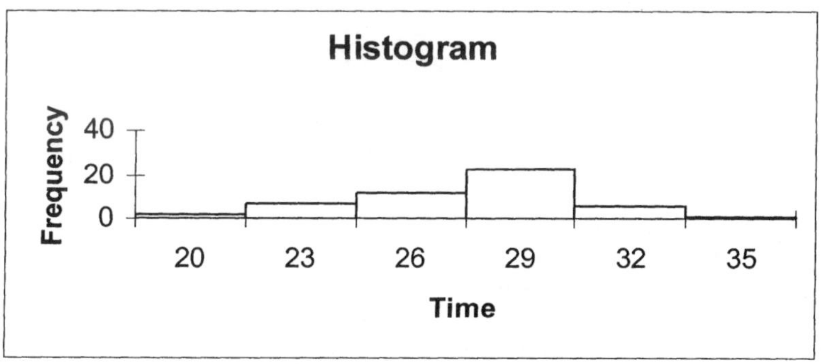

c The distribution is approximately bell shaped and slightly negatively skewed.

2.40 a

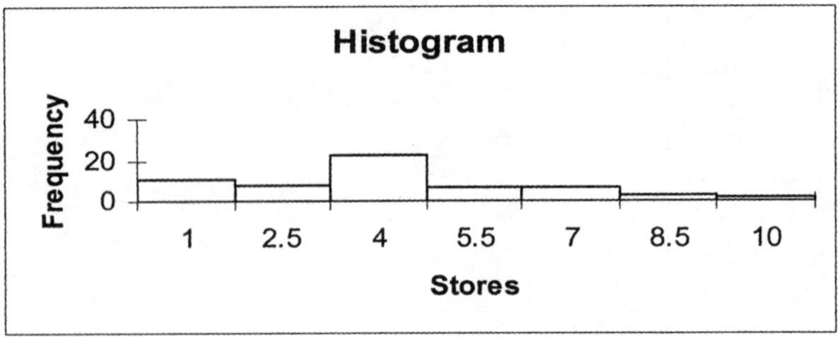

b

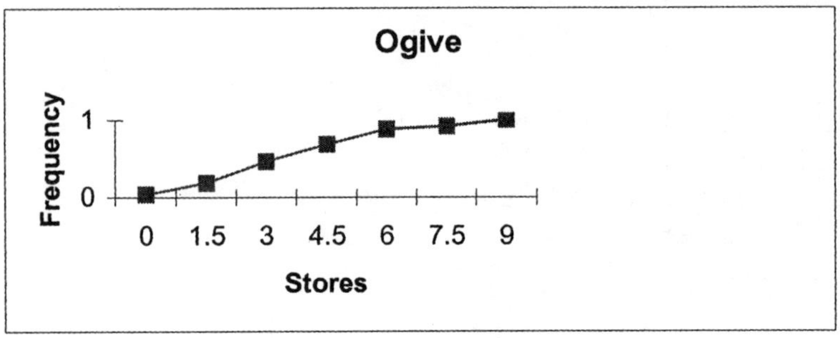

c The number of stores is bimodal and positively skewed.

2.42 a

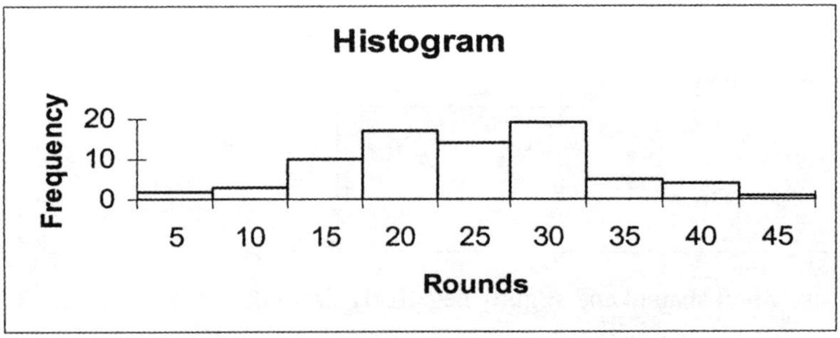

b

Stem & Leaf Display				
Stems	Leaves			
0	->359			
1	->0023334445556677888888899			
2	->00001223334444455566667888889999			
3	->00000112556668			
4	->2			

c

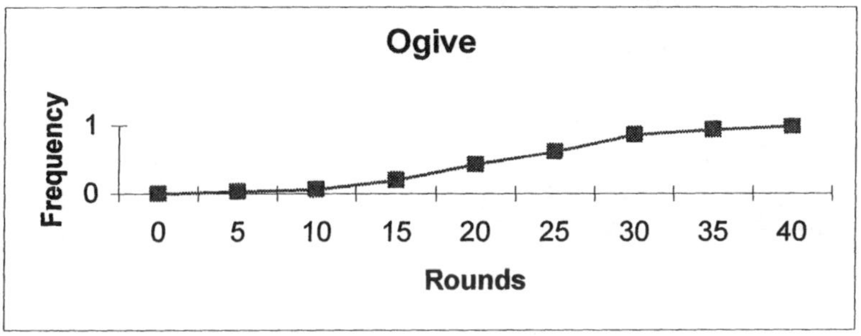

d The histogram is symmetric (approximately) and bimodal.

2.44

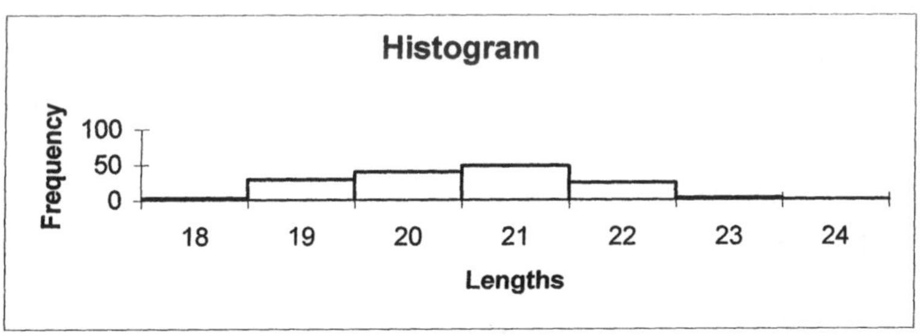

The histogram is unimodal, bell-shaped and roughly symmetric. Most of the lengths lie between 18 and 23 inches.

2.46

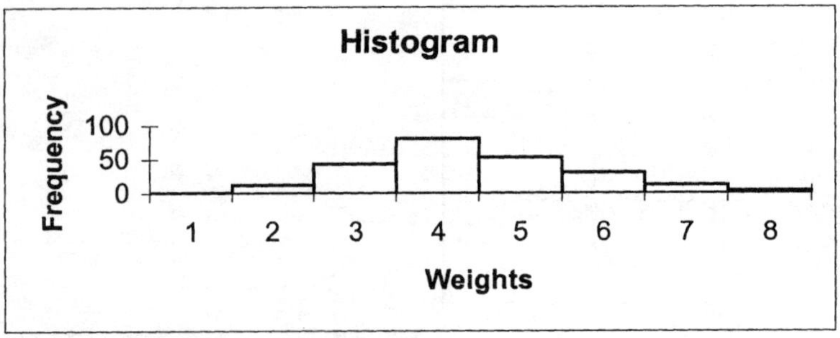

The histogram is unimodal, symmetric and bell-shaped. Most tomatoes weigh between 2 and 7 ounces with a small fraction weighing less than 2 ounces or more than 7 ounces.

2.48

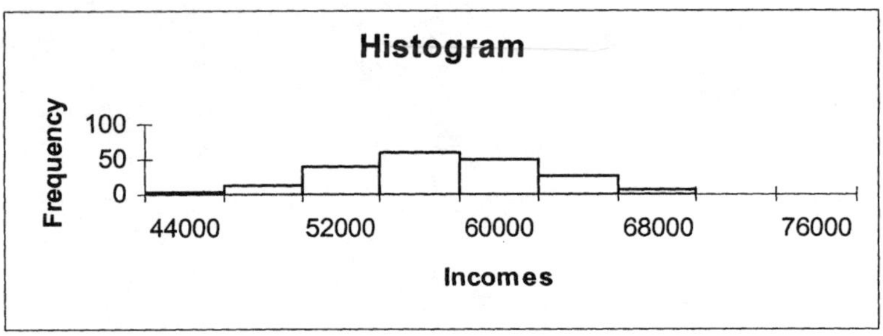

The histogram is symmetric, unimodal, and bell shaped.

2.50

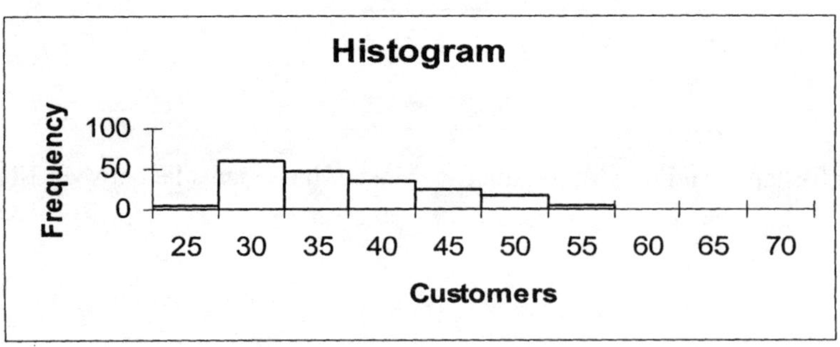

The histogram is unimodal and positively skewed.

2.52

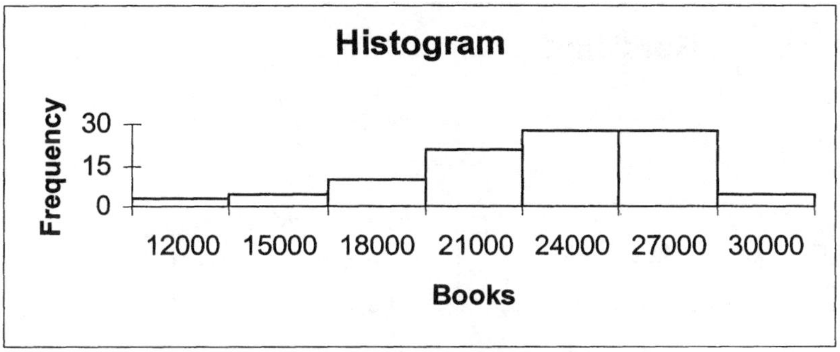

The histogram of the number of books shipped daily is negatively skewed, It appears that there is a maximum number that the company can ship.

2.54 a

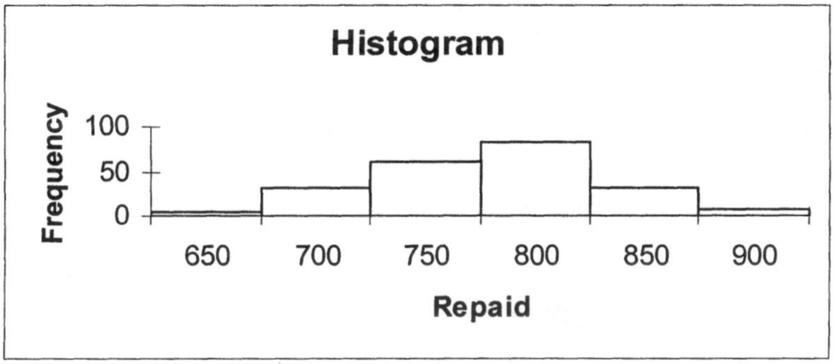

b

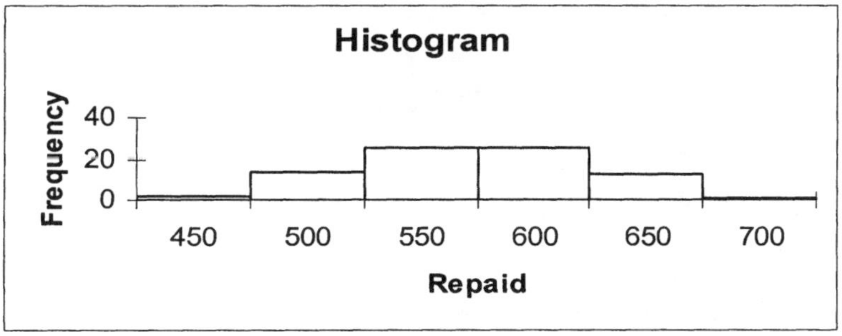

d This scorecard is a much better predictor.

2.56

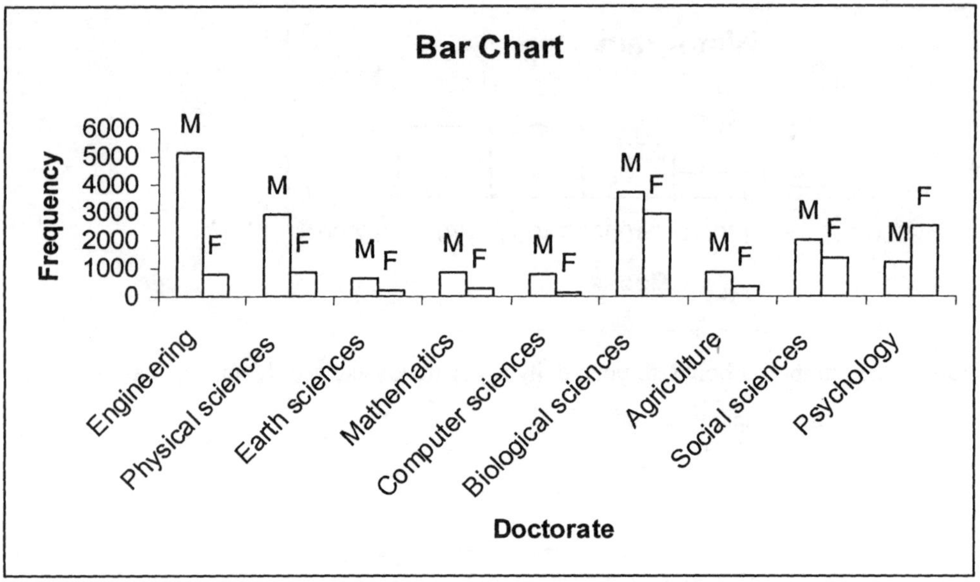

The two bar charts are somewhat dissimilar. There is a weak relationship.

2.58 a

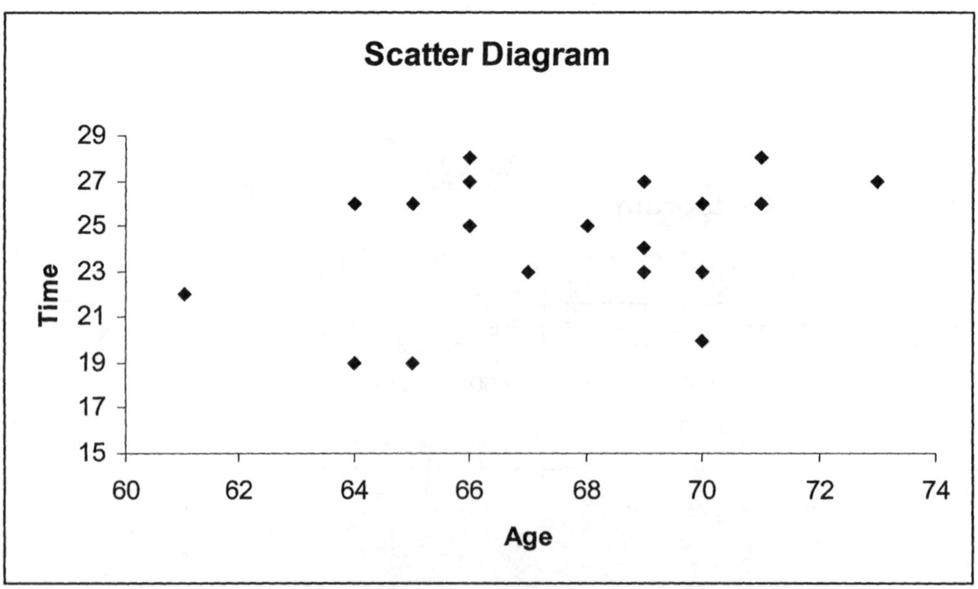

b There is a weak positive linear relationship between age and time.

2.60

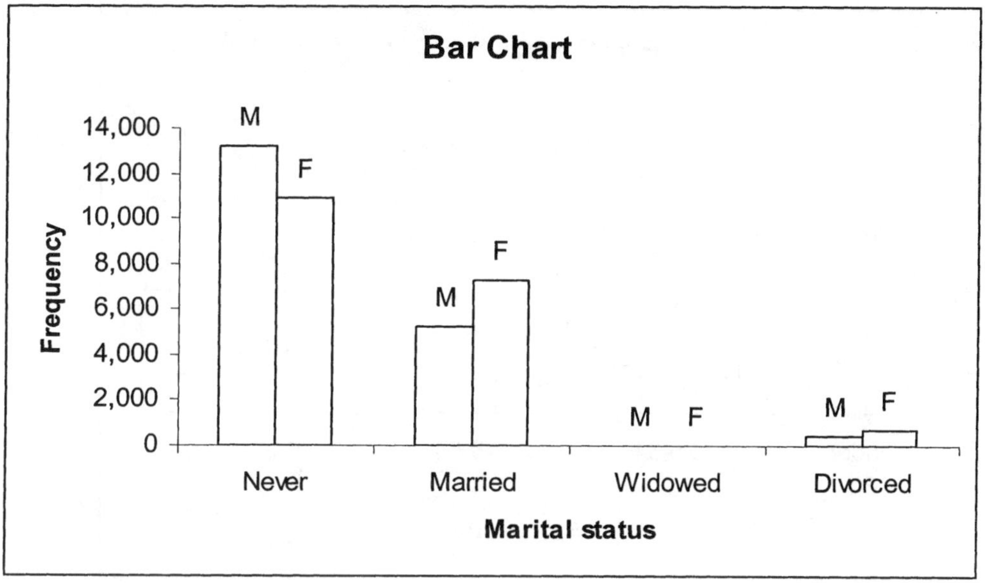

Gender and marital status are unrelated.

2.62

Age Group	Accident rate (per driver)	Fatal accident rate (per 1,000 drivers)
Under 20	.373	.643
20 – 24	.173	.352
25 – 34	.209	.305
35- 44	.162	.251
45 – 54	.133	.214
55 – 64	.108	.208
65 – 74	.095	.177
Over 74	.093	.304

b

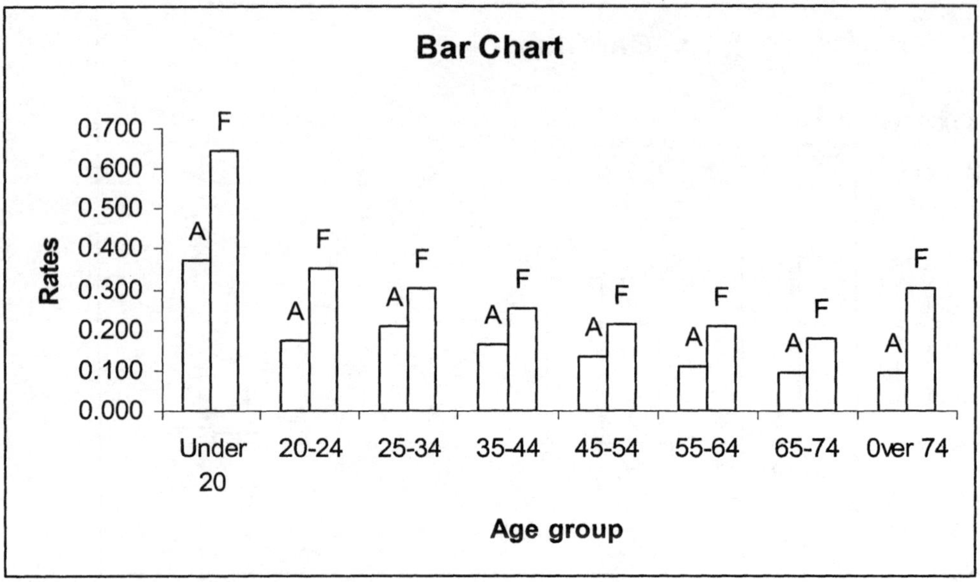

c The accident rate generally decreases as the ages increase. The fatal accident rate decreases until the over 74 age category where there is an increase. As drivers age they become less likely to be involved in an accident. As a result the fatal accident rate also decreases except for the over 74 age group. Perhaps because of other health issues older drivers are more likely than other drivers to die as a result of the accident.

2.64

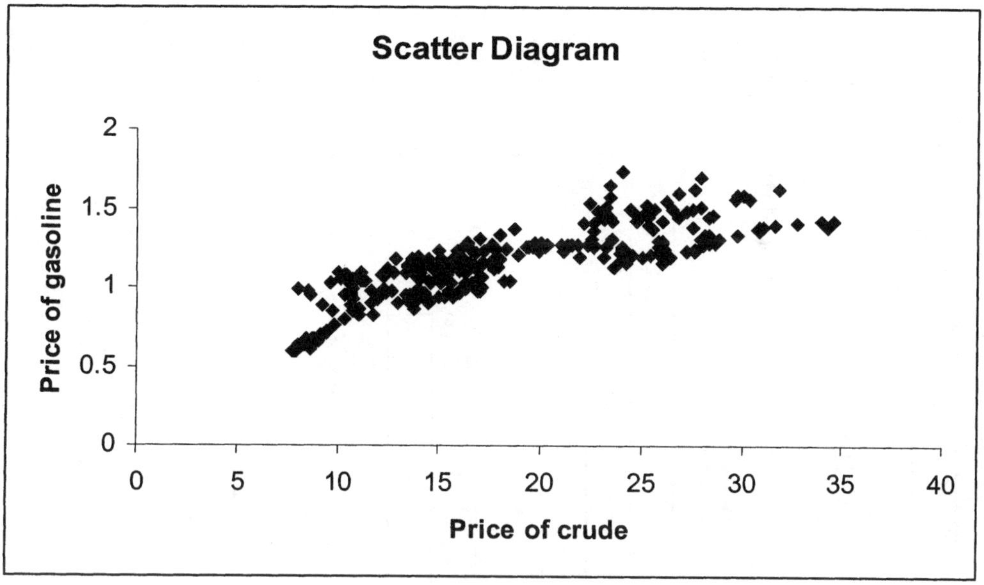

There is a strong positive linear relationship between the prices of crude oil and gasoline.

2.66a

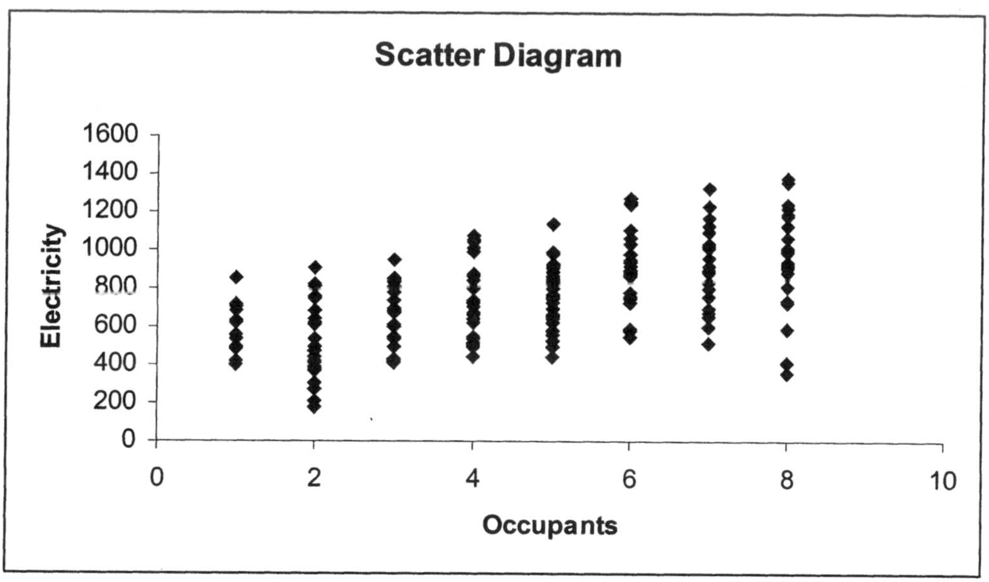

b There is moderately strong positive linear relationship between the number of occupants and electricity use.

2.68

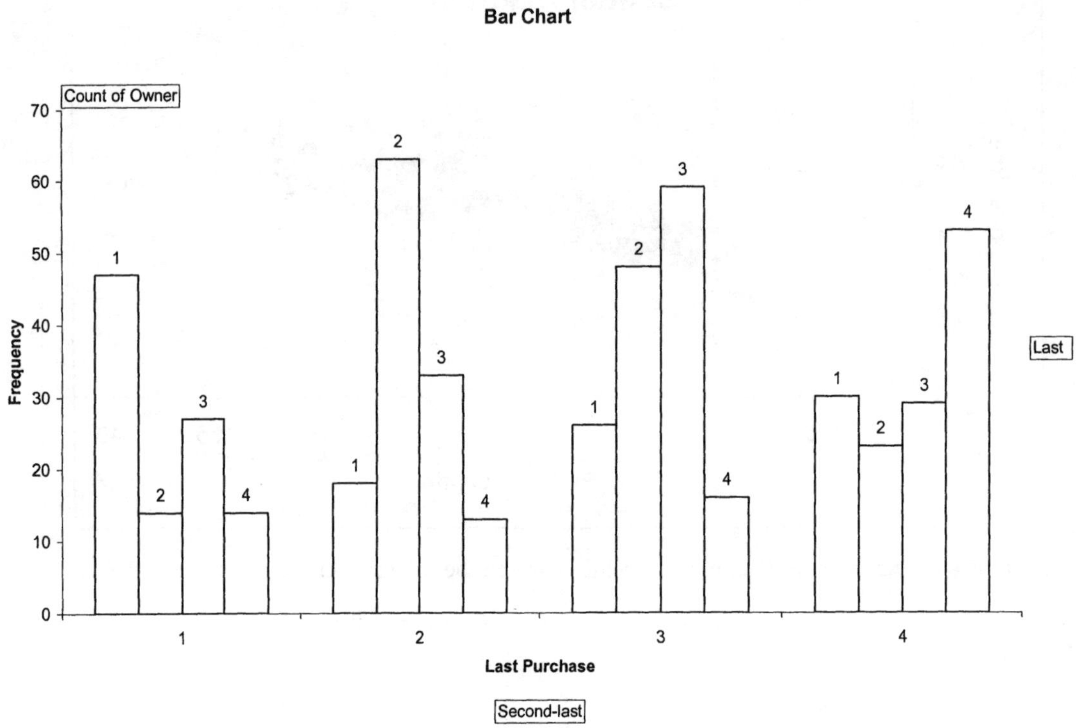

There is a relationship between the last two purchases. There is some brand loyalty.

2.70 a

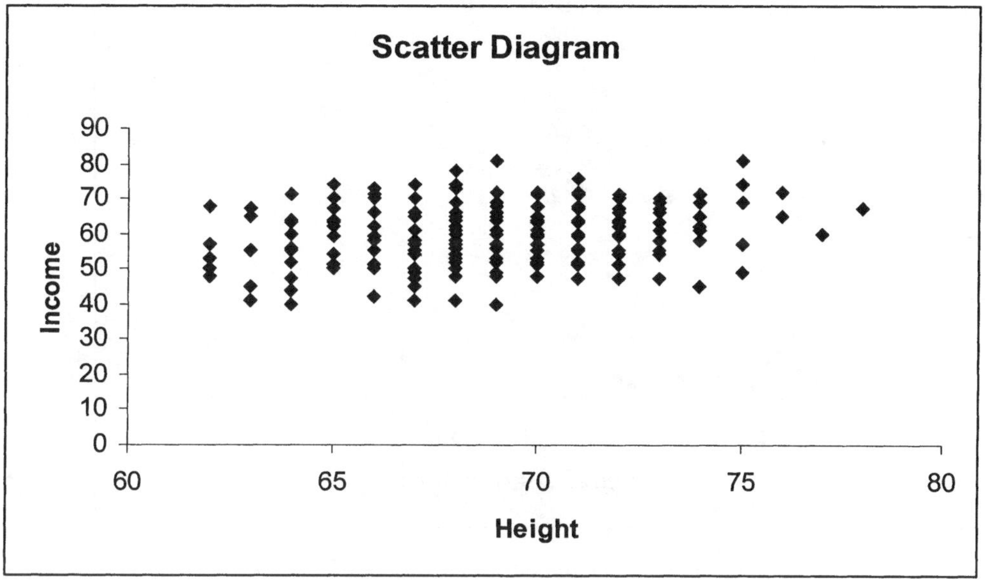

b There is a no linear relationship between the two variables.

2.72

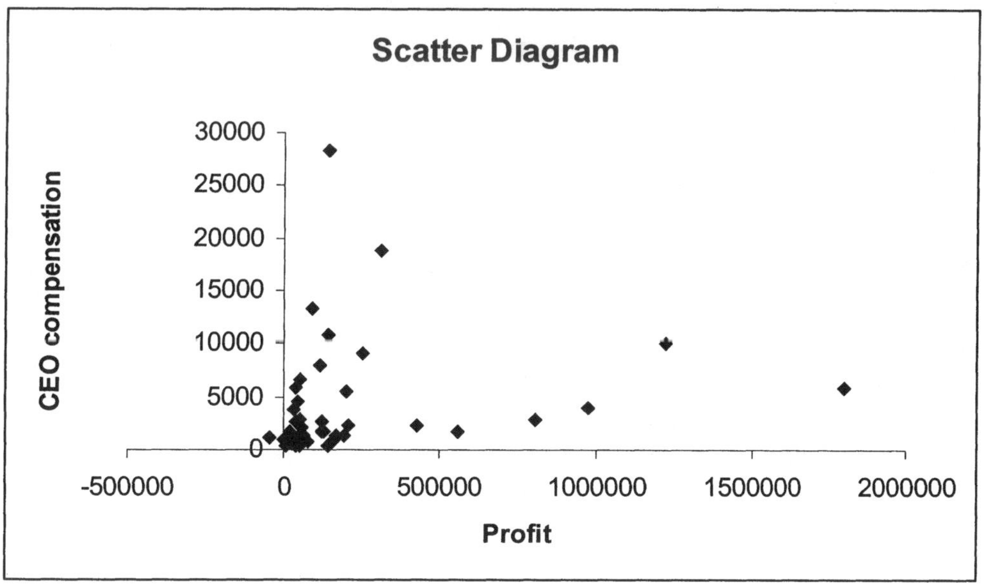

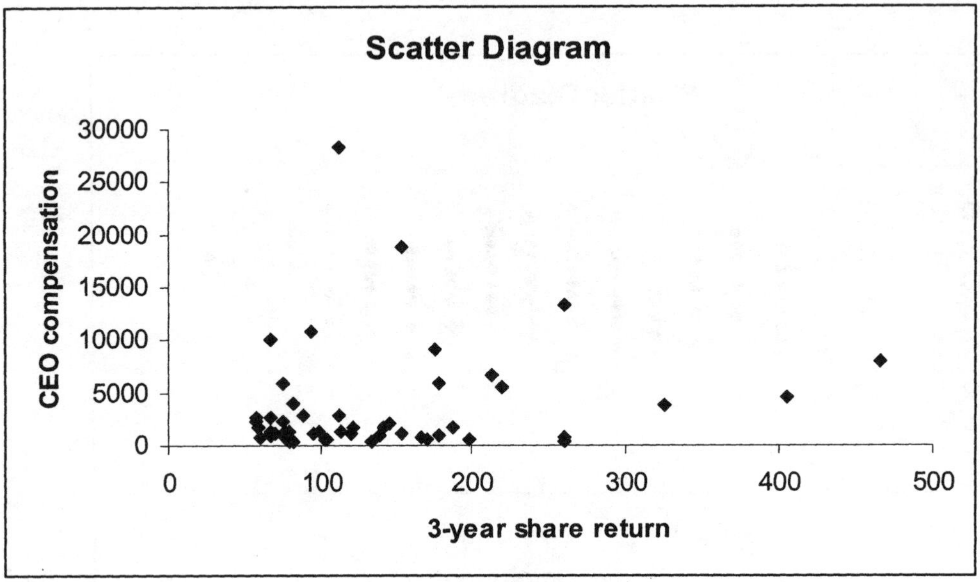

There does not appear to be a linear relationship between profit and CEO compensation or between 3-year share return and CEO compensation.

2.74

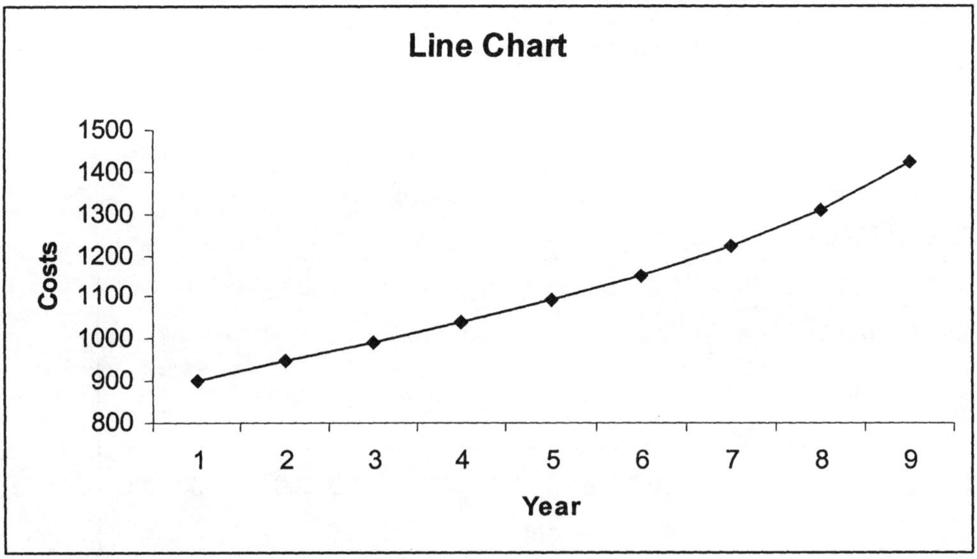

Costs have increased dramatically and appear to be accelerating.

2.76

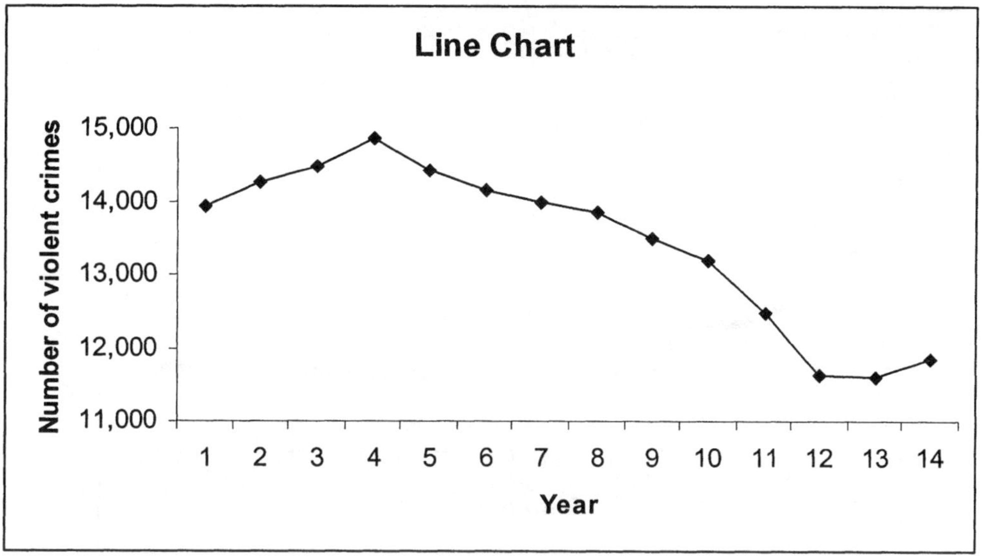

After rising for 3 years, the number of crimes has steadily decreased until year 12, where is started to rise again.

2.78

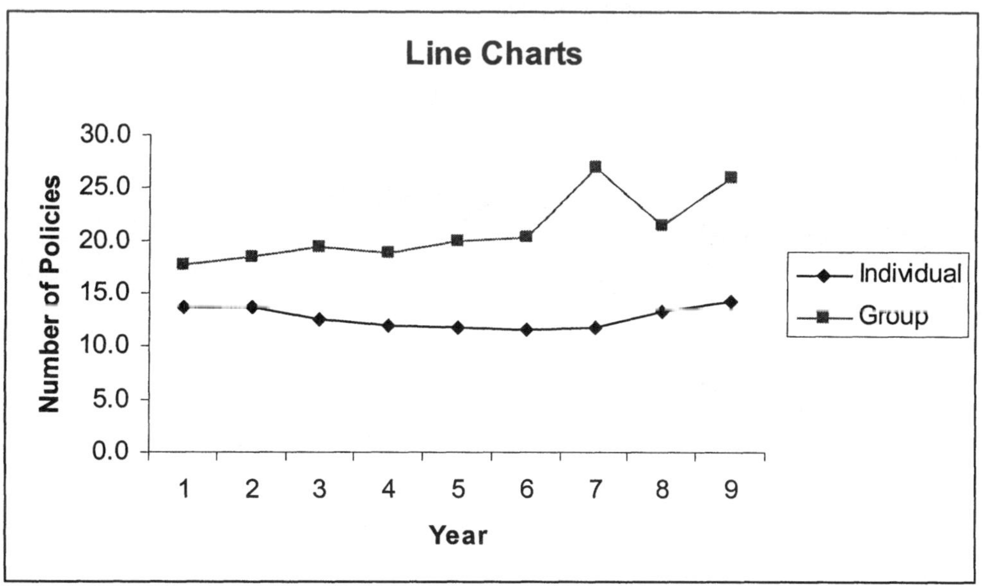

The number of individual policies has been stable while group policies are increasing.

2.80a

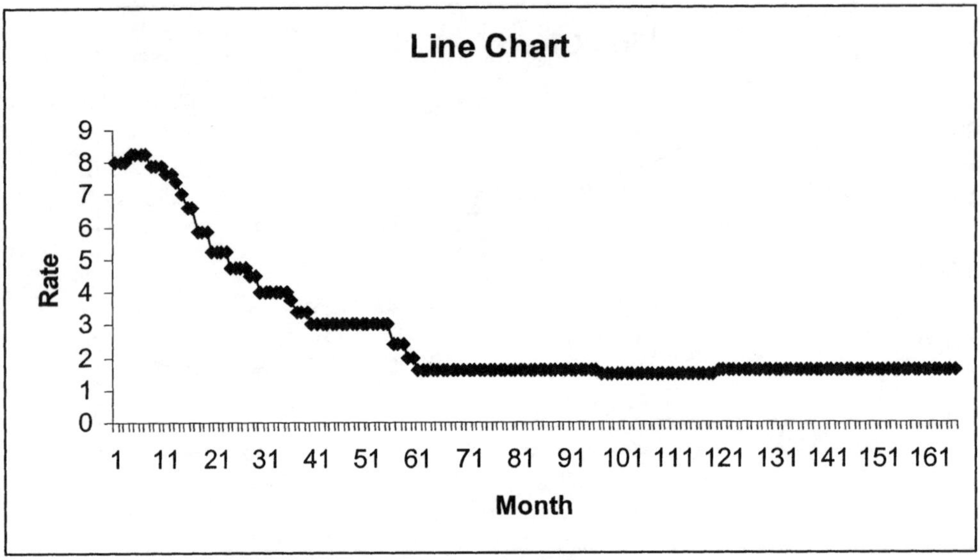

b There was a large decrease over the first half of the period, but has leveled since.

2.82a

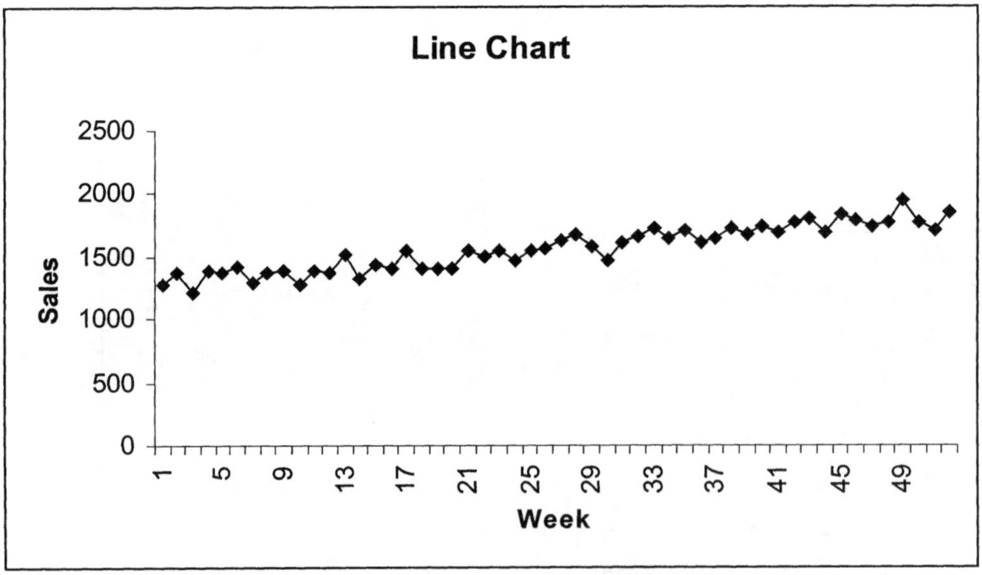

b There has been a gradual weekly increase in sales.

2.84

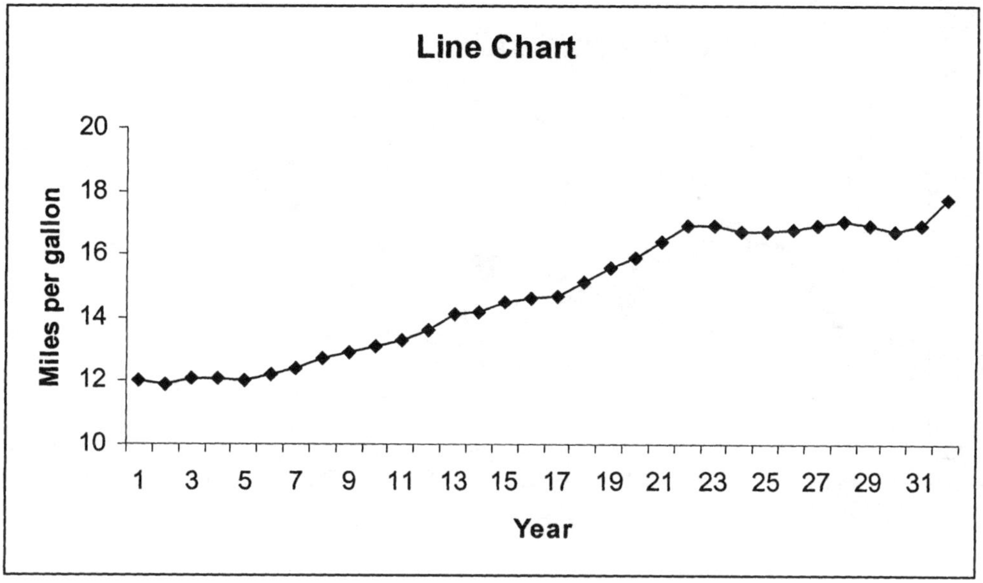

Gas mileage has steadily improved over the past 31 years.

2.86

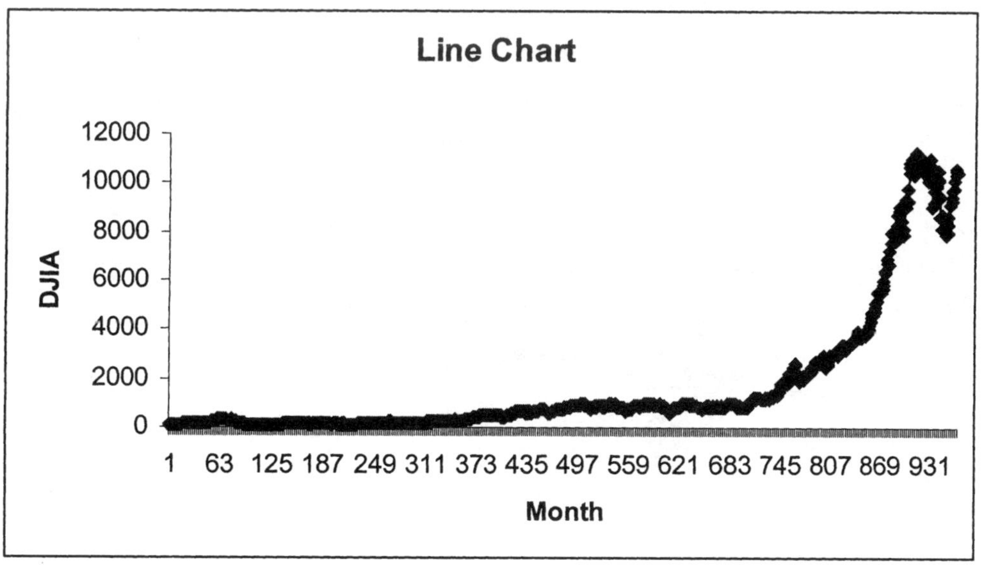

The trend until month 700 (1982) was slow but steady. Then the index grew exponentially until month 900, (1999), at which point there was a significant decrease and recovery.

2.88

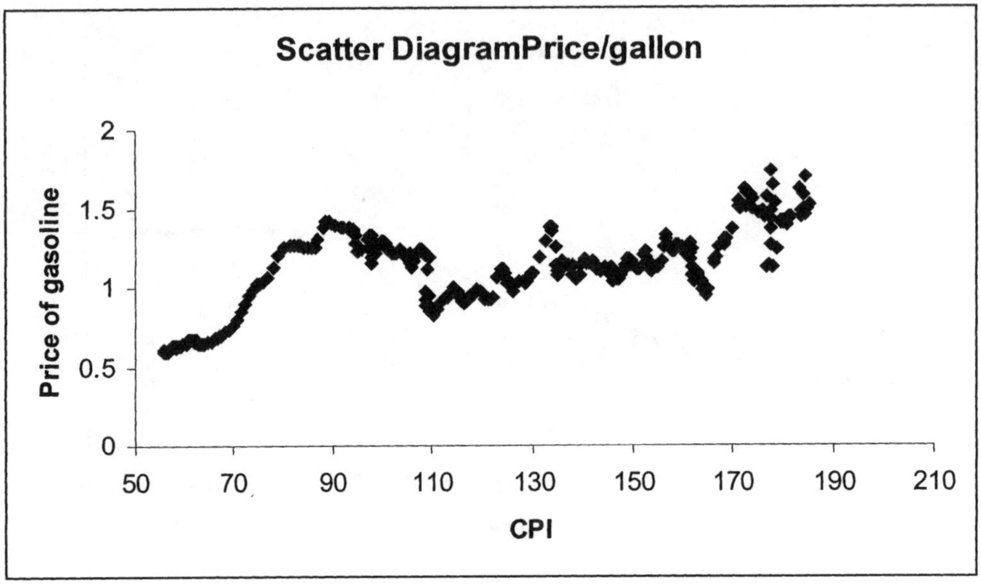

There is a moderately strong linear relationship suggesting that the some of the price increase is due to inflation.

2.90

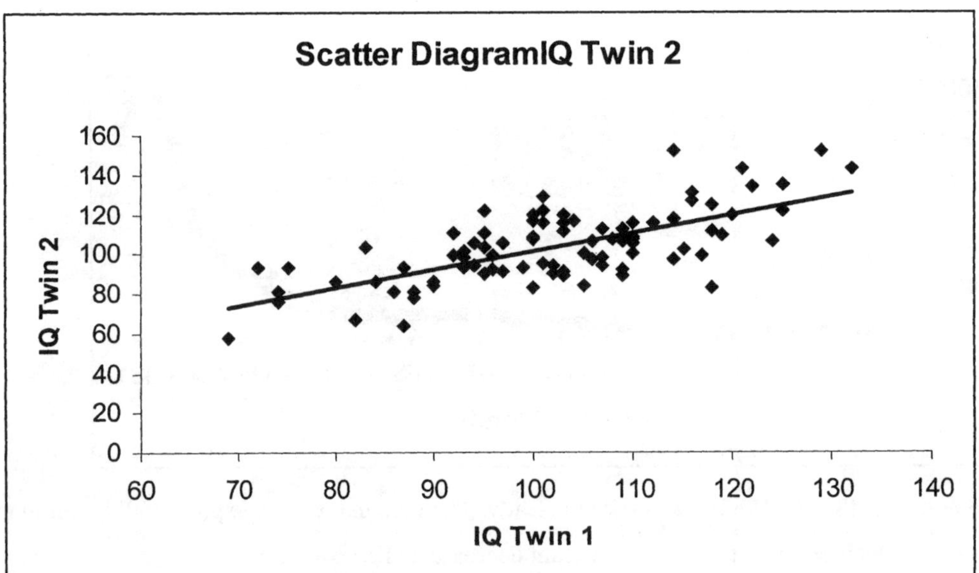

There is a moderately strong linear relationship between the IQs of twins.

2.92 Although there are year-to-year fluctuations the winning time appears to be constant.

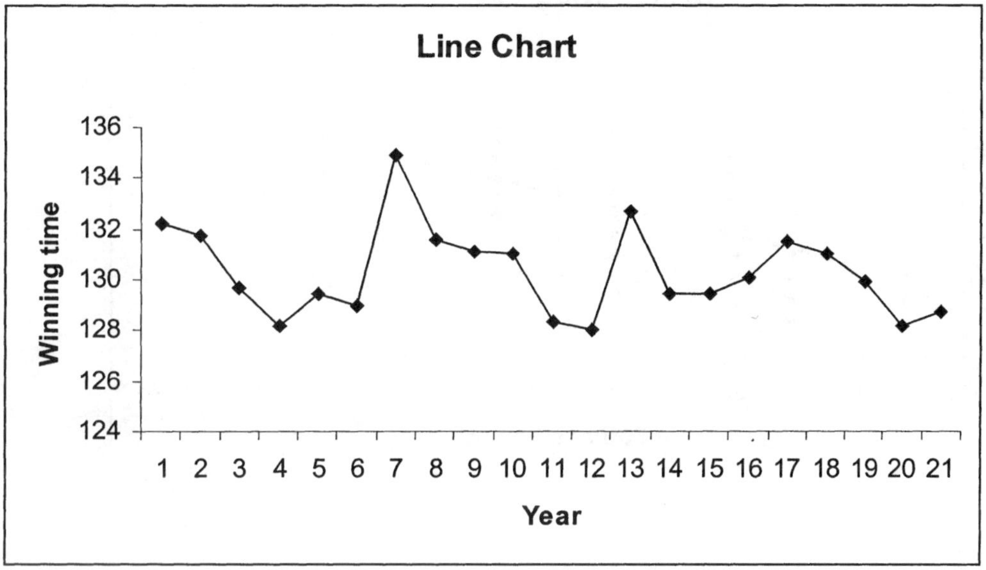

2.94

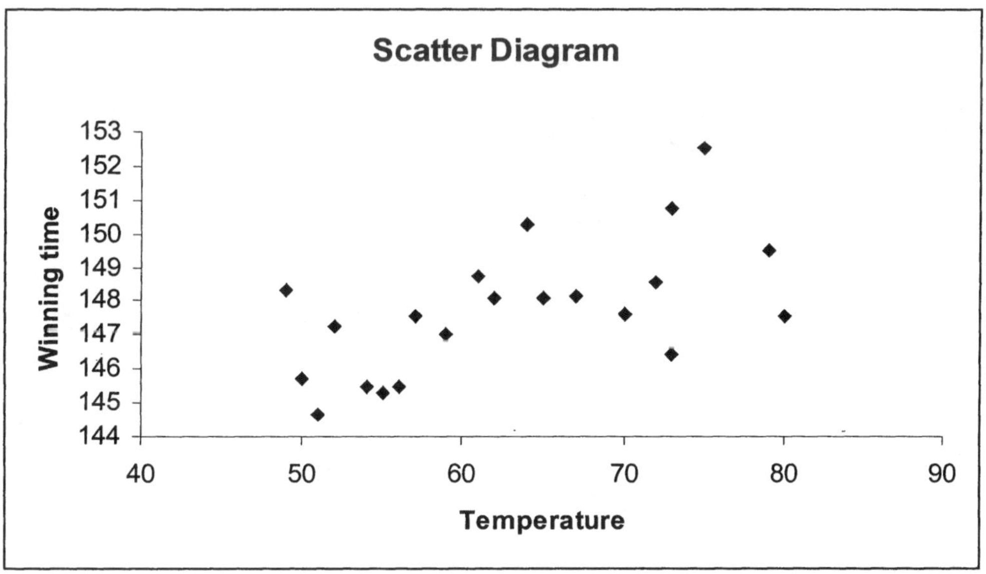

There is a moderately strong positive linear relationship between temperature and winning time.

2.96a

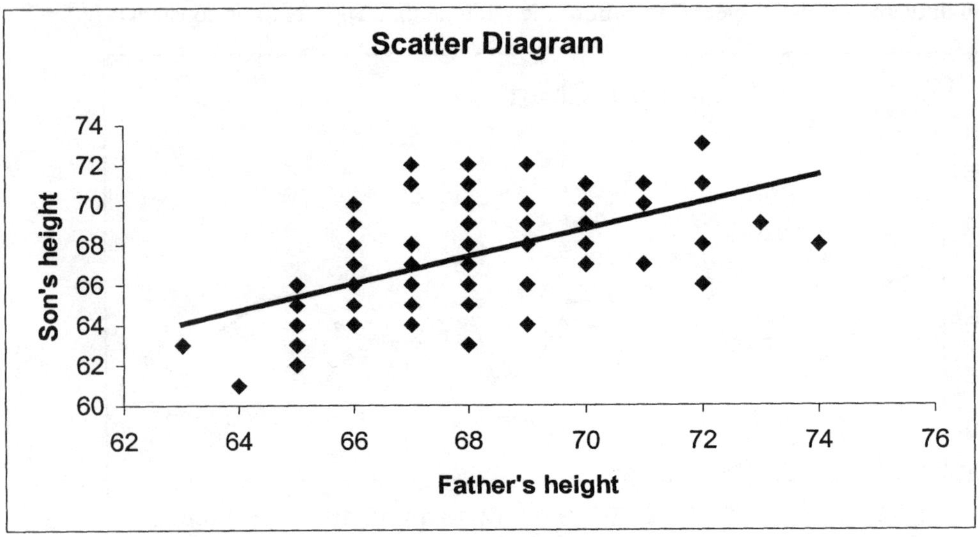

b The direction is positive.

c There does appear to be a linear relationship.

2.98 Canada

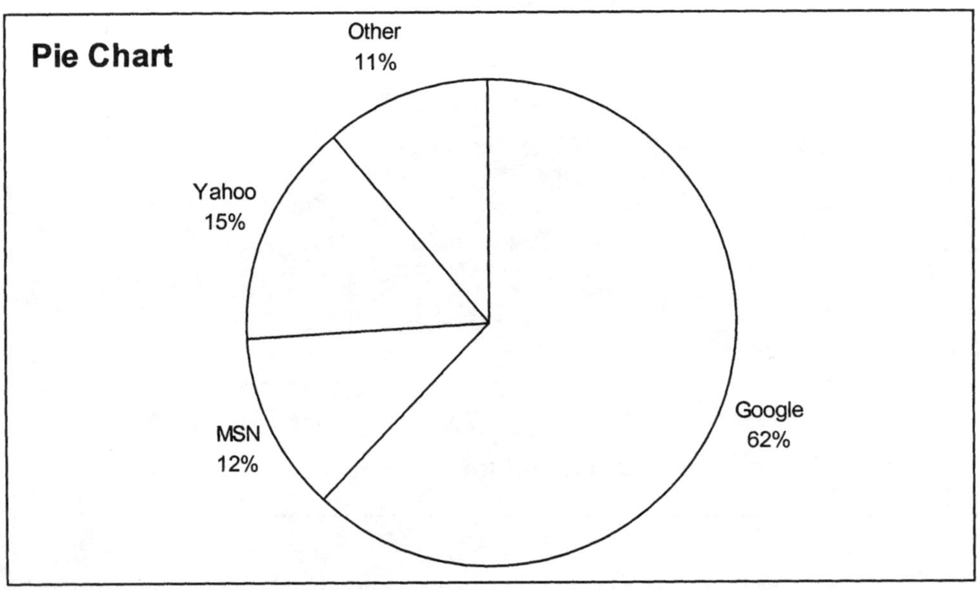

U.S.

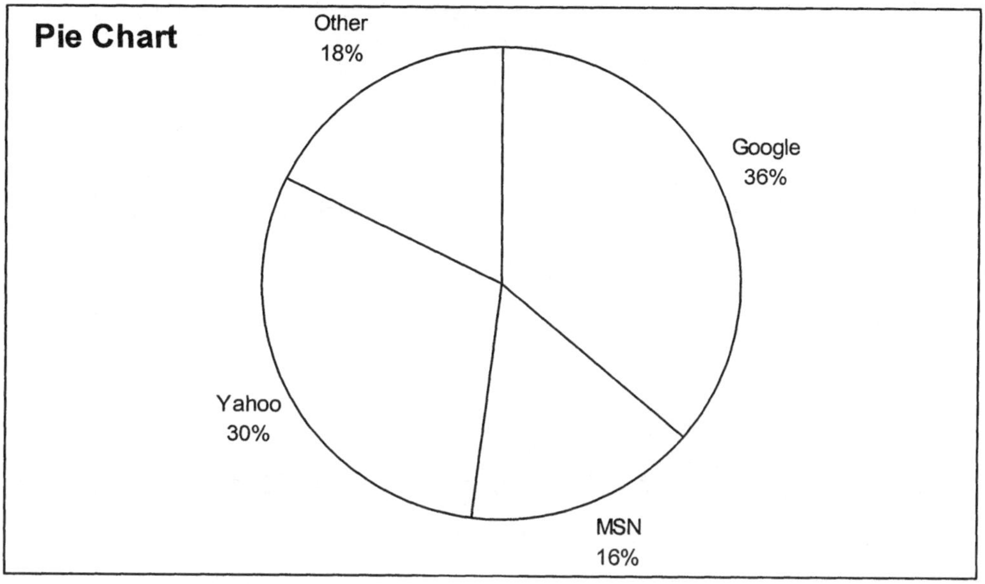

In Canada Google is the most popular by a wide margin. In the United States Google and Yahoo are the leaders.

2.100

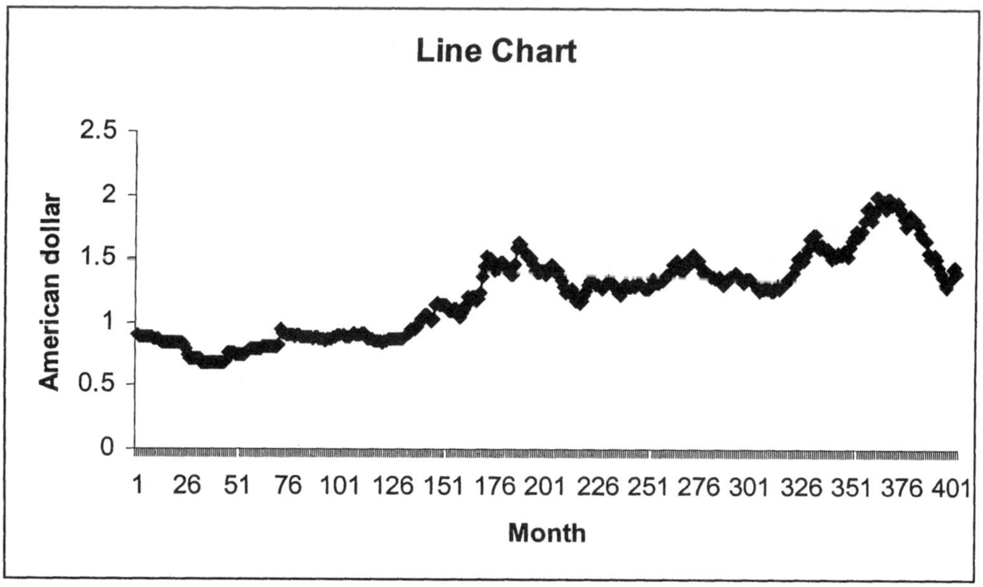

The value of the American dollar has risen over the years.

2.102

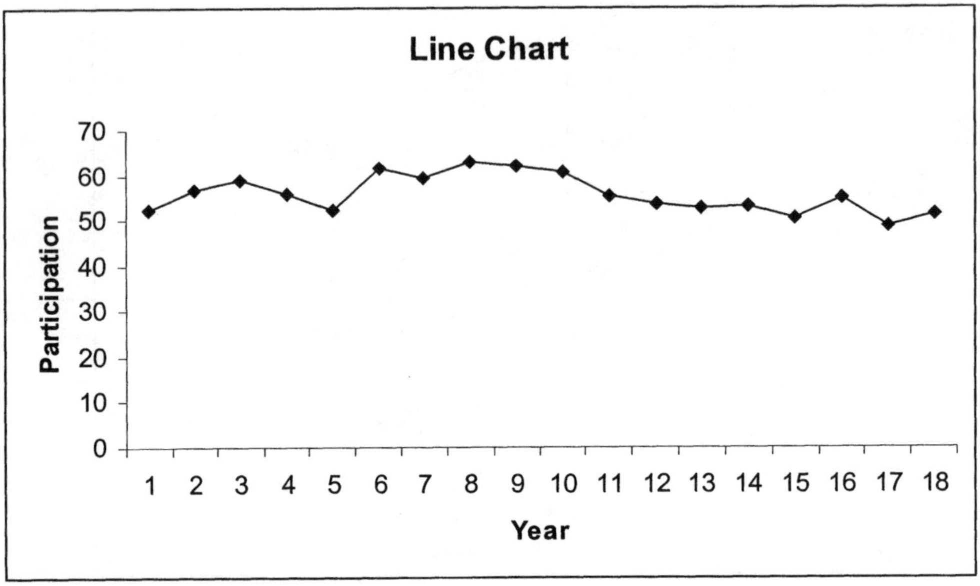

The participation rate varies between 50 and 60%.

2.104

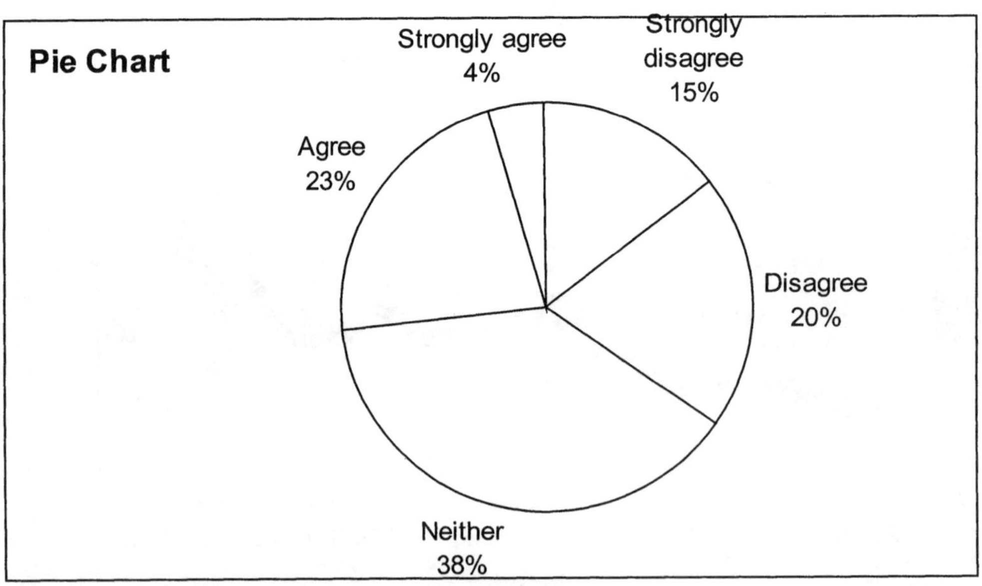

Most students would not agree.

2.106

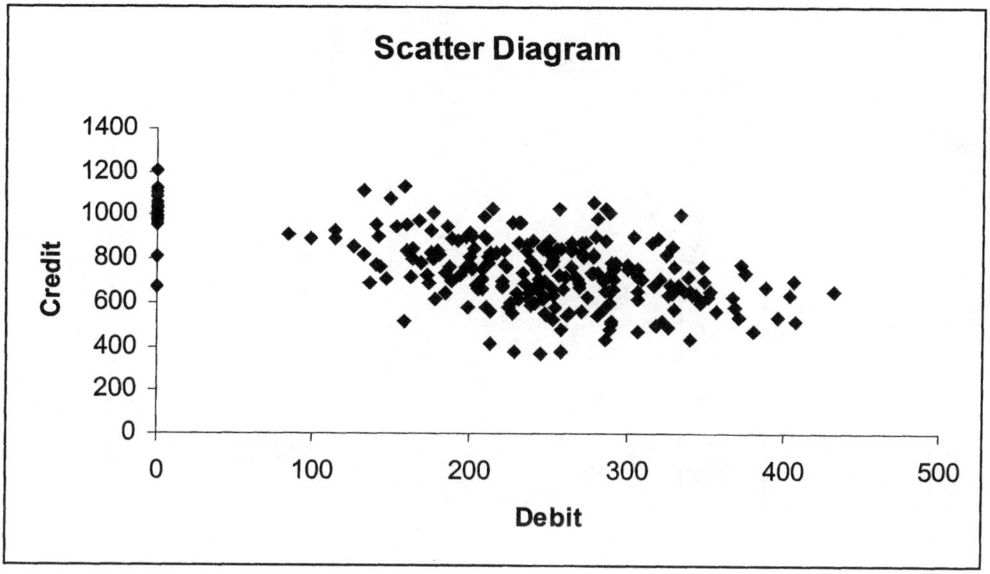

There is a moderately strong negative linear relationship.

2.108

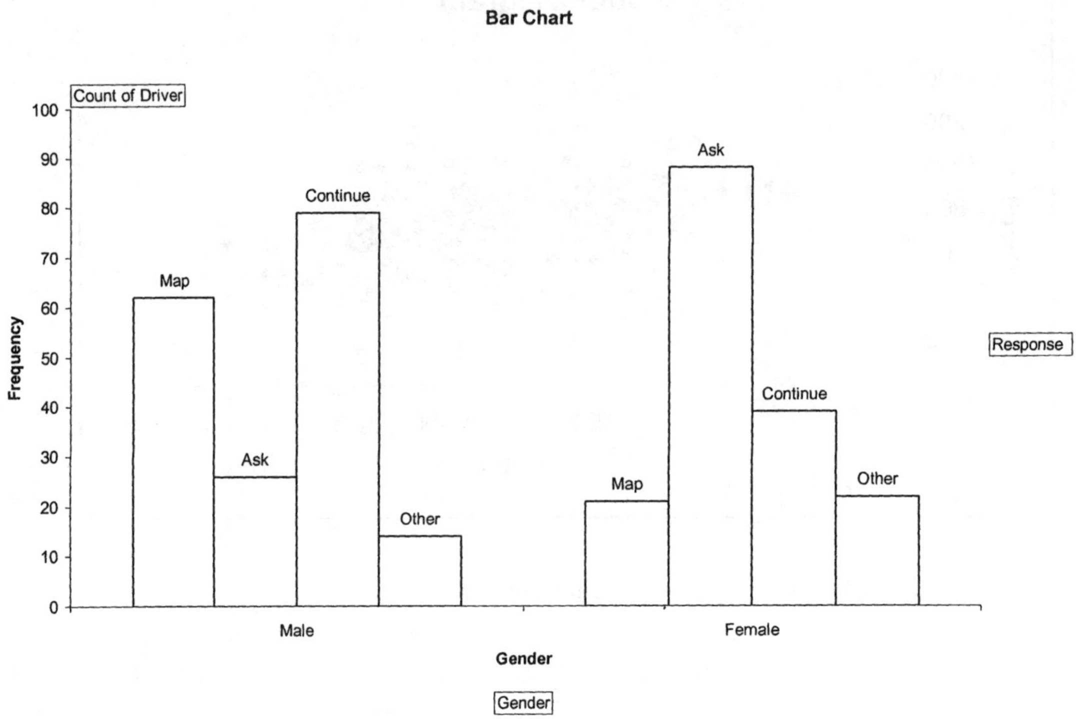

There are large differences between male and female responses. There is a strong relationship between gender and what drivers do when lost.

2.110

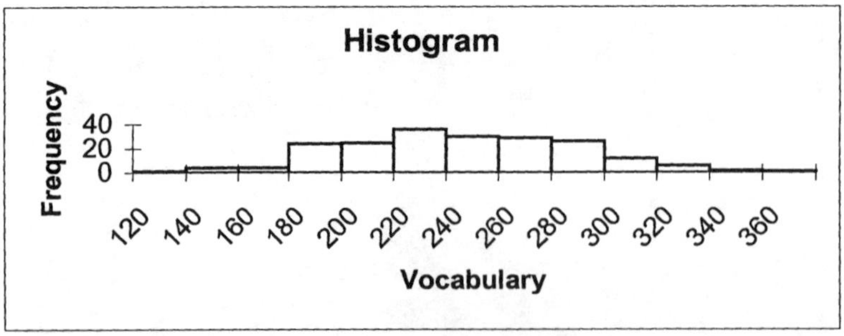

Most vocabularies lie between 160 and 280 words.

2.112

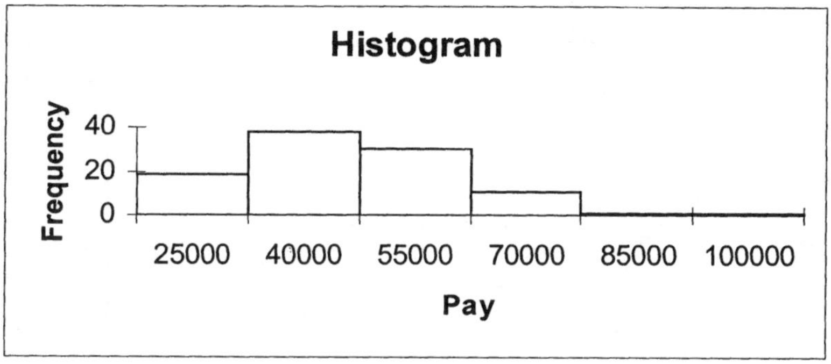

Most directors earned between \$25,000 and \$55,000.

2.114 Fatal accidents

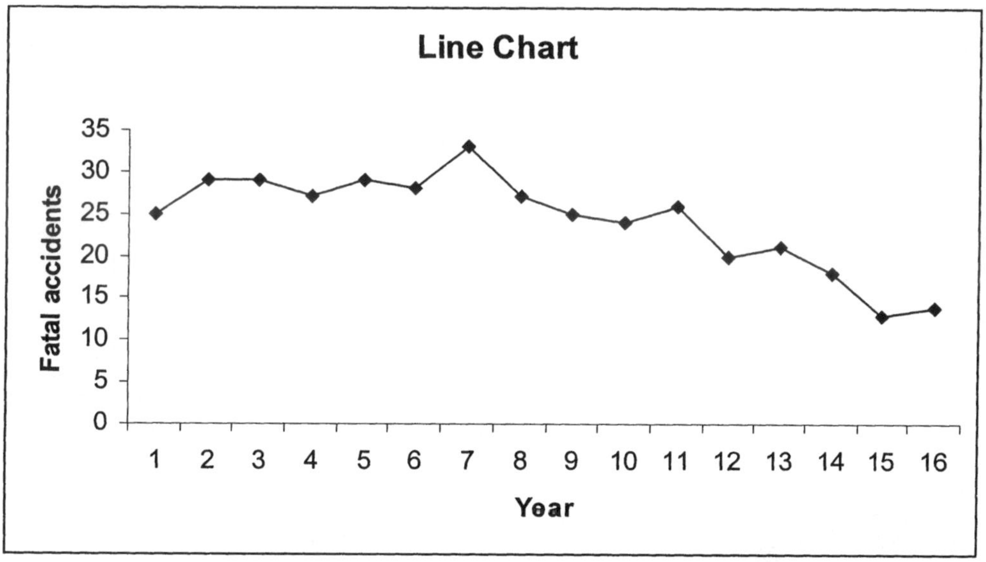

Passenger deaths

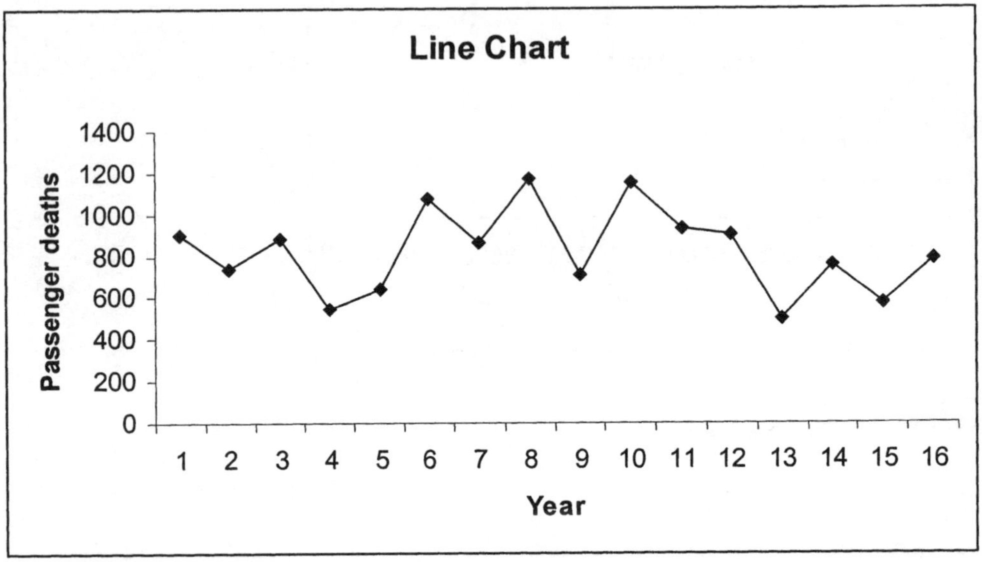

Safety has not improved using the number of passenger deaths. However, using the number of fatal accidents, safety has improved.

2.116

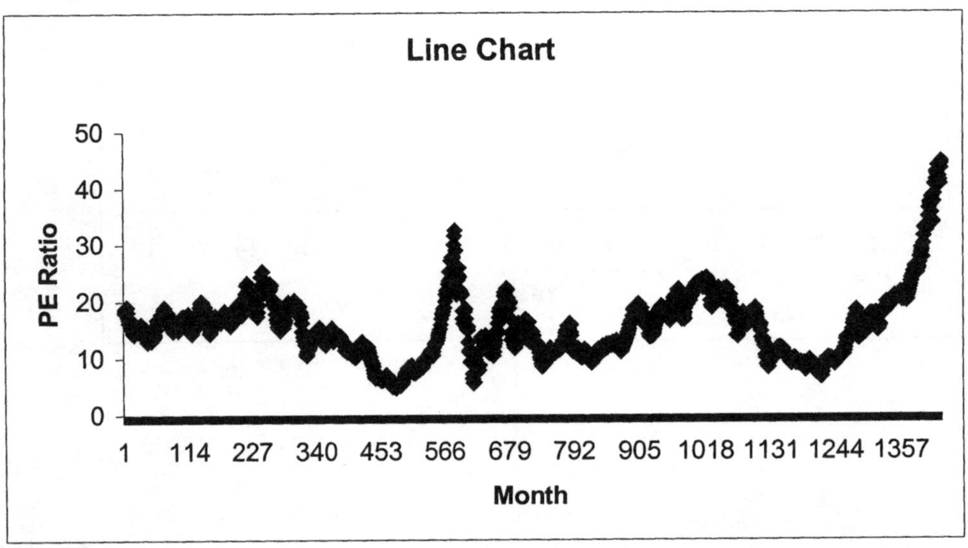

The average PE ratio appears to lie between 5 and 25 except for two periods, just before the 1929 stock market crash and in the 1990's.

2.118 Business Statistics course (Example 2.6)

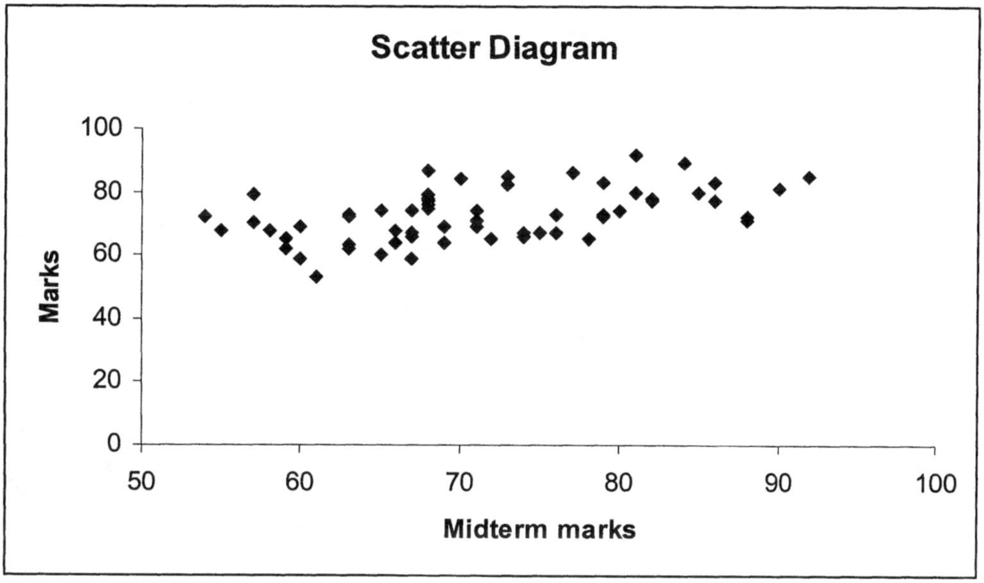

Mathematical Statistics course (Example 2.7)

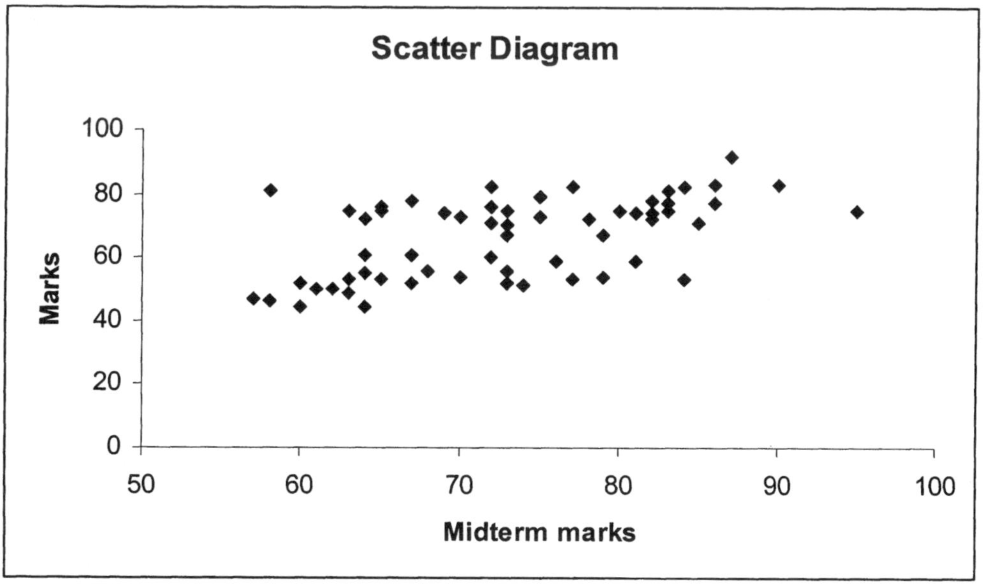

The relationship between midterm marks and final marks appear to be similar for both statistics courses.

Chapter 3

3.2 Region: Sales: Last year

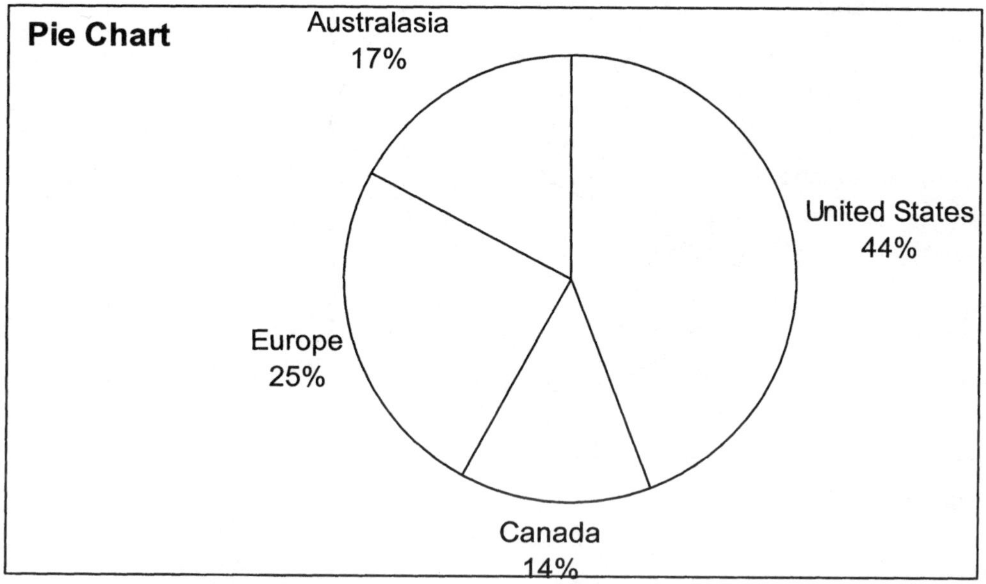

Region: Sales: Previous year

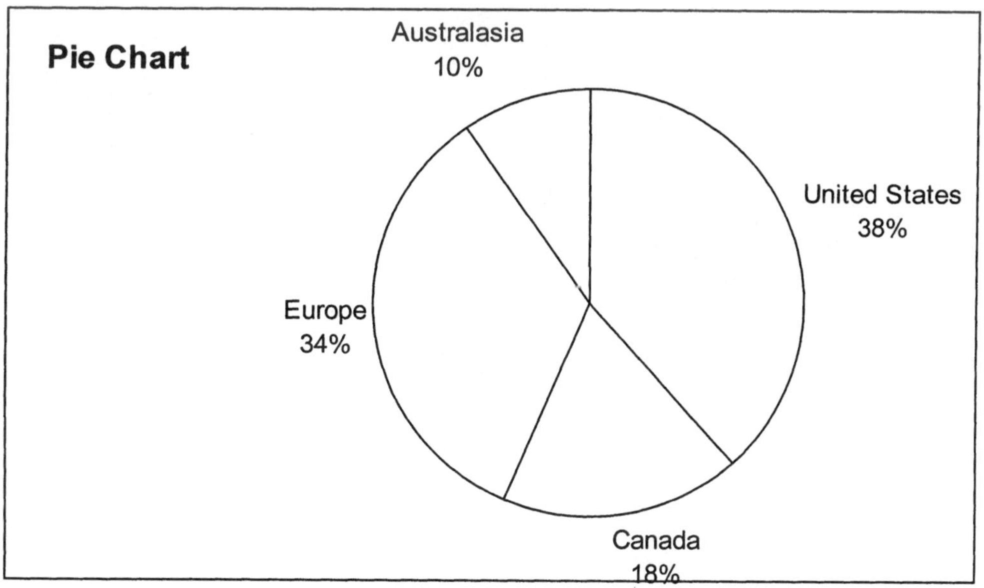

Division: Sales: Last Year

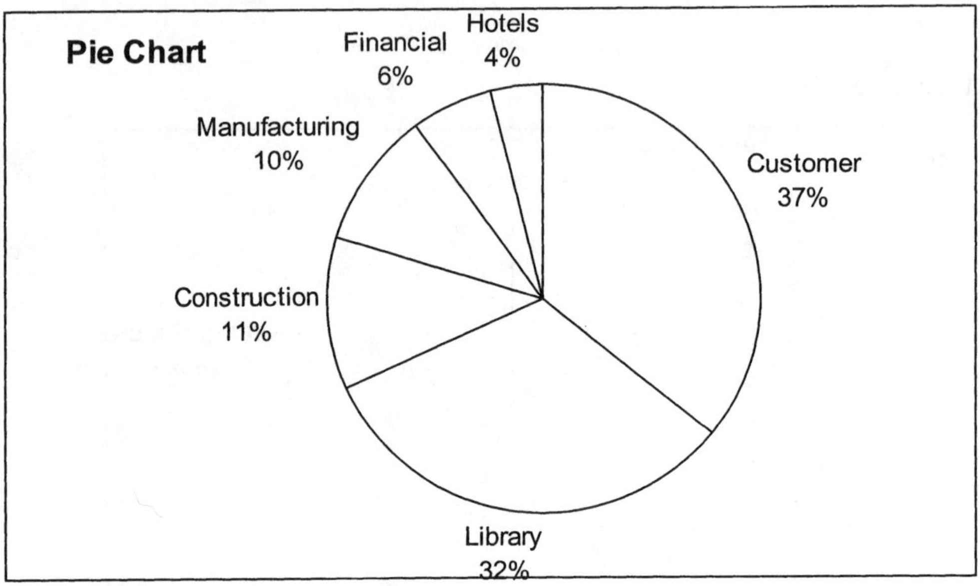

Division: Sales: Previous year

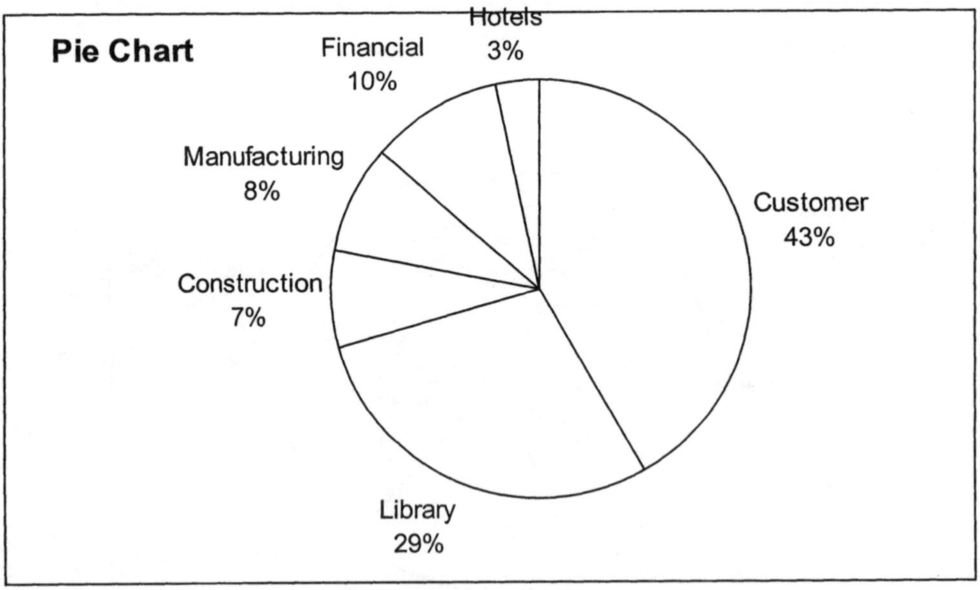

3.4 a

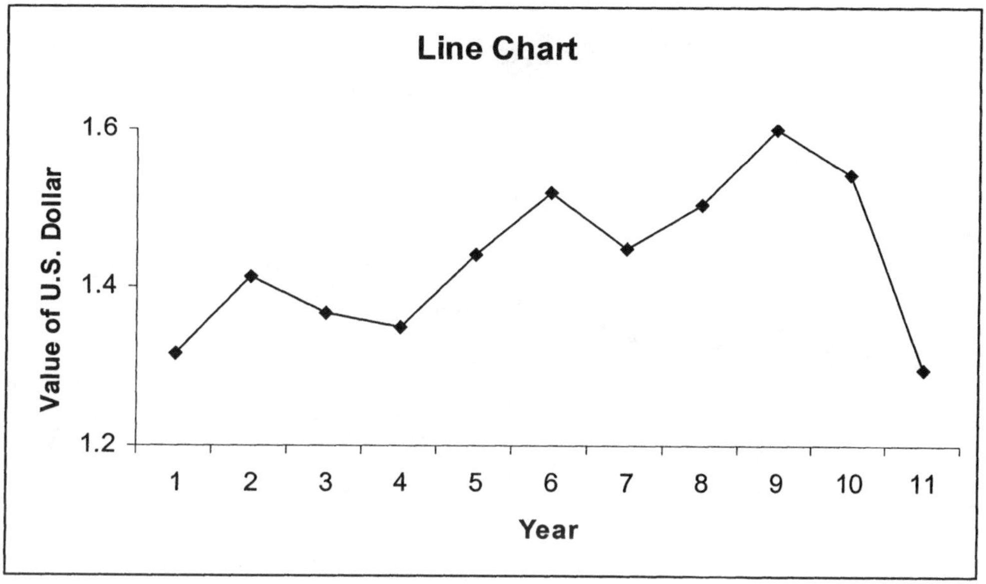

b In the first year (1994) the U.S. dollar was worth $1.3173 Canadian. It decreased over the next 2 years and rose for the following 2 years. This was followed by a decrease and 2 increases. It decreased slightly in 2003 and fell sharply to 1.2958 in 2004.

c There is a small amount of information, particularly useful for Canadian and American shoppers who cross-border shop.

d The chart can be made more informative if we include other variables that may explain the fluctuations. For example, we could include interest rates in both countries as well as other economic variables.

3.6

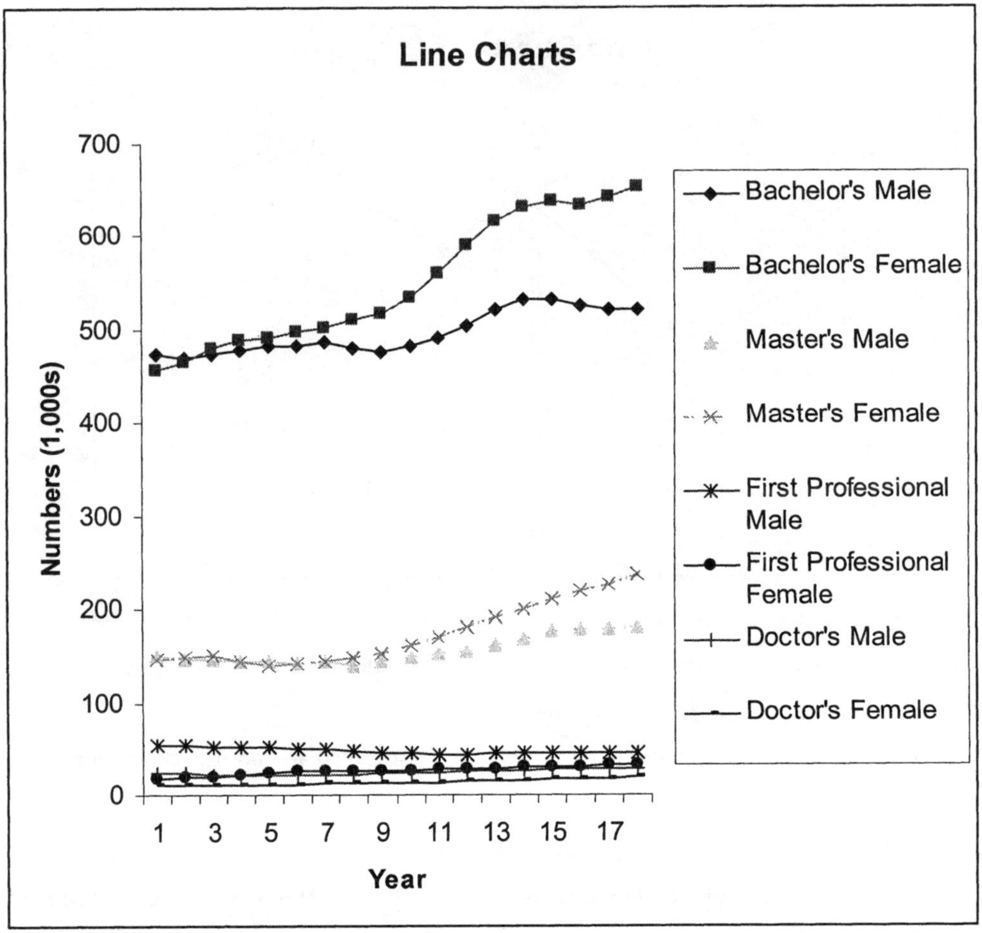

We enlarged this line chart to make it easier to see the trends. However, it may be batter to separate Bachelor's degrees in a bar chart and the other three designations in line charts.

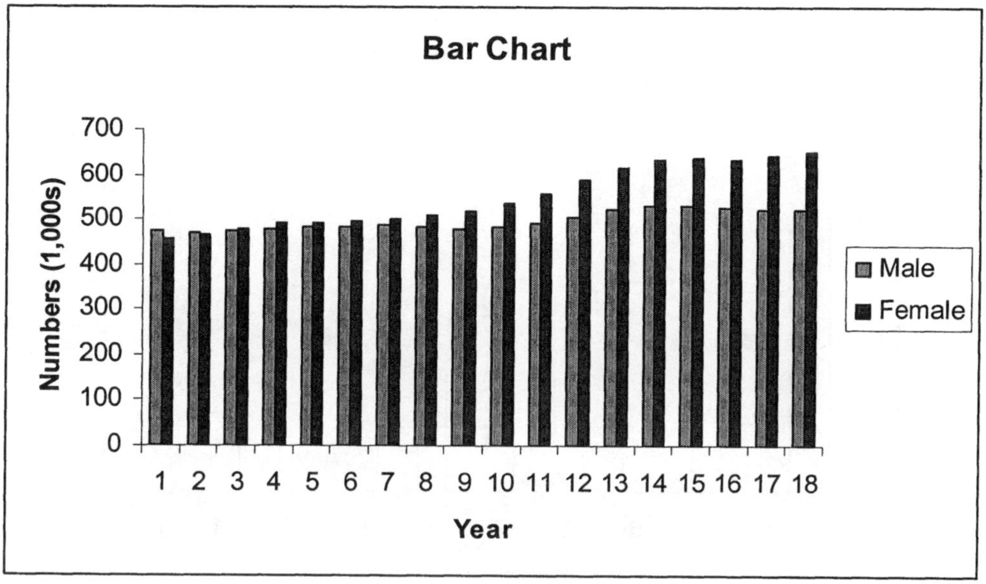
Bar Chart
700
600
500
400
300
200
100
0
Numbers (1,000s)
1 2 3 4 5 6 7 8 9 10 11 12 13 14 15 16 17 18
Year
Male
Female

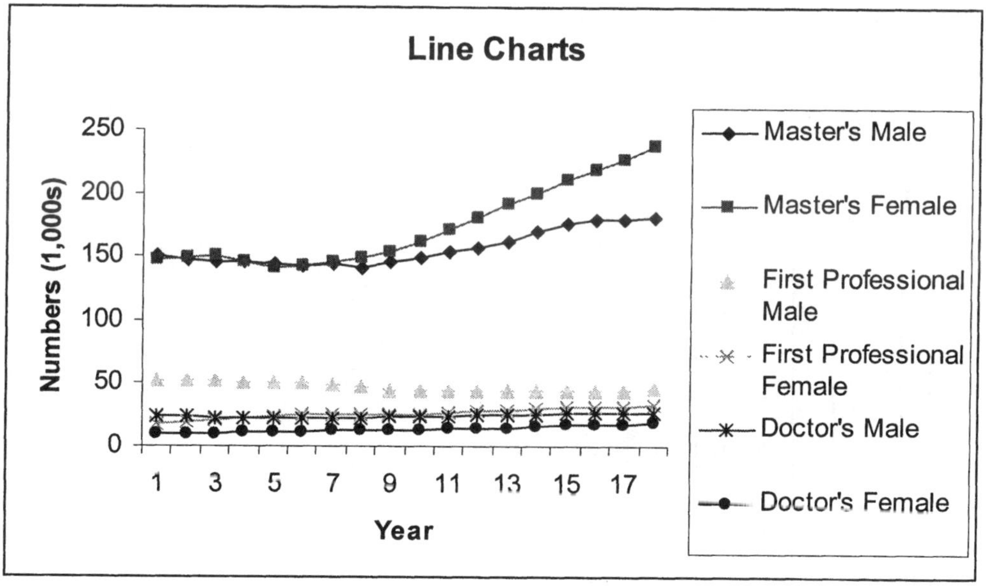
Line Charts
250
200
150
100
50
0
Numbers (1,000s)
1 3 5 7 9 11 13 15 17
Year
Master's Male
Master's Female
First Professional Male
First Professional Female
Doctor's Male
Doctor's Female

3.8 a

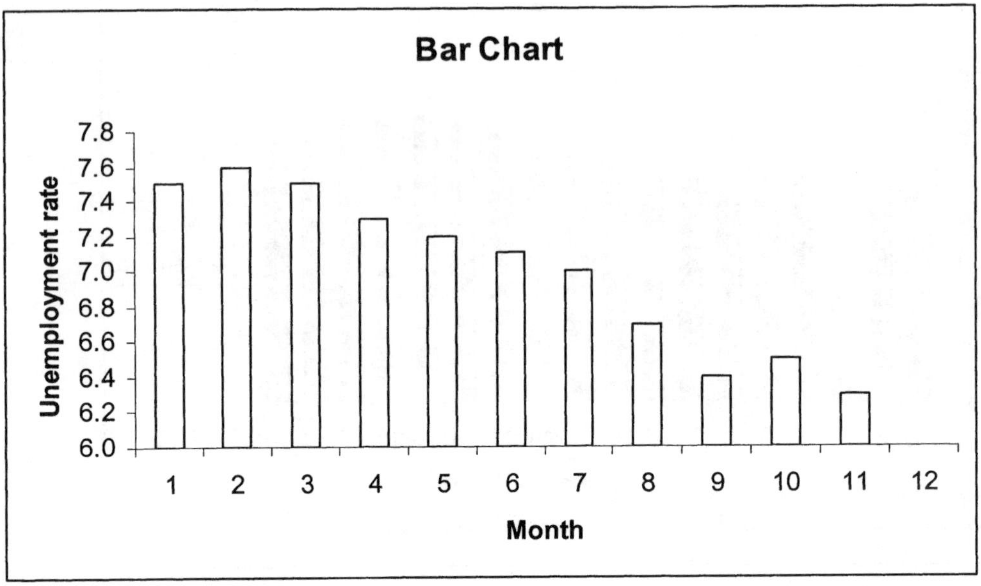

b

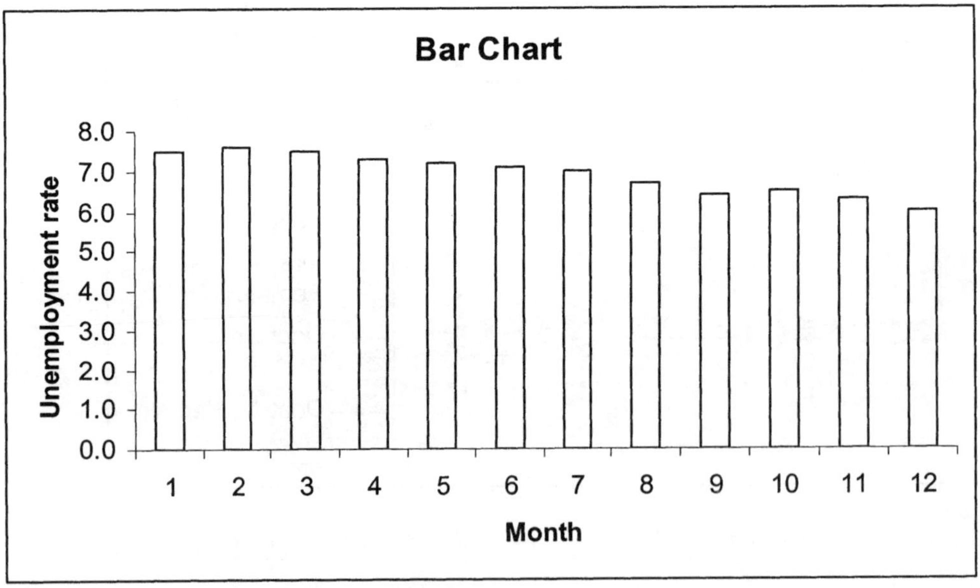

c Caption a: Unemployment rate falling rapidly. Caption b: Unemployment rate virtually unchanged.

d The chart in a is more honest.

3.10 a

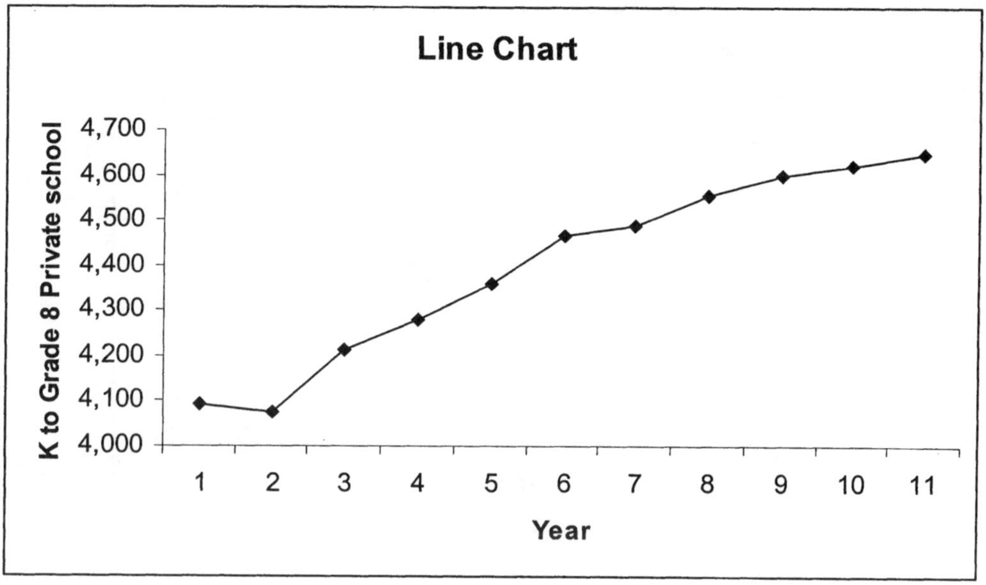
Line Chart
K to Grade 8 Private school
4,700
4,600
4,500
4,400
4,300
4,200
4,100
4,000
1 2 3 4 5 6 7 8 9 10 11
Year

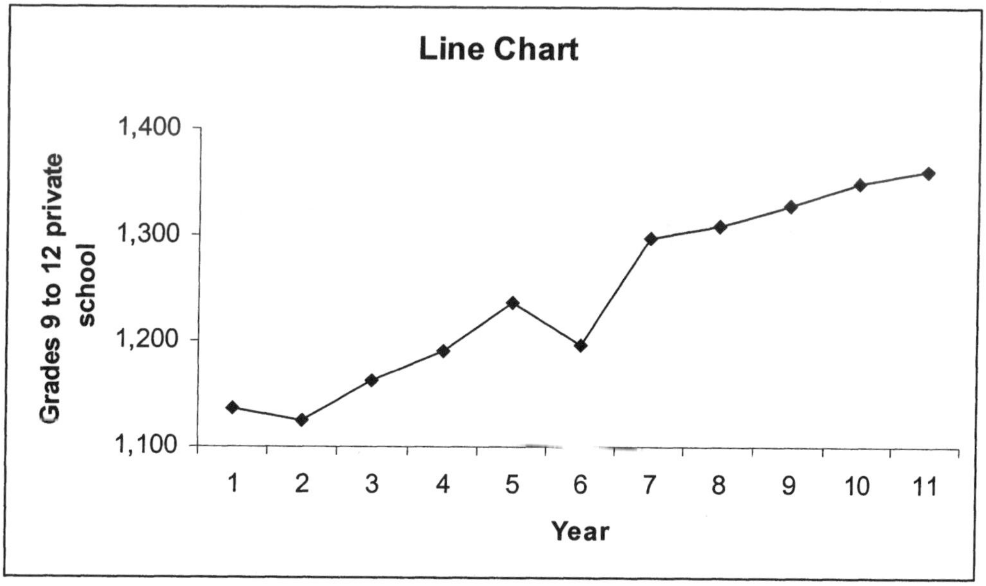
Line Chart
Grades 9 to 12 private school
1,400
1,300
1,200
1,100
1 2 3 4 5 6 7 8 9 10 11
Year

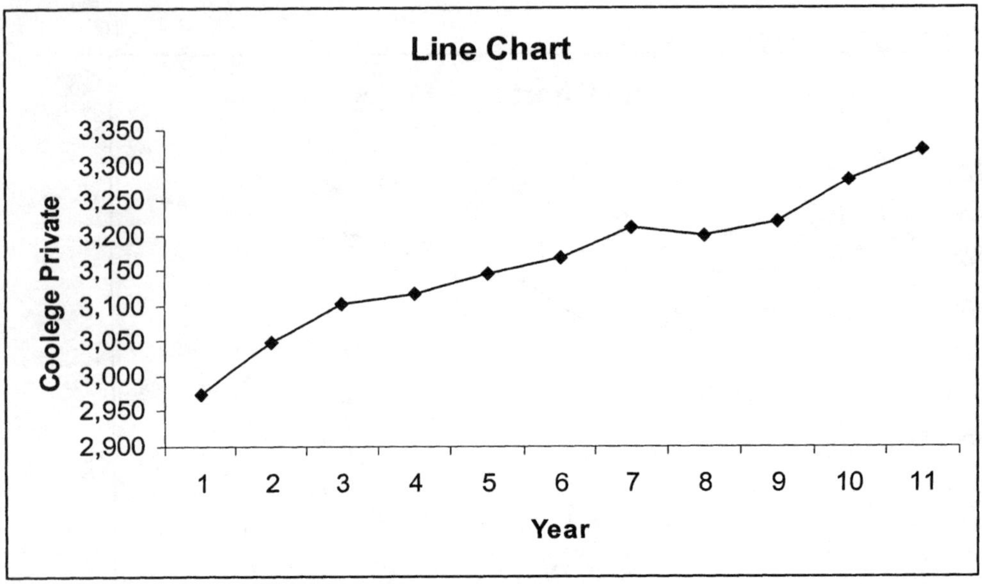
Line Chart
Coolege Private
3,350
3,300
3,250
3,200
3,150
3,100
3,050
3,000
2,950
2,900
1
2
3
4
5
6
7
8
9
10
11
Year

b

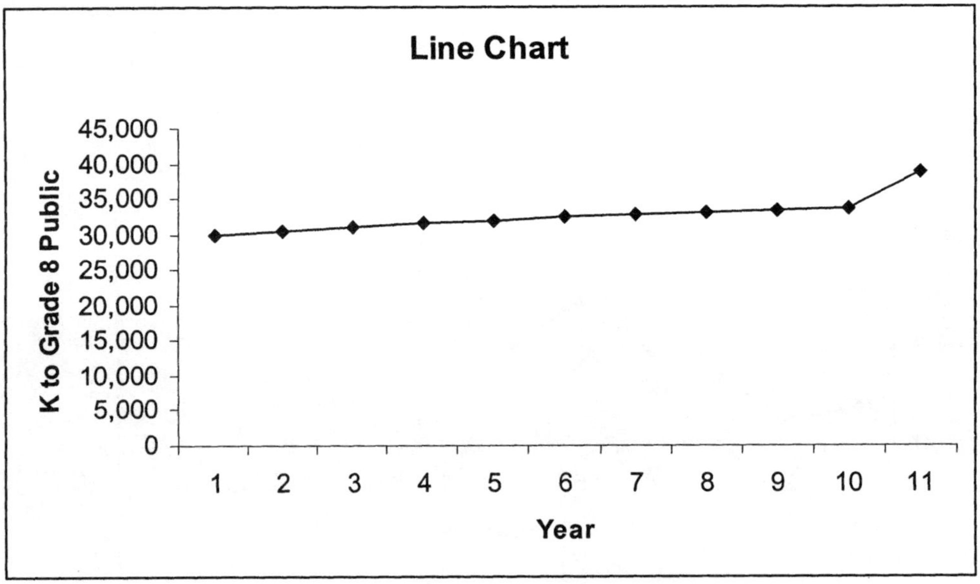
Line Chart
K to Grade 8 Public
45,000
40,000
35,000
30,000
25,000
20,000
15,000
10,000
5,000
0
1
2
3
4
5
6
7
8
9
10
11
Year

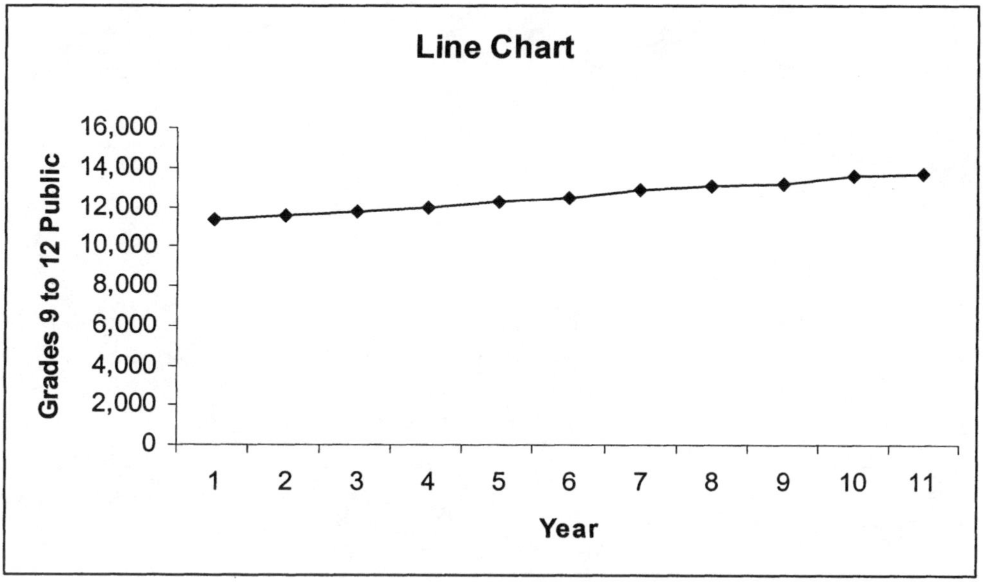
Line Chart
16,000
14,000
12,000
10,000
8,000
6,000
4,000
2,000
0
Grades 9 to 12 Public
1
2
3
4
5
6
7
8
9
10
11
Year

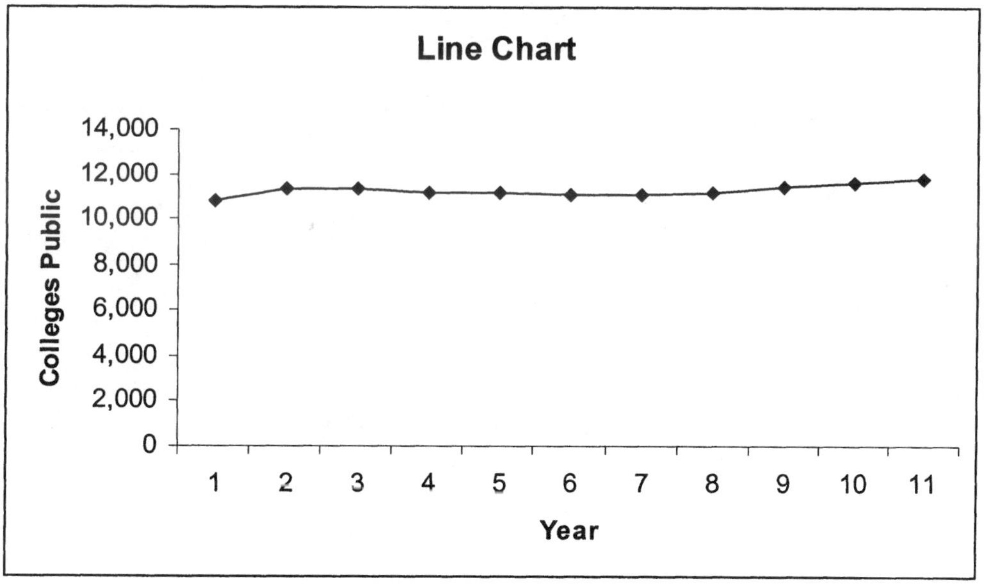
Line Chart
14,000
12,000
10,000
8,000
6,000
4,000
2,000
0
Colleges Public
1
2
3
4
5
6
7
8
9
10
11
Year

Chapter 4

4.2 $\bar{x} = \frac{\sum x_i}{n} = \frac{0+5+3+8+6+3+12+8+4+9+16+8+0+6+2}{15} = \frac{90}{15} = 6.0$

Ordered data: 0, 0, 2, 3, 3, 4, 5, 6, 6, 8, 8, 8, 9, 12, 16; Median = 6

Mode = 8

4.4 a $\bar{x} = \frac{\sum x_i}{n} = \frac{10+6+5+2+6+4+9+13+10+12+7+4+9+13+15+8+11+12+4+0}{20}$

$= \frac{160}{20} = 8.0$

Ordered data: 0, 2, 4, 4, 4, 5, 6, 6, 7, 8, 9, 9, 10, 10, 11, 12, 12, 13, 13, 15; Median = 8.5

Mode = 4

b The mean number of days to submit grades is 8.2, the median is 8.5, and the mode is 4.

4.6 $R_g = \sqrt[3]{(1+R_1)(1+R_2)(1+R_3)} - 1 = \sqrt[3]{(1+.25)(1-.10)(1+.50)} - 1 = .19$

4.8 a $\bar{x} = \frac{\sum x_i}{n} = \frac{.10+.22+.06-.05+.20}{5} = \frac{.53}{5} = .106$

Ordered data: –.05, .06, .10, .20, .22; Median = .10

b $R_g = \sqrt[5]{(1+R_1)(1+R_2)(1+R_3)(1+R_4)(1+R_5)} - 1 = \sqrt[5]{(1+.10)(1+.22)(1+.06)(1-.05)(1+.20)} - 1 =$

.102

c The geometric mean

4.10 a Year 1 rate of return = $\frac{1200-1000}{1000} = .20$

Year 2 rate of return = $\frac{1200-1200}{1200} = 0$

Year 3 rate of return = $\frac{1500-1200}{1200} = .25$

Year 4 rate of return = $\frac{2000-1500}{1500} = .33$

b $\bar{x} = \frac{\sum x_i}{n} = \frac{.20+0+.25+.33}{4} = \frac{.78}{4} = .195$

Ordered data: 0, .20, .25, .33; Median = .225

c $R_g = \sqrt[4]{(1+R_1)(1+R_2)(1+R_3)(1+R_4)} - 1 = \sqrt[4]{(1+.20)(1+0)(1+.25)(1+.33)} - 1 = .188$

d The geometric mean is because $1000(1.188)^4 = 2000$

4.12 a $\bar{x} = 24{,}329$; median = 24,461

b The mean starting salary is $24,329. Half the sample earned less than $24,461.

4.14a $\bar{x} = 32.91$; median = 32; mode = 32

b The mean speed is 32.91 mph. Half the sample traveled slower than 32 mph and half traveled faster. The mode is 32.

4.16 a $\bar{x} = 11.19$; median = 11

b The mean number of days is 11.19 and half the sample took less than 11 days and half took more than 11 days to pay.

14.18a $\bar{x} = 29.48$; median = 30.00

b $\bar{x} = 40.18$; median = 41.00

b The mean commuting time in New York is larger than that in Los Angeles.

4.20 $\bar{x} = \frac{\sum x_i}{n} = \frac{8+9+3+6+5+6+5+6}{8} = \frac{48}{8} = 6$

$$s^2 = \frac{\sum (x_i - \bar{x})^2}{n-1} = \frac{[(8-6)^2 + (9-6)^2 + \ldots + (6-5)^2}{8-1} = \frac{24}{7} = 3.43$$

4.22 $\bar{x} = \frac{\sum x_i}{n} = \frac{7+(-5)+(-3)+8+4+(-4)+1+(-5)+9+3}{10} = \frac{15}{10} = 1.5$

$$s^2 = \frac{\sum (x_i - \bar{x})^2}{n-1} = \frac{[(7-1.5)^2 + ((-5)-1.5)^2 + \ldots + (3-1.5)^2}{10-1} = \frac{272.5}{9} = 30.28$$

$s = \sqrt{s^2} = \sqrt{30.28} = 5.50$

4.24 a: $s^2 = 51.5$

b: $s^2 = 6.5$

c: $s^2 = 174.5$

4.26 5, 5, 5, 5, 5

4.28 a From the empirical rule we know that approximately 68% of the observations fall between 46 and 54. Thus 16% are less than 46 (the other 16% are above 54).

b Approximately 95% of the observations are between 42 and 58. Thus, only 2.5% are above 58 and all the rest, 97.5% are below 58.

c See (a) above; 16% are above 54.

4.30 a Nothing

b At least 75% lie between 60 and 180.

c At least 88.9% lie between 30 and 210.

4.32 Range = 25.85, $s^2 = 29.46$, and s = 5.43; there is considerable variation between prices; at least 75% of the prices lie within 10.86 of the mean; at least 88.9% of the prices lie within 16.29 of the mean.

4.34 $\bar{x} = 175.73, s^2 = 3{,}851.82$; s = 62.1; At least 75% of the withdrawals lie within \$124.20 of the mean; at least 88.9% of the withdrawals lie within \$186.30 of the mean..

4.36a s = 15.01

b In approximately 68% of the days the number of arrivals falls within 30.02 of the mean; on approximately 95% of the hours the number of arrivals falls within 45.03 of the mean

4.38 Third decile: $L_{30} = (15+1)\frac{30}{100} = (16)(.30) = 4.8$; the third decile is 5 + .8(7 – 5) = 6.6.

Sixth decile: $L_{60} = (15+1)\frac{60}{100} = (16)(.60) = 9.6$; the sixth decile is 17 + .6(18 – 17) = 17.6.

4.40 30th percentile: $L_{30} = (10+1)\frac{30}{100} = (11)(.30) = 3.3$; the 30th percentile is 22.3.

80th percentile: $L_{80} = (10+1)\frac{80}{100} = (11)(.80) = 8.8$; the 80th percentile 30.8.

4.42 Interquartile range = 15.6 –13.05 = 2.55

4.44 First quartile = 5.75, third quartile = 15; interquartile range = 15 – 5.75 = 9.25

4.46

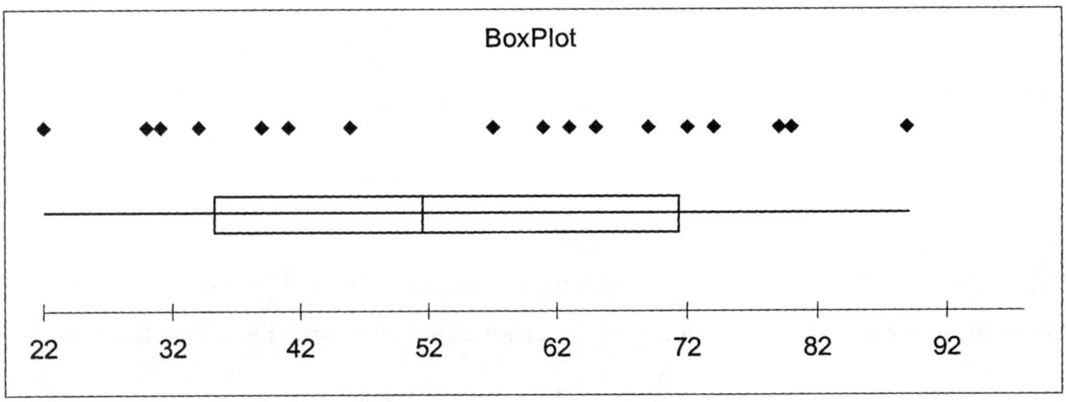

4.48 Dogs

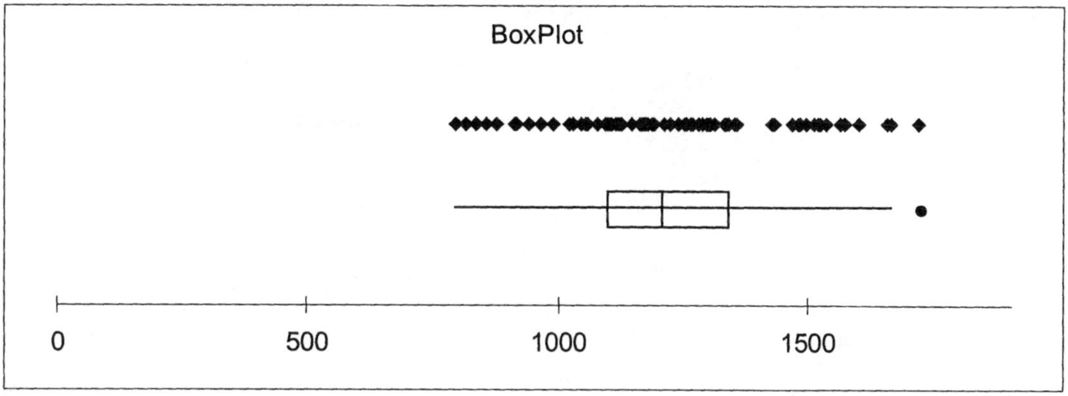

Cats

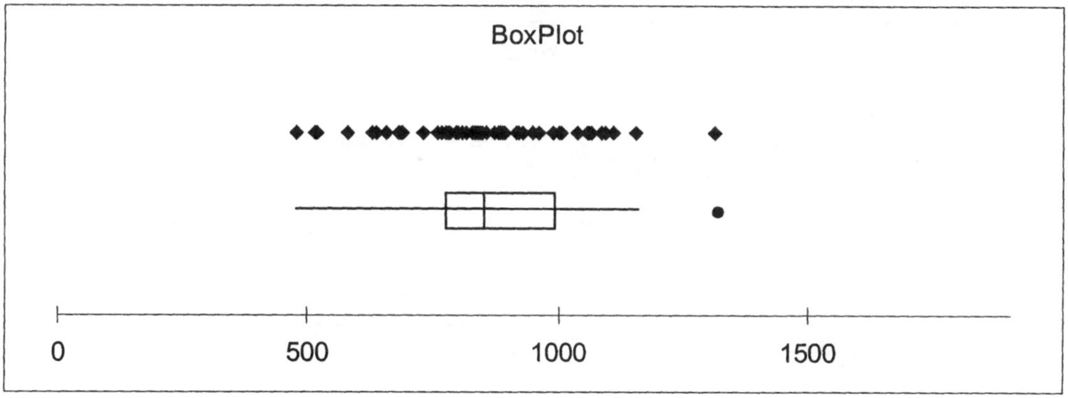

Dogs cost more money than cats. Both sets of expenses are positively skewed.

4.50 BA

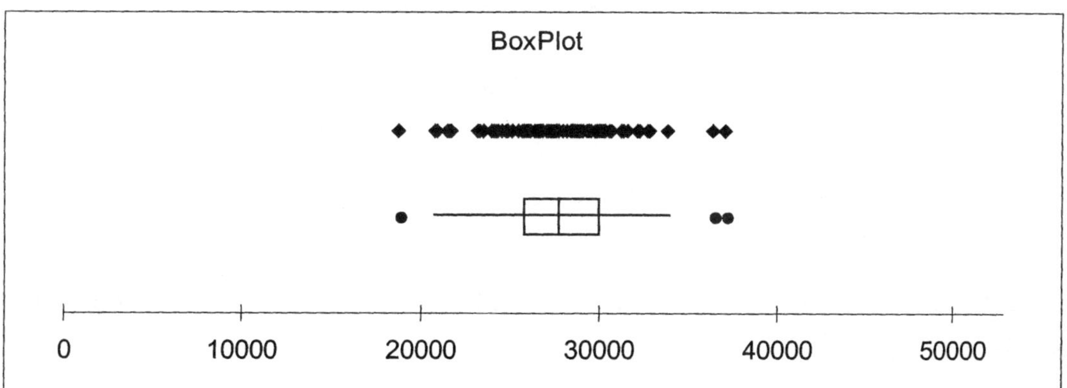

BSc

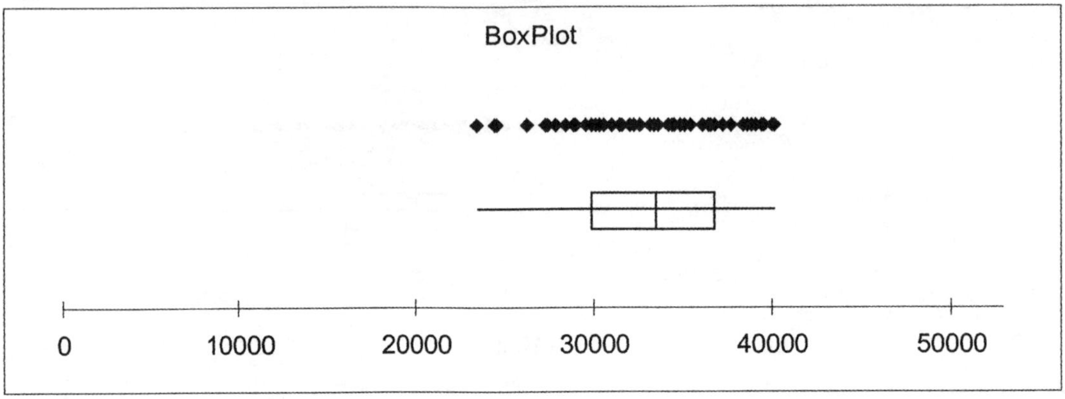

BBA

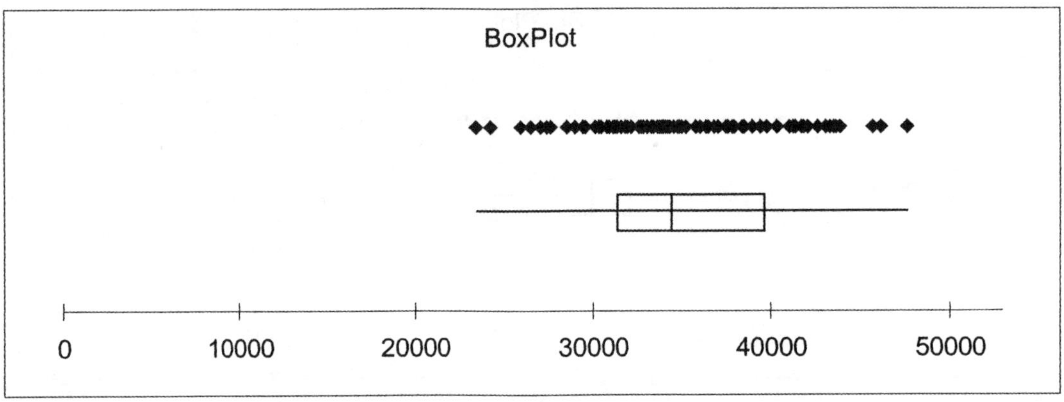

Other

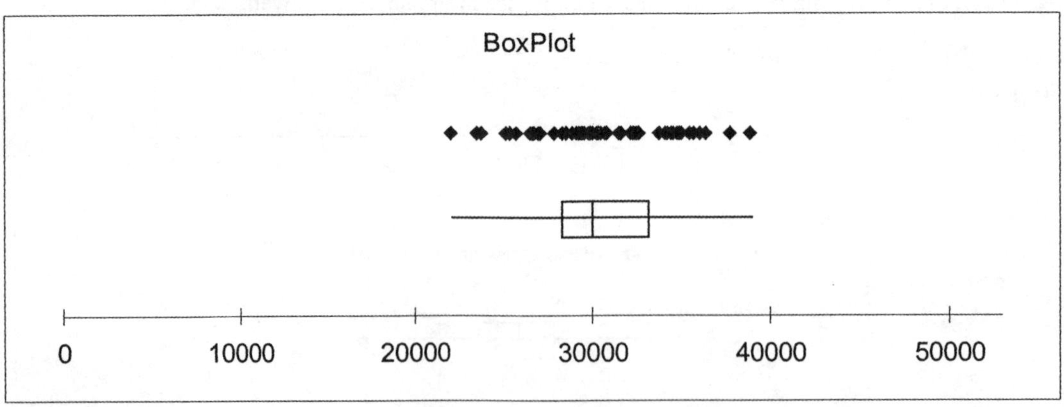

The starting salaries of BA and other are the lowest and least variable. Starting salaries for BBA and BSc are higher.

4.52a

Private course:

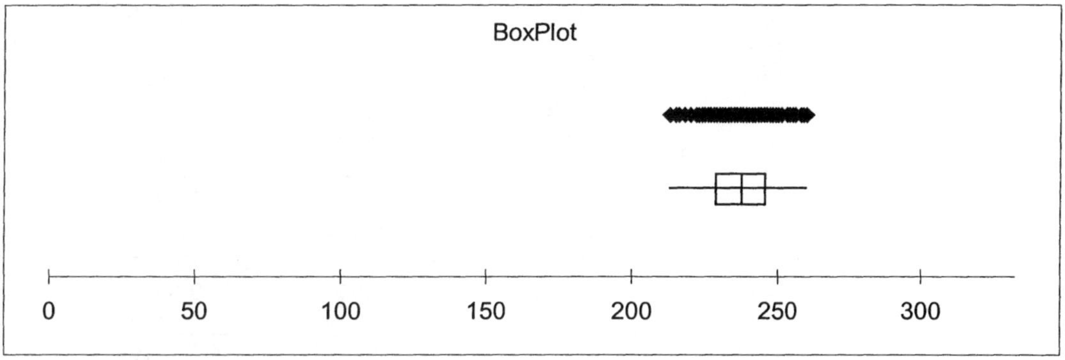

Public course:

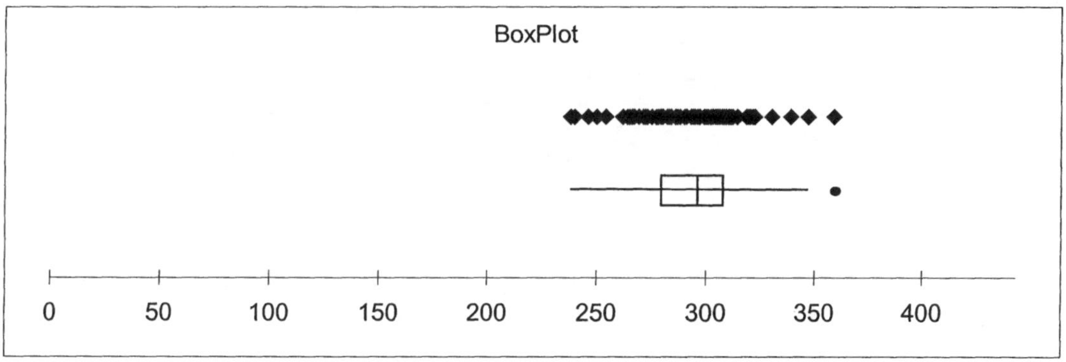

b The amount of time taken to complete rounds on the public course are larger and more variable than those played on private courses.

4.54 The quartiles are 697.19, 804.90, and 909.38. One-quarter of mortgage payments are less than \$607.19 and one quarter exceed \$909.38.

4.56 $r = \frac{s_{xy}}{s_x s_y} = \frac{-14}{(3)(7)} = -.667$

There is a moderately strong negative linear relationship.

4.58

	x_i	y_i	x_i^2	y_i^2	x_iy_i
	60	260	3,600	67,600	15,600
	45	266	2,025	70,756	11,970
	55	257	3,025	66,049	14,135
	35	199	1,225	39,601	6,965
	55	271	3,025	73,441	14,905
	60	322	3,600	103,684	19,320
	35	165	1,225	27,225	5,775
	60	388	3,600	150,544	23,280
	50	233	2,500	54,289	11,650
	45	243	2,025	59,049	10,935
	40	242	1,600	58,564	9,680
	45	233	2,025	54,289	10,485
Total	585	3,079	29,475	825,091	154,700

$\sum_{i=1}^{n} x_i = 585 \quad \sum_{i=1}^{n} y_i = 3{,}079 \quad \sum_{i=1}^{n} x_i^2 = 29{,}475 \quad \sum_{i=1}^{n} y_i^2 = 825{,}091 \quad \sum_{i=1}^{n} x_i y_i =$
154,700

a $$s_{xy} = \frac{1}{n-1}\left[\sum_{i=1}^{n} x_i y_i - \frac{\sum_{i=1}^{n} x_i \sum_{i=1}^{n} y_i}{n}\right] = \frac{1}{12-1}\left[154{,}700 - \frac{(585)(3{,}079)}{12}\right] = 418.1$$

$$s_x^2 = \frac{1}{n-1}\left[\sum_{i=1}^{n} x_i^2 - \frac{\left(\sum_{i=1}^{n} x_i\right)^2}{n}\right] = \frac{1}{12-1}\left[29{,}475 - \frac{(585)^2}{12}\right] = 86.93$$

$$s_y^2 = \frac{1}{n-1}\left[\sum_{i=1}^{n} y_i^2 - \frac{\left(\sum_{i=1}^{n} y_i\right)^2}{n}\right] = \frac{1}{12-1}\left[825{,}091 - \frac{(3{,}079)^2}{12}\right] = 3{,}188$$

$$r = \frac{s_{xy}}{s_x s_y} = \frac{418.1}{\sqrt{(86.93)(3{,}188)}} = .7942$$

b $$b_1 = \frac{s_{xy}}{s_x^2} = \frac{418.1}{86.93} = 4.809$$

$$\bar{x} = \frac{\sum x_i}{n} = \frac{585}{12} = 48.75$$

$$\bar{y} = \frac{\sum y_i}{n} = \frac{3{,}079}{12} = 256.6$$

$$b_0 = \bar{y} - b_1\bar{x} = 256.6 - (4.809)(48.75) = 22.16$$

The least squares line is

$$\hat{y} = 22.16 + 4.809x$$

For each additional minute of exercise the metabolic rate increases on average by 4.809.

4.60 a

	A	B	C
1		*Age*	*Expense*
2	Age	228.1	
3	Expense	51.49	179.7

Covariance: $s_{xy} = \frac{n(\text{Excel covariance})}{n-1} = \frac{(1{,}348)(51.49)}{1{,}347} = 51.53$

	A	B	C
1		*Age*	*Expense*
2	Age	1	
3	Expense	0.2543	1

Coefficient of correlation = .2543

b There is a weak linear relationship between age and medical expenses.

c

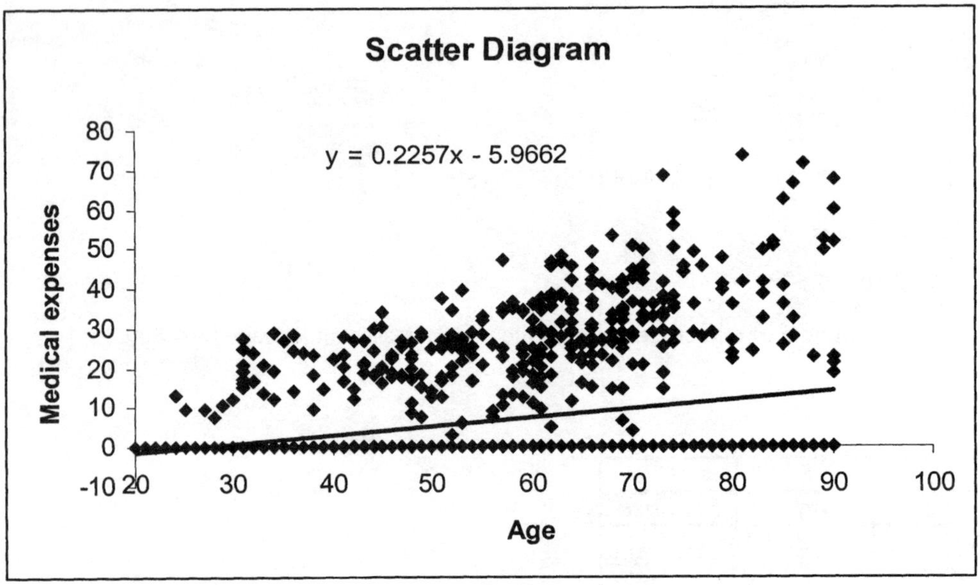

The least squares line is $\hat{y} = -5.966 + .2257x$

d For each additional year of age mean medical expenses increase on average by $.2257 or 23 cents.

e Charge 25 cents per day per year of age.

4.62 a

	A	B	C
1		*Rate*	*Houses*
2	Rate	10.21	
3	Houses	-13.96	230.5

Covariance: $s_{xy} = \frac{n(\text{Excel covariance})}{n-1} = \frac{492(-13.96)}{491} = -13.99$

	A	B	C
1		*Rate*	*Houses*
2	Rate	1	
3	Houses	-0.2878	1

Coefficient of correlation $= -.2878$

There is a weak negative linear relationship between the number of houses built and the prime bank rate

4.64

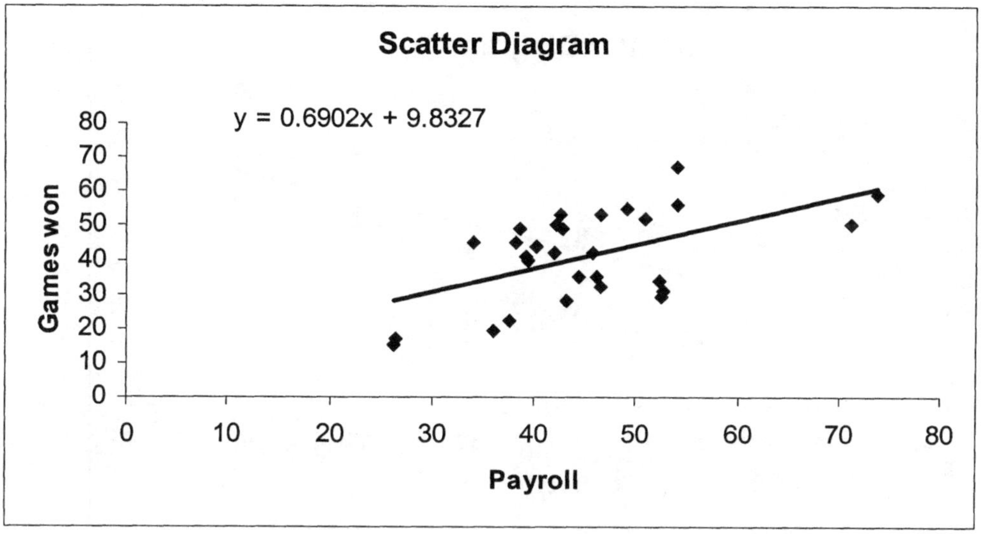

$\hat{y} = 9.8327 + .6902x$; Cost to win one more game = 1million/.6902 = $1,448,855

4.66

	A	B	C
1		*Index*	*Rate*
2	Index	1	
3	Rate	0.0669	1

There is a very weak positive linear relationship between the unemployment rate and the index. We would have expected a negative linear relationship.

4.68

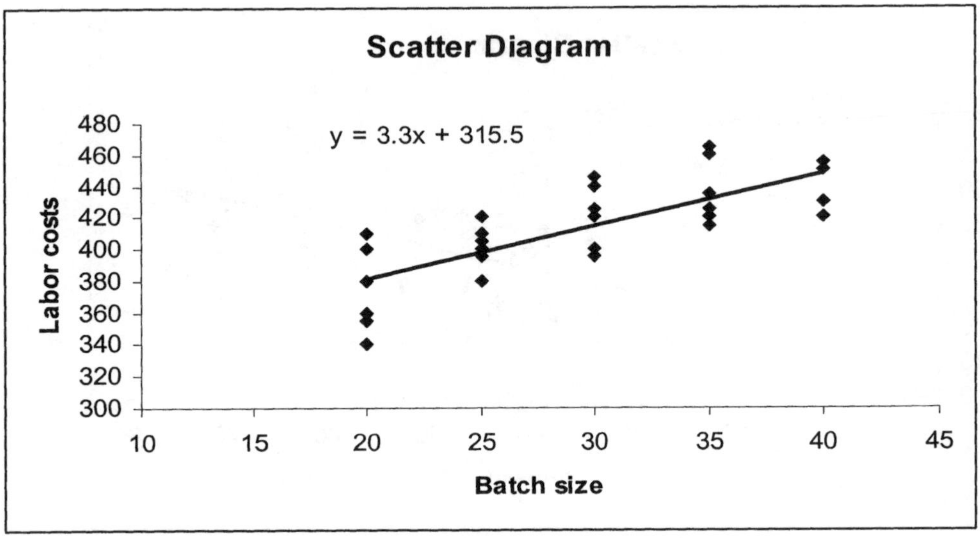

$\hat{y} = 315.5 + 3.3x$; Fixed costs = \$315.50, variable costs = \$3.30

4.70 a

	A	B	C	D	E
1	*Repaid*			*Defaulted*	
2					
3	Mean	751.5		Mean	545.7
4	Standard Error	3.75		Standard Error	6.07
5	Median	753		Median	549.5
6	Mode	753		Mode	552
7	Standard Deviation	49.16		Standard Deviation	54.25
8	Sample Variance	2416		Sample Variance	2943
9	Kurtosis	0.177		Kurtosis	-0.673
10	Skewness	-0.170		Skewness	-0.094
11	Range	253		Range	237
12	Minimum	625		Minimum	419
13	Maximum	878		Maximum	656
14	Sum	129265		Sum	43658
15	Count	172		Count	80

b We can see that among those who repaid the mean score is larger than that of those who did not and the standard deviation is smaller. This information is similar but more precise than that obtained in Exercise 2.54.

4.72

	A	B	C
1		*Calculus*	*Statistics*
2	Calculus	1	
3	Statistics	0.6784	1

The coefficient of correlation provides a more precise indication of the strength of the linear relationship. However, we cannot define exactly what this value tells us.

4.74

	A	B	C
1		*Price:Gasoline*	*Price: Crude*
2	Price:Gasoline	0.05782	
3	Price: Crude	1.374	46.51

Covariance: $s_{xy} = \frac{n(\text{Excel cov ariance})}{n-1} = \frac{336(1.374)}{335} = 1.378$

	A	B	C
1		*Price:Gasoline*	*Price: Crude*
2	Price:Gasoline	1	
3	Price: Crude	0.8376	1

The coefficient of correlation .8376 provides a somewhat more precise measure of the strength of the linear relationship.

4.76

	A	B	C
1		*Height*	*Income*
2	Height	1	
3	Income	0.2248	1

The coefficient of correlation .2248 is more precise than the scatter diagram. However, the information is limited.

4.78

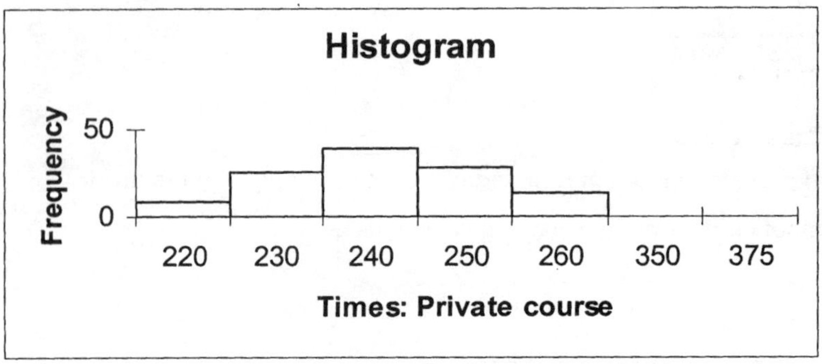

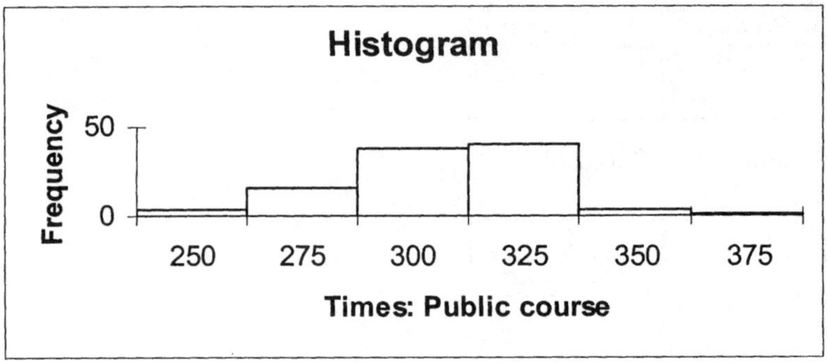

The information obtained here is more detailed than the information provided by the box plots.

4.80

	A	B
1	*Coffees*	
2		
3	Mean	29,913
4	Standard Error	1,722
5	Median	30,660
6	Mode	#N/A
7	Standard Deviation	12,174
8	Sample Variance	148,213,791
9	Kurtosis	0.12
10	Skewness	0.22
11	Range	59,082
12	Minimum	3,647
13	Maximum	62,729
14	Sum	1,495,639
15	Count	50

a $\bar{x} = 29,913$, median = 30,660

b $s^2 = 148{,}213{,}791$; s = 12,174

c

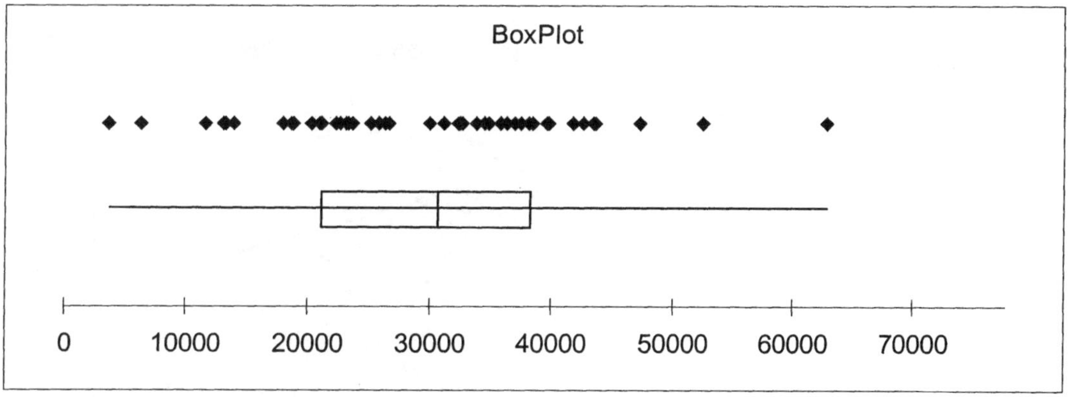

d The number of coffees sold varies considerably.

4.82a

	A	B	C
1		*Coffees*	*Temperature*
2	Coffees	145,249,515	
3	Temperature	-144,003	260

$$s_{xy} = \frac{\text{n(Excel cov ariance)}}{n-1} = \frac{50(-144{,}003)}{49} = -146{,}942$$

	A	B	C
1		*Coffees*	*Temperature*
2	Coffees	1	
3	Temperature	-0.7409	1

r = –.7409

b $\hat{y} = 49{,}337 - 553.7x$

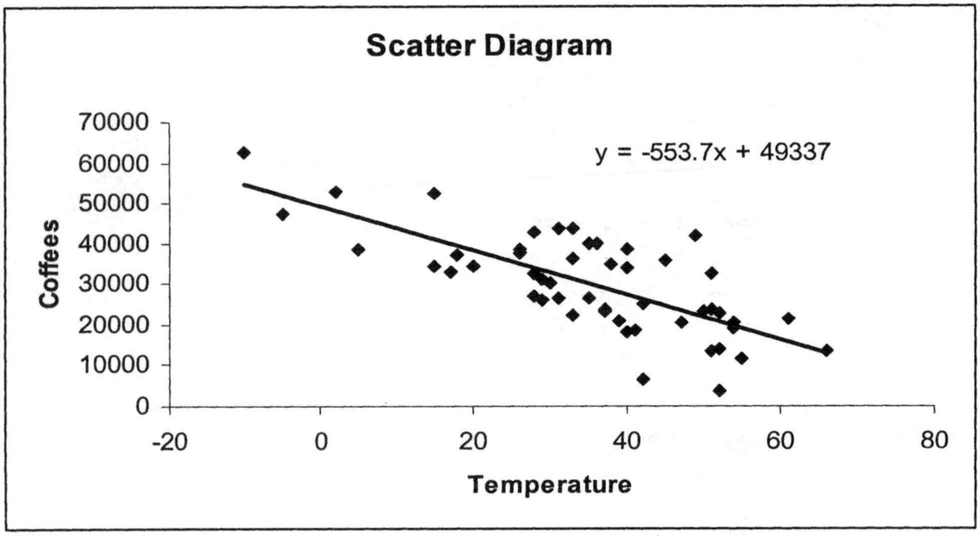

c There is a moderately strong negative linear relationship. For each additional degree of temperature the number of coffees sold decreases on average by 554 cups.

d In this exercise we determined that the number of cups of coffee sold is related to temperature, which may explain the variability in coffee sales. .

4.84

	A	B
1	*Internet*	
2		
3	Mean	26.32
4	Standard Error	0.60
5	Median	26
6	Mode	21
7	Standard Deviation	9.41
8	Sample Variance	88.57
9	Kurtosis	-0.071
10	Skewness	0.15
11	Range	52
12	Minimum	2
13	Maximum	54
14	Sum	6579
15	Count	250

a $\bar{x} = 26.32$ and median = 26

b $s^2 = 88.57$, $s = 9.41$

c

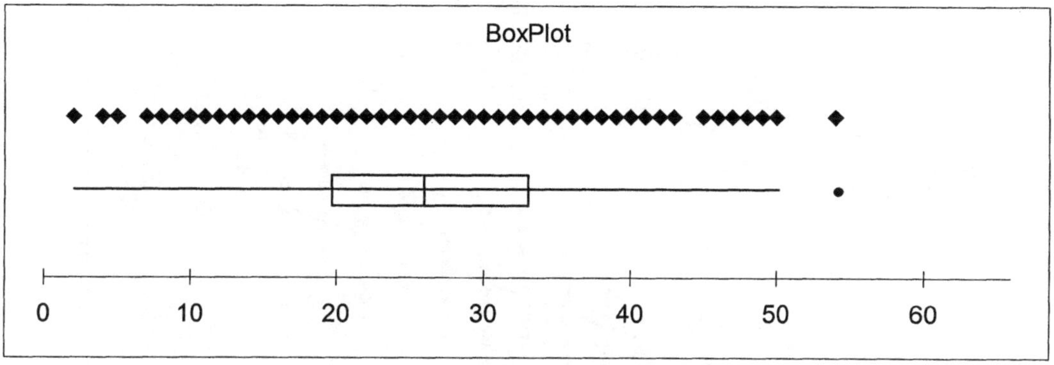

d The times are positively skewed. Half the times are above 26 hours.

4.86a

	A	B	C
1		*Internet*	*Education*
2	Internet	88.22	
3	Education	11.55	3.67

$$s_{xy} = \frac{n(\text{Excel cov ariance})}{n-1} = \frac{250(11.55)}{249} = 11.60$$

	A	B	C
1		*Internet*	*Education*
2	Internet	1	
3	Education	0.6418	1

b

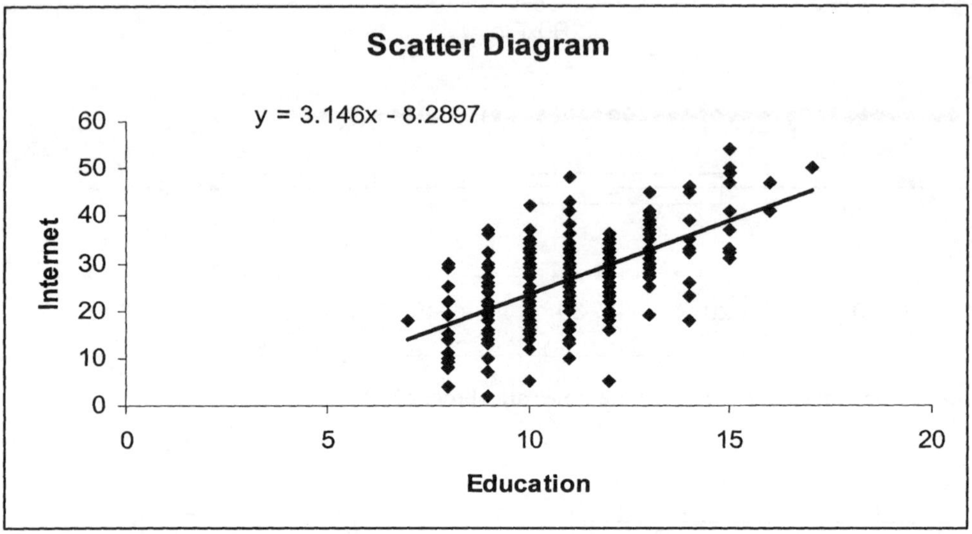

c There is a moderately strong positive linear relationship between Internet use and education. For each additional year of education Internet use increases on average by 3.15 hours per month.

d This exercise helps explain the variation in Internet use.

4.88a

	Corn	*Rainfall*
Corn	387.78	
Rainfall	1,118.57	8,738.66

$$s_{xy} = \frac{n(\text{Excel covariance})}{n-1} = \frac{150(1{,}118.57)}{149} = 1{,}126.07$$

	A	B	C
1		*Corn*	*Rainfall*
2	Corn	1	
3	Rainfall	0.6076	1

b

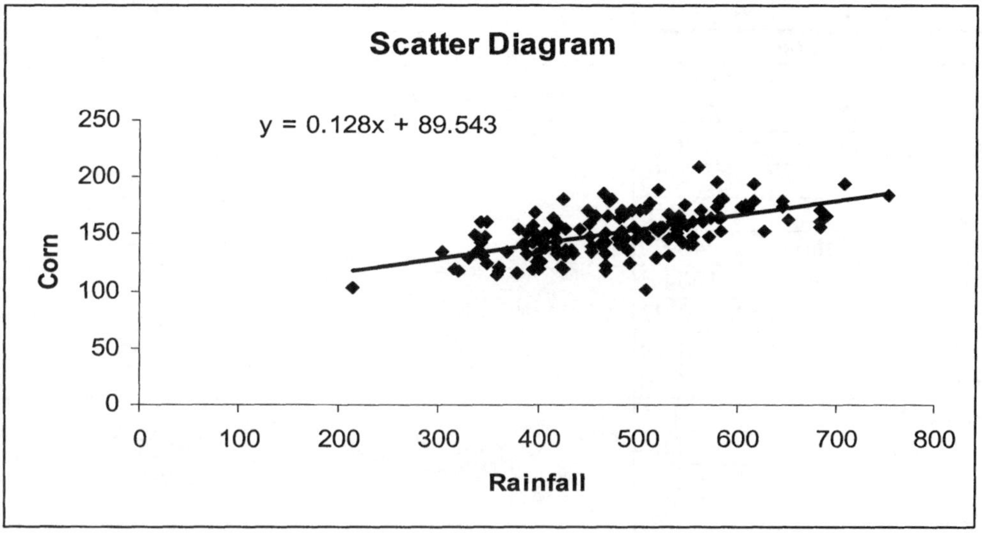

$\hat{y}$ = 89.54 + .128 Rainfall

c There is a moderately strong positive linear relationship between yield and rainfall. For each additional inch of rainfall yield increases on average by .13 bushels.

d In this exercise we determined that yield is related to rainfall, which helps explain the variability in corn yield.

4.90a, b, and c

	A	B
1	*Vocabulary*	
2		
3	Mean	226.49
4	Standard Error	3.11
5	Median	223
6	Mode	215
7	Standard Deviation	43.99
8	Sample Variance	1934.8
9	Kurtosis	-0.27
10	Skewness	0.089
11	Range	240
12	Minimum	114
13	Maximum	354
14	Sum	45,297
15	Count	200
16	Largest(50)	259
17	Smallest(50)	193

a The mean vocabulary is 226.49 words. The median is 223, which tells us that half the children had vocabularies greater than 223 words and half had less.

b The variance is 1934.8 and the standard deviation is 43.99. Both indicate a great deal of variation between children.

c The quartiles are 193, 223, and 259.

4.92a

	A	B	C
1		*Temperature*	*Winning times*
2	Temperature	1	
3	Winning times	0.5984	1

b There is a moderately strong positive linear relationship between the winning times of women and temperatures.

c They appear to provide the same type of information.

4.94a

	A	B
1	*Debts*	
2		
3	Mean	12,067
4	Standard Error	179.9
5	Median	12,047
6	Mode	11,621
7	Standard Deviation	2,632
8	Sample Variance	6,929,745
9	Kurtosis	-0.41325
10	Skewness	-0.2096
11	Range	12,499
12	Minimum	4,626
13	Maximum	17,125
14	Sum	2,582,254
15	Count	214

b The mean debt is \$12,067. Half the sample incurred debts below \$12,047 and half incurred debts above. The mode is \$11,621.

Chapter 5

5.2a The study is observational. The statistics practitioner did not randomly assign stores to buy cans or bottles.
b Randomly assign some stores to receive only cans and others to receive only bottles.

5.4a A survey can be conducted by means of a personal interview, a telephone interview, or a self-administered questionnaire.
b A personal interview has a high response rate relative to other survey methods, but is expensive because of the need to hire well-trained interviewers and possibly pay travel-related costs if the survey is conducted over a large geographical area. A personal interview also will likely result in fewer incorrect responses that arise when respondents misunderstand some questions. A telephone interview is less expensive, but will likely result in a lower response rate. A self-administered questionnaire is least expensive, but suffers from lower response rates and accuracy than interviews.

5.6a The sampled population will exclude those who avoid large department stores in favor or smaller shops, as well as those who consider their time too valuable to spend participating in a survey. The sampled population will therefore differ from the target population of all customers who regularly shop at the mall.
b The sampled population will contain a disproportionate number of thick books, because of the manner in which the sample is selected.
c The sampled population consists of those eligible voters who are at home in the afternoon, thereby excluding most of those with full-time jobs (or at school).

5.8a A self-selected sample is a sample formed primarily on the basis of voluntary inclusion, with little control by the designer of the survey.
b Choose any recent radio or television poll based on responses of listeners who phone in on a volunteer basis.
c Self-selected samples are usually biased, because those who participate are more interested in the issue than those who don't, and therefore probably have a different opinion.

5.10 No, because the sampled population consists of the responses about the professor's course. We cannot make draw inferences about all courses.

5.12 We used Excel to generate 30 six-digit random numbers. Because we will ignore any duplicate numbers generated, we generated 30 six-digit random numbers and will use the first 20 unique random numbers to select our sample. The 30 numbers generated are shown below.

169,470	744,530	22,554	918,730	320,262	503,129
318,858	698,203	822,383	938,262	800,806	56,643
836,116	123,936	80,539	154,211	391,278	940,154
110,630	856,380	222,145	692,313	949,828	561,511
909,269	811,274	288,553	749,627	858,944	39,308

5.14 Use cluster sampling, letting each city block represent a cluster.

5.18 Three types of nonsampling errors:

(1) Error due to incorrect responses

(2) Nonresponse error, which refers to error introduced when responses are not obtained from some members of the sample. This may result in the sample being unrepresentative of the target population.

(3)Error due to selection bias, which arises when the sampling plan is such that some members of the target population cannot possibly be selected for inclusion in the sample.

Chapter 6

6.2 a Subjective approach

b If all the teams in major league baseball have exactly the same players the New York Yankees will win 25% of all World Series.

6.4 a Subjective approach

b The Dow Jones Industrial Index will increase on 60% of the days if economic conditions remain unchanged.

6.6 {Adams wins. Brown wins, Collins wins, Dalton wins}

6.8 a {0, 1, 2, 3, 4, 5}

b {4, 5}

c P(5) = .10

d P(2, 3, or 4) = P(2) + P(3) + P(4) = .26 + .21 + .18 = .65

e P(6) = 0

6.10 P(Contractor 1 wins) = 2/6, P(Contractor 2 wins) = 3/6, P(Contractor 3 wins) = 1/6

6.12 a P(shopper does not use credit card) = P(shopper pays cash) + P(shopper pays by debit card)

= .30 + .10 = .40

b P(shopper pays cash or uses a credit card) = P(shopper pays cash) + P(shopper pays by credit card)

= .30 + .60 = .90

6.14 a P(single) = .15, P(married) = .50, P(divorced) = .25, P(widowed) = .10

b Relative frequency approach

6.16 $P(A_1) = .4 + .2 = .6$, $P(A_2) = .3 + .1 = .4$. $P(B_1) = .4 + .3 = .7$, $P(B_2) = .2 + .1 = .3$.

6.18 a $P(A_1 \mid B_1) = \dfrac{P(A_1 \text{ and } B_1)}{P(B_1)} = \dfrac{.4}{.7} = .57$

b $P(A_2 \mid B_1) = \dfrac{P(A_2 \text{ and } B_1)}{P(B_1)} = \dfrac{.3}{.7} = .43$

c Yes. It is not a coincidence. Given B_1 the events A_1 and A_2 constitute the entire sample space.

6.20 The events are not independent because $P(A_1 \mid B_2) \neq P(A_1)$.

6.22 $P(A_1 \mid B_1) = \dfrac{P(A_1 \text{ and } B_1)}{P(B_1)} = \dfrac{.20}{.20 + .15} = .571$; $P(A_1) = .20 + .60 = .80$; the events are dependent.

6.24 $P(A_1) = .20 + .25 = .45$, $P(A_2) = .15 + .25 = .40$, $P(A_3) = .10 + .05 = .15$.

$P(B_1) = .20 + 15 + .10 = .45$, $P(B_2) = .25 + .25 + .05 = .55$.

6.26 a $P(A_1 \text{ or } A_2) = P(A_1) + P(A_2) = .45 + .40 = .85$

b $P(A_2 \text{ or } B_2) = P(A_2) + P(B_2) - P(A_2 \text{ and } B_2) = .40 + .55 - .25 = .70$

c $P(A_3 \text{ or } B_1) = P(A_3) + P(B_1) - P(A_3 \text{ and } B_1) = .15 + .45 - .10 = .50$

6.28 a $P(\text{promoted} \mid \text{female}) = \dfrac{P(\text{promoted and female})}{P(\text{female})} = \dfrac{.05}{.05 + .12} = .294$

b $P(\text{promoted} \mid \text{male}) = \dfrac{P(\text{promoted and male})}{P(\text{male})} = \dfrac{.15}{.15 + .68} = .181$

c Yes, because promotion and gender are not independent events.

6.30 a P(He is a smoker) = .10 + .21 = .31

b P(He does not have lung disease) = .21 + .66 = .87

c $P(\text{He has lung disease} \mid \text{he is a smoker}) = \dfrac{P(\text{he has lung disease and he is a smoker})}{P(\text{he is a smoker})} = \dfrac{.10}{.31} = .323$

d P(He has lung disease | he does not smoke) =

$$\frac{P(\text{he has lung disease and he does not smoke})}{P(\text{he does not smoke})} = \frac{.03}{.69} = .044$$

6.32 a $P(\text{manual} \mid \text{math-stats}) = \dfrac{P(\text{manual and math}-\text{stats})}{P(\text{math}-\text{stats})} = \dfrac{.23}{.23+.36} = .390$

b P(computer) = .36 + .30 = .66

c No, because P(manual) = .23 + .11 = .34, which is not equal to P(manual | math-stats).

6.34 a $P(\text{ask} \mid \text{male}) = \dfrac{P(\text{ask and male})}{P(\text{male})} = \dfrac{.12}{.23+.12+.15} = \dfrac{.12}{.50} = .24$

b P(consult a map) = .23 + .14 = .37

c No, because $P(\text{consult map} \mid \text{male}) = \dfrac{P(\text{consult a map and male})}{P(\text{male})} = \dfrac{.23}{.23+.12+.15} = \dfrac{.25}{.50} = .46$, which

is not equal to P(consult map)

6.36 a P(remember) = .12 + .18 = .30

b $P(\text{remember} \mid \text{violent}) = \dfrac{P(\text{remember and violent})}{P(\text{violent})} = \dfrac{.12}{.12+.38} = \dfrac{.12}{.50} = .24$

c Yes, the events are dependent.

6.38 a P(uses a spreadsheet) = .311 + .312 = .623

b $P(\text{uses a spreadsheet} \mid \text{male}) = \dfrac{P(\text{uses a spreadsheet and male})}{P(\text{male})} = \dfrac{.312}{.312+.168} = \dfrac{.312}{.480} = .650$

c b $P(\text{female} \mid \text{uses a spreadsheet}) = \dfrac{P(\text{uses a spreadsheet and female})}{P(\text{uses a spreadsheet})} = \dfrac{.311}{.311+.209} = \dfrac{.311}{.520} = .598$

6.40 a P(under 20) = .2307 + .0993 + .5009 = .8309

b P(retail) = .5009 + .0876 + .0113 = .5998

c $P(\text{20 to 99} \mid \text{construction}) = \dfrac{P(\text{20 to 99 and construction})}{P(\text{construction})} = \dfrac{.0189}{.2307+.0189+.0019} = \dfrac{.0189}{.2515} = .0751$

6.42 a $P(\text{new} \mid \text{overdue}) = \dfrac{P(\text{new and overdue})}{P(\text{overdue})} = \dfrac{.08}{.08+.50} = \dfrac{.08}{.58} = .138$

b $P(\text{overdue} \mid \text{new}) = \dfrac{P(\text{new and overdue})}{P(\text{new})} = \dfrac{.08}{.08+.13} = \dfrac{.08}{.21} = .381$

c Yes, because P(new) = .21 $\neq$ P(new | overdue)

6.44 a P(unemployed | high school graduate) =

$$\frac{\text{P(unemployed and high school graduate)}}{\text{P(high school graduate)}} = \frac{.0128}{.3108 + .0128} = \frac{.0128}{.3236} = .0396$$

b P(employed) = .0975 + .3108 + .1785 + .0849 + .1959 + .0975 = .9651

c P(advanced degree | unemployed) =

$$\frac{\text{P(advanced degree and unemployed)}}{\text{P(unemployed)}} = \frac{.0015}{.0080 + .0128 + .0062 + .0023 + .0041 + .0015} = \frac{.0015}{.0349} = .0430$$

d P(not a high school graduate) = .0975 + .0080 = .1055

6.46 a P(bachelor's degree | west)

$$= \frac{\text{P(bachelor's degree and west)}}{\text{P(west)}} = \frac{.0418}{.0359 + .0608 + .0456 + .0181 + .0418 + .0180} = \frac{.0418}{.2202} = .1898$$

b P(northwest | high school graduate)

$$= \frac{\text{P(northwest and high school graduate)}}{\text{P(high school graduate)}} = \frac{.0711}{.0711 + .0843 + .1174 + .0608} = \frac{.0711}{.3336} = .2131$$

c P(south) = .0683 + .1174 + .0605 + .0248 + .0559 + .0269 = .3538

6.48

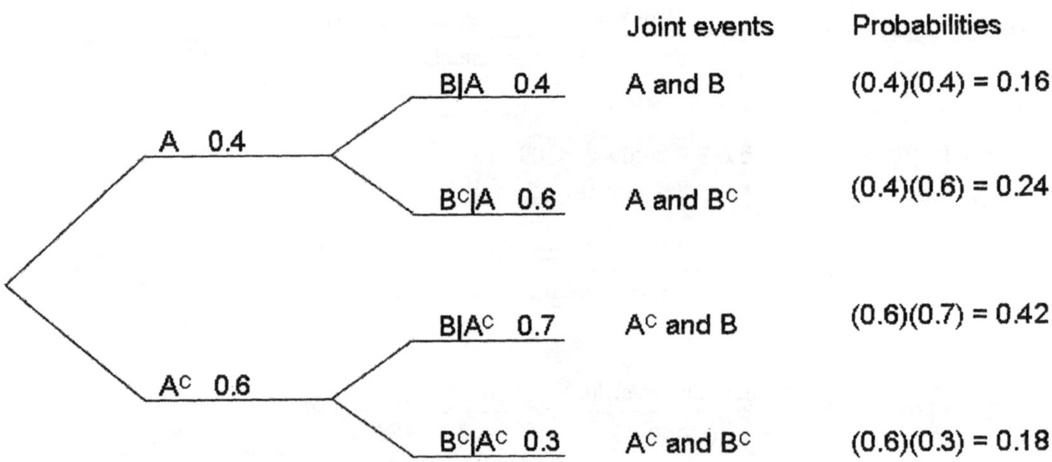

6.50

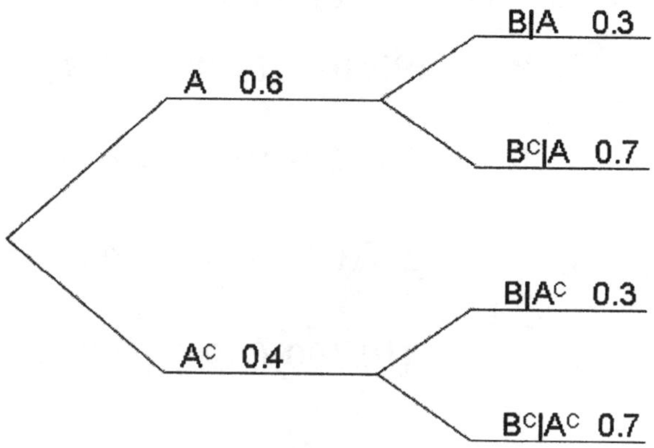

Joint events	Probabilities
A and B	(0.6)(0.3) = 0.18
A and B^c	(0.6)(0.7) = 0.42
A^c and B	(0.4)(0.3) = 0.12
A^c and B^c	(0.4)(0.7) = 0.28

6.52

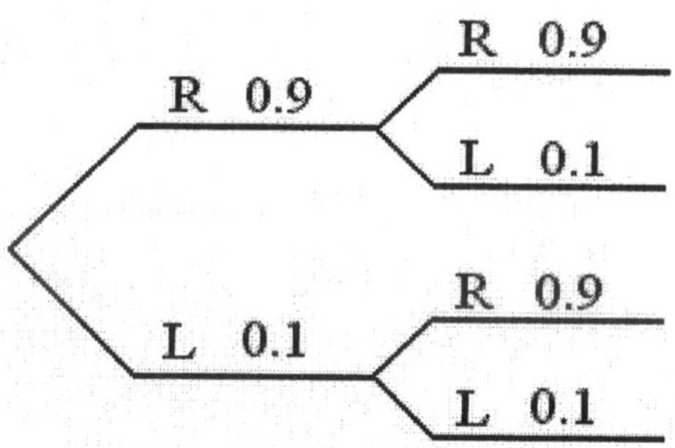

Joint events	Probabilities
R and R	(0.9)(0.9) = 0.81
R and L	(0.9)(0.1) = 0.09
L and R	(0.1)(0.9) = 0.09
L and L	(0.1)(0.1) = 0.01

a P(R and R) = .81

b P(L and L) = .01

c P(R and L) + P(L and R) = .09 + .09 = .18

d P(Rand L) + P(L and R) + P(R and R) = .09 + .09 + .81 = .99

6.54a

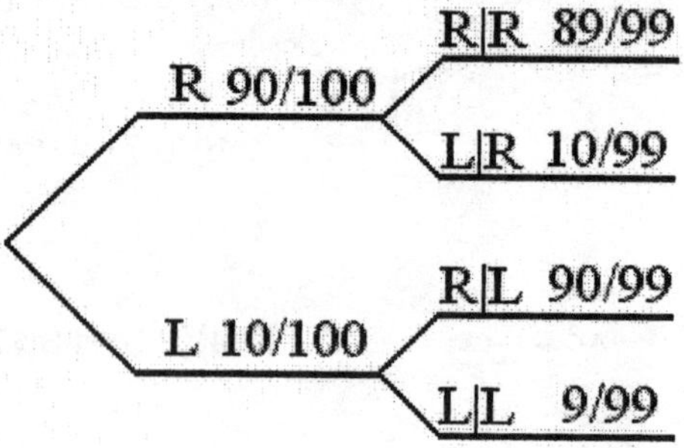

Joint events	Probabilities
R R	(90/100)(89/99) = 0.8091
R L	(90/100)(10/99) = 0.0909
L R	(10/100)(90/99) = 0.0909
L L	(10/100)(9/99) = 0.0091

b P(RR) = .8091

c P(LL) = .0091

d P(RL) + P(LR) = .0909 + .0909 = .1818

e P(RL) + P(LR) + P(RR) = .0909 + .0909 + .8091 = .9909

6.56

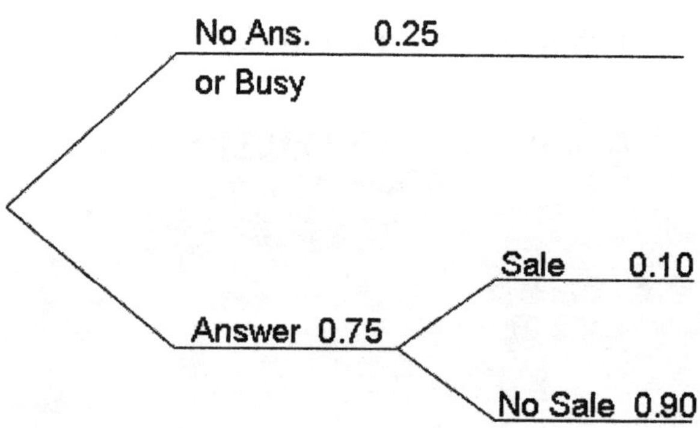

Joint events	Probabilities
	0.25
Answer and Sale	(0.75)(0.10) = 0.075

P(sale) = .075

6.58

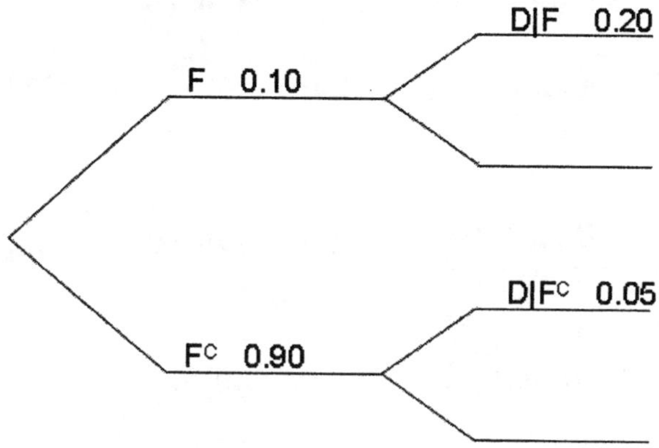

Joint events	Probabilities
F and D	(0.10)(0.20) = 0.02
F^C and D	(0.90)(0.05) = 0.045

P(D) = .02 + .045 = .065

6.60

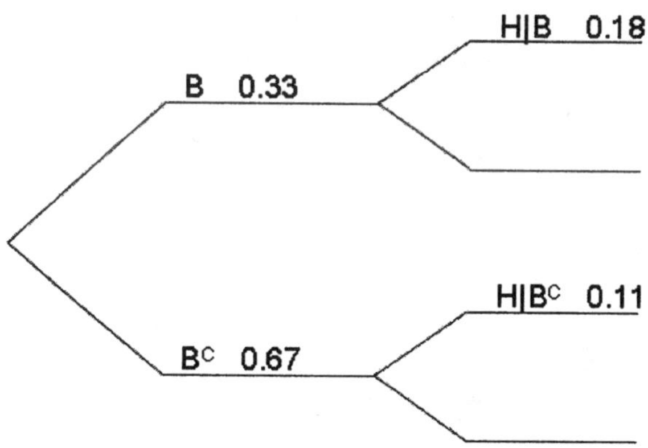

Joint events	Probabilities
B and H	(0.33)(0.18) = 0.0594
B^C and H	(0.67)(0.11) = 0.0737

P(heart attack) = .0594 + .0737 = .1331

6.62

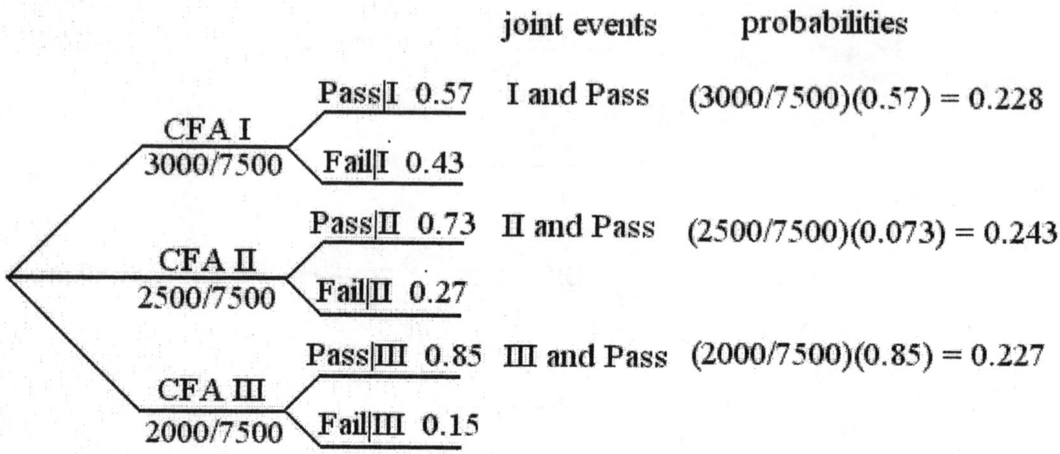

P(pass) = .228 + .243 + .227 = .698

6.64

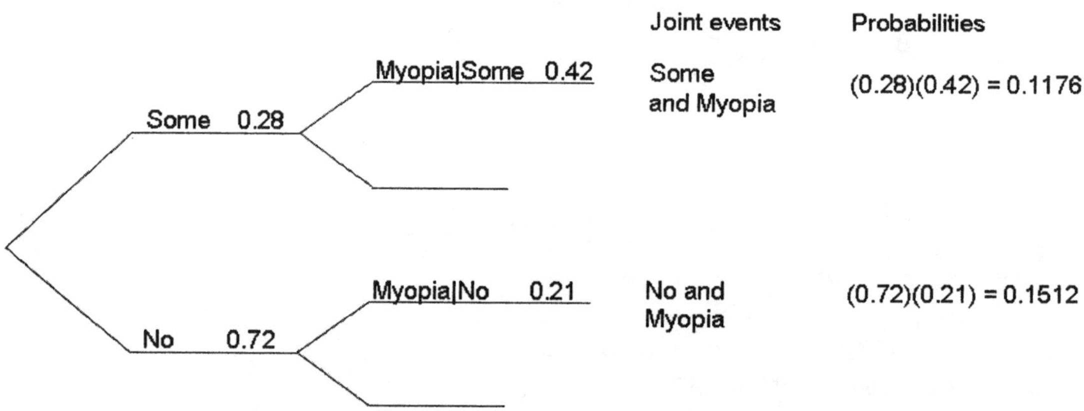

P(myopic) = .1176 + .1512 = .2688

6.66 Let A = mutual fund outperforms the market in the first year

B = mutual outperforms the market in the second year

P(A and B) = P(A)P(B | A) = (.15)(.22) = .033

6.68 Define the events:

M: The main control will fail.

B_1: The first backup will fail.

B_2: The second backup will fail

The probability that the plane will crash is

$P(M \text{ and } B_1 \text{ and } B_2) = [P(M)][P(B_1)][P(B_2)]$

$= (.0001)(.01)(.01)$

$= .00000001$

We have assumed that the 3 systems will fail independently of one another.

6.70

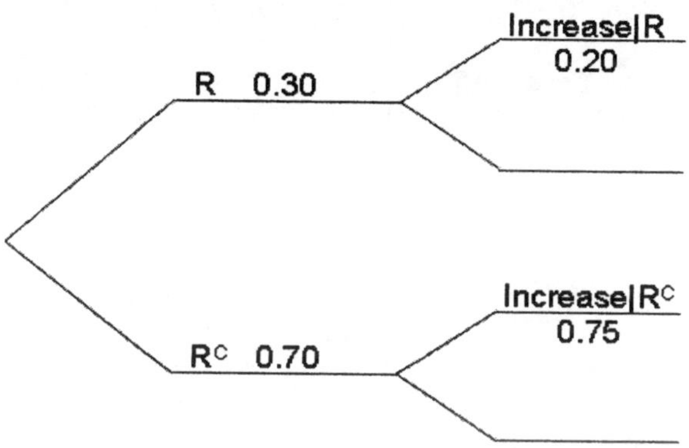

Joint events	Probabilities
R and Increase	(0.30)(0.20) = 0.06
R^C and Increase	(0.70)(0.75) = 0.525

P(Increase) = .06 + .525 = .585

6.72 P(A and B) = .32, $P(A^C \text{ and } B) = .14$, P(B) = .46, $P(B^C) = .54$

a $P(A \mid B) = \dfrac{P(A \text{ and } B)}{P(B)} = \dfrac{.32}{.46} = .696$

b $P(A^C \mid B) = \dfrac{P(A^C \text{ and } B)}{P(B)} = \dfrac{.14}{.46} = .304$

c $P(A \text{ and } B^C) = .48$; $P(A \mid B^C) = \dfrac{P(A \text{ and } B^C)}{P(B^C)} = \dfrac{.48}{.54} = .889$

d $P(A^C \text{ and } B^C) = .06$; $P(A^C \mid B^C) = \dfrac{P(A^C \text{ and } B^C)}{P(B^C)} = \dfrac{.06}{.54} = .111$

6.74 $P(F \mid D) = \dfrac{P(F \text{ and } D)}{P(D)} = \dfrac{.020}{.038} = .526$

6.76 $P(\text{CFA I} \mid \text{passed}) = \dfrac{P(\text{CFA I and passed})}{P(\text{passed})} = \dfrac{.228}{.698} = .327$

6.78 $P(A) = .40$, $P(B \mid A) = .85$, $P(B \mid A^C) = .29$

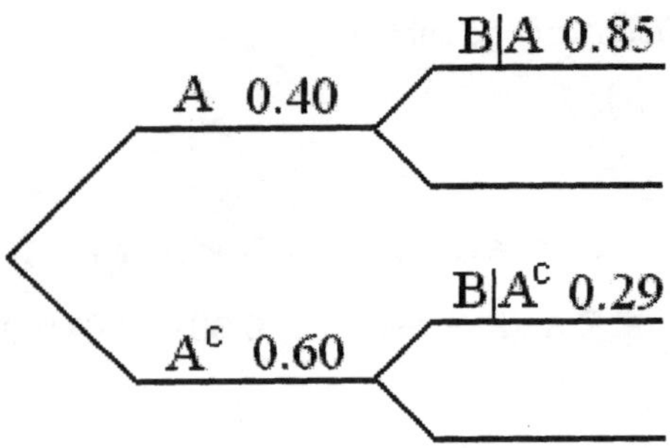

Joint events	Probabilities
A and B	(0.40)(0.85) = 0.34
A^C and B	(0.60)(0.29) = 0.174

$P(B) = .34 + .174 = .514$

$P(A \mid B) = \dfrac{P(A \text{ and } B)}{P(B)} = \dfrac{.34}{.514} = .661$

6.80 Define events: A, B, C = airlines A, B, and C, D = on time

$P(A) = .50$, $P(B) = .30$, $P(C) = .20$, $P(D \mid A) = .80$, $P(D \mid B) = .65$, $P(D \mid C) = .40$

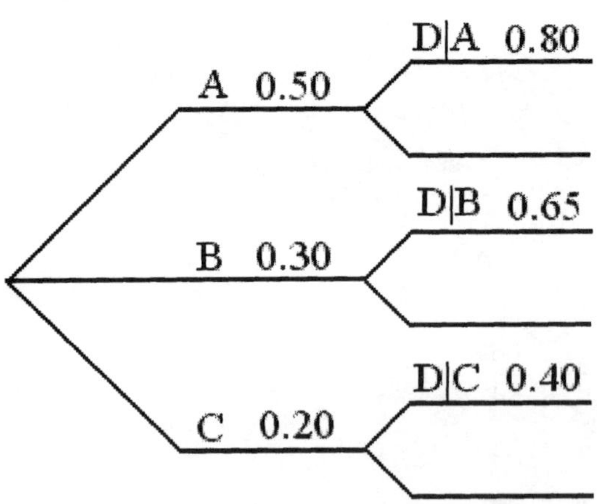

Joint events	Probabilities
AD	(0.50)(0.80) = 0.40
BD	(0.30)(0.65) = 0.195
CD	(0.20)(0.40) = 0.08

$P(D) = .40 + .195 + .08 = .675$

$$P(A \mid D) = \frac{P(A \text{ and } D)}{P(D)} = \frac{.40}{.675} = .593$$

6.82

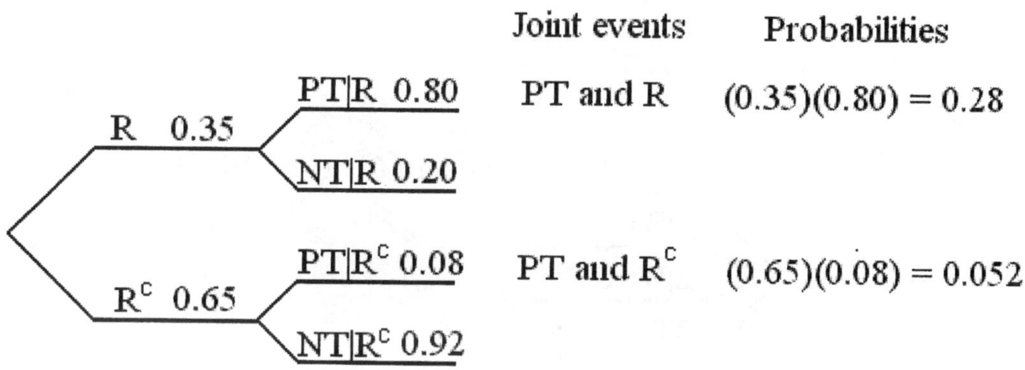

$P(PT) = .28 + .052 = .332$

$$P(R \mid PT) = \frac{P(R \text{ and } PT)}{P(PT)} = \frac{.28}{.332} = .843$$

6.84 Sensitivity = $P(PT \mid H) = .920$

Specificity = $P(NT \mid H^C) = .973$

Positive predictive value = $P(H \mid PT) = .1460$

Negative predictive value = $P H^C \mid NT) = \frac{P(H^C \text{ and } NT)}{P(NT)} = \frac{.9681}{.0004 + .9681} = \frac{.9681}{.9685} = .9996$

6.86 a P(Marketing-A) = .06 + .23 = .29

b P(Marketing A | Statistics not A) = $\frac{\text{P(Marketing A and Statistics not A)}}{\text{P(Statistics not A)}} = \frac{.23}{.23 + .58} = \frac{.23}{.81} = .2840$

c No, the probabilities in (a) and (b) differ

6.88 a P(second) = .05 + .14 = .19

b P(successful | −8 or less) = $\frac{\text{P(successful and } -8 \text{ or less)}}{\text{P}(-8 \text{ or less})} = \frac{.15}{.15 + .14} = \frac{.15}{.29} = .517$

c No, because P(successful) = .66 + .15 = .81, which is not equal to P(successful | –8 or less) .

6.90 $P(A^C \mid B) = \dfrac{P(A^C \text{ and } B)}{P(B)} = \dfrac{.221}{.749} = .295$

6.92

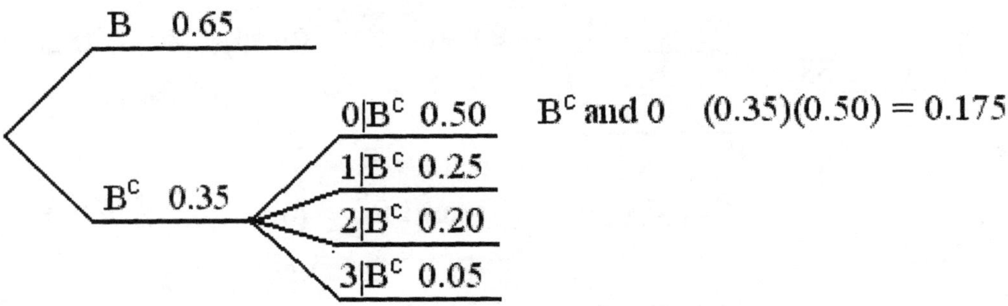

P(no sale) = .65 + .175 = .825

6.94

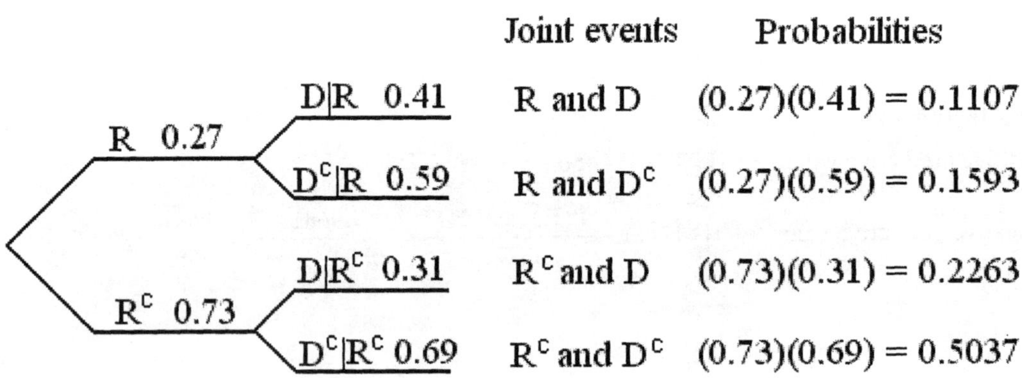

a $P(D) = P(R \text{ and } D) + P(R^C \text{ and } D) = .1107 + .2263 = .3370$

$P(R \mid D) = \dfrac{P(R \text{ and } D)}{P(D)} = \dfrac{.1107}{.3370} = .3285$

b $P(D^C) = P(R \text{ and } D^C) + P(R^C \text{ and } D^C) = .1593 + .5037 = .6630$

$$P(R|D^C) = \frac{P(R \text{ and } D^C)}{P(D^C)} = \frac{.1593}{.6630} = .2403$$

6.96

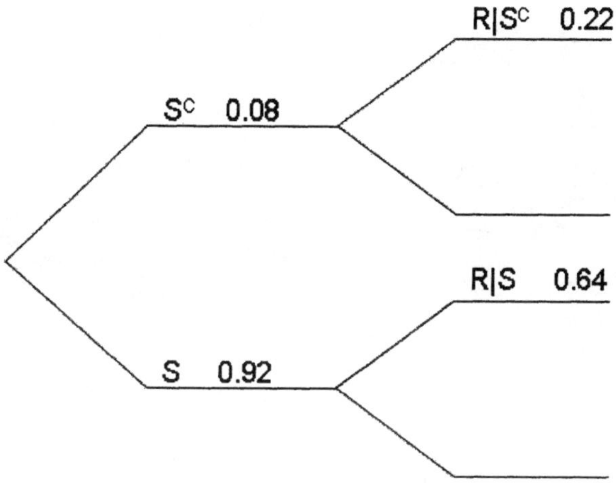

P(R) = .0176 + .5888 = .6064

$$P(S | R) = \frac{P(S \text{ and } R)}{P(R)} = \frac{.5888}{.6064} = .9710$$

6.98 Define the events: A_1 = envelope containing two Maui brochures is selected, A_2 = envelope containing two Oahu brochures is selected, A_3 = envelope containing one Maui and one Oahu brochures is selected. B = a Maui brochure is removed from the selected envelope.

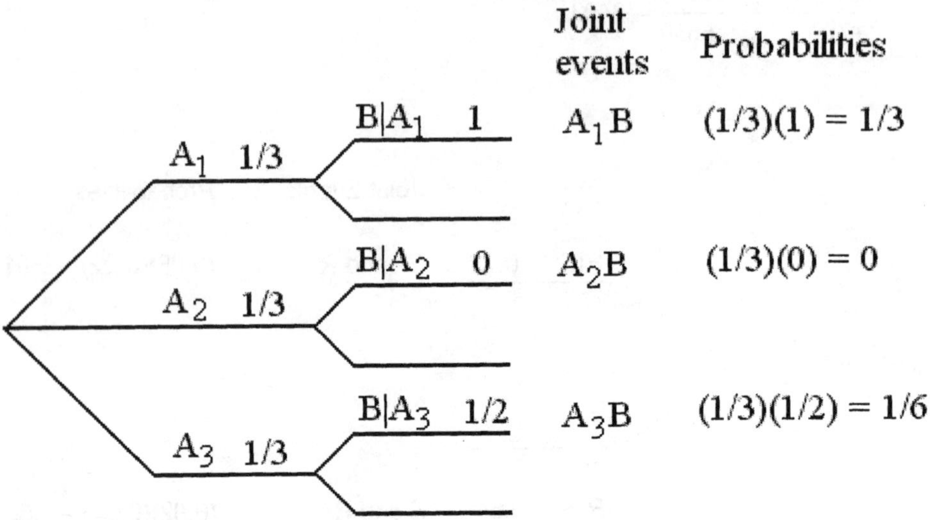

P(B) = 1/3 + 0 + 1/6 = 1/2

$$P(A_1 \mid B) = \frac{P(A_1 \text{ and } B)}{P(B)} = \frac{1/3}{1/2} = 2/3$$

6.100 Define events: A = company fail, B = predict bankruptcy

$P(A) = .08$, $P(B \mid A) = .85$, $P(B^C \mid A^C) = .74$

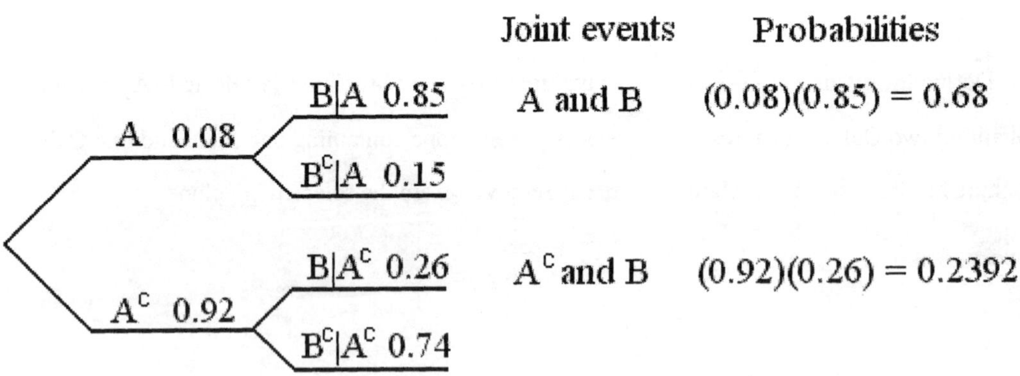

P(B) = .068 + .2392 = .3072

$$P(A \mid B) = \frac{P(A \text{ and } B)}{P(B)} = \frac{.068}{.3072} = .2214$$

6.102 Probabilities of outcomes: P(HH) = .25, P(HT) = .25, P(TH) = .25, P(TT) .25

P(TT | HH is not possible) = .25/(.25 + .25 + .25) = .333

Chapter 7

7.2 a 0, 1, 2, …, 100

b Yes.

c Yes, there are 101 values.

d The variable is discrete because it is countable.

7.4 a any value between 0 and several hundred miles

b No, because we cannot identify the second value or any other value larger than 0.

c No, uncountable means infinite.

d The variable is continuous.

7.6 P(x) = 1/6 for x = 1, 2, 3, 4, 5, and 6

7.8 a $P(2 \le X \le 5) = P(2) + P(3) + P(4) + P(5) = .310 + .340 + .220 + .080 = .950$

$P(X > 5) = P(6) + P(7) = .019 + .001 = .020$

$P(X < 4) = P(0) + P(1) + P(2) + P(3) = .005 + .025 + .310 + .340 = .680$

b. b. $E(X) = \sum xP(x) = 0(.005) + 1(.025) + 2(.310) + 4(.340) +5(.080) + 6(.019) + 7(.001) = 3.066$

c. $\sigma^2 = V(X) = \sum (x-\mu)^2 P(x) = (0–3.066)^2(.005) + (1–3.066)^2(.025) + (2–3.066)^2(.310)$

$+ (3–3.066)^2(.340) + (4–3.066)^2(.220) + (5–3.066)^2(.080) + (6–3.066)^2(.019)$

$+ (7–3.066)^2(.001) = 1.178$

$\sigma = \sqrt{\sigma^2} = \sqrt{1.178} = 1.085$

7.10 a $P(X > 0) = P(2) + P(6) + P(8) = .2 + .4 + .1 = .7$

b $P(X \ge 1) = P(2) + P(6) + P(8) = .2 + .4 + .1 = .7$

c $P(X \ge 2) = P(2) + P(6) + P(8) = .2 + .4 + .1 = .7$

d $P(2 \le X \le 5) = P(2) = .2$

7.12 P(Losing 6 in a row) = $.5^6 = .0156$

7.14

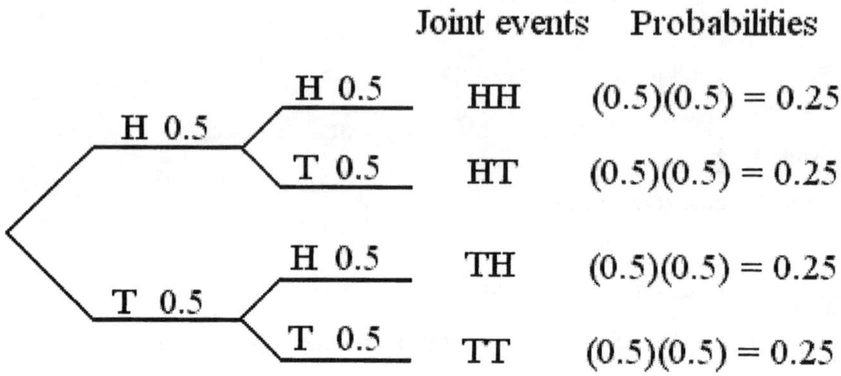

a P(HH) = .25

b P(HT) = .25

c P(TH) = .25

d P(TT) = .25

7.16

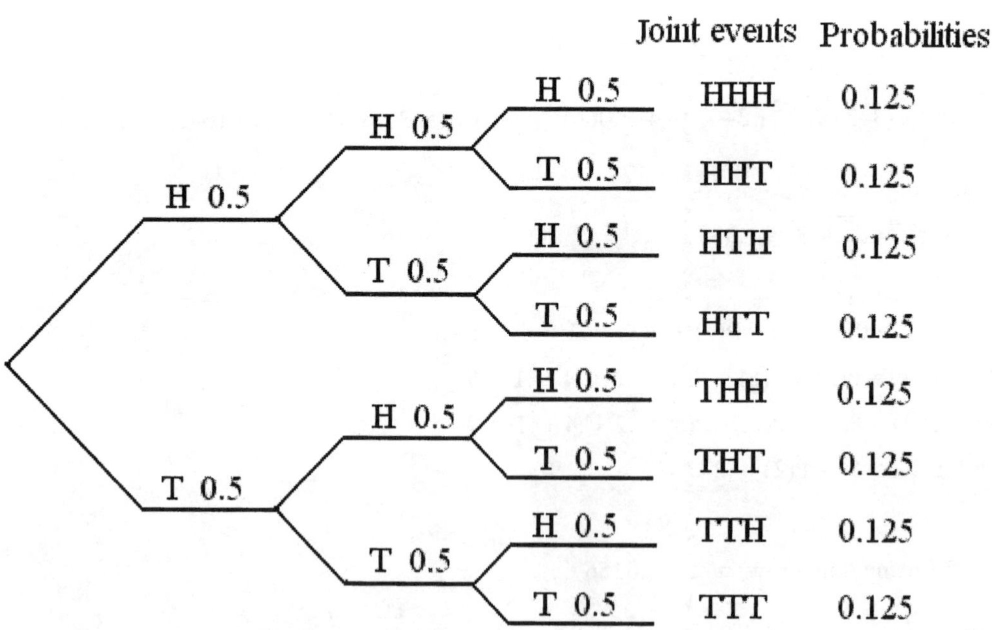

7.18a. $\mu = E(X) = \sum xP(x) = -4(.59) + 5(.15) + 7(.25) + 8(.01) = .22$

$\sigma^2 = V(X) = \sum (x-\mu)^2 P(x) = (-4-.22)^2(.59) + (5-.22)^2(.15) + (7-.22)^2(.25) + (8-.22)^2(.01)$

$= 26.03$

b.

x	–4	5	7	8
y	–20	25	35	40
P(y)	.59	.15	.25	.01

c. $E(Y) = \sum yP(y) = -20(.59) + 25(.15) + 35(.25) + 40(.01) = 1.10$

$V(Y) = \sum (y-\mu)^2 P(y) = (-20-1.10)^2(.59) + (25-1.10)^2(.15) + (35-1.1)^2(.25)$

$+ (40-1.1)^2(.01) = 650.8$

d. $E(Y) = E(5X) = 5E(X) = 5(.22) = 1.10$

$V(Y) = V(5X) = 5^2 V(X) = 25(26.03) = 650.8.$

7.20a. $P(X \geq 2) = P(2) + P(3) = .4 + .2 = .6$

b. $\mu = E(X) = \sum xP(x) = 0(.2) + 1(.3) + 2(.4) + 3(.1) = 1.4$

$\sigma^2 = V(X) = \sum (x-\mu)^2 P(x) = (0-1.4)^2(.2) + (1-1.4)^2(.3) + (2-1.4)^2(.4) + (3-1.4)^2(.1) = .84$

7.22 a $P(X > 4) = P(5) + P(6) + P(7) = .20 + .10 + .10 = .40$

b $P(X \geq 2) = 1 - P(X \leq 1) = 1 - P(1) = 1 - .05 = .95$

7.24 $Y = .25X$; $E(Y) = .25E(X) = .25(4.1) = 1.025$

$V(Y) = V(.25X) - (.25)^2(2.69) = .168$

7.26 a $P(4) = .06$

b $P(8) = 0$

c $P(0) = .35$

d $P(X \geq 1) = 1 - P(0) = 1 - .35 = .65$

7.28 a $P(X = 3) = P(3) = .21$

b $P(X \geq 5) = P(5) + P(6) + P(7) + P(8) = .12 + .08 + .06 + .05 = .31$

c $P(5 \leq X \leq 7) = P(5) + P(6) + P(7) = .12 + .08 + .06 = .26$

7.30 $\mu = E(X) = \sum xP(x) = 0(.04) + 1(.19) + 2(.22) + 3(.28) + 4(.12) + 5(.09) + 6(.06) = 2.76$

$\sigma^2 = V(X) = \sum (x - \mu)^2 P(x) = (1–2.76)^2 (.04) + (2–2.76)^2 (.19) + (3–2.76)^2 (.28)$

$+ (4–2.76)^2 (.12) + (5–2.76)^2 (.09) + (6–2.76)^2 (.06) = 2.302$

$\sigma = \sqrt{\sigma^2} = \sqrt{2.302} = 1.517$

7.32 $\mu = E(X) = \sum xP(x) = 1(.24) + 2(.18) + 3(.13) + 4(.10) + 5(.07) + 6(.04) + 7(.04) + 8(.20) =$ 3.86

$\sigma^2 = V(X) = \sum (x - \mu)^2 P(x) = (1–3.86)^2 (.24) + (2–3.86)^2 (.18) + (3–3.86)^2 (.13) + (4–3.86)^2 (.10)$

$+ (5–3.86)^2 (.07) +(6–3.86)^2 (.04) + (7–3.86)^2 (.04) + (8–3.86)^2 (.20) = 6.78$

$\sigma = \sqrt{\sigma^2} = \sqrt{6.78} = 2.60$

7.34 E(Value of coin) = 400(.40) + 900(.30) + 100(.30) = 460. Take the $500.

7.36 E(damage costs) = .01(400) + .02(200) + .10(100) + .87(0) = 18. The owner should pay up to $18 for the device.

7.38 $\mu = E(X) = \sum xP(x) = 1(.05) + 2(.12) + 3(.20) + 4(.30) + 5(.15) + 6(.10) + 7\,(.08) = 4.00$

$\sigma^2 = V(X) = \sum (x - \mu)^2 P(x) = (1–4.0)^2 (.05) + (2–4.0)^2 (.12) + (3–4.0)^2 (.20) + (4–4.0)^2 (.30)$

$+ (5–4.0)^2 (.15) +(6–4.0)^2 (.10) + (7–4.0)^2 (.08) = 2.40$

7.40 $\mu = E(X) = \sum xP(x) = 0(.10) + 1(.25) + 2(.40) + 3(.20) + 4(.05) = 1.85$

7.42 Breakeven point = 15,000/(7.40 – 3.00) = 3,409

7.44 a $\sum_{\text{all x}} \sum_{\text{all y}} xyP(x, y) = (1)(1)(.5) + (1)(2)(.1) + (2)(1)(.1) + (2)(2)(.3) = 2.1$

$COV(X, Y) = \sum_{\text{all x}} \sum_{\text{all y}} xyP(x, y) - \mu_x\mu_y = 2.1 - (1.4)(1.4) = .14$

$\sigma_x = \sqrt{\sigma_x^2} = \sqrt{.24} = .49,\ \sigma_y = \sqrt{\sigma_y^2} = \sqrt{.24} = .49$

$$\rho = \frac{COV(X, Y)}{\sigma_x \sigma_y} = \frac{.14}{(.49)(.49)} = .58$$

7.46 a

x + y	P(x + y)
2	.5
3	.2
4	.3

b $\mu_{x+y} = E(X+Y) = \sum (x+y)P(x+y) = 2(.5) + 3(.2) + 4(.3) = 2.8$

$\sigma_{x+y}^2 = V(X+Y) = \sum [(x+y) - \mu_{x+y}]^2 P(x+y) = (2-2.8)^2(.5) + (3-2.8)^2(.2) + (4-2.8)^2(.3) = .76$

c Yes

7.48 a $\sum_{\text{all } x} \sum_{\text{all } y} xyP(x, y) = (1)(1)(.28) + (1)(2)(.12) + (2)(1)(.42) + (2)(2)(.18) = 2.08$

$COV(X, Y) = \sum_{\text{all } x} \sum_{\text{all } y} xyP(x, y) - \mu_x \mu_y = 2.08 - (1.6)(1.3) = 0$

$\sigma_x = \sqrt{\sigma_x^2} = \sqrt{.24} = .49,\ \sigma_y = \sqrt{\sigma_y^2} = \sqrt{.21} = .46$

$$\rho = \frac{COV(X, Y)}{\sigma_x \sigma_y} = \frac{0}{(.49)(.46)} = 0$$

7.50 a

x + y	P(x + y)
2	.28
3	.54
4	.18

b $\mu_{x+y} = E(X+Y) = \sum (x+y)P(x+y) = 2(.28) + 3(.54) + 4(.18) = 2.9$

$\sigma_{x+y}^2 = V(X+Y) = \sum [(x+y) - \mu_{x+y}]^2 P(x+y) = (2-2.9)^2(.28) + (3-2.9)^2(.54) + (4-2.9)^2(.18)$

$= .45$

c Yes

7.52

y	x = 0	1	2
1	.42	.21	.07
2	.18	.09	.03

7.54 a

Refrigerators, x	P(x)
0	.22
1	.49
2	.29

b

Stoves, y	P(y)
0	.34
1	.39
2	.27

c $\mu_x = E(X) = \sum xP(x) = 0(.22) + 1(.49) + 2(.29) = 1.07$

$\sigma^2 = V(X) = \sum (x - \mu)^2 P(x) = (0\text{–}1.07)^2(.22) + (1\text{–}1.07)^2(.49) + (2\text{–}1.07)^2(.29) = .505$

d $\mu_y = E(Y) = \sum yP(y) = 0(.34) + 1(.39) + 2(.27) = .93$

$\sigma^2 = V(Y) = \sum (y - \mu)^2 P(y) = (0\text{–}.93)^2(.34) + (1\text{–}.93)^2(.39) + (2\text{–}.93)^2(.27) = .605$

e $\sum_{\text{all } x} \sum_{\text{all } y} xyP(x, y) = (0)(0)(.08) + (0)(1)(.09) + (0)(2)(.05) + (1)(0)(.14) + (1)(1)(.17)$

$+ (1)(2)(18) + (2)(0)(.12) + (21)(1)(13) + (2)(2)(.04) = .95$

$COV(X, Y) = \sum_{\text{all } x} \sum_{\text{all } y} xyP(x, y) - \mu_x\mu_y = .95 - (1.07)(.93) = -.045$

$\sigma_x = \sqrt{\sigma_x^2} = \sqrt{.505} = .711, \ \sigma_y = \sqrt{\sigma_y^2} = \sqrt{.605} = .778$

$$\rho = \frac{COV(X, Y)}{\sigma_x \sigma_y} = \frac{-.045}{(.711)(.778)} = -.081$$

7.56 a P(X = 1 | Y = 0) = P(X =1 and Y = 0)/P(Y = 0) = .14/.34 = .412

b P(Y = 0 | X = 1) = P(X =1 and Y = 0)/P(X = 1) = .14/.49 = .286

c P(X = 2 | Y = 2) = P(X =2 and Y = 2)/P(Y = 2) = .04/.27 = .148

7.58 $E\left(\sum X_i\right)=\sum E(X_i)=35+20+20+50+20=145$

$V\left(\sum X_i\right)=\sum V(X_i)=8+5+4+12+2=31$

$\sigma=\sqrt{31}=5.57$

7.60 $E\left(\sum X_i\right)=\sum E(X_i)=10+3+30+5+100+20=168$

$V\left(\sum X_i\right)=\sum V(X_i)=9+0+100+1+400+64=574$

$\sigma=\sqrt{574}=24.0$

7.62 $E(R_p) = .211$

$V(R_p) = w_1^2\,\sigma_1^2 + w_2^2\,\sigma_2^2 + 2\,w_1\,w_2\,\rho\,\sigma_1\,\sigma_2$

$= (.30)^2(.02)^2+(.70)^2(.15^2)+2(.30)(.70)(.25)(.02)(.15)=.0114$

$\sigma_{R_p}=\sqrt{.0114}=.1067$

7.64 The expected value does not change. The standard deviation decreases.

7.66 $E(R_p) = w_1E(R_1) + w_2E(R_2) = (.60)(.09) + (.40)(.13) = .1060$

$V(R_p) = w_1^2\,\sigma_1^2 + w_2^2\,\sigma_2^2 + 2\,w_1\,w_2\,\rho\,\sigma_1\,\sigma_2$

$= (.60)^2(.15)^2+(.40)^2(.21^2)+2(.60)(.40)(.4)(.15)(.21)=.0212$

The statistics used in Exercises 7.68 to 7.80 were computed by Excel. The variances were taken from the variance-covariance matrix. As a result they are the population parameters. To convert to statistics multiply the variance of the portfolio returns by n/(n–1).

7.68 a

Stock	1	2	3
Means	.0463	.1293	–.0016
Variances	.0148	.0100	.0039

b Invest all your money in stock 2; it has the largest mean return.

c Invest all your money in stock 3; it has the smallest variance.

7.70 a

	A	B	C	D	E
1	**Portfolio of 3 Stocks**				
2			**Stock 1**	**Stock 2**	**Stock 3**
3	**Variance-Covariance Matrix**	**Stock 1**	0.0148		
4		**Stock 2**	0.0037	0.0100	
5		**Stock 3**	0.0015	-0.0012	0.0039
6					
7	**Expected Returns**		0.0463	0.1293	-0.0016
8					
9	**Weights**		0.5	0.3	0.2
10					
11	**Portfolio Return**				
12	**Expected Value**	**0.0616**			
13	**Variance**	**0.0060**			
14	**Standard Deviation**	**0.0777**			

b The mean return on this portfolio is greater than the mean returns on stocks 1 and 3 and the portfolio in Exercise 7.69, but smaller than that of stock 2. The variance of the returns on this portfolio is smaller than that for stocks 1 and 2 and larger than that of stock 3 and the portfolio in Exercise 7.69.

7.72 a

	A	B	C	D	E
1	**Portfolio of 3 Stocks**				
2			**Stock 1**	**Stock 2**	**Stock 3**
3	**Variance-Covariance Matrix**	**Stock 1**	0.0957		
4		**Stock 2**	-0.0288	0.2345	
5		**Stock 3**	0.0004	0.0243	0.0515
6					
7	**Expected Returns**		0.0232	0.0601	0.0136
8					
9	**Weights**		0.3	0.4	0.3
10					
11	**Portfolio Return**				
12	**Expected Value**	**0.0351**			
13	**Variance**	**0.0498**			
14	**Standard Deviation**	**0.2231**			

b The mean return on the portfolio is greater than the mean returns on stocks 1 and 3, but smaller than that of stock 2. The variance of the returns on the portfolio is smaller than that for the three stocks.

7.74 a

Stock	1	2	3	4
Means	.0187	−.0176	.0153	.0495
Variances	.0615	.0232	.0228	.0517

b Invest all your money in stock 4; it has the largest mean return.

c Invest all your money in stock 3; it has the smallest variance.

7.76 a

	A	B	C	D	E	F
1	**Portfolio of 4 Stocks**					
2			**Stock 1**	**Stock 2**	**Stock 3**	**Stock 4**
3	**Variance-Covariance Matrix**	**Stock 1**	0.0615			
4		**Stock 2**	-0.0012	0.0232		
5		**Stock 3**	0.0168	-0.0022	0.0228	
6		**Stock 4**	0.0129	0.0179	-0.0005	0.0517
7						
8	**Expected Returns**		0.0187	-0.0176	0.0153	0.0495
9						
10	**Weights**		0.20	0.20	0.10	0.50
11						
12	**Portfolio Return**					
13	**Expected Value**	**0.0265**				
14	**Variance**	**0.0231**				
15	**Standard Deviation**	**0.1521**				

b The mean return on this portfolio is greater than the mean return on stocks 1, 2, and 3, and the mean return on the portfolio in Exercise 7.75. It is smaller than the mean return on stock 4. The variance of the returns on this portfolio is smaller than that for stocks 1, 2, and 4, but larger than the variance on the returns of stock 3 and the variance of the returns on the portfolio in Exercise 7.75.

7.78 a

	GE	*SEAGRAM*	*COKE*	*MCDONALDS*
GE	0.0019			
SEAGRAM	0.0004	0.0043		
COKE	0.0004	-0.0005	0.0017	
MCDONALDS	0.0004	0.0011	0.0002	0.0025

b Invest in General Electric and Coca-Cola.

7.80 We created a portfolio with the following weights

General Electric	40%
Seagram	10%
Coca-Cola	40%
McDonald's	10%

	A	B	C	D	E	F
1	**Portfolio of 4 Stocks**					
2			**GE**	**SEAGRAM**	**COKE**	**MCDONALDS**
3	**Variance-Covariance Matrix**	**GE**	0.0019			
4		**SEAGRAM**	0.0004	0.0043		
5		**COKE**	0.0004	-0.0005	0.0017	
6		**MCDONALDS**	0.0004	0.0011	0.0002	0.0025
7						
8	**Expected Returns**		0.0231	0.0148	0.0213	0.0156
9						
10	**Weights**		0.40	0.10	0.40	0.10
11						
12	**Portfolio Return**					
13	**Expected Value**	**0.0208**				
14	**Variance**	**0.0008**				
15	**Standard Deviation**	**0.0289**				

7.82 a $P(X = 3) = P(X \le 3) - P(X \le 2) = .650 - .383 = .267$

b $P(X = 5) = P(X \le 5) - P(X \le 4) = .953 - .850 = .103$

c $P(X = 8) = P(X \le 8) - P(X \le 7) = 1.000 - .998 = .002$

7.84 $P(X = x) = \frac{n!}{x!(n-x)!} p^x (1-p)^{n-x}$

a $P(X = 0) = \frac{5!}{0!(5-0)!} (.4)^0 (1-.4)^{5-0} = .0778$

b a $P(X = 2) = \frac{5!}{2!(5-2)!} (.4)^2 (1-.4)^{5-2} = .3456$

c $P(X \le 3) = P(0) + P(1) + P(2) + P(3) = .0778 + .2592 + .3456 + .2304 = .9130$

d $P(X \ge 2) = P(2) + P(3) + P(4) + P(5) = .3456 + .2304 + .0768 + .0102 = .6630$

7.86 a .07776

b .34560

c .91296

d .66304

7.88 a .17119

b .09164

c .90953

d .81056

7.90 Binomial distribution with p = .20

a $P(X = 1) = \frac{4!}{1!(4-1)!}(.20)^1(1-.20)^{4-1} = .4096$

b Table 1 with n = 8: $p(2) = P(X \le 2) - P(X \le 1) = .797 - .503 = .294$

c Excel: $P(10) = .10745$

7.92 a $P(X = 2) = \frac{5!}{2!(5-2)!}(.45)^2(1-.45)^{5-2} = .3369$

b Excel with n = 25 and p = .45: $P(X \ge 10) = 1 - P(X \le 9) = 1 - .2424 = .7576$

7.94 a $P(X = 2) = \frac{5!}{2!(5-2)!}(.52)^2(1-.52)^{5-2} = .2990$

b Excel with n = 25 and p = .52: $P(X \ge 10) = 1 - P(X \le 9) = 1 - .08033 = .91967$

7.96 Table 1 with n = 25 and p = .3: $P(X \le 10) = .902$

7.98 $P(X = 0) = \frac{4!}{01!(4-0)!}(.8)^0(1-.8)^{4-0} = .0016$

7.100 Table 1 with n = 25 and p = .60: $P(X \ge 15) = 1 - P(X \le 14) = 1 - .414 = .586$

7.102 Table 1 with n = 25 and p = .10

a $P(X = 0) = P(X \le 0) = .072$

b $P(X < 5) = P(X \le 4) = .902$

c $P(X > 2) = P(X \ge 3) = 1 - P(X \le 2) = 1 - .537 = .463$

7.104 $P(X = 20) = \dfrac{20!}{20!(20-20)!}(.75)^{20}(1-.75)^{20-20} = .00317$

7.106 Excel with n = 100 and p = .25: $P(X > 25) = P(X \geq 26) = 1 - P(X \leq 25) = 1 - .55347$
$= .44653$

7.108 Excel with n = 50 and p = .45: $P(X \geq 19) = 1 - P(X \leq 18) = 1 - .12735 = .87265$

7.110 a $P(X = 0) = \dfrac{e^{-\mu}\mu^x}{x!} = \dfrac{e^{-2}2^0}{0!} = .1353$

b $P(X = 3) = \dfrac{e^{-\mu}\mu^x}{x!} = \dfrac{e^{-2}2^3}{3!} = .1804$

c $P(X = 5) = \dfrac{e^{-\mu}\mu^x}{x!} = \dfrac{e^{-2}2^5}{5!} = .0361$

7.112 a Table 2 with $\mu = 3.5$: $P(X = 0) = P(X \leq 0) = .030$

b Table 2 with $\mu = 3.5$: $P(X \geq 5) = 1 - P(X \leq 4) = 1 - .725 = .275$

c Table 2 with $\mu = 3.5/7$: $P(X = 1) = P(X \leq 1) - P(X \leq 0) = .910 - .607 = .303$

7.114 $P(X = 0 \text{ with } \mu = 2) = \dfrac{e^{-\mu}\mu^x}{x!} = \dfrac{e^{-2}(2)^0}{0!} = .1353$

7.116 a $P(X = 0 \text{ with } \mu = 3) = \dfrac{e^{-\mu}\mu^x}{x!} = \dfrac{e^{-3}(3)^0}{0!} = .0498$

b $P(X = 10 \text{ with } \mu = 21) = \dfrac{e^{-\mu}\mu^x}{x!} = \dfrac{e^{-21}(21)^{10}}{10!} = .0035$

7.118 $P(X = 0 \text{ with } \mu = 80/200) = \dfrac{e^{-\mu}\mu^x}{x!} = \dfrac{e^{-.4}(.4)^0}{0!} = .6703$

7.120 a Table 2 with $\mu = 1.5$: $P(X \geq 2) = 1 - P(X \leq 1) = 1 - .558 = .442$

b Table 2 $\mu = 6$: $P(X < 4) = P(X \le 3) = .151$

7.122 a $P(X = 0 \text{ with } \mu = 1.5) = \frac{e^{-\mu}\mu^x}{x!} = \frac{e^{-1.5}(1.5)^0}{0!}$ .2231

b Table 2 with $\mu = 4.5$: $P(X \le 5) = .703$

c Table 2 with $\mu = 3.0$: $P(X \ge 3) = 1 - P(X \le 2 = 1 - .423 = .577$

7.124 a $E(X) = np = 40(.02) = .8$

b $P(X = 0) = \frac{40!}{0!(40-0)!}(.02)^0(1-.02)^{40-0} = .4457$

7.126 a $P(X = 10 \text{ with } \mu = 8) = \frac{e^{-\mu}\mu^x}{x!} = \frac{e^{-8}(8)^{10}}{10!} = .0993$

b Table 2 with $\mu = 8$: $P(X > 5) = P(X \ge 6) = 1 - P(X \le 5) = 1 - .191 = .809$

c Table 2 with $\mu = 8$: $P(X < 12) = P(X \le 11) = .888$

7.128 Table 1 with n = 10 and p = .3: $P(X > 5) = P(X \ge 6) = 1 - P(X \le 5) = 1 - .953 = .047$

7.130 Table 1 with n = 10 and p = .20: $P(X \ge 6) = 1 - P(X \le 5) = 1 - .994 = .006$

7.132 a Excel with n = 80 and p = .70: $P(X > 65) = P(X \ge 66) = 1 - P(X \le 65) = 1 - .99207 =$ .00793

b $E(X) = np = 80(.70) = 56$

c $\sigma = \sqrt{np(1-p)^2} = \sqrt{80(.70)(1-.70)} = 4.10$

7.134 Table 1 with n = 25 and p = .40:

a $P(X = 10) = P(X \le 10) - P(X \le 9) = .586 - .425 = .161$

b $P(X < 5) = P(X \le 4) = .009$

c $P(X > 15) = P(X \ge 16) = 1 - P(X \le 15) = 1 - .987 = .013$

7.136 a $\mu = E(X) = \sum xP(x) = 0(.36) + 1(.22) + 2(.20) + 3(.09) + 4(.08) + 5(.05) = 1.46$

$\sigma^2 = V(X) = \sum(x-\mu)^2 P(x) = (0-1.46)^2(.36) + (1-1.46)^2(.22) + (2-1.46)^2(.20)$

$+ (3-1.46)^2(.09) + (4-1.46)^2(.08) + (5-1.46)^2(.05) = 2.23$

$\sigma = \sqrt{\sigma^2} = \sqrt{2.23} = 1.49$

b $\mu = E(X) = \sum xP(x) = 0(.15) + 1(.18) + 2(.23) + 3(.26) + 4(.10) + 5(.08) = 2.22$

$\sigma^2 = V(X) = \sum(x-\mu)^2 P(x) = (0-2.22)^2(.15) + (1-2.22)^2(.18) + (2-2.22)^2(.23)$

$+ (3-2.22)^2(.26) + (4-2.22)^2(.10) + (5-2.22)^2(.08) = 2.11$

$\sigma = \sqrt{\sigma^2} = \sqrt{2.11} = 1.45$

c Viewers of nonviolent shows remember more about the product that was advertised.

7.138 $p = .08755$ because $P(X \geq 1) = 1 - P(X = 0 \text{ with } n = 10 \text{ and } p = .08755) = 1 - .40 = .60$

7.140 Binomial with $n = 5$ and $p = .01$.

x	p(x)
0	.95099
1	.04803
2	.00097
3	.00001
4	0
5	0

Chapter 8

8.2 a $P(X > 45) \approx \frac{(60-45)\times 2}{50\times 15} + \frac{(75-60)\times 2}{50\times 15} = .0800$

b $P(10 < X < 40) \approx \frac{(15-10)\times 17}{50\times 15} + \frac{(30-15)\times 7}{50\times 15} + \frac{(40-30)\times 6}{50\times 15} = .3333$

c $P(X < 25) \approx \frac{(-15-[-30])\times 6}{50\times 15} + \frac{(0-[-15])\times 10}{50\times 15} + \frac{(15-0)\times 17}{50\times 15} + \frac{(25-15)\times 7}{50\times 15} = .7533$

d $P(35 < X < 65) \approx \frac{(45-35)\times 6}{50\times 15} + \frac{(60-45)\times 2}{50\times 15} + \frac{(65-60)\times 2}{50\times 15} = .1333$

8.4 a

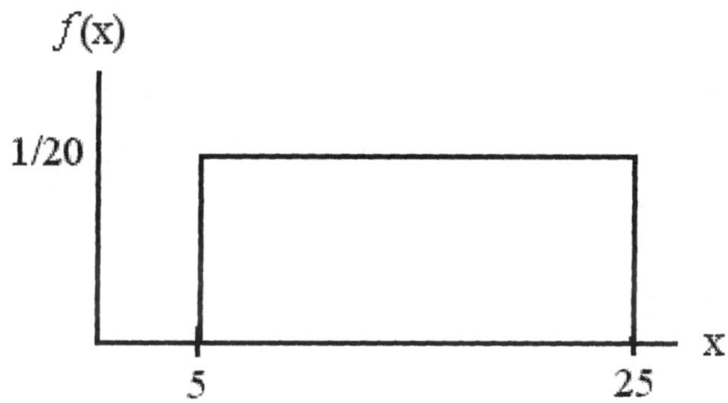

b $P(X > 25) = 0$

c $P(10 < X < 15) = (15-10)\frac{1}{20} = .25$

d $P(5.0 < X < 5.1) = (5.1-5)\frac{1}{20} = .005$

8.6 $f(x) = \frac{1}{(60-30)} = \frac{1}{30} \quad 30 < x < 60$

a $P(X > 55) = (60-55)\frac{1}{30} = .1667$

b $P(30 < X < 40) = (40 - 30)\frac{1}{30} = .3333$

c $P(X = 37.23) = 0$

8.8 $.10 \times (60 - 30) = 3$; The top decile = 60–3 = 57 minutes

8.10 .20(175–110) = 13. Bottom 20% lie below (110 + 13) = 123

For Exercises 8.12 and 8.14 we calculate probabilities by determining the area in a triangle. That is,

Area in a triangle = (.5)(height)(base)

8.12 a

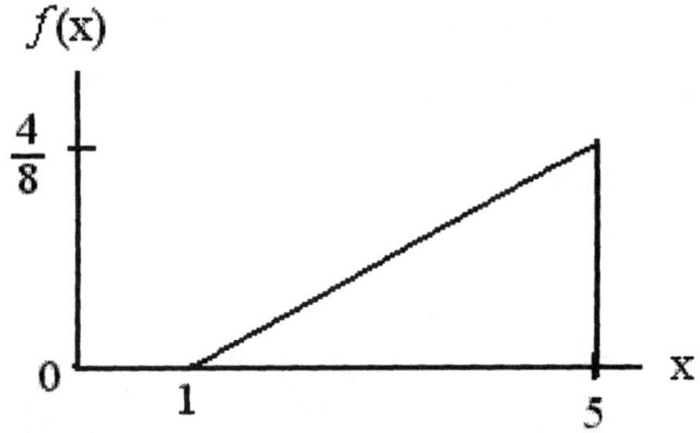

b $P(2 < X < 4) = P(X < 4) - P(X < 2) = (.5)(3/8)(4–1) - (.5)(1/8)(2–1) = .5625 - .0625 = .5$

c $P(X < 3) = (.5)(2/8)(3–1) = .25$

8.14 a $f(x) = .10 - .005x \quad 0 \le x \le 20$

b $P(X > 10) = (.5)(.05)(20–10) = .25$

c $P(6 < X < 12) = P(X > 6) - PX > 12) = (.5)(.07)(20–6) - (.5)(.04)(20–12) = .49 - .16 = .33$

8.16 $P(0 < Z < 1.61) = .4463$

8.18 $P(0 < Z < 1.69) = .4545$

8.20 $P(0 < Z < 2.3) = .4893$

8.22 $P(Z > -1.24) = P(Z < 1.24) = .5 + P(0 < Z < 1.24) = .5 + .3925 = .8925$

8.24 $P(Z > 1.57) = .5 - P(0 < Z < 1.57) = .5 - .4418 = .0582$

8.26 $P(.34 < Z < 2.06) = P(0 < Z < 2.06) - P(0 < Z < .34) = .4803 - .1331 = .3472$

8.28 $P(Z > 3.09) = .5 - P(0 < Z < 3.09) = .5 - .4990 = .0010$

8.30 $P(Z > 4.0) = 0$

8.32 $P(0 < Z < z_{.045}) = .5 - .045 = .4550$; $z_{.045} = 1.70$

8.34 $P(X > 145) = P\left(\frac{X-\mu}{\sigma} > \frac{145-100}{25}\right) = P(Z > 1.80) = .5 - P(0 < Z < 1.80) = .5 - .4641 = .0359$

8.36 $P(800 < X < 1100) = P\left(\frac{800-1{,}000}{400} < \frac{X-\mu}{\sigma} < \frac{1{,}100-1{,}000}{400}\right) = P(-.5 < Z > .25)$

$= P(0 < Z < .5) + P(0 < Z < .25) = .1915 + .0987 = .2902$

8.38 a $P(5 < X < 10) = P\left(\frac{5-7.2}{1.9} < \frac{X-\mu}{\sigma} < \frac{10-7.2}{1.9}\right) = P(-1.16 < Z > 1.47)$

$= P(0 < Z < 1.16) + P(0 < Z < 1.47) = .3770 + .4292 = .8062$

b $P(X > 7) = P\left(\frac{X-\mu}{\sigma} > \frac{7-7.2}{1.9}\right) = P(Z > -.11) = .5 + P(0 < Z < .11) = .5 + .0438 = .5438$

c $P(X < 4) = P\left(\frac{X-\mu}{\sigma} < \frac{4-7.2}{1.9}\right) = P(Z < -1.68) = .5 - P(0 < Z < 1.68) = .5 - .4535 = .0465$

8.40 $P(X > 5{,}000) = P\left(\frac{X-\mu}{\sigma} > \frac{5{,}000-5{,}100}{200}\right) = P(Z > -.5) = .5 + P(0 < Z < .5) = .5 + .1915 = .6915$

8.42 a $P(X > 12{,}000) = P\left(\frac{X-\mu}{\sigma} > \frac{12{,}000-10{,}000}{2{,}400}\right) = P(Z > .83) = .5 - P(0 < Z < .83) = .5 - .2967$

$= .2033$

b $P(X < 9{,}000) = P\left(\frac{X-\mu}{\sigma} < \frac{9{,}000-10{,}000}{2{,}400}\right) = P(Z < -.42) = .5 - P(0 < Z < .42) = .5 - .1628 = .3372$

8.44 a $P(X > 70) = P\left(\frac{X-\mu}{\sigma} > \frac{70-65}{4}\right) = P(Z > 1.25) = .5 - P(0 < Z < 1.25) = .5 - .3944 = .1056$

b $P(X < 60) = P\left(\frac{X-\mu}{\sigma} < \frac{60-65}{4}\right) = P(Z < -1.25) = .5 - P(0 < Z < 1.25) = .5 - .3944 = .1056$

c $P(55 < X < 70) = P\left(\frac{55-65}{4} < \frac{X-\mu}{\sigma} < \frac{70-65}{4}\right) = P(-2.50 < Z < 1.25)$

$= P(0 < Z < 2.50) + P(0 < Z < 1.25) = .4938 + .3944 = .8882$

8.46 Top 5%: $P(0 < Z < z_{.05}) = .5 - .05 = .4500$; $z_{.05} = 1.645$; $z_{.05} = \frac{x-\mu}{\sigma}$; $1.645 = \frac{x-80}{4}$;

$x = 86.58$

Bottom 5%: $P(-z_{05} < Z < 0) = .5 - .05 = .4500$; $-z_{.05} = -1.645$; $-z_{05} = \frac{x-\mu}{\sigma}$; $-1.645 = \frac{x-80}{4}$;

$x = 73.42$

8.48 $P(X > 8) = P\left(\frac{X-\mu}{\sigma} > \frac{8-7.2}{.667}\right) = P\ Z > 1.2) = .5 - P(0 < Z < 1.2) = .5 - .3849 = .1151$

8.50 a $P(X > 9) = P\left(\frac{X-\mu}{\sigma} > \frac{9-7.5}{1.8}\right) = P\ Z > .83) = .5 - P(0 < Z < .83) = .5 - .2967 = .2033$

b $P(6 < X < 9) = P\left(\frac{6-7.5}{1.8} < \frac{X-\mu}{\sigma} < \frac{9-7.5}{1.8}\right) = P(-.83 < Z < .83)$

$= 2P(0 < Z < .83) = 2(.2967) = .5934$

c $P(X < 4) = P\left(\frac{X-\mu}{\sigma} < \frac{4-7.5}{1.81}\right) = P\ Z < -1.94) = .5 - P(0 < Z < 1.94) = .5 - .4738 = .0262$

d $P(-z_{.10} < Z < 0) = .5 - .10 = .4000$; $-z_{.10} = -1.28$; $-z_{.10} = \frac{x-\mu}{\sigma}$; $-1.28 = \frac{x-7.5}{1.8}$;

$x = 5.20$ hours

8.52 $P(-z_{.01} < Z < 0) = .5 - .01 = .4900$; $-z_{.01} = -2.33$; $-z_{.01} = \frac{x-\mu}{\sigma}$; $-2.33 = \frac{x-11{,}500}{800}$;

$x = 9{,}636$

8.54 a $P(X > 30) = P\left(\frac{X-\mu}{\sigma} > \frac{30-27}{7}\right) = P(Z > .43) = .5 - P(0 < Z < .43)$

$= .5 - .1664 = .3336$

b $P(X > 40) = P\left(\frac{X-\mu}{\sigma} > \frac{40-27}{7}\right) = P(Z > 1.86) = .5 - P(0 < Z < 1.86)$

$= .5 - .4686 = .0314$

c $P(X < 15) = P\left(\frac{X-\mu}{\sigma} < \frac{15-27}{7}\right) = P(Z < -1.71) = .5 - P(0 < Z < 1.71)$

$= .5 - .4564 = .0436$

d $P(0 < Z < z_{.20}) = .5 - .20 = .3000$; $z_{.20} = .84$; $z_{.20} = \frac{x-\mu}{\sigma}$; $.84 = \frac{x-27}{7}$; $x = 32.88$

8.56 $P(X < 45{,}000) = P\left(\frac{X-\mu}{\sigma} < \frac{45{,}000-41{,}825}{13{,}444}\right) = P(Z < .24) = .5 + P(0 < Z < .24) = .5 + .0948$

$= .5948$

8.58 a $P(X < 4) = P\left(\frac{X-\mu}{\sigma} < \frac{4-7.5}{1.2}\right) = P(Z < -2.92) = .5 - P(0 < Z < 2.92) = .5 - .4982 = .0018$

b $P(7 < X < 10) = P\left(\frac{7-7.5}{1.2} < \frac{X-\mu}{\sigma} < \frac{10-7.5}{1.2}\right) = P(-.42 < Z < 2.08) = P(0 < Z < .42)$

$+ P(0 < Z < 2.08) = .1628 + .4812 = .6440$

8.60 A: $P(0 < Z < z_{.10}) = .5 - .10 = .4000$; $z_{.10} = 1.28$; $z_{.10} = \frac{x-\mu}{\sigma}$; $1.28 = \frac{x-70}{10}$; $x = 82.8$

B: $P(0 < Z < z_{40}) = .5 - .40 = .1000;\ z_{40} = .25;\ z_{40} = \frac{x-\mu}{\sigma};\ .25 = \frac{x-70}{10};\ x = 72.5$

C: $P(-z_{20} < Z < 0) = .5 - .20 = .3000;\ -z_{20} = -.84;\ -z_{20} = \frac{x-\mu}{\sigma};\ -.84 = \frac{x-70}{10};\ x = 61.6;$

D: $P(-z_{05} < Z < 0) = .5 - .05 = .4500;\ -z_{05} = -1.645;\ -z_{05} = \frac{x-\mu}{\sigma};\ -1.645 = \frac{x-70}{10};\ x = 53.55$

8.62 $P(x > 150{,}000) = P\left(\frac{X-\mu}{\sigma} < \frac{150{,}000-99{,}700}{30{,}000}\right) = P(Z > 1.68) = .5 - P(0 < Z < 1.68) = .5 - .4535$

$= .0465$

8.64 $P(0 < Z < z_{20}) = .5 - .20 = .3000;\ z_{20} = .84;\ z_{20} = \frac{x-\mu}{\sigma};\ .84 = \frac{x-150}{25};\ x = 171$

8.66 $P(0 < Z < z_{40}) = .5 - .40 = .1000;\ z_{40} = .25;\ z_{40} = \frac{x-\mu}{\sigma};\ .25 = \frac{x-850}{90};\ .x = 872.5$

(rounded to 873)

8.68 $P(X < 150) = P\left(\frac{X-\mu}{\sigma} < \frac{150-145}{5.57}\right) = P(Z < .90) = .5 + P(0 < Z < .90) = .5 + .3159 = .8159$

8.70 a. $P(X < 0) = P\left(\frac{X-\mu}{\sigma} < \frac{0-21.1}{10.67}\right) = P(Z < -1.98) = .5 - P(0 < Z < 1.98) = .5 - .4761 = .0239$

b. $P(X > 20) = P\left(\frac{X-\mu}{\sigma} > \frac{20-21.1}{10.67}\right) = P(Z > -.10) = .5 + P(0 < Z < .10) = .5 + .0398 = .5398$

8.72

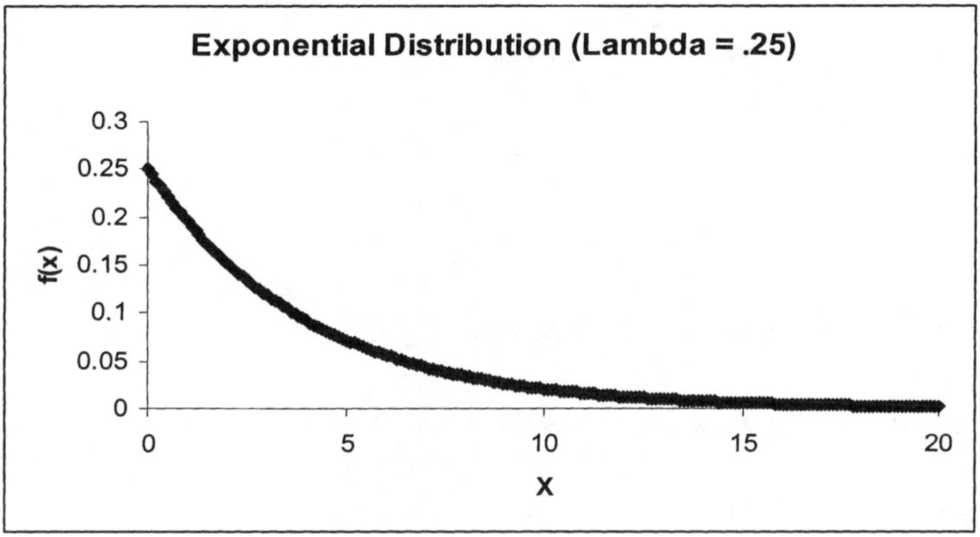

8.74 a $P(X>2)=e^{-3(2)}=e^{-.6}=.5488$

b $P(X<4)=1-e^{-3(4)}=1-e^{-1\,2}=1-.3012=.6988$

c $P(1<X<2)=e^{-.3(1)}-e^{-.3(2)}=e^{-3}-e^{-6}=.7408-.5488=.1920$

d $P(X=3)=0$

8.76 $\mu=1/\lambda=25$ hours; $\lambda=.04$ breakdowns/hour

$P(X>50)=e^{-04(50)}=e^{-2}=.1353$

8.78 $\mu=1/\lambda=5$ minutes; $\lambda=.2$ customer/minute

$P(X<10)=1-e^{-2(10)}=1-e^{-2}=1-.1353=.8647$

8.80 $\mu=1/\lambda=7.5$ minutes; $\lambda=.133$ service/minute

$P(X<5)=1-e^{-133(5)}=1-e^{-.665}=1-.5143=.4857$

8.82 $\mu=1/\lambda=6$ minutes; $\lambda=.167$ customers/minute

$P(X>10)=e^{-167(10)}=e^{-1.67}=.1889$

8.84	a 2.724	b 1.282	c 2.132	d 2.528
8.86	a 1.6556	b 2.6810	c 1.9600	d 1.6602
8.88	a .1744	b .0231	c .0251	d .0267
8.90	a 17.2919	b 50.8922	c 2.70554	d 53.5400
8.92	a 33.5705	b 866.911	c 24.3976	d 261.058
8.94	a .4881	b .9158	c .9988	d .9077
8.96	a 2.84	b 1.93	c 3.60	d 3.37
8.98	a 1.5204	b 1.5943	c 2.8397	d 1.1670
8.100	a .1050	b .1576	c .0001	d .0044

Chapter 9

9.2 a $P(\overline{X}=1)$ =P(1,1)= 1/36

b $P(\overline{X}=6) = P(6,6) = 1/36$

9.4 The variance of $\overline{X}$ is smaller than the variance of X.

9.6 No, because the sample mean is approximately normally distributed.

9.8 a $P(\overline{X}>1050) = P\left(\frac{\overline{X}-\mu}{\sigma/\sqrt{n}} > \frac{1050-1000}{200/\sqrt{25}}\right) = P(Z>1.25) = .5 - P(0<Z<1.25) = .5 - .3944$

$= .1056$

b $P(\overline{X}<960) = P\left(\frac{\overline{X}-\mu}{\sigma/\sqrt{n}} < \frac{960-1000}{200/\sqrt{25}}\right) = P(Z<-1.00) = .5 - P(0<Z<1.00) = .5 - .3413 = .1587$

c $P(\overline{X}>1100) = P\left(\frac{\overline{X}-\mu}{\sigma/\sqrt{n}} > \frac{1100-1000}{200/\sqrt{25}}\right) = P(Z>2.50) = .5 - P(0<Z<2.50) = .5 - .4938 = .0062$

9.10 a $P(49<\overline{X}<52) = P\left(\frac{49-50}{5/\sqrt{4}} < \frac{\overline{X}-\mu}{\sigma/\sqrt{n}} < \frac{52-50}{5/\sqrt{4}}\right) = P(-.40<Z<.80)$

$= P(0<Z<.40) + P(0<Z<.80) = .1554 + .2881 = .4435$

b $P(49<\overline{X}<52) = P\left(\frac{49-50}{5/\sqrt{16}} < \frac{\overline{X}-\mu}{\sigma/\sqrt{n}} < \frac{52-50}{5/\sqrt{16}}\right) = P(-.80<Z<1.60)$

$= P(0<Z<.80) + P(0<Z<1.60) = .2881 + .4452 = .7333$

c $P(49<\overline{X}<52) = P\left(\frac{49-50}{5/\sqrt{25}} < \frac{\overline{X}-\mu}{\sigma/\sqrt{n}} < \frac{52-50}{5/\sqrt{25}}\right) = P(-1.00<Z<2.00)$

$= P(0<Z<1.00) + P(0<Z<2.00) = .3413 + .4772 = .8185$

9.12 a $P(49 < \overline{X} < 52) = P\left(\frac{49-50}{20/\sqrt{4}} < \frac{\overline{X}-\mu}{\sigma/\sqrt{n}} < \frac{52-50}{20/\sqrt{4}}\right) = P(-.10 < Z < .20)$

$= P(0 < Z < .10) + P(0 < Z < .20) = .0398 + .0793 = .1191$

b $P(49 < \overline{X} < 52) = P\left(\frac{49-50}{20/\sqrt{16}} < \frac{\overline{X}-\mu}{\sigma/\sqrt{n}} < \frac{52-50}{20/\sqrt{16}}\right) = P(-.20 < Z < .40)$

$= P(0 < Z < .20) + P(0 < Z < .40) = .0793 + .1554 = .2347$

c $P(49 < \overline{X} < 52) = P\left(\frac{49-50}{20/\sqrt{25}} < \frac{\overline{X}-\mu}{\sigma/\sqrt{n}} < \frac{52-50}{20/\sqrt{25}}\right) = P(-.25 < Z < .50)$

$= P(0 < Z < .25) + P(0 < Z < .50) = .0987 + .1915 = .2902$

9.14 a $\sigma_{\overline{x}} = \frac{\sigma}{\sqrt{n}}\sqrt{\frac{N-n}{N-1}} = \frac{500}{\sqrt{1,000}}\sqrt{\frac{10,000-1,000}{10,000-1}} = 15.00$

b $\sigma_{\overline{x}} = \frac{\sigma}{\sqrt{n}}\sqrt{\frac{N-n}{N-1}} = \frac{500}{\sqrt{500}}\sqrt{\frac{10,000-500}{10,000-1}} = 21.80$

c $\sigma_{\overline{x}} = \frac{\sigma}{\sqrt{n}}\sqrt{\frac{N-n}{N-1}} = \frac{500}{\sqrt{100}}\sqrt{\frac{10,000-100}{10,000-1}} = 49.75$

9.16 We can answer part (c) and possibly part (b) depending on how nonnormal the population is.

9.18 a $P(X > 12) = P\left(\frac{X-\mu}{\sigma} > \frac{12-10}{3}\right) = P(Z > .67) = .5 - P(0 < Z < .67) = .5 - .2486 = .2514$

b $P(\overline{X} > 275/25) = P(\overline{X} > 11) = P\left(\frac{\overline{X}-\mu}{\sigma/\sqrt{n}} > \frac{11-10}{3/\sqrt{25}}\right) = P(Z > 1.67) = .5 - P(0 < Z < 1.67)$

$= .5 - .4525 = .0475$

9.20 a $P(X < 75) = P\left(\frac{X-\mu}{\sigma} < \frac{75-78}{6}\right) = P(Z < -.50) = .5 - P(0 < Z < .50) = .5 - .1915 = .3085$

b $P(\overline{X} < 75) = P\left(\frac{\overline{X}-\mu}{\sigma/\sqrt{n}} < \frac{75-78}{6/\sqrt{50}}\right) = P(Z < -3.54) = .5 - P(0 < Z < 3.54) = .5 - .5 = 0$

9.22 $P(\overline{X} > 10{,}000/16) = P(\overline{X} > 625) = P\left(\frac{\overline{X}-\mu}{\sigma/\sqrt{n}} > \frac{625-600}{200/\sqrt{16}}\right) = P(Z > .50)$

$= .5 - P(0 < Z < .50) = .5 - .1915 = .3085$

9.24 The professor needs to know the mean and standard deviation of the population of the weights of elevator users and that the distribution is not extremely nonnormal.

9.26 $P(\text{Total time} > 300) = P(\overline{X} > 300/60) = P(\overline{X} > 5) = P\left(\frac{\overline{X}-\mu}{\sigma/\sqrt{n}} > \frac{5-4.8}{1.3/\sqrt{60}}\right) = P(Z > 1.19)$

$= .5 - P(0 < Z < 1.19) = .5 - .3830 = .1170$

9.28 $P(\text{Total number of faxes} > 1500) = P(\overline{X} > 1500/5) = P(\overline{X} > 300) = P\left(\frac{\overline{X}-\mu}{\sigma/\sqrt{n}} > \frac{300-275}{75/\sqrt{5}}\right)$

$= P(Z > .75) = .5 - P(0 < Z < .75) = .5 - .2734 = .2266$

9.30a $P(\hat{P} > .60) = P\left(\frac{\hat{P}-p}{\sqrt{p(1-p)/n}} > \frac{.60-.5}{\sqrt{(.5)(1-.5)/300}}\right) = P(Z > 3.46) = 0$

b. $P(\hat{P} > .60) = P\left(\frac{\hat{P}-p}{\sqrt{p(1-p)/n}} > \frac{.60-.55}{\sqrt{(.55)(1-.55)/300}}\right) = P(Z > 1.74) = .5 - P(0 < Z < 1.74)$

$= .5 - .4591 = .0409$

c. $P(\hat{P} > .60) = P\left(\frac{\hat{P}-p}{\sqrt{p(1-p)/n}} > \frac{.60-.6}{\sqrt{(.6)(1-.6)/300}}\right) = P(Z > 0) = .5$

9.32 $P(\hat{P} < .75) = P\left(\frac{\hat{P}-p}{\sqrt{p(1-p)/n}} > \frac{.75-.80}{\sqrt{(.80)(1-.80)/100}}\right) = P(Z < -1.25) = .5 - P(0 < Z < 1.25)$

$= .5 - .3944 = .1056$

9.34 $P(\hat{P} < .49) = P\left(\frac{\hat{P}-p}{\sqrt{p(1-p)/n}} < \frac{.49-.52}{\sqrt{(.52)(1-.52)/500}}\right) = P(Z < -1.34) = .5 - P(0 < Z < 1.34)$

$= .5 - .4099 = .0901$

9.36 a $P(\hat{P} < .50) = P\left(\frac{\hat{P}-p}{\sqrt{p(1-p)/n}} < \frac{.50-.52}{\sqrt{(.52)(1-.52)/400}}\right) = P(Z < -.80) = .5 - P(0 < Z < .80)$

$= .5 - .2881 = .2119$; the claim may be true.

b $P(\hat{P} < .50) = P\left(\frac{\hat{P}-p}{\sqrt{p(1-p)/n}} < \frac{.50-.52}{\sqrt{(.52)(1-.52)/1{,}000}}\right) = P(Z < -1.27) = .5 - P(0 < Z < 1.27)$

$= .5 - .3980 = .1020$; the claim may be true.

9.38 $P(\hat{P} > .05) = P\left(\frac{\hat{P}-p}{\sqrt{p(1-p)/n}} > \frac{.05-.03}{\sqrt{(.03)(1-.03)/400}}\right) = P(Z > 2.34) = .5 - P(0 < Z < 2.34)$

$= .5 - .4904 = .0096$; the commercial appears to be dishonest

9.40 a $P(\hat{P} < .45) = P\left(\frac{\hat{P}-p}{\sqrt{p(1-p)/n}} < \frac{.45-.50}{\sqrt{(.50)(1-.50)/600}}\right) = P(Z < -2.45) = .5 - P(0 < Z < 2.45)$

$= .5 - .4929 = .0071$

b The claim appears to be false.

9.42 $P(\hat{P} < .75) = P\left(\frac{\hat{P}-p}{\sqrt{p(1-p)/n}} < \frac{.75-.80}{\sqrt{(.80)(1-.80)/350}}\right) = P(Z < -2.34)$

$= .5 - P(0 < Z < 2.34) = .5 - .4904 = .0096$

9.44 The claim appears to be false.

9.46 $P(\bar{X}_1 - \bar{X}_2 > 25) = P\left(\frac{(\bar{X}_1 - \bar{X}_2) - (\mu_1 - \mu_2)}{\sqrt{\frac{\sigma_1^2}{n_1} + \frac{\sigma_2^2}{n_2}}} > \frac{25 - (280 - 270)}{\sqrt{\frac{25^2}{50} + \frac{30^2}{50}}}\right) = P(Z > 2.72)$

$= .5 - P(0 < Z < 2.72) = .5 - .4967 = .0033$

9.48 $P(\overline{X}_1 - \overline{X}_2 > 0) = P\left(\frac{(\overline{X}_1 - \overline{X}_2) - (\mu_1 - \mu_2)}{\sqrt{\frac{\sigma_1^2}{n_1} + \frac{\sigma_2^2}{n_2}}} > \frac{0 - (40 - 38)}{\sqrt{\frac{6^2}{25} + \frac{8^2}{25}}}\right) = P(Z > -1.00) = .5 + P(0 < Z < 1.00)$

$= .5 + .3413 = .8413$

9.50 $P(\overline{X}_1 - \overline{X}_2 > 0) = P\left(\frac{(\overline{X}_1 - \overline{X}_2) - (\mu_1 - \mu_2)}{\sqrt{\frac{\sigma_1^2}{n_1} + \frac{\sigma_2^2}{n_2}}} > \frac{0 - (140 - 138)}{\sqrt{\frac{6^2}{25} + \frac{8^2}{25}}}\right) = P(Z > -1.00)$

$= .5 + P(0 < Z < 1.00) = .5 + .3413 = .8413$

9.52 $P(\overline{X}_1 - \overline{X}_2 > 0) = P\left(\frac{(\overline{X}_1 - \overline{X}_2) - (\mu_1 - \mu_2)}{\sqrt{\frac{\sigma_1^2}{n_1} + \frac{\sigma_2^2}{n_2}}} > \frac{0 - (73 - 77)}{\sqrt{\frac{12^2}{4} + \frac{10^2}{4}}}\right) = P(Z > .51) = .5 - P(0 < Z < .51)$

$= .5 - .1950 = .3050$

9.54 $P(\overline{X}_1 - \overline{X}_2 < 0) = P\left(\frac{(\overline{X}_1 - \overline{X}_2) - (\mu_1 - \mu_2)}{\sqrt{\frac{\sigma_1^2}{n_1} + \frac{\sigma_2^2}{n_2}}} < \frac{0 - (10 - 15)}{\sqrt{\frac{3^2}{25} + \frac{3^2}{25}}}\right) = P(Z < 5.89) = 1$

Chapter 10

10.2 An unbiased estimator of a parameter is an estimator whose expected value equals the parameter.

10.4

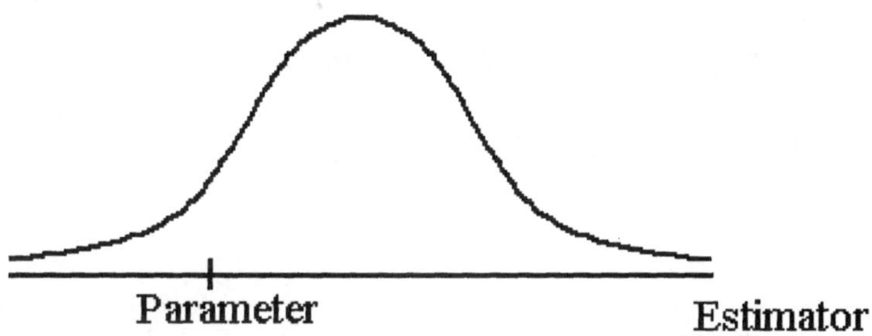

10.6

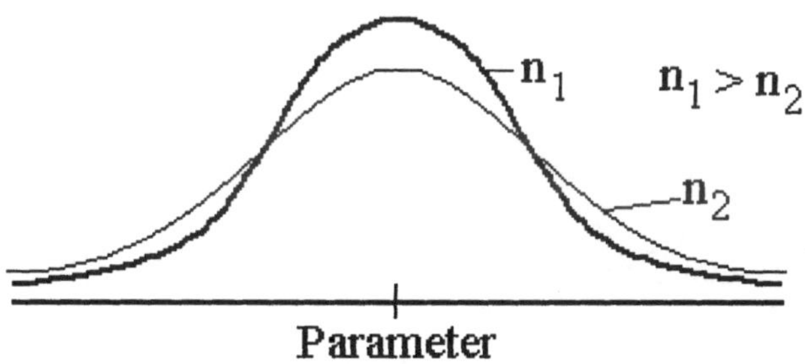

10.8

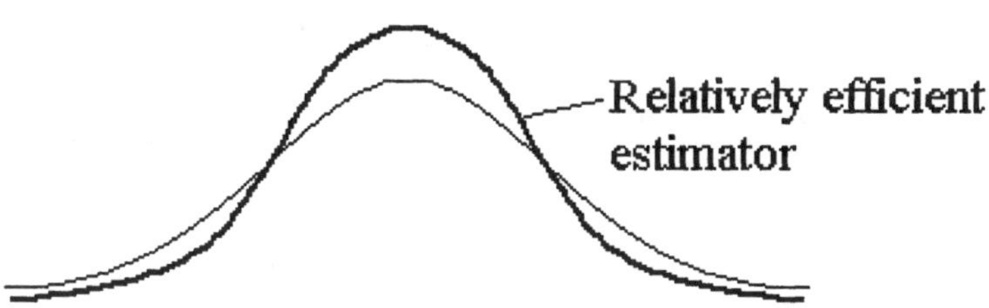

10.10 a. $\bar{x} \pm z_{\alpha/2}\sigma/\sqrt{n} = 200 \pm 1.96(40/\sqrt{25}) = 200 \pm 15.68$; LCL = 184.32.40, UCL = 215.68

b. $\bar{x} \pm z_{\alpha/2}\sigma/\sqrt{n} = 200 \pm 1.96(25/\sqrt{25}) = 200 \pm 9.80$; LCL = 190.20, UCL = 209.80

c. $\bar{x} \pm z_{\alpha/2}\sigma/\sqrt{n} = 200 \pm 1.96(10/\sqrt{25}) = 200 \pm 3.92$; LCL = 196.08, UCL = 203.92

d. The interval narrows.

10.12 a. $\bar{x} \pm z_{\alpha/2}\sigma/\sqrt{n} = 500 \pm 2.33(20/\sqrt{50}) = 500 \pm 6.59$; LCL = 493.41, UCL = 506.59

b. $\bar{x} \pm z_{\alpha/2}\sigma/\sqrt{n} = 500 \pm 1.96(20/\sqrt{50}) = 500 \pm 5.54$; LCL = 494.46, UCL = 505.54

c. $\bar{x} \pm z_{\alpha/2}\sigma/\sqrt{n} = 500 \pm 1.645(20/\sqrt{50}) = 500 \pm 4.65$; LCL = 495.35, UCL = 504.65

d. The interval narrows.

10.14 a. $\bar{x} \pm z_{\alpha/2}\sigma/\sqrt{n} = 10 \pm 1.645(5/\sqrt{100}) = 10 \pm .82$; LCL = 9.18, UCL = 10.82

b. $\bar{x} \pm z_{\alpha/2}\sigma/\sqrt{n} = 10 \pm 1.645(5/\sqrt{25}) = 10 \pm 1.64$; LCL = 8.36, UCL = 11.64

c. $\bar{x} \pm z_{\alpha/2}\sigma/\sqrt{n} = 10 \pm 1.645(5/\sqrt{10}) = 10 \pm 2.60$; LCL = 7.40, UCL = 12.60

d. The interval widens.

10.16 a. $\bar{x} \pm z_{\alpha/2}\sigma/\sqrt{n} = 400 \pm 2.575(5/\sqrt{100}) = 400 \pm 1.29$; LCL = 398.71, UCL = 401.29

b. $\bar{x} \pm z_{\alpha/2}\sigma/\sqrt{n} = 200 \pm 2.575(5/\sqrt{100}) = 200 \pm 1.29$; LCL = 198.71, UCL = 201.29

c. $\bar{x} \pm z_{\alpha/2}\sigma/\sqrt{n} = 100 \pm 2.575(5/\sqrt{100}) = 100 \pm 1.29$; LCL = 98.71, UCL = 101.29

d. The width of the interval is unchanged.

10.18 Yes, because as the sample size increases the variance decreases, which means that the difference between the estimator and the parameter grows smaller as the sample size grows larger.

10.20 a sample median $\pm z_{\alpha/2}\dfrac{1.2533\,\sigma}{\sqrt{n}} = 500 \pm 1.645\dfrac{1.2533(12)}{\sqrt{50}} = 500 \pm 3.50$

b. The 90% confidence interval estimate of the population mean using the sample mean is 500 ± 2.79. The 90% confidence interval of the population mean using the sample median is wider than that using the sample mean because the variance of the sample median is larger. The median is calculated by placing all the observations in order. Thus, the median loses the potential information contained in the actual values in the sample. This results in a wider interval estimate.

10.22 $\bar{x} \pm z_{\alpha/2}\sigma/\sqrt{n}$ = 6.33 ± 1.645(2/$\sqrt{9}$) = 6.33 ± 1.10; LCL = 5.23, UCL = 7.43

10.24 $\bar{x} \pm z_{\alpha/2}\sigma/\sqrt{n}$ = 22.83 ± 1.96(12/$\sqrt{12}$) = 22.83 ± 6.79; LCL = 16.04, UCL = 29.62

10.26 $\bar{x} \pm z_{\alpha/2}\sigma/\sqrt{n}$ = 16.9 ± 2.575(5/$\sqrt{10}$) = 16.9 ± 4.07; LCL = 12.83, UCL = 20.97

10.28 $\bar{x} \pm z_{\alpha/2}\sigma/\sqrt{n}$ = 13.15 ± 1.645(6/$\sqrt{13}$) = 13.15 ± 2.74; LCL = 10.41, UCL = 15.89

10.30 $\bar{x} \pm z_{\alpha/2}\sigma/\sqrt{n}$ = 252.38 ± 1.96(30/$\sqrt{400}$) = 252.38 ± 2.94; LCL = 249.44, UCL = 255.32

10.32 $\bar{x} \pm z_{\alpha/2}\sigma/\sqrt{n}$ = 10.21 ± 1.96(1.8/$\sqrt{100}$) = 10.21 ± .35; LCL = 9.86, UCL = 10.56

10.34 $\bar{x} \pm z_{\alpha/2}\sigma/\sqrt{n}$ = 26.81 ± 1.645(1.5/$\sqrt{50}$) = 26.81 ± .35; LCL = 26.46, UCL = 27.16. We estimate that the mean time to assemble a cell phone lies between 26.46 and 27.16 minutes. This type of estimate is correct 90% of the time.

10.36 $\bar{x} \pm z_{\alpha/2}\sigma/\sqrt{n}$ = 19.28 ± 1.645(6/$\sqrt{250}$) = 19.28 ± .62; LCL = 18.66, UCL = 19.90. We estimate that the mean leisure time per week of Japanese middle managers lies between 18.66 and 19.90 hours. This type of estimate is correct 90% of the time.

10.38 $\bar{x} \pm z_{\alpha/2}\sigma/\sqrt{n}$ = 585,063 ± 1.645(30,000/$\sqrt{80}$) = 585,063 ± 5,518; LCL = 579,545, UCL = 590,581. We estimate that the mean annual income of all company presidents lies between $579,545 and $590,581. This type of estimate is correct 90% of the time.

10.40 $\bar{x} \pm z_{\alpha/2}\sigma/\sqrt{n}$ = 27.19 ± 1.96(8/$\sqrt{100}$) = 27.19 ± 1.57; LCL = 25.62, UCL = 28.76

10.42 a The sample size increases.

b The sample size increases.

c The sample size decreases.

10.44 a The sample size decreases.

b the sample size decreases.

c The sample size increases.

10.46 a. $\bar{x} \pm z_{\alpha/2} \frac{\sigma}{\sqrt{n}} = 150 \pm 1.645 \frac{5}{\sqrt{271}} = 150 \pm .5$

b. $\bar{x} \pm z_{\alpha/2} \frac{\sigma}{\sqrt{n}} = 150 \pm 1.645 \frac{20}{\sqrt{271}} = 150 \pm 2$

10.48 a. $n = \left(\frac{z_{\alpha/2}\sigma}{W}\right)^2 = \left(\frac{1.96 \times 200}{10}\right)^2 = 1{,}537$

b. 500 $\pm$ 10

10.50 a The width of the confidence interval estimate is equal to what was specified.

b The width of the confidence interval estimate is smaller than what was specified.

c The width of the confidence interval estimate is larger than what was specified.

10.52 $n = \left(\frac{z_{\alpha/2}\sigma}{W}\right)^2 = \left(\frac{1.96 \times 10}{3}\right)^2 = 43$

10.54 $n = \left(\frac{z_{\alpha/2}\sigma}{W}\right)^2 = \left(\frac{2.575 \times 15}{1}\right)^2 = 1{,}492$

10.56 $n = \left(\frac{z_{\alpha/2}\sigma}{W}\right)^2 = \left(\frac{1.96 \times 30}{3}\right)^2 = 385$

Chapter 11

11.2 H_0: The drug is not safe and effective

H_1: The drug is safe and effective

11.4 H_1: The plane is on fire

H_1: The plane is not on fire

11.6 The defendant in both cases was O. J. Simpson. The verdicts were logical because in the criminal trial the amount of evidence to convict is greater than the amount of evidence required in a civil trial. The two juries concluded that there was enough (preponderance of) evidence in the civil trial, but not enough evidence (beyond a reasonable doubt) in the criminal trial.

All p-values and probabilities of Type II errors were calculated manually using Table 3 in Appendix B.

11.8 Rejection region: $z > z_{03} = 1.88$

$$z = \frac{\bar{x} - \mu}{\sigma / \sqrt{n}} = \frac{51 - 50}{5 / \sqrt{9}} = .60$$

p-value = P(Z > .60) = .5 – .2257 = .2743

There is not enough evidence to infer that $\mu > 50$.

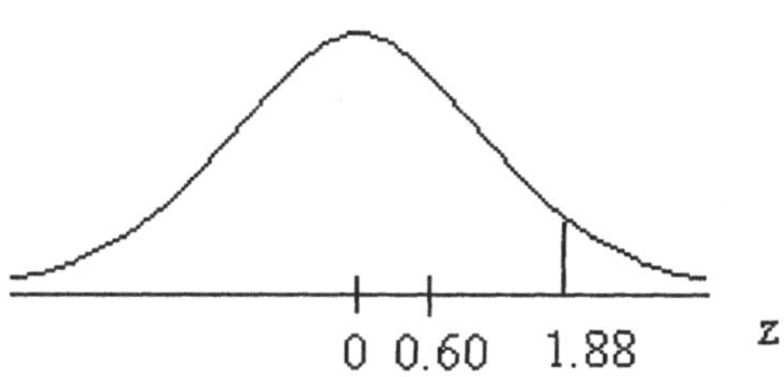

11.10 Rejection region: $z < -z_{.025} = -1.96$ or $z > z_{.025} = 1.96$

$$z = \frac{\bar{x}-\mu}{\sigma/\sqrt{n}} = \frac{100-100}{10/\sqrt{100}} = 0$$

p-value = 2P(Z > 0) = 2(.5) = 1.00

There is not enough evidence to infer that $\mu \neq 100$.

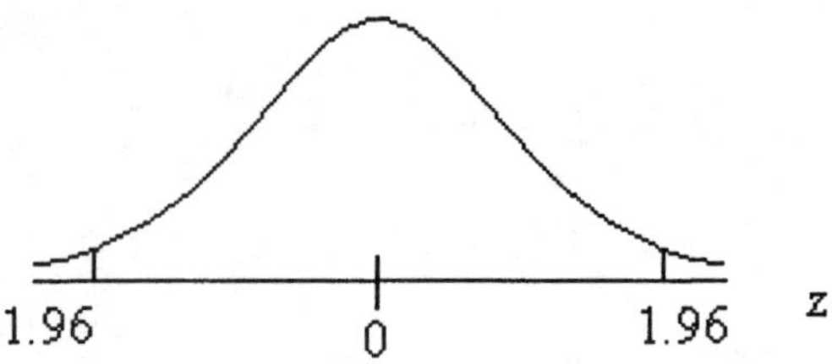

11.12 Rejection region: $z < -z_{.05} = -1.645$

$$z = \frac{\bar{x}-\mu}{\sigma/\sqrt{n}} = \frac{48-50}{15/\sqrt{100}} = -1.33$$

p-value = P(Z < −1.33) = .5 – .4082= .0918

There is not enough evidence to infer that $\mu < 50$.

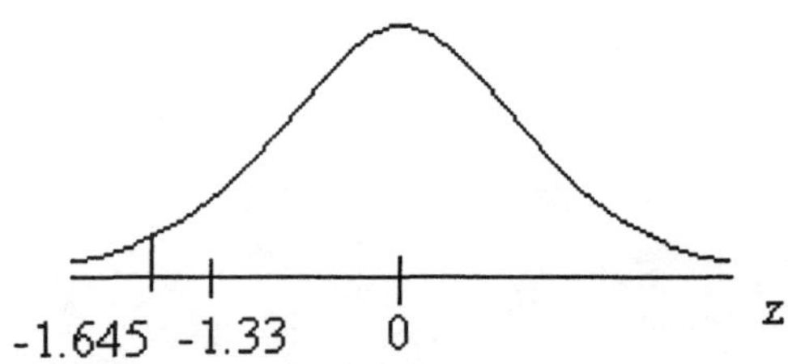

11.14a. $z = \frac{\bar{x}-\mu}{\sigma/\sqrt{n}} = \frac{310-300}{50/\sqrt{9}} = .60$

p-value = P(Z >.60) = .5 – .2257 = .2743

b. $z = \frac{\bar{x}-\mu}{\sigma/\sqrt{n}} = \frac{310-300}{30/\sqrt{9}} = 1.00$

p-value = P(Z > 1.00) = .5 – .3413 = .1587

c $z = \frac{\bar{x}-\mu}{\sigma/\sqrt{n}} = \frac{310-300}{10/\sqrt{9}} = 3.00$

p-value = P(Z > 3.00) = .5 – .4987 = .0013

d. The value of the test statistic increases and the p-value decreases.

11.16 a. $z = \frac{\bar{x}-\mu}{\sigma/\sqrt{n}} = \frac{99-100}{8/\sqrt{100}} = -1.25$

p-value = $2P(Z < -1.25) = 2(.5 - .3944) = .2112$

b. $z = \frac{\bar{x}-\mu}{\sigma/\sqrt{n}} = \frac{99-100}{8/\sqrt{50}} = -.88$

p-value = $2P(Z < -.88) = 2(.5 - .3106) = .3788$

c. $z = \frac{\bar{x}-\mu}{\sigma/\sqrt{n}} = \frac{99-100}{8/\sqrt{20}} = -.56$

p-value = $2P(Z < -.56) = 2(.5 - .2123) = .5754$

d. The value of the test statistic increases and the p-value increases.

11.18 a. $z = \frac{\bar{x}-\mu}{\sigma/\sqrt{n}} = \frac{58-70}{20/\sqrt{25}} = -3.00$

p-value = $P(Z < -3.00) = .5 - .4987 = .0013$

b. $z = \frac{\bar{x}-\mu}{\sigma/\sqrt{n}} = \frac{62-70}{20/\sqrt{25}} = -2.00$

p-value = $P(Z < -2.00) = .5 - .4772 = .0228$

c. $z = \frac{\bar{x}-\mu}{\sigma/\sqrt{n}} = \frac{66-70}{20/\sqrt{25}} = -1.00$

p-value = $P(Z < -1.00) = .5 - .3413 = .1587$

d. The value of the test statistic increases and the p-value increases.

11.20 a $z = \frac{\bar{x}-\mu}{\sigma/\sqrt{n}} = \frac{178-170}{35/\sqrt{400}} = 4.57$

p-value = $P(Z > 4.57) = 0$.

b $z = \frac{\bar{x}-\mu}{\sigma/\sqrt{n}} = \frac{178-170}{100/\sqrt{400}} = 1.60$

p-value = $P(Z > 1.60) = .5 - .4452 = .0548$.

The value of the test statistic decreases and the p-value increases.

11.22 a $z = \frac{\bar{x}-\mu}{\sigma/\sqrt{n}} = \frac{21.63-22}{6/\sqrt{100}} = -.62$

p-value = P(Z < –.62) = .5 – .2324 = .2676

b $z = \frac{\bar{x}-\mu}{\sigma/\sqrt{n}} = \frac{21.63-22}{6/\sqrt{500}} = -1.38$

p-value = P(Z < –1.38) = .5 – .4162 = .0838.

The value of the test statistic decreases and the p-value decreases.

11.24

$\bar{x}$	$z = \frac{\bar{x}-22}{6/\sqrt{220}}$	p-value
22.0	0	.5
21.8	–.49	.3121
21.6	–.99	.1611
21.4	–1.48	.0694
21.2	–1.98	.0239
21.0	–2.47	.0068
20.8	–2.97	.0015
20.6	–3.46	0
20.4	–3.96	0

11.26 a $z = \frac{\bar{x}-\mu}{\sigma/\sqrt{n}} = \frac{17.55-17.09}{2/\sqrt{100}} = 2.30$

p-value = 2P(Z > 2.30) = 2(.5 – .4893) = 2(.0107) = .0214.

b $z = \frac{\bar{x}-\mu}{\sigma/\sqrt{n}} = \frac{17.55-17.09}{10/\sqrt{100}} = .46$

p-value = 2P(Z > .46) = 2(.5 – .1772) = 2(.3228) = .6456.

The value of the test statistic decreases and the p-value increases.

11.28 $H_0: \mu = 50$

$H_1: \mu > 50$

$z = \frac{\bar{x}-\mu}{\sigma/\sqrt{n}} = \frac{60.11-50}{12/\sqrt{18}} = 3.89$

p-value = P(Z > 3.57) = 0

There is enough evidence to infer that the mean is greater than 50 minutes.

11.30 $H_0: \mu = 12$

$H_1: \mu < 12$

$$z = \frac{\bar{x} - \mu}{\sigma / \sqrt{n}} = \frac{11.00 - 12}{3 / \sqrt{15}} = -1.29$$

p-value = P(Z < –1.29) = .5 – .4015 = .0985

There is enough evidence to infer that the average number of golf balls lost is less than 12.

11.32 $H_0: \mu = 36$

$H_1: \mu < 36$

$$z = \frac{\bar{x} - \mu}{\sigma / \sqrt{n}} = \frac{35.42 - 36}{10 / \sqrt{12}} = -.20$$

p-value = P(Z < –.20) = .5 – .0793 = .4207

There is not enough evidence to infer that the average student spent less time than recommended.

11.34 $H_0: \mu = .50$

$H_1: \mu \neq .50$

$$z = \frac{\bar{x} - \mu}{\sigma / \sqrt{n}} = \frac{.486 - .50}{.04 / \sqrt{10}} = -1.11$$

p-value = 2P(Z < – 1.11) = 2(.5 – .3665) = 2(.1335) = .2670

There is not enough evidence to infer that the mean diameter is not .50 inch.

11.36 $H_0: \mu = 30{,}000$

$H_1: \mu < 30{,}000$

$$z = \frac{\bar{x} - \mu}{\sigma / \sqrt{n}} = \frac{29{,}120 - 30{,}000}{8{,}000 / \sqrt{350}} = -2.06$$

p-value = (P(Z < –2.06) = .5 – .4803 = .0197

There is enough evidence to infer that the president is correct

11.38a $H_0: \mu = 17.85$

$H_1: \mu > 17.85$

$$z = \frac{\bar{x}-\mu}{\sigma/\sqrt{n}} = \frac{19.13-17.85}{3.87/\sqrt{25}} = 1.65$$

p-value = P(Z > 1.65) = .5 – .4505 = .0495

There is enough evidence to infer that the campaign was successful.

b We must assume that the population standard deviation is unchanged.

11.40 $H_0 : \mu = 100$

$H_1 : \mu > 100$

$$z = \frac{\bar{x}-\mu}{\sigma/\sqrt{n}} = \frac{101.66-100}{8/\sqrt{200}} = 2.93$$

p-value = P(Z > 2.93) = .5 – .4983 = .0017

There is enough evidence to support the officer's belief.

11.42 $H_0 : \mu = 120$

$H_1 : \mu > 120$

$$z = \frac{\bar{x}-\mu}{\sigma/\sqrt{n}} = \frac{125.7-120}{16/\sqrt{40}} = 2.25$$

p-value = P(Z > 2.25) = .5 – .4878 = .0122

There is not enough evidence to infer that the site is acceptable

11.44 $H_0 : \mu = 4$

$H_1 : \mu \neq 4$

$$z = \frac{\bar{x}-\mu}{\sigma/\sqrt{n}} = \frac{4.84-4}{2/\sqrt{63}} = 3.33$$

p-value = 2P(Z > 3.33) = 0

There is enough evidence to infer that the average Alpine skier does not ski 4 times per year.

11.46 $H_0 : \mu = 32$

$H_1 : \mu < 32$

$$z = \frac{\bar{x}-\mu}{\sigma/\sqrt{n}} = \frac{29.92-32}{8/\sqrt{110}} = -2.73$$

p-value = P(Z < –2.73) = 5 – .4968 = .0032.

There is enough evidence to infer that there has been a decrease in the mean time away from desks. A type I error occurs when we conclude that the plan decreases the mean time away from desks when it actually does not. This error is quite expensive. Consequently we demand a low p-value. The p-value is small enough to infer that there has been a decrease.

11.48 Rejection region: $\frac{\bar{x}-\mu}{\sigma/\sqrt{n}} > z_{\alpha/2}$ or $\frac{\bar{x}-\mu}{\sigma/\sqrt{n}} < -z_{\alpha/2}$

$$\frac{\bar{x}-200}{10/\sqrt{100}} > z_{.025} = 1.96 \text{ or } \frac{\bar{x}-200}{10/\sqrt{100}} < -1.96$$

$\bar{x} > 201.96$ or $\bar{x} < 198.04$

$\beta = P(198.04 < \bar{x} < 201.96 \text{ given } \mu = 203)$

$$= P\left(\frac{198.04-203}{10/\sqrt{100}} < \frac{\bar{x}-\mu}{\sigma/\sqrt{n}} < \frac{201.96-203}{10/\sqrt{100}}\right) = P(-4.96 < z < -1.04) = .5 - .3508 = .1492$$

11.50 Rejection region: $\frac{\bar{x}-\mu}{\sigma/\sqrt{n}} < -z_{\alpha}$

$$\frac{\bar{x}-50}{10/\sqrt{40}} < -z_{.05} = -1.645$$

$\bar{x} < 47.40$

$$\beta = P(\bar{x} > 47.40 \text{ given } \mu = 48) = P\left(\frac{\bar{x}-\mu}{\sigma/\sqrt{n}} > \frac{47.40-48}{10/\sqrt{40}}\right) = P(z > -.38) = .5 + .1480 = .6480$$

Exercise 11.50

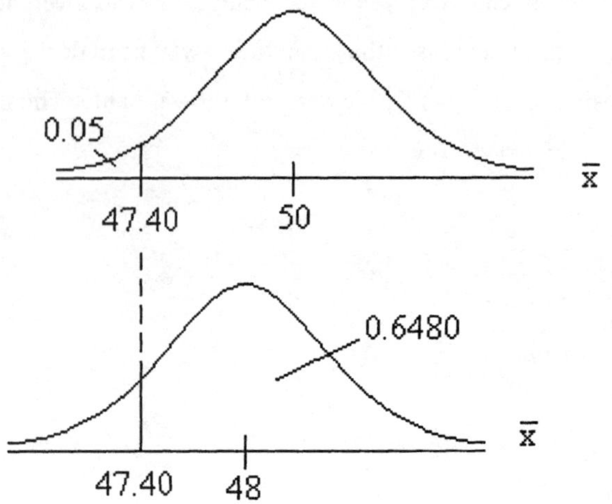

11.52 a. Rejection region: $\frac{\bar{x}-\mu}{\sigma/\sqrt{n}} > z_\alpha$

$\frac{\bar{x}-100}{20/\sqrt{100}} > z_{.10} = 1.28$

$\bar{x} > 102.56$

$\beta = P(\bar{x} < 102.56 \text{ given } \mu = 102) = P\left(\frac{\bar{x}-\mu}{\sigma/\sqrt{n}} < \frac{102.56-102}{20/\sqrt{100}}\right) = P(z < .28) = .5 + .1103 = .6103$

b. Rejection region: $\frac{\bar{x}-\mu}{\sigma/\sqrt{n}} > z_\alpha$

$\frac{\bar{x}-100}{20/\sqrt{100}} > z_{.02} = 2.55$

$\bar{x} > 104.11$

$\beta = P(\bar{x} < 104.11 \text{ given } \mu = 102) = P\left(\frac{\bar{x}-\mu}{\sigma/\sqrt{n}} < \frac{104.11-102}{20/\sqrt{100}}\right) = P(z < 1.06) = .5 + .3554 = .8554$

c. β increases.

11.54

Exercise 11.52 a

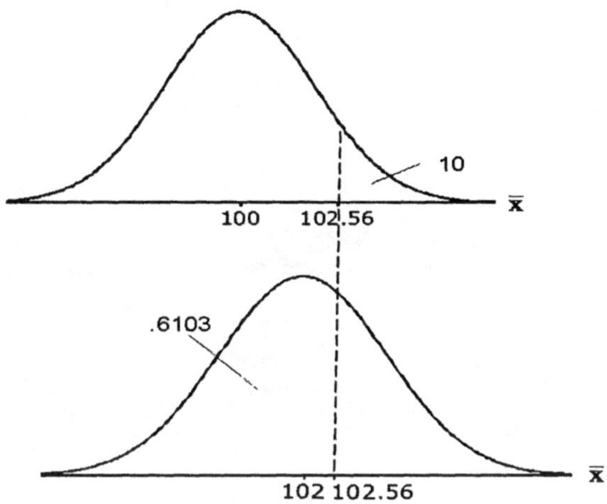

Exercise 11.52 b

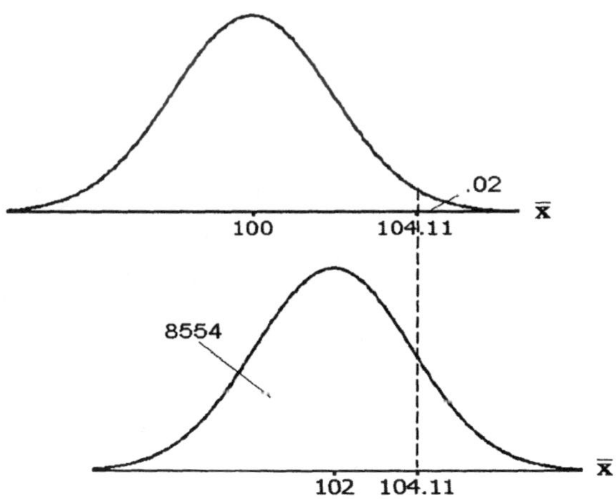

Exercise 11.53 a

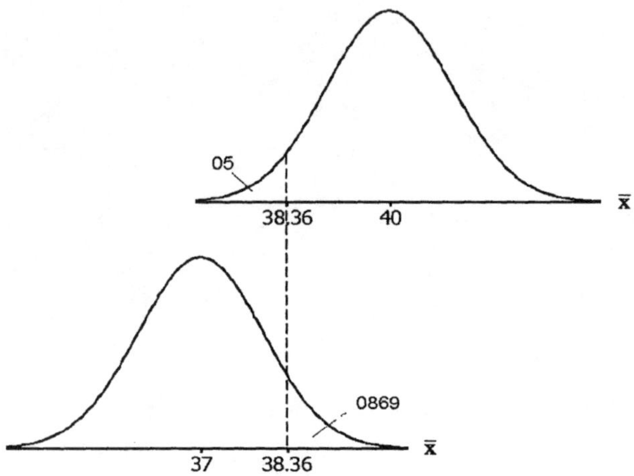

Exercise 11.53 b

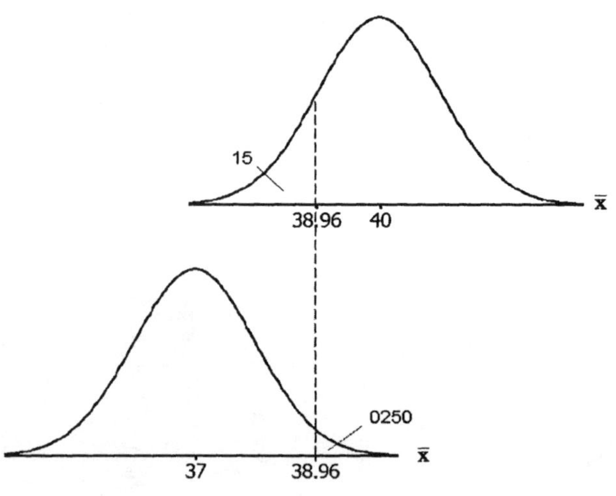

11.56 a. Rejection region: $\dfrac{\bar{x}-\mu}{\sigma/\sqrt{n}} > z_{\alpha}$

$\dfrac{\bar{x}-300}{50/\sqrt{81}} > z_{.05} = 1.645$

$\bar{x} > 309.14$

$\beta = P(\bar{x} < 309.14 \text{ given } \mu = 310) = P\left(\dfrac{\bar{x}-\mu}{\sigma/\sqrt{n}} < \dfrac{309.14-310}{50/\sqrt{81}}\right) = P(z < -.15) = .5 - .0596 = .4404$

b. Rejection region: $\frac{\bar{x}-\mu}{\sigma/\sqrt{n}} > z_\alpha$

$\frac{\bar{x}-300}{50/\sqrt{36}} > z_{.05} = 1.645$

$\bar{x} > 313.71$

$\beta = P(\bar{x} < 313.71 \text{ given } \mu = 310) = P\left(\frac{\bar{x}-\mu}{\sigma/\sqrt{n}} < \frac{313.71-310}{50/\sqrt{36}}\right) = P(z < .45) = .5 + .1736 = .6736$

c. β increases.

11.58

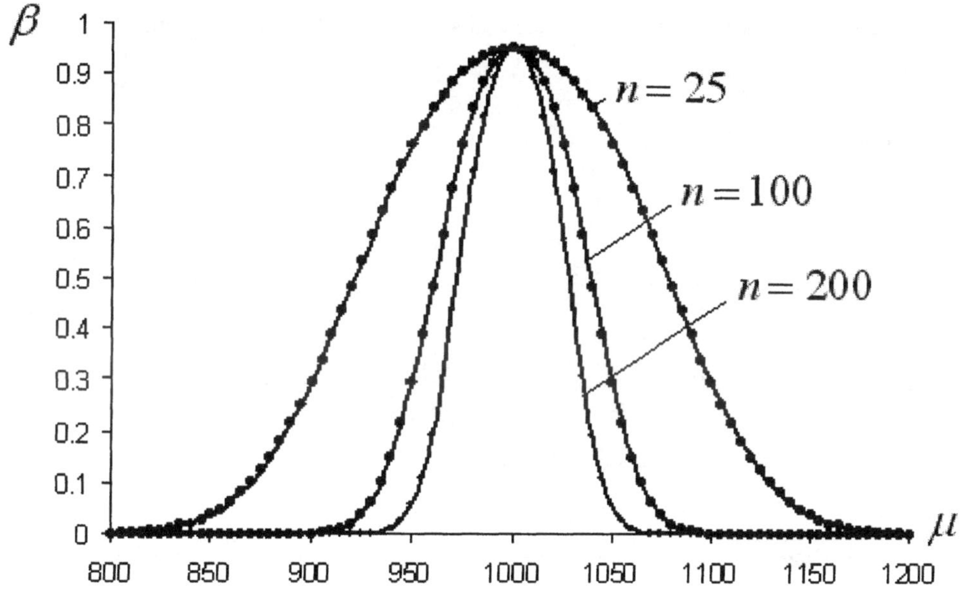

11.60 $H_0: \mu = 170$

$H_1: \mu < 170$

A Type I error occurs when we conclude that the new system is not cost effective when it actually is.

A Type II error occurs when we conclude that the new system is cost effective when it actually is not.

The test statistic is the same. However, the p-value equals 1 minus the p-value calculated Example 10.1. That is,

p-value = 1 – .0069 = .9931

We conclude that there is no evidence to infer that the mean is less than 170. That is, there is no evidence to infer that the new system will not be cost effective.

11.62 Rejection region: $\frac{\bar{x}-\mu}{\sigma/\sqrt{n}} < -z_{\alpha}$

$$\frac{\bar{x}-22}{6/\sqrt{220}} < -z_{.10} = -1.28$$

$\bar{x} < 21.48$

$$\beta = P(\bar{x} > 21.48 \text{ given } \mu = 21) = P\left(\frac{\bar{x}-\mu}{\sigma/\sqrt{n}} > \frac{21.48-21}{6/\sqrt{220}}\right) = P(z > 1.19) = .5 - .3830 = .1170$$

The company can decide whether the sample size and significance level are appropriate.

11.64 Rejection region: $\frac{\bar{x}-\mu}{\sigma/\sqrt{n}} < -z_{\alpha}$

$$\frac{\bar{x}-32}{8/\sqrt{110}} < -z_{05} = -1.645$$

$\bar{x} < 30.75$

$$\beta = P(\bar{x} > 30.75 \text{ given } \mu = 30) = P\left(\frac{\bar{x}-\mu}{\sigma/\sqrt{n}} > \frac{30.75-30)}{8/\sqrt{110}}\right) = P(z > .98) = .5 - .3365 = .1635$$

β can be decreased by increasing α and/or increasing the sample size.

11.66 A Type I error occurs when we conclude that the site is feasible when it is not. The consequence of this decision is to conduct further testing. A Type II error occurs when we do not conclude that a site is feasible when it actually is. We will do no further testing on this site, and as a result we will not build on a good site.

Chapter 12

12.2 a $\bar{x} \pm t_{\alpha/2} s/\sqrt{n}$ = 1,000 ± 2.626(300/$\sqrt{100}$) = 1,000 ± 78.78; LCL = 921.22, UCL = 1,078.78

b $\bar{x} \pm t_{\alpha/2} s/\sqrt{n}$ = 1,000 ± 2.626(200/$\sqrt{100}$) = 1,000 ± 52.52; LCL = 947.48, UCL = 1,052.52

c $\bar{x} \pm t_{\alpha/2} s/\sqrt{n}$ = 1,000 ± 2.626(100/$\sqrt{100}$) = 1,000 ± 26.26; LCL = 973.74, UCL = 1,026.26

d. The interval narrows.

12.4 a $\bar{x} \pm t_{\alpha/2} s/\sqrt{n}$ = 10 ± 1.984(1/$\sqrt{100}$) = 10 ± .20; LCL = 9.80, UCL = 10.20

b $\bar{x} \pm t_{\alpha/2} s/\sqrt{n}$ = 10 ± 1.984(4/$\sqrt{100}$) = 10 ± .79; LCL = 9.21, UCL = 10.79

c $\bar{x} \pm t_{\alpha/2} s/\sqrt{n}$ = 10 ± 1.984(10/$\sqrt{100}$) = 10 ± 1.98; LCL = 8.02, UCL = 11.98

d The interval widens.

12.6 a $\bar{x} \pm t_{\alpha/2} s/\sqrt{n}$ = 63 ± 1.990(8/$\sqrt{81}$) = 63 ± 1.77; LCL = 61.23, UCL = 64.77

b $\bar{x} \pm t_{\alpha/2} s/\sqrt{n}$ = 63 ± 2.000(8/$\sqrt{64}$) = 63 ± 2.00; LCL = 61.00, UCL = 65.00

c $\bar{x} \pm t_{\alpha/2} s/\sqrt{n}$ = 63 ± 2.030(8/$\sqrt{36}$) = 63 ± 2.71; LCL = 60.29, UCL = 65.71

d The interval widens.

12.8 $H_0: \mu = 220$

$H_1: \mu \neq 220$

Rejection region: $t < -t_{\alpha/2,n-1} = -t_{.025,199} \approx -1.972$ or $t > t_{\alpha/2,n-1} = t_{.025,199} = 1.972$

a $t = \dfrac{\bar{x}-\mu}{s/\sqrt{n}} = \dfrac{215-220}{22/\sqrt{200}} = -3.21$, p-value = .0015. There is enough evidence to infer that the population mean is not equal to 180.

b $t = \dfrac{\bar{x}-\mu}{s/\sqrt{n}} = \dfrac{215-220}{45/\sqrt{200}} = -1.57$, p-value = .1177. There is not enough evidence to infer that the population mean is not equal to 180.

c $t = \frac{\bar{x} - \mu}{s/\sqrt{n}} = \frac{215 - 220}{60/\sqrt{200}} = -1.18$, p-value = .2400. There is not enough evidence to infer that the population mean is not equal to 180.

d. As the s increases, the test statistic increases and the p-value increases.

12.10 $H_0 : \mu = 50$

$H_0 : \mu \neq 50$

a Rejection region: $t < -t_{\alpha/2,n-1} = -t_{.05,24} = -1.711$ or $t > t_{\alpha/2,n-1} = t_{.05,24} = 1.711$

$t = \frac{\bar{x} - \mu}{s/\sqrt{n}} = \frac{52 - 50}{15/\sqrt{25}} = .67$, p-value = .5113. There is not enough evidence to infer that the population mean is not equal to 50.

b Rejection region: $t < -t_{\alpha/2,n-1} = -t_{05,14} = -1.761$ or $t > t_{\alpha/2,n-1} = t_{05,14} = 1.761$

$t = \frac{\bar{x} - \mu}{s/\sqrt{n}} = \frac{52 - 50}{15/\sqrt{15}} = .52$, p-value = .6136. There is not enough evidence to infer that the population mean is not equal to 50.

c Rejection region: $t < -t_{\alpha/2,n-1} = -t_{05,4} = -2.132$ or $t > t_{\alpha/2,n-1} = t_{05,4} = -2.132$

$t = \frac{\bar{x} - \mu}{s/\sqrt{n}} = \frac{52 - 50}{15/\sqrt{5}} = .30$, p-value = .7804. There is not enough evidence to infer that the population mean is not equal to 50.

d The test statistic decreases and the p-value increases.

12.12 Rejection region: $t > t_{\alpha,n-1} = t_{.01,99} \approx 2.364$

a $t = \frac{\bar{x} - \mu}{s/\sqrt{n}} = \frac{106 - 100}{35/\sqrt{100}} = 1.71$, p-value = .0448. There is not enough evidence to infer that the population mean is greater than 100.

b $t = \frac{\bar{x} - \mu}{s/\sqrt{n}} = \frac{106 - 100}{25/\sqrt{100}} = 2.40$, p-value = .0091. There is enough evidence to infer that the population mean is greater than 100.

c $t = \frac{\bar{x} - \mu}{s/\sqrt{n}} = \frac{106 - 100}{15/\sqrt{100}} = 4.00$, p-value = .0001. There is enough evidence to infer that the population mean is greater than 100

d The test statistic increases and the p-value decreases.

12.14 a $\bar{x} \pm t_{\alpha/2} s/\sqrt{n} = 175 \pm 2.132(30/\sqrt{5}) = 175 \pm 28.60$; LCL = 146.40, UCL = 203.60

b $\bar{x} \pm z_{\alpha/2} \sigma/\sqrt{n} = 175 \pm 1.645(30/\sqrt{5}) = 175 \pm 22.07$; LCL = 152.93, UCL = 197.07

c The student t distribution is more widely dispersed than the standard normal; thus, $z_{\alpha/2}$ is smaller than $t_{\alpha/2}$.

12.16 a $\bar{x} \pm t_{\alpha/2} s/\sqrt{n} = 350 \pm 2.576(100/\sqrt{500}) = 350 \pm 11.52$; LCL = 338.48, UCL = 361.52

b $\bar{x} \pm z_{\alpha/2} \sigma/\sqrt{n} = 350 \pm 2.575(100/\sqrt{500}) = 350 \pm 11.52$; LCL = 338.48, UCL = 361.52

c With n = 500 the student t distribution with 999 degrees of freedom is almost identical to the standard normal distribution.

12.18 $H_0: \mu = 110$

$H_0: \mu < 110$

a Rejection region: $t < -t_{\alpha,n-1} = -t_{.10,9} = -1.383$

$t = \frac{\bar{x} - \mu}{s/\sqrt{n}} = \frac{103 - 110}{17/\sqrt{10}} = -1.30$, p-value = .1126. There is not enough evidence to infer that the population mean is less than 110.

b Rejection region: $z < -z_{\alpha} = z_{10} = -1.28$

$z = \frac{\bar{x} - \mu}{\sigma/\sqrt{n}} = \frac{103 - 110}{17/\sqrt{10}} = -1.30$, p-value = P(Z <–1.30) = .5 – P(0 <Z< 1.30) = .5 – .4032 = .0968.

There is enough evidence to infer that the population mean is less than 110.

c The Student t distribution is more dispersed than the standard normal.

12.20 a Rejection region: $t > t_{\alpha,n-1} = t_{.05,999} = 1.645$

$t = \frac{\bar{x} - \mu}{s/\sqrt{n}} = \frac{405 - 400}{100/\sqrt{1,000}} = 1.58$, p-value = .0569. There is not enough evidence to infer that the population mean is less than 15.

b Rejection region: $z > z_{\alpha} = z_{.05} = 1.645$

$t = \frac{\overline{x} - \mu}{s/\sqrt{n}} = \frac{405 - 400}{100/\sqrt{1{,}000}} = 1.58$, p-value = P(0 < Z < 1.58) = .5 – .4429 = .0571. There is not enough evidence to infer that the population mean is less than 15.

c With n = 1,000 the student t distribution with 999 degrees of freedom is almost identical to the standard normal distribution.

12.22 $\overline{x} \pm t_{\alpha/2} s/\sqrt{n} = 29{,}717 \pm 1.761(21{,}438/\sqrt{15}) = 29{,}717 \pm 9{,}748$; LCL = 19,969, UCL = 39,465

12.24 $H_0: \mu = 200$

$H_0: \mu < 200$

Rejection region: $t < -t_{\alpha,n-1} = -t_{01,17} = -2.567$

$t = \frac{\overline{x} - \mu}{s/\sqrt{n}} = \frac{199.21 - 200}{2.50/\sqrt{18}} = -1.34$, p-value = .0978. There is not enough evidence to conclude that the average container is mislabeled.

12.26 $\overline{x} \pm t_{\alpha/2} s/\sqrt{n} = 22.13 \pm 2.145(10.06)/\sqrt{15}) = 22.13 \pm 5.57$; LCL = 16.56, UCL =27.70

12.28 $H_0: \mu = 10$

$H_0: \mu < 10$

Rejection region: $t < -t_{\alpha,n-1} = -t_{10,9} = -1.383$

$t = \frac{\overline{x} - \mu}{s/\sqrt{n}} = \frac{7.10 - 10}{3.75/\sqrt{10}} = -2.45$, p-value = .0185. There is enough evidence to infer that the mean proportion of returns is less than 10%.

12.30 $\overline{x} \pm t_{\alpha/2} s/\sqrt{n} = 4.66 \pm 2.576(2.37/\sqrt{240}) = 4.66 \pm .39$; LCL = 4.27, UCL = 5.05

Total number: LCL = 100 million (4.27) = 427 million, UCL = 100 million (5.05) = 505 million

12.32 $H_0: \mu = 45$

$H_0: \mu > 45$

Rejection region: $t > t_{\alpha,n-1} = t_{05,143} \approx 1.656$

$t = \frac{\bar{x}-\mu}{s/\sqrt{n}} = \frac{53.78-45}{4.05/\sqrt{144}} = 26.01$, p-value = 0. There is enough evidence to infer that the mean time exceeds 45 hours.

12.34 $\bar{x} \pm t_{\alpha/2} s/\sqrt{n} = 2.67 \pm 1.973(2.50/\sqrt{188}) = 2.67 \pm .36$; LCL = 2.31, UCL = 3.03

12.36 $\bar{x} \pm t_{\alpha/2} s/\sqrt{n} = 29.14 \pm 2.009(4.62/\sqrt{49}) = 29.14 \pm 1.33$; LCL = 27.81, UCL = 30.47

12.38 $H_0 : \mu = 20$

$H_0 : \mu > 20$

Rejection region: $t > t_{\alpha,n-1} = t_{05,115} \approx 1.658$

$t = \frac{\bar{x}-\mu}{s/\sqrt{n}} = \frac{20.27-20}{5.72/\sqrt{116}} = .51$, p-value = .3061. There is not enough evidence to infer that the mean number of commercials is greater than 20.

12.40 $H_0 : \mu = 105$

$H_0 : \mu > 105$

Rejection region: $t > t_{\alpha,n-1} = t_{05,84} \approx 1.664$

$t = \frac{\bar{x}-\mu}{s/\sqrt{n}} = \frac{109.27-105}{17.30/\sqrt{85}} = 2.28$, p-value = .0127. There is enough evidence to infer that an e-grocery will be successful.

12.42 $H_0 : \sigma^2 = 300$

$H_1 : \sigma^2 \neq 300$

a Rejection region: $\chi^2 < \chi^2_{1-\alpha/2,n-1} = \chi^2_{975,99} \approx 74.2219$ or $\chi^2 > \chi^2_{\alpha/2,n-1} = \chi^2_{025,99} \approx 129.561$

$\chi^2 = \frac{(n-1)s^2}{\sigma^2} = \frac{(100-1)(220)}{300} = 72.60$, p-value = .0427. There is enough evidence to infer that the population variance differs from 300.

b Rejection region: $\chi^2 < \chi^2_{1-\alpha/2,n-1} = \chi^2_{.975,49} \approx 32.3574$ or $\chi^2 > \chi^2_{\alpha/2,n-1} = \chi^2_{.025,49} \approx 71.4202$

$\chi^2 = \frac{(n-1)s^2}{\sigma^2} = \frac{(50-1)(220)}{300} = 35.93$, p-value = .1643. There is not enough evidence to infer that the population variance differs from 300.

c Decreasing the sample size decreases the test statistic and increases the p-value of the test.

12.44 a $LCL = \frac{(n-1)s^2}{\chi^2_{\alpha/2,n-1}} = \frac{(n-1)s^2}{\chi^2_{.05,14}} = \frac{(15-1)(12)}{23.6848} = 7.09$

$UCL = \frac{(n-1)s^2}{\chi^2_{1-\alpha/2,n-1}} = \frac{(n-1)s^2}{\chi^2_{.95,14}} \frac{(15-1)(12)}{6.57063} = 25.57$

b $LCL = \frac{(n-1)s^2}{\chi^2_{\alpha/2,n-1}} = \frac{(n-1)s^2}{\chi^2_{.05,29}} = \frac{(30-1)(12)}{42.5569} = 8.18$

$UCL = \frac{(n-1)s^2}{\chi^2_{1-\alpha/2,n-1}} = \frac{(n-1)s^2}{\chi^2_{95,29}} = \frac{(30-1)(12)}{17.7083} = 19.65$

c Increasing the sample size narrows the interval.

12.46 $H_0: \sigma^2 = 200$

$H_1: \sigma^2 < 200$

Rejection region: $\chi^2 < \chi^2_{1-\alpha,n-1} = \chi^2_{.90,9} = 4.16816$

$\chi^2 = \frac{(n-1)s^2}{\sigma^2} = \frac{(10-1)(174.22)}{200} = 7.84$, p-value = .4497. There is not enough evidence to infer that the population variance has decreased.

12.48 $LCL = \frac{(n-1)s^2}{\chi^2_{\alpha/2,n-1}} = \frac{(n-1)s^2}{\chi^2_{025,9}} = \frac{(10-1)(.0098)}{19.0228} = .0046$

$UCL = \frac{(n-1)s^2}{\chi^2_{1-\alpha/2,n-1}} = \frac{(n-1)s^2}{\chi^2_{975,9}} = \frac{(10-1)(.0098)}{2.70039} = .0327$

12.50 $H_0: \sigma^2 = 45$

$H_1: \sigma^2 > 45$

Rejection region: $\chi^2 > \chi^2_{\alpha,n-1} = \chi^2_{.10,244} = 272.704$

$\chi^2 = \frac{(n-1)s^2}{\sigma^2} = \frac{(245-1)(57.92)}{45} = 314.06$; p-value = .0016. There is enough evidence to infer that the population variance is greater than 45.

12.52 $H_0: \sigma^2 = 200$

$H_1: \sigma^2 < 200$

Rejection region: $\chi^2 < \chi^2_{1-\alpha,n-1} = \chi^2_{.95,99} \approx 77.9295$

$\chi^2 = \frac{(n-1)s^2}{\sigma^2} = \frac{(100-1)(174.47)}{200} = 86.36$; p-value = .1863. There is not enough evidence to infer that the population variance is less than 200. Replace the bulbs as they burn out.

12.54 a $\hat{p} \pm z_{\alpha/2}\sqrt{\hat{p}(1-\hat{p})/n} = .48 \pm 1.96\sqrt{.48(1-.48)/500} = .48 \pm .0438$

b $\hat{p} \pm z_{\alpha/2}\sqrt{\hat{p}(1-\hat{p})/n} = .48 \pm 1.96\sqrt{.48(1-.48)/200} = .48 \pm .0692$

c $\hat{p} \pm z_{\alpha/2}\sqrt{\hat{p}(1-\hat{p})/n} = .48 \pm 1.96\sqrt{.48(1-.48)/1000} = .48 \pm .0310$

d The interval narrows.

12.56 $H_0: p = .60$

$H_1: p > .60$

a $z = \frac{\hat{p}-p}{\sqrt{p(1-p)/n}} = \frac{.63-.60}{\sqrt{.60(1-.60)/100}} = .61$, p-value = P(Z > .61) = .5 – .2291 =.2709

b $z = \frac{\hat{p}-p}{\sqrt{p(1-p)/n}} = \frac{.63-.60}{\sqrt{.60(1-.60)/200}} = .87$, p-value = P(Z > .87) = .5 – .3078 = .1922

c $z = \frac{\hat{p}-p}{\sqrt{p(1-p)/n}} = \frac{.63-.60}{\sqrt{.60(1-.60)/400}} = 1.22$, p-value = P(Z > 1.22) = .5 – .3888 = .1112

d The p-value decreases.

12.58 $n = \left(\frac{z_{\alpha/2}\sqrt{\hat{p}(1-\hat{p})}}{B}\right)^2 = \left(\frac{1.645\sqrt{.5(1-.5)}}{.03}\right)^2 = 752$

12.60 a $\hat{p} \pm z_{\alpha/2}\sqrt{\hat{p}(1-\hat{p})/n} = .75 \pm 1.645\sqrt{.75(1-.75)/752} = .75 \pm .0260$

b The interval is narrower.

c Yes, because the interval estimate is better than specified.

12.62 a.75 ± .03

b Yes, because the sample size was chosen to produce this interval.

12.64 a $\hat{p} \pm z_{\alpha/2}\sqrt{\hat{p}(1-\hat{p})/n} = .5 \pm 1.645\sqrt{.5(1-.5)/564} = .5 \pm .0346$

b The interval is wider.

c No because the interval estimate is wider (worse) than specified.

12.66 $\hat{p} = 217/418 = .52$

$\hat{p} \pm z_{\alpha/2}\sqrt{\hat{p}(1-\hat{p})/n} = .52 \pm 1.645\sqrt{.52(1-.52)/418} = .52 \pm .04$; LCL = .48, UCL = .56

12.68 $H_0: p = .92$

$H_1: p > .92$

$\hat{p} = 249/268 = .929$

$z = \frac{\hat{p}-p}{\sqrt{p(1-p)/n}} = \frac{.929-.92}{\sqrt{.92(1-.92)/268}} = .54$, p-value = P(Z > .54) = .5 – .2054 =.2946. There is not enough evidence to conclude that the airline's on-time performance has improved.

12.70 $\hat{p} = 68/400 = .17$

$\hat{p} \pm z_{\alpha/2}\sqrt{\hat{p}(1-\hat{p})/n} = .17 \pm 1.96\sqrt{.17(1-.17)/400} = .17 \pm .0368$; LCL = .1332, UCL = .2068

12.72 $\tilde{p} = \frac{x+2}{n+4} = \frac{1+2}{200+4} = .0147$

$\tilde{p} \pm z_{\alpha/2}\sqrt{\frac{\tilde{p}(1-\tilde{p})}{n+4}}$ = $.0147 \pm 1.96\sqrt{\frac{.0147(1-.0147)}{200+4}}$ = .0147 ± .0165; LCL = 0 (increased from –.0018), UCL = .0312

12.74 $\tilde{p} = \frac{x+2}{n+4} = \frac{1+2}{385+4} = .0077$

$\tilde{p} \pm z_{\alpha/2}\sqrt{\frac{\tilde{p}(1-\tilde{p})}{n+4}}$ = $.0077 \pm 2.575\sqrt{\frac{.0077(1-.0077)}{385+4}}$ = .0077 ± .0114; LCL = 0 (increased from –.0037), UCL = .0191

12.76 LCL = 75,000(.0792) =5,940, UCL = 75,000(.1320) = 9,900

12.78 $H_0: p = .90$

$H_1: p < .90$

$z = \frac{\hat{p} - p}{\sqrt{p(1-p)/n}} = \frac{.8644 - .90}{\sqrt{.90(1-.90)/177}}$ = –1.58, p-value =P(Z < –1.58) = .5 – .4429 = .0571. There is not enough evidence to infer that the satisfaction rate is less than 90%.

12.80 $H_0: p = .80$

$H_1: p > .80$

$z = \frac{\hat{p} - p}{\sqrt{p(1-p)/n}} = \frac{.8225 - .80}{\sqrt{.80(1-.80)/400}}$ = 1.13, p-value = P(Z > 1.13) = .5 – .3708 = .1292. There is not enough evidence to infer that the claim is true.

12.82 $H_0: p = .50$

$H_1: p > .50$

$z = \frac{\hat{p} - p}{\sqrt{p(1-p)/n}} = \frac{.57 - .50}{\sqrt{.50(1-.50)/100}} = 1.40$, p-value = P(Z > 1.40) = .5 – .4192 =.0808. There is enough evidence to conclude that more than 50% of all business students would rate the book as excellent.

12.84 $\hat{p} \pm z_{\alpha/2}\sqrt{\hat{p}(1-\hat{p})/n} = .0827 \pm 1.645\sqrt{.0827(1-.0827)/387} = .0827 \pm .0230$; LCL = .0597, UCL = .1057

12.86 $\hat{p} \pm z_{\alpha/2}\sqrt{\hat{p}(1-\hat{p})/n} = .1914 \pm 1.645\sqrt{.1914(1-.1914)/810} = .1914 \pm .0227$; LCL = .1687, UCL = .2141

Number: LCL = 270 million (.1687) = 45.55 million, UCL = 270 million (.2141) = 57.81 million

12.88 $\hat{p} \pm z_{\alpha/2}\sqrt{\hat{p}(1-\hat{p})/n} = .0975 \pm 1.96\sqrt{.0975(1-.0975)/2000} = .0975 \pm .0130$; LCL = .0845, UCL = .1105

Number: LCL = 100 million (.0845) = 8.45 million, UCL = 100 million (.1105) = 11.05 million

12.90 Code 2 was changed to 3.

$\hat{p} \pm z_{\alpha/2}\sqrt{\hat{p}(1-\hat{p})/n} = .5313 \pm 1.96\sqrt{.5313(1-.5313)/320} = .5313 \pm .0547$; LCL = .4766, UCL = .5860;

Market segment size: LCL = 15,517,000 (.4766) = 7,395,402 , UCL = 15,517,000 (.5860) = 9,092,962

12.92 $\hat{p} \pm z_{\alpha/2}\sqrt{\hat{p}(1-\hat{p})/n} = .1077 \pm 1.96\sqrt{.1077(1-.1077)/325} = .1077 \pm .0337$; LCL = .0740, UCL = .1414; Market segment size: LCL = 35.6 million(.0740) = 2.634 million, UCL = 35.6 million(.1414) = 5.034 million

12.94 $\hat{p} \pm z_{\alpha/2}\sqrt{\hat{p}(1-\hat{p})/n} = .1500 \pm 1.96\sqrt{.1500(1-.1500)/340} = .1500 \pm .0380$; LCL = .1120, UCL = .1880; Number: LCL = 187 million(.1120) = 20.944 million, UCL = 187 million(.1880) = 35.156 million

12.96 $\hat{p} = 29/559 = .0519$; $\hat{p} \pm z_{\alpha/2}\sqrt{\hat{p}(1-\hat{p})/n} = .0519 \pm 2.575\sqrt{.0519(1-.0519)/559}$

$= .0519 \pm .0242$; LCL = .0277, UCL = .0761; Number: LCL = 118,653(.0277) = 3,287, UCL = 118,653(.0761) = 9,029

12.98 $\hat{p} = 14/125 = .112$; $\hat{p} \pm z_{\alpha/2}\sqrt{\frac{\hat{p}(1-\hat{p})}{n}}\sqrt{\frac{N-n}{N-1}} = .112 \pm 1.645\sqrt{\frac{.112(1-.112)}{125}}\sqrt{\frac{2{,}490-125}{2{,}490-1}}$

$= .112 \pm .0452$; LCL = .0668, UCL = .1572; Number: LCL = 2,490(.0668) = 166, UCL = 2,490(.1572) = 391

12.100 $\bar{x} \pm t_{\alpha/2}\frac{s}{\sqrt{n}}\sqrt{\frac{N-n}{N-1}} = 313.47 \pm 1.984\frac{55.53}{\sqrt{100}}\sqrt{\frac{1{,}431-100}{1{,}431-1}} = 313.47 \pm 10.63$; LCL = 302.84, UCL = 324.10; Total: LCL = 1,431(302.84) = $433,364, UCL = 1,431(324.10) = $463,787

12.102 $\bar{x} \pm t_{\alpha/2}\frac{s}{\sqrt{n}}\sqrt{\frac{N-n}{N-1}} = 12{,}940 \pm 1.653\frac{4{,}139}{\sqrt{188}}\sqrt{\frac{2{,}684-100}{2{,}684-1}} = 12{,}940 \pm 490$; LCL = 12,450, UCL = 13,430; Total: LCL = 2,684(12,450) = $33,415,800, UCL = 2,684(13,430 = $36,046,120

12.104 a $H_0: \mu = 30$

$H_1: \mu > 30$

	A	B	C	D
1	**t-Test: Mean**			
2				
3				*Costs*
4	Mean			31.95
5	Standard Deviation			7.19
6	Hypothesized Mean			30
7	df			124
8	t Stat			3.04
9	P(T<=t) one-tail			0.0015
10	t Critical one-tail			1.6572
11	P(T<=t) two-tail			0.0030
12	t Critical two-tail			1.9793

t = 3.04, p-value = .0015; there is enough evidence to infer that the candidate is correct.

b

	A	B	C	D
1	**t-Estimate: Mean**			
2				
3				*Costs*
4	Mean			31.95
5	Standard Deviation			7.19
6	LCL			30.68
7	UCL			33.23

LCL = 30.68, UCL = 33.23

c The costs are required to be normally distributed.

12.106 $H_0 : \sigma^2 = 17$

$H_1 : \sigma^2 > 17$

	A	B	C	D
1	**Chi Squared Test: Variance**			
2				
3				*Times*
4	Sample Variance			27.47
5	Hypothesized Variance			17
6	df			19
7	chi-squared Stat			30.71
8	P (CHI<=chi) one-tail			0.0435
9	chi-squared Critical one tail	Left-tail		10.1170
10		Right-tail		30.1435
11	P (CHI<=chi) two-tail			0.0869
12	chi-squared Critical two tail	Left-tail		8.9065
13		Right-tail		32.8523

$\chi^2 = 30.71$, p-value = .0435. There is enough evidence to infer that problems are likely.

12.108 a

	A	B	C	D
1	**t-Estimate: Mean**			
2				
3				*Marks*
4	Mean			71.88
5	Standard Deviation			10.03
6	LCL			69.03
7	UCL			74.73

LCL = 69.03, UCL = 74.73

b $H_0 : \mu = 68$

$H_1 : \mu > 68$

	A	B	C	D
1	**t-Test: Mean**			
2				
3				*Marks*
4	Mean			71.88
5	Standard Deviation			10.03
6	Hypothesized Mean			68
7	df			49
8	t Stat			2.74
9	P(T<=t) one-tail			0.0043
10	t Critical one-tail			1.6766
11	P(T<=t) two-tail			0.0086
12	t Critical two-tail			2.0096

t = 2.74, p-value = .0043; there is enough evidence to infer that students with a calculus background would perform better in statistics than students with no calculus?

12.110

	A	B
1	**z-Estimate: Proportion**	
2		*Insurance*
3	Sample Proportion	0.632
4	Observations	250
5	LCL	0.582
6	UCL	0.682

LCL = .582, UCL = .682

12.112

	A	B	C	D
1	**t-Estimate: Mean**			
2				
3				*Time*
4	Mean			6.35
5	Standard Deviation			2.16
6	LCL			6.05
7	UCL			6.65

LCL = 6.05, UCL = 6.65

12.114

	A	B
1	**z-Estimate: Proportion**	
2		*Tourist*
3	Sample Proportion	0.667
4	Observations	72
5	LCL	0.558
6	UCL	0.776

LCL = .558, UCL = .776

12.116 $H_0: p = .90$

$H_1: p < .90$

	A	B	C	D
1	**z-Test: Proportion**			
2				
3				*Springs*
4	Sample Proportion			0.86
5	Observations			100
6	Hypothesized Proportion			0.9
7	z Stat			-1.33
8	P(Z<=z) one-tail			0.0912
9	z Critical one-tail			1.2816
10	P(Z<=z) two-tail			0.1824
11	z Critical two-tail			1.6449

z = –1.33, p-value = .0912; there is enough evidence to infer that less than 90% of the springs are the correct length.

12.118 a $H_0: \mu = 9.8$

$H_1: \mu < 9.8$

	A	B	C	D
1	**t-Test: Mean**			
2				
3				*Time*
4	Mean			9.16
5	Standard Deviation			2.64
6	Hypothesized Mean			9.8
7	df			149
8	t Stat			-2.97
9	P(T<=t) one-tail			0.0018
10	t Critical one-tail			1.2873
11	P(T<=t) two-tail			0.0036
12	t Critical two-tail			1.6551

t = –2.97, p-value = .0018; there is enough evidence to infer that enclosure of preaddressed envelopes improves the average speed of payments?

b $H_0: \sigma^2 = 10.24\ (3.2^2)$

$H_1: \sigma^2 < 10.24$

	A	B	C	D
1	**Chi Squared Test: Variance**			
2				
3				*Time*
4	Sample Variance			6.98
5	Hypothesized Variance			10.24
6	df			149
7	chi-squared Stat			101.58
8	P (CHI<=chi) one-tail			0.0011
9	chi-squared Critical one tail	Left-tail		127.3493
10		Right-tail		171.5069
11	P (CHI<=chi) two-tail			0.0021
12	chi-squared Critical two tail	Left-tail		121.7870
13		Right-tail		178.4854

$\chi^2 = 101.58$, p-value = .0011; there is enough evidence to infer that the variability in payment speeds decreases when a preaddressed envelope is sent.

12.120

	A	B
1	**z-Estimate: Proportion**	
2		*Concert*
3	Sample Proportion	0.1533
4	Observations	600
5	LCL	0.1245
6	UCL	0.1822

Proportion: LCL = .1245, UCL = .1822

Total: LCL = 400,000(.1245) = 49,800 UCL = 400,000(.1822) = 72,880

Chapter 13

13.2 $H_0: (\mu_1 - \mu_2) = 0$

$H_1: (\mu_1 - \mu_2) \neq 0$

a Equal-variances test statistic

Rejection region: $t < -t_{\alpha/2,\nu} = -t_{.025,22} = -2.074$ or $t > t_{\alpha/2,\nu} = t_{.025,22} = 2.074$

$$t = \frac{(\bar{x}_1 - \bar{x}_2) - (\mu_1 - \mu_2)}{\sqrt{s_p^2\left(\frac{1}{n_1} + \frac{1}{n_2}\right)}} = \frac{(74-71)-0}{\sqrt{\left(\frac{(12-1)18^2 + (12-1)16^2}{12+12-2}\right)\left(\frac{1}{12} + \frac{1}{12}\right)}} = .43$$

, p-value = .6703. There is not enough evidence to infer that the population means differ.

b Equal-variances test statistic

Rejection region: $t < -t_{\alpha/2,\nu} = -t_{.025,22} = -2.074$ or $t > t_{\alpha/2,\nu} = t_{.025,22} = 2.074$

$$t = \frac{(\bar{x}_1 - \bar{x}_2) - (\mu_1 - \mu_2)}{\sqrt{s_p^2\left(\frac{1}{n_1} + \frac{1}{n_2}\right)}} = \frac{(74-71)-0}{\sqrt{\left(\frac{(12-1)210^2 + (12-1)198^2}{12+12-2}\right)\left(\frac{1}{12} + \frac{1}{12}\right)}} = .04$$

, p-value = .9716. There is not enough evidence to infer that the population means differ.

c The value of the test statistic decreases and the p-value increases.

d Equal-variances test statistic

Rejection region: $t < -t_{\alpha/2,\nu} = -t_{.025,298} = -1.960$ or $t > t_{\alpha/2,\nu} = t_{.025,298} = 1.960$

$$t = \frac{(\bar{x}_1 - \bar{x}_2) - (\mu_1 - \mu_2)}{\sqrt{s_p^2\left(\frac{1}{n_1} + \frac{1}{n_2}\right)}} = \frac{(74-71)-0}{\sqrt{\left(\frac{(150-1)18^2 + (150-1)16^2}{150+150-2}\right)\left(\frac{1}{150} + \frac{1}{150}\right)}} = 1.53$$

, p-value = .1282.

There is not enough evidence to infer that the population means differ.

e The value of the test statistic increases and the p-value decreases.

f Rejection region: $t < -t_{\alpha/2,\nu} = -t_{.025,22} = -2.074$ or $t > t_{\alpha/2,\nu} = t_{.025,22} = 2.074$

$$t = \frac{(\bar{x}_1 - \bar{x}_2) - (\mu_1 - \mu_2)}{\sqrt{s_p^2\left(\frac{1}{n_1} + \frac{1}{n_2}\right)}} = \frac{(76-71)-0}{\sqrt{\left(\frac{(12-1)18^2 + (12-1)16^2}{12+12-2}\right)\left(\frac{1}{12} + \frac{1}{12}\right)}} = .72$$

, p-value = .4796. There is not enough evidence to infer that the population means differ.

g The value of the test statistic increases and the p-value decreases.

13.4 a Unequal-variances estimator

$$\nu = \frac{(s_1^2/n_1 + s_2^2/n_2)^2}{\frac{(s_1^2/n_1)^2}{n_1 - 1} + \frac{(s_2^2/n_2)^2}{n_2 - 1}} = 64.8 \text{ (rounded to 65, approximated by } \nu = 70\text{)}$$

$$(\bar{x}_1 - \bar{x}_2) \pm t_{\alpha/2}\sqrt{\left(\frac{s_1^2}{n_1} + \frac{s_2^2}{n_2}\right)} = (63 - 60) \pm 1.667\sqrt{\left(\frac{18^2}{50} + \frac{7^2}{45}\right)} = 3 \pm 4.59$$

b Unequal-variances estimator

$$\nu = \frac{(s_1^2/n_1 + s_2^2/n_2)^2}{\frac{(s_1^2/n_1)^2}{n_1 - 1} + \frac{(s_2^2/n_2)^2}{n_2 - 1}} = 63.1 \text{ (rounded to 63, approximated by } \nu = 60\text{)}$$

$$(\bar{x}_1 - \bar{x}_2) \pm t_{\alpha/2}\sqrt{\left(\frac{s_1^2}{n_1} + \frac{s_2^2}{n_2}\right)} = (63 - 60) \pm 1.671\sqrt{\left(\frac{41^2}{50} + \frac{15^2}{45}\right)} = 3 \pm 10.38$$

c The interval widens.

d Unequal-variances estimator

$$\nu = \frac{(s_1^2/n_1 + s_2^2/n_2)^2}{\frac{(s_1^2/n_1)^2}{n_1 - 1} + \frac{(s_2^2/n_2)^2}{n_2 - 1}} = 131 \text{ (approximated by } \nu = 140\text{)}$$

$$(\bar{x}_1 - \bar{x}_2) \pm t_{\alpha/2}\sqrt{\left(\frac{s_1^2}{n_1} + \frac{s_2^2}{n_2}\right)} = (63 - 60) \pm 1.656\sqrt{\left(\frac{18^2}{100} + \frac{7^2}{90}\right)} = 3 \pm 3.22$$

e The interval narrows.

13.6 a In all cases the equal-variances t-test degrees of freedom is greater than the unequal-variances t-test degrees of freedom.

13.8 $H_0: (\mu_1 - \mu_2) = 0$

$H_1: (\mu_1 - \mu_2) \neq 0$

Two-tail F test: F = 1.04, p-value = .9873; use equal-variances test statistic

Rejection region: $t < -t_{\alpha/2,\nu} = -t_{.05,13} = -1.771$ or $t > t_{\alpha/2,\nu} = t_{.05,13} = 1.771$

$$t = \frac{(\bar{x}_1 - \bar{x}_2) - (\mu_1 - \mu_2)}{\sqrt{s_p^2\left(\frac{1}{n_1} + \frac{1}{n_2}\right)}} = \frac{(3{,}372 - 4{,}093) - 0}{\sqrt{\left(\frac{(9-1)755{,}196 + (6-1)725{,}778}{9+6-2}\right)\left(\frac{1}{9} + \frac{1}{6}\right)}} = -1.59, \text{p-value} = .1368.$$

There is not enough evidence to infer a difference between the two types of vacation expenses.

13.10 $H_0 : (\mu_1 - \mu_2) = 0$

$H_1 : (\mu_1 - \mu_2) < 0$

Two-tail F test: F = 1.02, p-value = .9823; use equal-variances test statistic

Rejection region: $t < -t_{\alpha,\nu} = -t_{.10,18} = -1.330$

$$t = \frac{(\bar{x}_1 - \bar{x}_2) - (\mu_1 - \mu_2)}{\sqrt{s_p^2\left(\frac{1}{n_1} + \frac{1}{n_2}\right)}} = \frac{(5.10 - 7.30) - 0}{\sqrt{\left(\frac{(10-1)5.88 + (10-1)5.79}{10+10-2}\right)\left(\frac{1}{10} + \frac{1}{10}\right)}} = -2.04, \text{p-value} = .0283.$$ There is enough evidence to infer that there are fewer errors when the yellow ball is used.

13.12 $H_0 : (\mu_1 - \mu_2) = 0$

$H_1 : (\mu_1 - \mu_2) \neq 0$

Two-tail F test: F = .99, p-value = .9571; use equal-variances test statistic

Rejection region: $t < -t_{\alpha/2,\nu} = -t_{.025,238} = -1.960$ or $t > t_{\alpha/2,\nu} = t_{025,238} = 1.960$

$$t = \frac{(\bar{x}_1 - \bar{x}_2) - (\mu_1 - \mu_2)}{\sqrt{s_p^2\left(\frac{1}{n_1} + \frac{1}{n_2}\right)}} = \frac{(10.01 - 9.12) - 0}{\sqrt{\left(\frac{(120-1)4.43^2 + (120-1)4.45^2}{120+120-2}\right)\left(\frac{1}{120} + \frac{1}{120}\right)}} = 1.55, \quad \text{p-value} = .1218.$$

There is not enough evidence to infer that oat bran is different from other cereals in terms of cholesterol reduction?

13.14 a $H_0 : (\mu_1 - \mu_2) = 0$

$H_1 : (\mu_1 - \mu_2) > 0$

Two-tail F test: F = 1.01, p-value = .9619; use equal-variances test statistic

Rejection region: $t > t_{\alpha,\nu} = t_{05,282} \approx 1.645$

$$t = \frac{(\bar{x}_1 - \bar{x}_2) - (\mu_1 - \mu_2)}{\sqrt{s_p^2\left(\frac{1}{n_1} + \frac{1}{n_2}\right)}} = \frac{(59.81 - 57.40) - 0}{\sqrt{\left(\frac{(125-1)7.02^2 + (159-1)6.99^2}{125 + 159 - 2}\right)\left(\frac{1}{125} + \frac{1}{159}\right)}} = 2.88, \text{ p-value} = .0021.$$

There is enough evidence to infer that the cruise ships are attracting younger customers.

b $(\bar{x}_1 - \bar{x}_2) \pm t_{\alpha/2}\sqrt{s_p^2\left(\frac{1}{n_1} + \frac{1}{n_2}\right)} = (59.81 - 57.40)$

$$\pm 2.576\sqrt{\left(\frac{(125-1)7.02^2 + (159-1)6.99^2}{125 + 159 - 2}\right)\left(\frac{1}{125} + \frac{1}{159}\right)} = 2.41 \pm 2.16;$$

LCL = .25, UCL = 4.57

13.16 $H_0: (\mu_1 - \mu_2) = 0$

$H_1: (\mu_1 - \mu_2) > 0$

Two-tail F test: F = .98, p-value = .9520; use equal-variances test statistic

Rejection region: $t > t_{\alpha,\nu} = t_{.05,58} \approx 1.671$

$$t = \frac{(\bar{x}_1 - \bar{x}_2) - (\mu_1 - \mu_2)}{\sqrt{s_p^2\left(\frac{1}{n_1} + \frac{1}{n_2}\right)}} = \frac{(115.50 - 110.20) - 0}{\sqrt{\left(\frac{(30-1)21.69^2 + (30-1)21.93^2}{30 + 30 - 2}\right)\left(\frac{1}{30} + \frac{1}{30}\right)}} = .94, \text{ p-value} = .1753.$$

There is not enough evidence to retain supplier A - switch to supplier B.

13.18a $H_0: (\mu_1 - \mu_2) = 0$

$H_1: (\mu_1 - \mu_2) \neq 0$

Two-tail F test: F = 5.18, p-value = .0019; use unequal-variances test statistic

$$\nu = \frac{(s_1^2/n_1 + s_2^2/n_2)^2}{\frac{(s_1^2/n_1)^2}{n_1 - 1} + \frac{(s_2^2/n_2)^2}{n_2 - 1}} = 33.9 \text{ (rounded to 34)}$$

Rejection region: $t < -t_{\alpha/2,\nu} = -t_{005,34} \approx -2.724$ or $t > t_{\alpha/2,\nu} = t_{005,34} \approx 2.724$

$$t = \frac{(\bar{x}_1 - \bar{x}_2) - (\mu_1 - \mu_2)}{\sqrt{\left(\frac{s_1^2}{n_1} + \frac{s_2^2}{n_2}\right)}} = \frac{(70.42 - 56.44) - 0}{\sqrt{\left(\frac{20.54^2}{24} + \frac{9.03^2}{16}\right)}} = 2.94$$, p-value = .0060. There is enough evidence to conclude that the two packages differ in the amount of time needed to learn how to use them.

b $$(\bar{x}_1 - \bar{x}_2) \pm t_{\alpha/2}\sqrt{\left(\frac{s_1^2}{n_1} + \frac{s_2^2}{n_2}\right)} = (70.42 - 56.44) \pm 2.030\sqrt{\left(\frac{20.54^2}{24} + \frac{9.03^2}{16}\right)} = 13.98 \pm 9.67;$$

LCL = 4.31, UCL = 23.65

c The amount of time is required to be normally distributed.

d The histograms are somewhat bell shaped.

13.20 $H_0 : (\mu_1 - \mu_2) = 0$

$H_1 : (\mu_1 - \mu_2) > 0$

Two-tail F test: F = .73, p-value = .0699; use equal-variances test statistic

Rejection region: $t > t_{\alpha,\nu} = t_{.05,268} \approx 1.645$

$$t = \frac{(\bar{x}_1 - \bar{x}_2) - (\mu_1 - \mu_2)}{\sqrt{s_p^2\left(\frac{1}{n_1} + \frac{1}{n_2}\right)}} = \frac{(.646 - .601) - 0}{\sqrt{\left(\frac{(125-1).045^2 + (145-1).053^2}{125+145-2}\right)\left(\frac{1}{125} + \frac{1}{145}\right)}} = 7.54$$, p-value = 0.

There is enough evidence to conclude that the reaction time of drivers using cell phones is slower that for non-cell phone users.

13.22 $H_0 : (\mu_1 - \mu_2) = 0$

$H_1 : (\mu_1 - \mu_2) > 0$

Two-tail F test: F = .97, p-value = .9054; use equal-variances test statistic

Rejection region: $t > t_{\alpha,\nu} = t_{.05,143} \approx 1.656$

$$t = \frac{(\bar{x}_1 - \bar{x}_2) - (\mu_1 - \mu_2)}{\sqrt{s_p^2\left(\frac{1}{n_1} + \frac{1}{n_2}\right)}} = \frac{(6.18 - 5.94) - 0}{\sqrt{\left(\frac{(64-1)1.59^2 + (81-1)1.61^2}{64+81-2}\right)\left(\frac{1}{64} + \frac{1}{81}\right)}} = .90$$, p-value = .1858. There is not enough evidence to infer that people spend more time researching for a financial planner than they do for a stock broker.

13.24 $H_0: (\mu_1 - \mu_2) = 0$

$H_1: (\mu_1 - \mu_2) \neq 0$

Two-tail F test: F = .85, p-value = .2494; use equal-variances test statistic

Rejection region: $t < -t_{\alpha/2,\nu} = -t_{.025,413} \approx -1.960$ or $t > t_{\alpha/2,\nu} = t_{.025,413} \approx 1.960$

$$t = \frac{(\bar{x}_1 - \bar{x}_2) - (\mu_1 - \mu_2)}{\sqrt{s_p^2\left(\frac{1}{n_1} + \frac{1}{n_2}\right)}} = \frac{(149.85 - 154.43) - 0}{\sqrt{\left(\frac{(213-1)21.82^2 + (202-1)23.64^2}{213+202-2}\right)\left(\frac{1}{213} + \frac{1}{202}\right)}} = -2.05$$, p-value = .0412. There is enough evidence to conclude that there are differences in service times between the two chains.

13.26 a $H_0: (\mu_1 - \mu_2) = 0$

$H_1: (\mu_1 - \mu_2) \neq 0$

Two-tail F test: F = 1.51, p-value = .0402; use unequal-variances test statistic

$$\nu = \frac{(s_1^2/n_1 + s_2^2/n_2)^2}{\frac{(s_1^2/n_1)^2}{n_1 - 1} + \frac{(s_2^2/n_2)^2}{n_2 - 1}} = 190$$

Rejection region: $t < -t_{\alpha/2,\nu} = -t_{.025,190} \approx -1.973$ or $t > t_{\alpha/2,\nu} = t_{.025,190} \approx 1.973$

$$t = \frac{(\bar{x}_1 - \bar{x}_2) - (\mu_1 - \mu_2)}{\sqrt{\left(\frac{s_1^2}{n_1} + \frac{s_2^2}{n_2}\right)}} = \frac{(130.93 - 126.14) - 0}{\sqrt{\left(\frac{31.99^2}{100} + \frac{26.00^2}{100}\right)}} = 1.16$$, p-value = .2467. There is not enough evidence to infer that differences exist between the two types of customers.

13.28 $H_0: (\mu_1 - \mu_2) = 0$

$H_1: (\mu_1 - \mu_2) < 0$

Two-tail F test: F = 1.51, p-value = .0402; use unequal-variances test statistic

$$\nu = \frac{(s_1^2/n_1 + s_2^2/n_2)^2}{\frac{(s_1^2/n_1)^2}{n_1 - 1} + \frac{(s_2^2/n_2)^2}{n_2 - 1}} = 531$$

Rejection region: $t < -t_{\alpha,\nu} = -t_{.05,531} \approx -1.645$

$$t = \frac{(\bar{x}_1 - \bar{x}_2) - (\mu_1 - \mu_2)}{\sqrt{\left(\frac{s_1^2}{n_1} + \frac{s_2^2}{n_2}\right)}} = \frac{(237.99 - 251.99) - 0}{\sqrt{\left(\frac{12.24^2}{263} + \frac{14.84^2}{279}\right)}} = -12.01$$, p-value = 0. There is enough evidence to infer that British golfers play golf in less time than do American golfers.

13.30 $H_0: (\mu_1 - \mu_2) = 0$

$H_1: (\mu_1 - \mu_2) < 0$

Two-tail F test: F = .35, p-value = .0061; use unequal-variances test statistic

$$\nu = \frac{(s_1^2/n_1 + s_2^2/n_2)^2}{\frac{(s_1^2/n_1)^2}{n_1 - 1} + \frac{(s_2^2/n_2)^2}{n_2 - 1}} = 53$$

Rejection region: $t < -t_{\alpha,\nu} = -t_{.05,53} \approx -1.676$

$$t = \frac{(\bar{x}_1 - \bar{x}_2) - (\mu_1 - \mu_2)}{\sqrt{\left(\frac{s_1^2}{n_1} + \frac{s_2^2}{n_2}\right)}} = \frac{(7{,}137.2 - 9{,}303.7) - 0}{\sqrt{\left(\frac{195.07^2}{28} + \frac{331.89^2}{33}\right)}} = -31.61$$, p-value = 0. There is enough evidence to conclude that the total distance of American golf courses is greater than that of British courses.

13.32 Assuming that the volunteers were randomly assigned to eat either oat bran or another grain cereal the data are experimental.

13.34 a The data are observational because the students decided themselves which package each would use.

b The professor can randomly assign one of the two packages to each student.

c Better students tend to choose Program B and better students learn how to use computer software more quickly.

13.36a Let students select the section they wish to attend and compare test results.

b Randomly assign students to either section and compare test results.

13.38a Randomly select finance and marketing MBA graduates and determine their starting salaries.

b Randomly assign some MBA students to major in finance and others to major in marketing. Compare starting salaries after they graduate.

c Better students may be attracted to finance and better students draw higher starting salaries.

13.40 $H_0: \mu_D = 0$

$H_1: \mu_D < 0$

Rejection region: $t < -t_{\alpha,\nu} = -t_{.05,7} = -1.895$

$t = \frac{\bar{x}_D - \mu_D}{s_D / \sqrt{n_D}} = \frac{-4.75 - 0}{4.17 / \sqrt{8}} = -3.22$, p-value = .0073. There is enough evidence to infer that the Brand A is better than Brand B.

13.42 $H_0: \mu_D = 0$

$H_1: \mu_D > 0$

Rejection region: $t > t_{\alpha,\nu} = t_{.05,6} = 1.943$

$t = \frac{\bar{x}_D - \mu_D}{s_D / \sqrt{n_D}} = \frac{2.43 - 0}{3.41 / \sqrt{7}} = 1.89$, p-value = .0538. There is not enough evidence to infer that the camera reduces the number of red-light runners.

13.44 a $H_0: \mu_D = 0$

$H_1: \mu_D > 0$

Rejection region: $t > t_{\alpha,\nu} = t_{.05,11} = 1.796$

$t = \frac{\bar{x}_D - \mu_D}{s_D / \sqrt{n_D}} = \frac{3.08 - 0}{5.88 / \sqrt{12}} = 1.82$, p-value = .0484. There is enough evidence to infer that companies with exercise programs have lower medical expenses.

b $\bar{x}_D \pm t_{\alpha/2} \frac{s_D}{\sqrt{n_D}} = 3.08 \pm 2.201 \frac{5.88}{\sqrt{12}} = 3.08 \pm 3.74$; LCL = –.66, UCL = 6.82

c Yes because medical expenses will vary by the month of the year.

13.46 $H_0: \mu_D = 0$

$H_1: \mu_D \neq 0$

Rejection region: $t < -t_{\alpha/2,\nu} = -t_{025,49} \approx -2.009$ or $t > t_{\alpha/2,\nu} = t_{.025,49} \approx 2.009$

$t = \frac{\bar{x}_D - \mu_D}{s_D / \sqrt{n_D}} = \frac{-1.16 - 0}{2.22 / \sqrt{50}} = -3.70$, p-value = .0006. There is enough evidence to infer that waiters and waitresses earn different amounts in tips.

13.48a $H_0: \mu_D = 0$

$H_1: \mu_D > 0$

Rejection region: $t > t_{\alpha,\nu} = t_{.10,14} = 1.345$

$t = \frac{\bar{x}_D - \mu_D}{s_D / \sqrt{n_D}} = \frac{57.40 - 0}{13.14 / \sqrt{15}} = 16.92$, p-value = 0. There is enough evidence to conclude that heating costs for insulated homes is less than that for uninsulated homes.

b $\bar{x}_D \pm t_{\alpha/2} \frac{s_D}{\sqrt{n_D}} = 57.40 \pm 2.145 \frac{13.14}{\sqrt{15}} = 57.40 \pm 7.28$; LCL = 50.12, UCL = 64.68

c Differences are required to be normally distributed.

13.50 $H_0: \mu_D = 0$

$H_1: \mu_D < 0$

Rejection region: $t < -t_{\alpha,\nu} = -t_{05,169} \approx -1.654$

$t = \frac{\bar{x}_D - \mu_D}{s_D / \sqrt{n_D}} = \frac{-183.35 - 0}{1568.94 / \sqrt{170}} = -1.52$, p-value = .0647. There is not enough to infer stock holdings have decreased.

13.52 $H_0: \mu_D = 0$

$H_1: \mu_D > 0$

Rejection region: $t > t_{\alpha,\nu} = t_{.05,54} \approx 1.676$

$t = \frac{\bar{x}_D - \mu_D}{s_D / \sqrt{n_D}} = \frac{520.85 - 0}{1854.92 / \sqrt{55}} = 2.08$, p-value = .0210. There is enough evidence to infer that company 1's calculated tax payable is higher than company 2's.

13.54 The matched pairs experiment reduced the variation caused by different drivers.

13.56 Salary offers and undergraduate GPA are not as strongly linked as are salary offers and MBA GPA.

13.58 a LCL = $\left(\frac{s_1^2}{s_2^2}\right)\frac{1}{F_{\alpha/2,\nu_1,\nu_2}} = \left(\frac{28}{19}\right)\frac{1}{4.03} = .366$, UCL = $\left(\frac{s_1^2}{s_2^2}\right)F_{\alpha/2,\nu_2,\nu_1} = \left(\frac{28}{19}\right)4.03 = 5.939$

b LCL = $\left(\frac{s_1^2}{s_2^2}\right)\frac{1}{F_{\alpha/2,\nu_1,\nu_2}} = \left(\frac{28}{19}\right)\frac{1}{2.27} = .649$, UCL = $\left(\frac{s_1^2}{s_2^2}\right)F_{\alpha/2,\nu_2,\nu_1} = \left(\frac{28}{19}\right)2.27 = 3.345$

c The interval narrows.

13.60 $H_0 : \sigma_1^2 / \sigma_2^2 = 1$

$H_1 : \sigma_1^2 / \sigma_2^2 \neq 1$

Rejection region: $F > F_{\alpha/2,\nu_1,\nu_2} = F_{.025,8,5} = 6.76$ or

$F < F_{1-\alpha/2,\nu_1,\nu_2} = 1/F_{\alpha/2,\nu_2,\nu_1} = 1/F_{.025,5,8} = 1/4.82 = .21$

$F = s_1^2 / s_2^2 = 755{,}196/725{,}778 = 1.04$, p-value = .9873. The equal-variances t-test in Exercise 13.10 was justified.

13.62 $H_0 : \sigma_1^2 / \sigma_2^2 = 1$

$H_1 : \sigma_1^2 / \sigma_2^2 \neq 1$

Rejection region: $F > F_{\alpha/2,\nu_1,\nu_2} = F_{.025,10,10} = 3.72$ or

$F < F_{1-\alpha/2,\nu_1,\nu_2} = 1/F_{\alpha/2,\nu_2,\nu_1} = 1/F_{.025,10,10} = 1/3.72 = .269$

$F = s_1^2 / s_2^2 = 193.67/60.00 = 3.23$, p-value = .0784. There is not enough evidence to infer that the variances of the marks differ between the two sections.

13.64 $H_0: \sigma_1^2/\sigma_2^2 = 1$

$H_1: \sigma_1^2/\sigma_2^2 \neq 1$

Rejection region: $F > F_{\alpha/2,\nu_1,\nu_2} = F_{.025,212,201} \approx 1.43$ or

$F < F_{1-\alpha/2,\nu_1,\nu_2} = 1/F_{\alpha/2,\nu_2,\nu_1} = 1/F_{.025,212,201} \approx 1/1.43 = .70$

$F = s_1^2/s_2^2 = 476.1/558.9 = .85$, p-value = .2494. There is not enough evidence to infer a difference between variances; the equal-variance t test in Exercise 13.24 was justified.

13.66 $H_0: \sigma_1^2/\sigma_2^2 = 1$

$H_1: \sigma_1^2/\sigma_2^2 \neq 1$

Rejection region: $F > F_{\alpha/2,\nu_1,\nu_2} = F_{.025,99,99} \approx 1.43$ or

$F < F_{1-\alpha/2,\nu_1,\nu_2} = 1/F_{\alpha/2,\nu_2,\nu_1} = 1/F_{025,99,99} \approx 1/1.43 = .70$

$F = s_1^2/s_2^2 = 1{,}023/676 = 1.51$, p-value = .0405. There is enough evidence to infer a difference between variances; the unequal-variance t test in Exercise 13.26 was appropriate.

13.68 $H_0: \sigma_1^2/\sigma_2^2 = 1$

$H_1: \sigma_1^2/\sigma_2^2 \neq 1$

Rejection region: $F > F_{\alpha/2,\nu_1,\nu_2} = F_{025,27,32} \approx 2.14$ or

$F < F_{1-\alpha/2,\nu_1,\nu_2} = 1/F_{\alpha/2,\nu_2,\nu_1} = 1/F_{.025,32,27} \approx 1/2.13 = .47$

$F = s_1^2/s_2^2 = 38{,}051/110{,}151 = .35$, p-value = .0061. There is enough evidence to infer a difference between variances; the unequal-variance t test in Exercise 13.30 was the correct technique.

13.70 $H_0: (p_1 - p_2) = 0$

$H_1: (p_1 - p_2) \neq 0$

a $z = \dfrac{(\hat{p}_1 - \hat{p}_2)}{\sqrt{\hat{p}(1-\hat{p})\left(\dfrac{1}{n_1} + \dfrac{1}{n_2}\right)}} = \dfrac{(.45 - .40)}{\sqrt{.425(1-.425)\left(\dfrac{1}{100} + \dfrac{1}{100}\right)}} = .72$, p-value = $2P(Z > .72)$

$= 2(.5 - .2642) = .4716.$

b $z = \frac{(\hat{p}_1 - \hat{p}_2)}{\sqrt{\hat{p}(1-\hat{p})\left(\frac{1}{n_1}+\frac{1}{n_2}\right)}} = \frac{(.45-.40)}{\sqrt{.425(1-.425)\left(\frac{1}{400}+\frac{1}{400}\right)}} = 1.43$, p-value = 2P(Z > 1.43)

= 2(.5 – .4236) = .1528.

c The p-value decreases.

13.72 a $(\hat{p}_1 - \hat{p}_2) \pm z_{\alpha/2}\sqrt{\frac{\hat{p}_1(1-\hat{p}_1)}{n_1}+\frac{\hat{p}_2(1-\hat{p}_2)}{n_2}} = (.18–.22) \pm 1.645\sqrt{\frac{.18(1-.18)}{100}+\frac{.22(1-.22)}{100}}$

$= -.040 \pm .0929$

b $(\hat{p}_1 - \hat{p}_2) \pm z_{\alpha/2}\sqrt{\frac{\hat{p}_1(1-\hat{p}_1)}{n_1}+\frac{\hat{p}_2(1-\hat{p}_2)}{n_2}} = (.48–.52) \pm 1.645\sqrt{\frac{.48(1-.48)}{100}+\frac{.52(1-.52)}{100}}$

$= -.040 \pm .1162$

c The interval widens.

13.74a $H_0 : (p_1 - p_2) = 0$

$H_1 : (p_1 - p_2) > 0$

Rejection region: $z > z_\alpha = z_{05} = 1.645$

$z = \frac{(\hat{p}_1 - \hat{p}_2)}{\sqrt{\hat{p}(1-\hat{p})\left(\frac{1}{n_1}+\frac{1}{n_2}\right)}} = \frac{(.54-.43)}{\sqrt{.496(1-.496)\left(\frac{1}{900}+\frac{1}{600}\right)}} = 4.17$, p-value = 0. There is enough evidence to infer that the leader's popularity has decreased.

b $H_0 : (p_1 - p_2) = .05$

$H_1 : (p_1 - p_2) > .05$

Rejection region: $z > z_\alpha = z_{.05} = 1.645$

$z = \frac{(\hat{p}_1 - \hat{p}_2) - (p_1 - p_2)}{\sqrt{\frac{\hat{p}_1(1-\hat{p}_1)}{n_1}+\frac{\hat{p}_2(1-\hat{p}_2)}{n_2}}} = \frac{(.54-.43)-.05}{\sqrt{\frac{.54(1-.54)}{900}+\frac{.43(1-.43)}{600}}} = 2.29$, p-value = P(Z > 2.16)

= .5 – .4890 = .0110.

There is enough evidence to infer that the leader's popularity has decreased by more than 5%.

c $(\hat{p}_1 - \hat{p}_2) \pm z_{\alpha/2}\sqrt{\frac{\hat{p}_1(1-\hat{p}_1)}{n_1} + \frac{\hat{p}_2(1-\hat{p}_2)}{n_2}} = (.54-.43) \pm 1.96\sqrt{\frac{.54(1-.54)}{900} + \frac{.43(1-.43)}{600}}$

$= .11 \pm .051$

13.76 a $H_0: (p_1 - p_2) = 0$

$H_1: (p_1 - p_2) < 0$

Rejection region: $z < -z_{\alpha} = -z_{.05} = -1.645$

$z = \frac{(\hat{p}_1 - \hat{p}_2)}{\sqrt{\hat{p}(1-\hat{p})\left(\frac{1}{n_1} + \frac{1}{n_2}\right)}} = \frac{(.093 - .115)}{\sqrt{.104(1-.104)\left(\frac{1}{6281} + \frac{1}{6281}\right)}} = -4.04$, p-value = 0. There is enough evidence to infer that Plavix is effective.

13.78 $H_0: (p_1 - p_2) = 0$

$H_1: (p_1 - p_2) > 0$

Rejection region: $z > z_{\alpha} = z_{.05} = 1.645$

$\hat{p}_1 = \frac{1{,}084}{11{,}000} = .0985$ $\hat{p}_2 = \frac{997}{11{,}000} = .0906$ $\hat{p} = \frac{1{,}084 + 997}{22{,}000} = .0946$

$z = \frac{(\hat{p}_1 - \hat{p}_2)}{\sqrt{\hat{p}(1-\hat{p})\left(\frac{1}{n_1} + \frac{1}{n_2}\right)}} = \frac{(.0985 - .0906)}{\sqrt{.0946(1-.0946)\left(\frac{1}{11{,}000} + \frac{1}{11{,}000}\right)}} = 2.00$, p-value = $P(Z > 2.00)$

$= .5 - .4772 = .0228$. There is enough evidence to infer that aspirin leads to more cataracts.

13.80 $H_0: (p_1 - p_2) = 0$

$H_1: (p_1 - p_2) < 0$

Rejection region: $z < -z_{\alpha} = -z_{.05} = -1.645$

$\hat{p}_1 = \frac{88}{395} = .2228$ $\hat{p}_2 = \frac{105}{406} = .2586$ $\hat{p} = \frac{88 + 105}{395 + 406} = .2409$

$z = \frac{(\hat{p}_1 - \hat{p}_2)}{\sqrt{\hat{p}(1-\hat{p})\left(\frac{1}{n_1} + \frac{1}{n_2}\right)}} = \frac{(.2228 - .2586)}{\sqrt{.2409(1-.2409)\left(\frac{1}{395} + \frac{1}{406}\right)}} = -1.19$, p-value = $P(Z < -1.19)$

$= .5 - .3830 = .1170.$

There is not enough evidence to infer that exercise training reduces mortality.

13.82 $H_0: (p_1 - p_2) = 0$

$H_1: (p_1 - p_2) > 0$

Rejection region: $z > z_\alpha = z_{.10} = 1.28$

$z = \frac{(\hat{p}_1 - \hat{p}_2)}{\sqrt{\hat{p}(1-\hat{p})\left(\frac{1}{n_1} + \frac{1}{n_2}\right)}} = \frac{(.2632 - .0741)}{\sqrt{.11(1-.11)\left(\frac{1}{38} + \frac{1}{162}\right)}} = 3.35$, p-value = 0. There is enough evidence to conclude that smokers have a higher incidence of heart diseases than nonsmokers.

b $(\hat{p}_1 - \hat{p}_2) \pm z_{\alpha/2}\sqrt{\frac{\hat{p}_1(1-\hat{p}_1)}{n_1} + \frac{\hat{p}_2(1-\hat{p}_2)}{n_2}}$

$= (.2632–0741) \pm 1.645\sqrt{\frac{.2632(1-.2632)}{38} + \frac{.0741(1-.0741)}{162}} = .1891 \pm .1223$; LCL = .0668,

UCL = .3114

13.84 $H_0: (p_1 - p_2) = 0$

$H_1: (p_1 - p_2) > 0$

Rejection region: $z > z_\alpha = z_{.05} = 1.645$

$z = \frac{(\hat{p}_1 - \hat{p}_2)}{\sqrt{\hat{p}(1-\hat{p})\left(\frac{1}{n_1} + \frac{1}{n_2}\right)}} = \frac{(.3585 - .3420)}{\sqrt{.3504(1-.3504)\left(\frac{1}{477} + \frac{1}{462}\right)}} = .53$, p-value = $P(Z > .53) = .5 - .2019$

$= .2981.$

There is not enough evidence to infer that the use of illicit drugs in the United States has increased in the past decade.

13.86 $H_0: (p_1 - p_2) = 0$

$H_1: (p_1 - p_2) > 0$

Rejection region: $z > z_\alpha = z_{.05} = 1.645$

$$z = \frac{(\hat{p}_1 - \hat{p}_2)}{\sqrt{\hat{p}(1-\hat{p})\left(\frac{1}{n_1} + \frac{1}{n_2}\right)}} = \frac{(.1385 - .0905)}{\sqrt{.1035(1-.1035)\left(\frac{1}{231} + \frac{1}{619}\right)}}$$ $z = 2.04$, p-value = $P(Z > 2.04)$

$= .5 - .4793 = .0207.$

There is enough evidence to conclude that health conscious adults are more likely to buy Special X.

13.88 $H_0: (p_1 - p_2) = 0$

$H_1: (p_1 - p_2) \neq 0$

Rejection region: $z < -z_{\alpha/2} = -z_{.025} = -1.96$ or $z > z_{\alpha/2} = z_{.025} = 1.96$

$$z = \frac{(\hat{p}_1 - \hat{p}_2)}{\sqrt{\hat{p}(1-\hat{p})\left(\frac{1}{n_1} + \frac{1}{n_2}\right)}} = \frac{(.0995 - .1297)}{\sqrt{.1132(1-.1132)\left(\frac{1}{382} + \frac{1}{316}\right)}} = -1.25$$, p-value = $2P(Z < -1.25)$

$= 2(.5 - .3944) = .2112.$

There is not enough evidence to infer differences between the two sources.

13.90 Gross sales must increase by 50/.20 = $250 to pay for ads.

$H_0: (\mu_1 - \mu_2) = 250$

$H_1: (\mu_1 - \mu_2) > 250$

	A	B	C
1	t-Test: Two-Sample Assuming Equal Variances		
2			
3		*During*	*Before*
4	Mean	5746.07	5372.13
5	Variance	167289	194772
6	Observations	15	24
7	Pooled Variance	184373	
8	Hypothesized Mean Difference	250	
9	df	37	
10	t Stat	0.88	
11	P(T<=t) one-tail	0.1931	
12	t Critical one-tail	1.6871	
13	P(T<=t) two-tail	0.3862	
14	t Critical two-tail	2.0262	

$t = .88$, p-value = .1931. There is not enough evidence to conclude that the ads are profitable.

13.92 $H_0: \mu_D = 0$

$H_1: \mu_D < 0$

	A	B	C
1	t-Test: Paired Two Sample for Means		
2			
3		*Drug*	*Placebo*
4	Mean	18.43	22.03
5	Variance	30.39	66.37
6	Observations	100	100
7	Pearson Correlation	0.69	
8	Hypothesized Mean Difference	0	
9	df	99	
10	t Stat	-6.09	
11	P(T<=t) one-tail	0.0000	
12	t Critical one-tail	1.6604	
13	P(T<=t) two-tail	0.0000	
14	t Critical two-tail	1.9842	

t = –6.09, p-value = 0. There is enough evidence to infer that the new drug is effective.

13.94 $H_0: (p_1 - p_2) = 0$

$H_1: (p_1 - p_2) < 0$

	A	B	C	D
1	**z-Test: Two Proportions**			
2				
3			*Last Year*	*This Year*
4	Sample Proportions		0.6758	0.7539
5	Observations		327	382
6	Hypothesized Difference		0	
7	z Stat		-2.30	
8	P(Z<=z) one tail		0.0106	
9	z Critical one-tail		1.6449	
10	P(Z<=z) two-tail		0.0212	
11	z Critical two-tail		1.96	

z = –2.30, p-value = .0106. There is enough evidence to infer an increase in seatbelt use.

13.96a $H_0: (\mu_1 - \mu_2) = 0$

$H_1: (\mu_1 - \mu_2) \neq 0$

	A	B	C
1	t-Test: Two-Sample Assuming Equal Variances		
2			
3		*Male*	*Female*
4	Mean	39.75	49.00
5	Variance	803.88	733.16
6	Observations	20	20
7	Pooled Variance	768.52	
8	Hypothesized Mean Difference	0	
9	df	38	
10	t Stat	-1.06	
11	P(T<=t) one-tail	0.1490	
12	t Critical one-tail	1.3042	
13	P(T<=t) two-tail	0.2980	
14	t Critical two-tail	1.6860	

t = –1.06, p-value = .2980. There is not enough evidence to conclude that men and women differ in the amount of time spent reading magazines.

b $H_0: (\mu_1 - \mu_2) = 0$

$H_1: (\mu_1 - \mu_2) < 0$

	A	B	C
1	t-Test: Two-Sample Assuming Unequal Variances		
2			
3		*Low*	*High*
4	Mean	33.10	56.84
5	Variance	278.69	1047.81
6	Observations	21.00	19
7	Hypothesized Mean Difference	0.00	
8	df	26.00	
9	t Stat	-2.87	
10	P(T<=t) one-tail	0.0040	
11	t Critical one-tail	1.3150	
12	P(T<=t) two-tail	0.0080	
13	t Critical two-tail	1.7056	

t = –2.87, p-value = .0040. There is enough evidence to conclude that high-income individuals devote more time to reading magazines than do low-income individuals.

13.98 $H_0: (p_1 - p_2) = 0$

$H_1: (p_1 - p_2) > 0$

	A	B	C	D
1	**z-Test: Two Proportions**			
2				
3			*This Year*	*3 Years Ago*
4	Sample Proportions		0.4351	0.3558
5	Observations		393	385
6	Hypothesized Difference		0	
7	z Stat		2.26	
8	P(Z<=z) one tail		0.0119	
9	z Critical one-tail		1.2816	
10	P(Z<=z) two-tail		0.0238	
11	z Critical two-tail		1.6449	

$z = 2.26$, p-value = .0119. There is enough evidence to infer that Americans have become more distrustful of television and newspaper reporting this year than they were three years ago.

13.100 $H_0: (p_1 - p_2) = 0$

$H_1: (p_1 - p_2) \neq 0$

The totals in columns A through D are 5788, 265, 5154, and 332, respectively.

	A	B	C	D	E
1	**z-Test of the Difference Between Two Proportions (Case 1)**				
2					
3		**Sample 1**	**Sample 2**	**z Stat**	**-4.28**
4	**Sample proportion**	0.045800	0.064400	**P(Z<=z) one-tail**	**0.0000**
5	**Sample size**	5788	5154	**z Critical one-tail**	**1.6449**
6	**Alpha**	0.05		**P(Z<=z) two-tail**	**0.0000**
7				**z Critical two-tail**	**1.9600**

$z = -4.28$, p-value = 0. There is enough evidence to infer that the defective rate differs between the two machines.

13.102a $H_0: (\mu_1 - \mu_2) = 0$

$H_1: (\mu_1 - \mu_2) < 0$

	A	B	C
1	t-Test: Two-Sample Assuming Equal Variances		
2			
3		20-year-old	40-year-old
4	Mean	125.74	129.93
5	Variance	31.90	31.95
6	Observations	26	24
7	Pooled Variance	31.92	
8	Hypothesized Mean Difference	0	
9	df	48	
10	t Stat	-2.62	
11	P(T<=t) one-tail	0.0059	
12	t Critical one-tail	1.2994	
13	P(T<=t) two-tail	0.0119	
14	t Critical two-tail	1.6772	

t = –2.62, p-value = .0059. There is enough evidence to infer that 40-year-old men have more iron in their bodies than do 20-year-old men.

b $H_0: (\mu_1 - \mu_2) = 0$

$H_1: (\mu_1 - \mu_2) < 0$

	A	B	C
1	t-Test: Two-Sample Assuming Equal Variances		
2			
3		20-year-old	40-year-old
4	Mean	134.02	141.11
5	Variance	36.15	39.47
6	Observations	26	24
7	Pooled Variance	37.74	
8	Hypothesized Mean Difference	0	
9	df	48	
10	t Stat	-4.08	
11	P(T<=t) one-tail	0.0001	
12	t Critical one-tail	1.2994	
13	P(T<=t) two-tail	0.0002	
14	t Critical two-tail	1.6772	

t = –4.08, p-value = .0001. There is enough evidence to infer that 40-year-old women have more iron in their bodies than do 20-year-old women.

13.104 a $H_0: (\mu_1 - \mu_2) = 0$

$H_1: (\mu_1 - \mu_2) > 0$

	A	B	C
1	t-Test: Two-Sample Assuming Unequal Variances		
2			
3		*Exercise*	*Drug*
4	Mean	13.52	9.92
5	Variance	5.76	13.16
6	Observations	25	25
7	Hypothesized Mean Difference	0	
8	df	42	
9	t Stat	4.14	
10	P(T<=t) one-tail	0.0001	
11	t Critical one-tail	2.4185	
12	P(T<=t) two-tail	0.0002	
13	t Critical two-tail	2.6981	

t = 4.14, p-value = .0001. There is enough evidence that exercise is more effective than medication in reducing hypertension.

b

	A	B	C	D	E	F
1	**t-Estimate of the Difference Between Two Means (Unequal-Variances)**					
2						
3		**Sample 1**	**Sample 2**	**Confidence Interval Estimate**		
4	**Mean**	13.52	9.92	**3.60**	±	**1.76**
5	**Variance**	5.76	13.16	**Lower confidence limit**		**1.84**
6	**Sample size**	25	25	**Upper confidence limit**		**5.36**
7	**Degrees of freedom**	**41.63**				
8	**Confidence level**	0.95				

LCL = 1.84, UCL = 5.36

c The histograms are bell shaped.

13.106 $H_0: \mu_D = 0$

$H_1: \mu_D < 0$

	A	B	C
1	t-Test: Paired Two Sample for Means		
2			
3		*Group 1*	*Group 2*
4	Mean	7.53	8.57
5	Variance	29.77	43.37
6	Observations	50	50
7	Pearson Correlation	0.89	
8	Hypothesized Mean Difference	0	
9	df	49	
10	t Stat	-2.40	
11	P(T<=t) one-tail	0.0100	
12	t Critical one-tail	1.6766	
13	P(T<=t) two-tail	0.0201	
14	t Critical two-tail	2.0096	

$t = -2.40$, p-value = .0100. There is enough evidence to conclude that people who exercise moderately more frequently lose weight faster

13.108 $H_0: (p_1 - p_2) = 0$

$H_1: (p_1 - p_2) > 0$

	A	B	C	D
1	**z-Test: Two Proportions**			
2				
3			*Special K*	*Other*
4	Sample Proportions		0.575	0.515
5	Observations		200	200
6	Hypothesized Difference		0	
7	z Stat		1.20	
8	P(Z<=z) one tail		0.1141	
9	z Critical one-tail		1.6449	
10	P(Z<=z) two-tail		0.2282	
11	z Critical two-tail		1.9600	

$z = 1.20$, p-value = .1141. There is not enough evidence to conclude that Special K buyers are more likely to think the ad is effective.

13.110 $H_0: (\mu_1 - \mu_2) = 0$

$H_1: (\mu_1 - \mu_2) > 0$

	A	B	C
1	t-Test: Two-Sample Assuming Unequal Variances		
2			
3		*Computer*	*No Computer*
4	Mean	69,933	48,246
5	Variance	63,359,040	101,588,525
6	Observations	89	61
7	Hypothesized Mean Difference	0	
8	df	109	
9	t Stat	14.07	
10	P(T<=t) one-tail	0.0000	
11	t Critical one-tail	1.2894	
12	P(T<=t) two-tail	0.0000	
13	t Critical two-tail	1.6590	

t = 14.07, p-value = 0. There is enough evidence to conclude that single-person businesses that use a PC earn more.

13.112 $H_0: (\mu_1 - \mu_2) = 0$

$H_1: (\mu_1 - \mu_2) < 0$

	A	B	C
1	t-Test: Two-Sample Assuming Equal Variances		
2			
3		*Supplement*	*Placebo*
4	Mean	19.02	21.85
5	Variance	41.34	25.49
6	Observations	48	48
7	Pooled Variance	33.41	
8	Hypothesized Mean Difference	0	
9	df	94	
10	t Stat	-2.40	
11	P(T<=t) one-tail	0.0092	
12	t Critical one-tail	1.6612	
13	P(T<=t) two-tail	0.0183	
14	t Critical two-tail	1.9855	

t = –2.40, p-value = .0092. There is enough evidence to infer that taking vitamin and mineral supplements daily increases the body's immune system?

13.114 $H_0: (\mu_1 - \mu_2) = 0$

$H_1: (\mu_1 - \mu_2) \neq 0$

	A	B	C
1	t-Test: Two-Sample Assuming Equal Variances		
2			
3		*Female*	*Male*
4	Mean	7.27	7.02
5	Variance	2.57	2.85
6	Observations	103	97
7	Pooled Variance	2.71	
8	Hypothesized Mean Difference	0	
9	df	198	
10	t Stat	1.08	
11	P(T<=t) one-tail	0.1410	
12	t Critical one-tail	1.6526	
13	P(T<=t) two-tail	0.2820	
14	t Critical two-tail	1.9720	

t = 1.08, p-value = .2820. There is not enough evidence to conclude that female and male high school students differ in the amount of time spent at part-time jobs.

13.116 $H_0: (\mu_1 - \mu_2) = 0$

$H_1: (\mu_1 - \mu_2) > 0$

	A	B	C
1	t-Test: Two-Sample Assuming Unequal Variances		
2			
3		*Teenagers*	*20-to-30*
4	Mean	18.18	14.30
5	Variance	357.32	130.79
6	Observations	176	154
7	Hypothesized Mean Difference	0	
8	df	293	
9	t Stat	2.28	
10	P(T<=t) one-tail	0.0115	
11	t Critical one-tail	1.6501	
12	P(T<=t) two-tail	0.0230	
13	t Critical two-tail	1.9681	

t = 2.28, p-value = .0115.There is enough evidence to infer that teenagers see more movies than do twenty to thirty year olds.

13.118 $H_0: (\mu_1 - \mu_2) = 0$

$H_1: (\mu_1 - \mu_2) > 0$

	A	B	C
1	t-Test: Two-Sample Assuming Unequal Variances		
2			
3		*Group 1*	*Groups 2-4*
4	Mean	11.58	10.60
5	Variance	9.28	21.41
6	Observations	269	981
7	Hypothesized Mean Difference	0	
8	df	644	
9	t Stat	4.15	
10	P(T<=t) one-tail	0.0000	
11	t Critical one-tail	1.6472	
12	P(T<=t) two-tail	0.0000	
13	t Critical two-tail	1.9637	

t = 4.15, p-value = 0. There is enough evidence to conclude that on average the market segment concerned about eating healthy food (group 1) outspends the other market segments.

13.120 $H_0: (\mu_1 - \mu_2) = 0$

$H_1: (\mu_1 - \mu_2) < 0$

	A	B	C
1	t-Test: Two-Sample Assuming Equal Variances		
2			
3		*No*	*Yes*
4	Mean	91,467	97,836
5	Variance	461,917,705	401,930,840
6	Observations	466	55
7	Pooled Variance	455,676,297	
8	Hypothesized Mean Difference	0	
9	df	519	
10	t Stat	-2.09	
11	P(T<=t) one-tail	0.0184	
12	t Critical one-tail	1.6478	
13	P(T<=t) two-tail	0.0369	
14	t Critical two-tail	1.9645	

t = –2.09, p-value = .0184. There is enough evidence to infer that professors aged 55 to 64 who plan to retire early have higher salaries than those who don't plan to retire early.

Chapter 14

14.2 a z-test of $p_1 - p_2$ (case 1)

$$H_0: (p_1 - p_2) = 0$$

$$H_1: (p_1 - p_2) > 0$$

$$z = \frac{(\hat{p}_1 - \hat{p}_2)}{\sqrt{\hat{p}(1-\hat{p})\left(\frac{1}{n_1} + \frac{1}{n_2}\right)}}$$

	A	B	C	D	E
1	**z-Test of the Difference Between Two Proportions (Case 1)**				
2					
3		**Sample 1**	**Sample 2**	**z Stat**	**2.83**
4	**Sample proportion**	0.4336	0.2414	**P(Z<=z) one-tail**	**0.0024**
5	**Sample size**	113	87	**z Critical one-tail**	**1.6449**
6	**Alpha**	0.05		**P(Z<=z) two-tail**	**0.0047**
7				**z Critical two-tail**	**1.9600**

z = 2.83, p-value = .0024. There is enough evidence to infer that customers who see the ad are more likely to make a purchase than those who do not see the ad.

b Equal-variances t-test of $\mu_1 - \mu_2$

$$H_0: (\mu_1 - \mu_2) = 0$$

$$H_1: (\mu_1 - \mu_2) > 0$$

$$t = \frac{(\bar{x}_1 - \bar{x}_2) - (\mu_1 - \mu_2)}{\sqrt{s_p^2\left(\frac{1}{n_1} + \frac{1}{n_2}\right)}}$$

	A	B	C
1	t-Test: Two-Sample Assuming Equal Variances		
2			
3		*Ad*	*No Ad*
4	Mean	97.38	92.01
5	Variance	621.97	283.26
6	Observations	49	21
7	Pooled Variance	522.35	
8	Hypothesized Mean Difference	0	
9	df	68	
10	t Stat	0.90	
11	P(T<=t) one-tail	0.1853	
12	t Critical one-tail	1.6676	
13	P(T<=t) two-tail	0.3705	
14	t Critical two-tail	1.9955	

t = .90, p-value = .1853. There is not enough evidence to infer that customers who see the ad and make a purchase spend more than those who do not see the ad and make a purchase.

c z-estimator of p

$$\hat{p} \pm z_{\alpha/2}\sqrt{\frac{\hat{p}(1-\hat{p})}{n}}$$

	A	B	C	D	E
1	**z-Estimate of a Proportion**				
2					
3	**Sample proportion**	0.4336	**Confidence Interval Estimate**		
4	**Sample size**	113	**0.4336**	±	**0.0914**
5	**Confidence level**	0.95	**Lower confidence limit**		**0.3423**
6			**Upper confidence limit**		**0.5250**

We estimate that between 34.23% and 52.50% of all customers who see the ad will make a purchase.

d t-estimator of μ

$$\bar{x} \pm t_{\alpha/2}\frac{s}{\sqrt{n}}$$

	A	B	C	D
1	**t-Estimate: Mean**			
2				
3				*Ad*
4	Mean			97.38
5	Standard Deviation			24.94
6	LCL			90.22
7	UCL			104.55

We estimate that the mean amount spent by customers who see the ad and make a purchase lies between \$90.22 and \$104.55.

14.4 a z-test of p

$$H_0: p = .95$$

$$H_1: p > .95$$

$$z = \frac{\hat{p} - p}{\sqrt{\frac{p(1-p)}{n}}}$$

	A	B	C	D
1	**z-Test: Proportion**			
2				
3				*Prority*
4	Sample Proportion			0.9714
5	Observations			245
6	Hypothesized Proportion			0.95
7	z Stat			1.54
8	P(Z<=z) one-tail			0.0619
9	z Critical one-tail			1.6449
10	P(Z<=z) two-tail			0.1238
11	z Critical two-tail			1.9600

z = 1.54, p-value = .0619. There is not enough evidence to infer that the spokesperson's claim is true.

b z-test of $p_1 - p_2$ (case 1)

$$H_0: (p_1 - p_2) = 0$$

$$H_1: (p_1 - p_2) > 0$$

$$z = \frac{(\hat{p}_1 \quad \hat{p}_2)}{\sqrt{\hat{p}(1-\hat{p})\left(\frac{1}{n_1} + \frac{1}{n_2}\right)}}$$

	A	B	C	D
1	**z-Test: Two Proportions**			
2				
3			*Prority*	*Ordinary*
4	Sample Proportions		0.9714	0.9101
5	Observations		245	378
6	Hypothesized Difference		0	
7	z Stat		3.02	
8	P(Z<=z) one tail		0.0013	
9	z Critical one-tail		1.6449	
10	P(Z<=z) two-tail		0.0026	
11	z Critical two-tail		1.9600	

z = 3.02, p-value = .0013. There is enough evidence to infer that Priority Mail delivers letters within two days more frequently than does ordinary mail.

14.6 Speeds: Equal-variances t-test of $\mu_1 - \mu_2$

$$H_0: (\mu_1 - \mu_2) = 0$$

$$H_1: (\mu_1 - \mu_2) > 0$$

$$t = \frac{(\bar{x}_1 - \bar{x}_2) - (\mu_1 - \mu_2)}{\sqrt{s_p^2\left(\frac{1}{n_1} + \frac{1}{n_2}\right)}}$$

	A	B	C
1	t-Test: Two-Sample Assuming Equal Variances		
2			
3		*Speeds Before*	*Speeds After*
4	Mean	31.74	31.42
5	Variance	4.50	4.41
6	Observations	100	100
7	Pooled Variance	4.45	
8	Hypothesized Mean Difference	0	
9	df	198	
10	t Stat	1.07	
11	P(T<=t) one-tail	0.1424	
12	t Critical one-tail	1.6526	
13	P(T<=t) two-tail	0.2849	
14	t Critical two-tail	1.9720	

t = 1.07, p-value = .1424. There is not enough evidence to infer that speed bumps reduce speeds.

Proper stops: Equal-variances t-test of $\mu_1 - \mu_2$

$$H_0: (\mu_1 - \mu_2) = 0$$

$$H_1: (\mu_1 - \mu_2) < 0$$

$$t = \frac{(\bar{x}_1 - \bar{x}_2) - (\mu_1 - \mu_2)}{\sqrt{s_p^2\left(\frac{1}{n_1} + \frac{1}{n_2}\right)}}$$

	A	B	C
1	t-Test: Two-Sample Assuming Equal Variances		
2			
3		*Stops Before*	*Stops After*
4	Mean	7.82	7.98
5	Variance	1.83	1.84
6	Observations	100	100
7	Pooled Variance	1.83	
8	Hypothesized Mean Difference	0	
9	df	198	
10	t Stat	-0.84	
11	P(T<=t) one-tail	0.2021	
12	t Critical one-tail	1.6526	
13	P(T<=t) two-tail	0.4042	
14	t Critical two-tail	1.9720	

$t = -.84$, p-value = .2021. There is not enough evidence to infer that speed bumps increase the number of proper stops.

14.8 t-test of μ_D

$$H_0: \mu_D = 0$$

$$H_1: \mu_D > 0$$

$$t = \frac{\bar{x}_D - \mu_D}{s_D / \sqrt{n_D}}$$

	A	B	C
1	t-Test: Paired Two Sample for Means		
2			
3		*Before*	*After*
4	Mean	28.94	26.22
5	Variance	61.45	104.30
6	Observations	50	50
7	Pearson Correlation	0.87	
8	Hypothesized Mean Difference	0	
9	df	49	
10	t Stat	3.73	
11	P(T<=t) one-tail	0.000	
12	t Critical one-tail	1.677	
13	P(T<=t) two-tail	0.000	
14	t Critical two-tail	2.010	

t = 3.73, p-value = .0002. There is enough evidence to infer that the law discourages bicycle use.

14.10 t-test of μ

$$H_0 : \mu = 200$$
$$H_1 : \mu > 200$$

$$t = \frac{\overline{x} - \mu}{s / \sqrt{n}}$$

	A	B	C	D
1	**t-Test: Mean**			
2				
3				*Pedestrians*
4	Mean			209.13
5	Standard Deviation			60.01
6	Hypothesized Mean			200
7	df			39
8	t Stat			0.96
9	P(T<=t) one-tail			0.1711
10	t Critical one-tail			1.6849
11	P(T<=t) two-tail			0.3422
12	t Critical two-tail			2.0227

t = .96, p-value = .1711. There is not enough evidence to infer that the franchiser should build on this site.

14.12 z-test of p

$$H_0: p = .5$$

$$H_1: p > .5$$

$$z = \frac{\hat{p} - p}{\sqrt{\frac{p(1-p)}{n}}}$$

	A	B	C	D
1	**z-Test: Proportion**			
2				
3				*Winner*
4	Sample Proportion			0.5296
5	Observations			625
6	Hypothesized Proportion			0.5
7	z Stat			1.48
8	P(Z<=z) one-tail			0.0694
9	z Critical one-tail			1.6449
10	P(Z<=z) two-tail			0.1388
11	z Critical two-tail			1.9600

z = 1.48, p-value = .0694. There is not enough evidence to conclude that more Floridians believe that Mr. Bush won than Floridians who believe Mr. Gore won.

14.14 Unequal-variances t-test of $\mu_1 - \mu_2$

$$H_0: (\mu_1 - \mu_2) = 0$$

$$H_1: (\mu_1 - \mu_2) > 0$$

$$t = \frac{(\bar{x}_1 - \bar{x}_2) - (\mu_1 - \mu_2)}{\sqrt{\frac{s_1^2}{n_1} + \frac{s_2^2}{n_2}}}$$

	A	B	C
1	t-Test: Two-Sample Assuming Unequal Variances		
2			
3		*Quit*	*Did not quit*
4	Mean	2.04	0.72
5	Variance	2.05	1.40
6	Observations	259	1626
7	Hypothesized Mean Difference	0	
8	df	316	
9	t Stat	14.06	
10	P(T<=t) one-tail	0.0000	
11	t Critical one-tail	1.6497	
12	P(T<=t) two-tail	0.0000	
13	t Critical two-tail	1.9675	

t = 14.06, p-value = 0. There is enough evidence to infer that quitting smoking results in weight gains.

14.16 a z-test of $p_1 - p_2$ (case 1) (Success = 2)

$$H_0: p_1 - p_2 = 0$$

$$H_1: p_1 - p_2 \neq 0$$

$$z = \frac{(\hat{p}_1 - \hat{p}_2)}{\sqrt{\hat{p}(1-\hat{p})\left(\frac{1}{n_1} + \frac{1}{n_2}\right)}}$$

	A	B	C	D
1	**z-Test: Two Proportions**			
2				
3			*Male most*	*Male less*
4	Sample Proportions		0.5962	0.8077
5	Observations		52	52
6	Hypothesized Difference		0	
7	z Stat		-2.36	
8	P(Z<=z) one tail		0.0092	
9	z Critical one-tail		1.6449	
10	P(Z<=z) two-tail		0.0184	
11	z Critical two-tail		1.96	

z = –2.36, p-value = .0184. There is enough evidence that men's choices are affected by the attractiveness of women's pictures

b z-test of $p_1 - p_2$ (case 1) (Success = 2)

$$H_0: p_1 - p_2 = 0$$

$$H_1: p_1 - p_2 \neq 0$$

$$z = \frac{(\hat{p}_1 - \hat{p}_2)}{\sqrt{\hat{p}(1-\hat{p})\left(\frac{1}{n_1} + \frac{1}{n_2}\right)}}$$

	A	B	C	D
1	**z-Test: Two Proportions**			
2				
3			*Female most*	*Female less*
4	Sample Proportions		0.7885	0.8269
5	Observations		52	52
6	Hypothesized Difference		0	
7	z Stat		-0.50	
8	P(Z<=z) one tail		0.3094	
9	z Critical one-tail		1.6449	
10	P(Z<=z) two-tail		0.6188	
11	z Critical two-tail		1.96	

$z = -.50$, p-value = .6188. There is not enough evidence to infer that women's choices are affected by the attractiveness of men's pictures.

14.18 t-estimator of μ

$$\bar{x} \pm t_{\alpha/2} \frac{s}{\sqrt{n}}$$

	A	B	C	D
1	**t-Estimate: Mean**			
2				
3				*Calls*
4	Mean			0.320
5	Standard Deviation			0.717
6	LCL			0.204
7	UCL			0.436

LCL = .204, UCL = .436. On average, each copier is estimated to require between .204 and .436 service calls in the first year.

Total number of service calls: LCL = 1000(.204) = 204, UCL = 1000(.436) = 436. It is estimated that the company's copiers will require between 204 and 436 service calls in the first year.

14.20 Unequal-variances t-test of $\mu_1 - \mu_2$

$$H_0: (\mu_1 - \mu_2) = 0$$

$$H_1: (\mu_1 - \mu_2) < 0$$

$$t = \frac{(\bar{x}_1 - \bar{x}_2) - (\mu_1 - \mu_2)}{\sqrt{\frac{s_1^2}{n_1} + \frac{s_2^2}{n_2}}}$$

	A	B	C
1	t-Test: Two-Sample Assuming Unequal Variances		
2			
3		*Leftover*	*Returned*
4	Mean	61.71	70.57
5	Variance	48.99	203.98
6	Observations	14	53
7	Hypothesized Mean Difference	0	
8	df	44	
9	t Stat	-3.27	
10	P(T<=t) one-tail	0.0011	
11	t Critical one-tail	1.6802	
12	P(T<=t) two-tail	0.0021	
13	t Critical two-tail	2.0154	

$t = -3.27$, p-value = .0011. There is enough evidence to support the professor's theory.

14.22 a z-test of p

$$H_0: p = 104{,}320/425{,}000 = .245$$

$$H_1: p > .245$$

$$z = \frac{\hat{p} - p}{\sqrt{\frac{p(1-p)}{n}}}$$

	A	B	C	D
1	**z-Test: Proportion**			
2				
3				*Deliver*
4	Sample Proportion			0.2825
5	Observations			400
6	Hypothesized Proportion			0.245
7	z Stat			1.74
8	P(Z<=z) one-tail			0.0406
9	z Critical one-tail			1.6449
10	P(Z<=z) two-tail			0.0812
11	z Critical two-tail			1.9600

z = 1.74, p-value = .0406. There is enough evidence to indicate that the campaign will increase home delivery sales.

b z-test of p

$$H_0 : p = 110{,}000/425{,}000 = .259$$

$$H_1 : p > .259$$

$$z = \frac{\hat{p} - p}{\sqrt{\frac{p(1-p)}{n}}}$$

	A	B	C	D
1	**z-Test: Proportion**			
2				
3				*Deliver*
4	Sample Proportion			0.2825
5	Observations			400
6	Hypothesized Proportion			0.259
7	z Stat			1.07
8	P(Z<=z) one-tail			0.1417
9	z Critical one-tail			1.6449
10	P(Z<=z) two-tail			0.2834
11	z Critical two-tail			1.9600

z = 1.07, p-value = .1417. There is not enough evidence to conclude that the campaign will be successful.

14.24a Equal-variances t-test of $\mu_1 - \mu_2$

$$H_0: (\mu_1 - \mu_2) = 0$$

$$H_1: (\mu_1 - \mu_2) < 0$$

$$t = \frac{(\bar{x}_1 - \bar{x}_2) - (\mu_1 - \mu_2)}{\sqrt{s_p^2\left(\frac{1}{n_1} + \frac{1}{n_2}\right)}}$$

	A	B	C
1	t-Test: Two-Sample Assuming Equal Variances		
2			
3		*Expenses MSA*	*Expenses Regular*
4	Mean	347.24	479.25
5	Variance	21043	21128
6	Observations	63	141
7	Pooled Variance	21102	
8	Hypothesized Mean Difference	0	
9	df	202	
10	t Stat	-6.00	
11	P(T<=t) one-tail	0.0000	
12	t Critical one-tail	1.6524	
13	P(T<=t) two-tail	0.0000	
14	t Critical two-tail	1.9718	

$t = -6.00$, p-value = 0. There is enough evidence to infer that medical expenses for those under the MSA plan are lower than those who are not.

b z-test of $p_1 - p_2$ (case 1)

$$H_0: p_1 - p_2 = 0$$

$$H_1: p_1 - p_2 < 0$$

$$z = \frac{(\hat{p}_1 - \hat{p}_2)}{\sqrt{\hat{p}(1-\hat{p})\left(\frac{1}{n_1} + \frac{1}{n_2}\right)}}$$

	A	B	C	D
1	**z-Test: Two Proportions**			
2				
3			*Health MSA*	*Health Regular*
4	Sample Proportions		0.7619	0.7801
5	Observations		63	141
6	Hypothesized Difference		0	
7	z Stat		-0.29	
8	P(Z<=z) one tail		0.3867	
9	z Critical one-tail		1.6449	
10	P(Z<=z) two-tail		0.7734	
11	z Critical two-tail		1.9600	

z = –.29, p-value = .3867. There is not enough evidence to support the critics of MSA.

14.26 Time to solve the 48 problems: Equal-variances t-test of $\mu_1 - \mu_2$

$$H_0 : (\mu_1 - \mu_2) = 0$$

$$H_1 : (\mu_1 - \mu_2) > 0$$

$$t = \frac{(\bar{x}_1 - \bar{x}_2) - (\mu_1 - \mu_2)}{\sqrt{s_p^2\left(\frac{1}{n_1} + \frac{1}{n_2}\right)}}$$

	A	B	C
1	t-Test: Two-Sample Assuming Equal Variances		
2			
3		*Diet*	*Not*
4	Mean	581.95	551.5
5	Variance	2716.6	2221.5
6	Observations	20	20
7	Pooled Variance	2469.1	
8	Hypothesized Mean Difference	0	
9	df	38	
10	t Stat	1.94	
11	P(T<=t) one-tail	0.0300	
12	t Critical one-tail	1.6860	
13	P(T<=t) two-tail	0.0601	
14	t Critical two-tail	2.0244	

t = 1.94, p-value = .0300. There is enough evidence to conclude that dieters take longer to solve the 48 problems than do nondieters.

Successfully repeat string of five letters: z-test of $p_1 - p_2$ (case 1)

$$H_0: p_1 - p_2 = 0$$

$$H_1: p_1 - p_2 < 0$$

$$z = \frac{(\hat{p}_1 - \hat{p}_2)}{\sqrt{\hat{p}(1-\hat{p})\left(\frac{1}{n_1} + \frac{1}{n_2}\right)}}$$

	A	B	C	D
1	**z-Test: Two Proportions**			
2				
3			*Diet*	*Not*
4	Sample Proportions		0.50	0.80
5	Observations		20	20
6	Hypothesized Difference		0	
7	z Stat		-1.99	
8	P(Z<=z) one tail		0.0234	
9	z Critical one-tail		1.6449	
10	P(Z<=z) two-tail		0.0468	
11	z Critical two-tail		1.96	

$z = -1.99$, p-value = .0234. There is enough evidence to conclude that dieters are less successful at repeating string of five letters.

Successfully repeat string of five words: z-test of $p_1 - p_2$ (case 1)

$$H_0: p_1 - p_2 = 0$$

$$H_1: p_1 - p_2 > 0$$

$$z = \frac{(\hat{p}_1 - \hat{p}_2)}{\sqrt{\hat{p}(1-\hat{p})\left(\frac{1}{n_1} + \frac{1}{n_2}\right)}}$$

	A	B	C	D
1	**z-Test: Two Proportions**			
2				
3			*Diet*	*Not*
4	Sample Proportions		0.35	0.60
5	Observations		20	20
6	Hypothesized Difference		0	
7	z Stat		-1.58	
8	P(Z<=z) one tail		0.0567	
9	z Critical one-tail		1.6449	
10	P(Z<=z) two-tail		0.1134	
11	z Critical two-tail		1.96	

$z = -1.58$, p-value = .0567. There is not enough evidence to conclude that dieters are less successful at repeating string of five words.

Chapter 15

15.2 a $\bar{\bar{x}} = \frac{4(20)+4(22)+4(25)}{4+4+4} = 22.33$

$$SST = \sum n_j(\bar{x}_j - \bar{\bar{x}})^2 = 4(20-22.33)^2 + 4(22-22.33)^2 + 4(25-22.33)^2 = 50.67$$

$$SSE = \sum (n_j - 1)s_j^2 = (4-1)(10) + (4-1)(10) + (4-1)(10) = 90$$

ANOVA Table

Source	Degrees of Freedom	Sum of Squares	Mean Squares	F
Treatments	$k-1=2$	$SST = 50.67$	$\frac{SST}{k-1} = \frac{50.67}{2} = 25.33$	$\frac{MST}{MSE} = \frac{25.33}{10} = 2.53$
Error	$n-k=9$	$SSE = 90$	$\frac{SSE}{n-kl} = \frac{90}{9} = 10$	

b $SSE = \sum (n_j - 1)s_j^2 = (4-1)(25) + (4-1)(25) + (4-1)(25) = 225$

ANOVA Table

Source	Degrees of Freedom	Sum of Squares	Mean Squares	F
Treatments	$k-1=2$	$SST = 50.67$	$\frac{SST}{k-1} = \frac{50.67}{2} = 25.33$	$\frac{MST}{MSE} = \frac{25.33}{25.0} = 1.01$
Error	$n-k=9$	$SSE = 225$	$\frac{SSE}{n-k} = \frac{225}{9} = 25.0$	

c The F statistic decreases.

15.4 $H_0: \mu_1 = \mu_2 = \mu_3$

H_1: At least two means differ.

Rejection region: $F > F_{\alpha,k-1,n-k} = F_{.05,2,9} = 4.26$

	Finance	Marketing	Management
Mean	2.25	3.25	5.75
Variance	2.25	2.92	2.92

Grand mean = 3.75

$$SST = \sum n_j(\bar{x}_j - \bar{\bar{x}})^2 = 4(2.25-3.75)^2 + 4(3.25-3.75)^2 + 4(5.75-3.75)^2 = 26.00$$

$$SSE = \sum (n_j - 1)s_j^2 = (4-1)(2.25) + (4-1)(2.92) + (4-1)(2.92) = 24.25$$

ANOVA table

Source	Degrees of Freedom	Sum of Squares	Mean Squares	F
Treatments	$k-1=2$	SST = 26.00	$\frac{SST}{k-1}=\frac{26.00}{2}=13.00$	$\frac{MST}{MSE}=\frac{13.00}{2.69}=4.82$
Error	$n-k=9$	SSE = 24.25	$\frac{SSE}{n-k}=\frac{24.25}{9}=2.69$	

F = 4.82, p-value = .0377. There is enough evidence to conclude that there are differences in the number of job offers between the three MBA majors.

15.6 $H_0: \mu_1 = \mu_2 = \mu_3$

H_1: At least two means differ.

Rejection region: $F > F_{\alpha,k-1,n-k} = F_{.05,2,12} = 3.89$

	BA	BSc	BBA
Mean	3.94	4.78	5.76
Variance	1.26	.92	1.00

Grand mean = 4.83

$SST = \sum n_j(\bar{x}_j - \bar{\bar{x}})^2 = 5(3.94-4.83)^2 + 5(4.78-4.83)^2 + 5(5.76-4.83)^2 = 8.30$

$SSE = \sum (n_j - 1)s_j^2 = (5-1)(1.26) + (5-1)(.92) + (5-1)(1.00) = 12.73$

ANOVA table

Source	Degrees of Freedom	Sum of Squares	Mean Squares	F
Treatments	$k-1=2$	SST = 8.30	$\frac{SST}{k-1}=\frac{8.30}{2}=4.15$	$\frac{MST}{MSE}=\frac{4.15}{1.06}=3.91$
Error	$n-k=12$	SSE = 12.73	$\frac{SSE}{n-k}=\frac{12.73}{12}=1.06$	

F = 3.91, p-value = .0493. There is enough evidence to conclude that students in different degree program differ in their summer earnings.

15.8 $H_0: \mu_1 = \mu_2 = \mu_3$

H_1: At least two means differ.

Rejection region: $F > F_{\alpha,k-1,n-k} = F_{.05,3,8} = 4.07$

	IBM	Dell	HP	Other
Mean	13.33	11.00	9.67	17.00
Variance	12.33	79.00	22.33	39.00

Grand mean = 12.75

$SST = \sum n_j(\bar{x}_j - \bar{\bar{x}})^2 = 3(13.33 - 12.75)^2 + 3(11.00 - 12.75)^2 + 3(9.67 - 12.75)^2 + 3(17.00 - 12.75)^2 = 92.92$

$SSE = \sum (n_j - 1)s_j^2 = (3-1)(12.33) + (3-1)(79.00) + (3-1)(22.33) + (3-1)(39.00) = 305.33$

ANOVA table

Source	Degrees of Freedom	Sum of Squares	Mean Squares	F
Treatments	$k-1=3$	$SST = 92.92$	$\frac{SST}{k-1} = \frac{92.92}{3} = 30.97$	$\frac{MST}{MSE} = \frac{30.97}{38.17} = .81$
Error	$n-k=8$	$SSE = 305.33$	$\frac{SSE}{n-k} = \frac{305.33}{8} = 38.17$	

F = .81, p-value = .5224. There is not enough evidence to conclude that there are differences in age between the computer brands.

15.10a $H_0: \mu_1 = \mu_2 = \mu_3 = \mu_4$

H_1: At least two means differ.

Rejection region: $F > F_{\alpha,k-1,n-k} = F_{.05,3,116} \approx 2.68$

Grand mean = 101.0

$SST = \sum n_j(\bar{x}_j - \bar{\bar{x}})^2 = 30(90.17 - 101.0)^2 + 30(95.77 - 101.0)^2 + 30(106.8 - 101.0)^2$

$+ 30(111.17 - 101.0)^2 = 8,464$

$SSE = \sum (n_j - 1)s_j^2 = (30-1)(991.52) + (30-1)(900.87) + (30-1)(928.70) + (30-1)(1,023.04)$

$= 111,480$

ANOVA table

Source	Degrees of Freedom	Sum of Squares	Mean Squares	F
Treatments	$k-1=3$	SST = 8,464	$\frac{SST}{k-1}=\frac{8,464}{3}=2,821$	$\frac{MST}{MSE}=\frac{2,821}{961.0}=2.94$
Error	$n-k=116$	SSE = 111,480	$\frac{SSE}{n-k}=\frac{111,480}{116}=961.0$	

F = 2.94, p-value = .0363. There is enough evidence to infer that there are differences between the completion times of the four income tax forms.

b The times for each form must be normally distributed with the same variance.

c The histograms are approximately bell-shaped and the sample variances are similar.

15.12 $H_0: \mu_1 = \mu_2 = \mu_3 = \mu_4$

H_1 : At least two means differ.

Rejection region: $F > F_{\alpha,k-1,n-k} = F_{.05,3,297} \approx 2.68$

Grand mean = 16.11

$$SST = \sum n_j(\bar{x}_j - \bar{\bar{x}})^2 = 39(22.21 - 16.11)^2 + 114(18.46 - 16.11)^2 + 81(15.49 - 16.11)^2 + 67(9.31 - 16.11)^2 = 5,202$$

$$SSE = \sum (n_j - 1)s_j^2 = (39 - 1)(121.64) + (114 - 1)(90.39) + (81 - 1)(85.25) + (67 - 1)(65.40) = 25,973$$

ANOVA table

Source	Degrees of Freedom	Sum of Squares	Mean Squares	F
Treatments	$k-1=3$	SST = 5,202	$\frac{SST}{k-1}=\frac{5,202}{3}=1,734$	$\frac{MST}{MSE}=\frac{1,734}{87.45}=19.83$
Error	$n-k=297$	SSE = 25,973	$\frac{SSE}{n-k}=\frac{25,973}{297}=87.45$	

F = 19.83, p-value = 0. There is enough evidence to infer that there are differences exist between the four groups.

15.14 $H_0: \mu_1 = \mu_2 = \mu_3$

H_1 : At least two means differ.

Rejection region: $F > F_{\alpha,k-1,n-k} = F_{.05,2,57} \approx 3.15$

Grand mean = 562.6

$$SST = \sum n_j(\bar{x}_j - \bar{\bar{x}})^2 = 20(551.50 - 562.6)^2 + 20(576.75 - 562.6)^2 + 20(559.45 - 562.6)^2 = 6,667$$

$$SSE = \sum (n_j - 1)s_j^2 = (20-1)(2,741.95) + (20-1)(2,641.14) + (20-1)(3,129.31) = 161,736$$

ANOVA table

Source	Degrees of Freedom	Sum of Squares	Mean Squares	F
Treatments	$k-1=2$	SST = 6,667	$\frac{SST}{k-1} = \frac{6,667}{2} = 3,334$	$\frac{MST}{MSE} = \frac{3,334}{2,837} = 1.17$
Error	$n-k=57$	SSE = 161,736	$\frac{SSE}{n-k} = \frac{161,736}{57} = 2,837$	

F = 1.17, p-value = .3162. There is not enough evidence of a difference between fertilizers in terms of crop yields.

15.16 $H_0: \mu_1 = \mu_2 = \mu_3 = \mu_4$

H_1: At least two means differ.

Rejection region: $F > F_{\alpha,k-1,n-k} = F_{05,3,116} \approx 2.68$

Grand mean = 77.39

$$SST = \sum n_j(\bar{x}_j - \bar{\bar{x}})^2 = 30(74.10 - 77.39)^2 + 30(75.67 - 77.39)^2 + 30(78.50 - 77.39)^2$$

$$+ 30(81.30 - 77.39)^2 = 909.42$$

$$SSE = \sum (n_j - 1)s_j^2 = (30-1)(249.96) + (30-1)(184.23) + (30-1)(233.36) + (30-1)(242.91)$$

$$= 26,403$$

ANOVA table

Source	Degrees of Freedom	Sum of Squares	Mean Squares	F
Treatments	$k-1=3$	SST = 909.4	$\frac{SST}{k-1} = \frac{909.4}{3} = 303.1$	$\frac{MST}{MSE} = \frac{303.1}{227.6} = 1.33$
Error	$n-k=116$	SSE = 26,403	$\frac{SSE}{n-k} = \frac{26,403}{116} = 227.6$	

F = 1.33, p-value = .2675. There is not enough evidence of a difference between the four groups of companies.

15.18 $H_0: \mu_1 = \mu_2 = \mu_3 = \mu_4$

H_1 : At least two means differ.

a Ages: Rejection region: $F > F_{\alpha,k-1,n-k} = F_{.05,3,291} \approx 2.68$

Grand mean = 36.23

$$SST = \sum n_j(\bar{x}_j - \bar{\bar{x}})^2 = 63(31.30 - 36.23)^2 + 81(34.42 - 36.23)^2 + 40(37.38 - 36.23)^2$$

$$+ 111(39.93 - 36.23)^2 = 3,366$$

$$SSE = \sum (n_j - 1)s_j^2 = (63 - 1)(28.34) + (81 - 1)(23.20) + (40 - 1)(31.16) + (111 - 1)(72.03) = 12,752$$

ANOVA table

Source	Degrees of Freedom	Sum of Squares	Mean Squares	F
Treatments	$k - 1 = 3$	SST =3,366	$\frac{SST}{k-1} = \frac{3,366}{3} = 1,122$	$\frac{MST}{MSE} = \frac{1,122}{43.82} = 25.60$
Error	$n - k = 291$	SSE = 12,752	$\frac{SSE}{n-k} = \frac{12,752}{291} = 43.82$	

F = 25.60, p-value = 0. There is sufficient evidence to infer that the ages of the four groups of cereal buyers differ.

b Incomes: Rejection region: $F > F_{\alpha,k-1,n-k} = F_{.05,3,291} \approx 2.68$

Grand mean = 39.97

$$SST = \sum n_j(\bar{x}_j - \bar{\bar{x}})^2 = 63(37.22 - 39.97)^2 + 81(38.91 - 39.97)^2 + 40(41.48 - 39.97)^2$$

$$+ 111(41.75 - 39.97)^2 = 1,008$$

$$SSE = \sum (n_j - 1)s_j^2 = (63 - 1)(39.82) + (81 - 1)(40.85) + (40 - 1)(61.38) + (111 - 1)(46.59) = 13,256$$

ANOVA table

Source	Degrees of Freedom	Sum of Squares	Mean Squares	F
Treatments	$k - 1 = 3$	SST =1,008	$\frac{SST}{k-1} = \frac{1,008}{3} = 336.0$	$\frac{MST}{MSE} = \frac{336.0}{45.55} = 7.37$
Error	$n - k = 291$	SSE = 13,256	$\frac{SSE}{n-k} = \frac{13,256}{291} = 45.55$	

F = 7.37, p-value = .0001. There is sufficient evidence to conclude that incomes differ between the four groups of cereal buyers.

c Education: Rejection region: $F > F_{\alpha,k-1,n-k} = F_{05,3,291} \approx 2.68$

Grand mean = 11.98

$SST = \sum n_j(\bar{x}_j - \bar{\bar{x}})^2 = 63(11.75 - 11.98)^2 + 81(12.41 - 11.98)^2 + 40(11.73 - 11.98)^2$

$+ 111(11.89 - 11.98)^2 = 21.71$

$SSE = \sum (n_j - 1)s_j^2 = (63 - 1)(3.93) + (81 - 1)(3.39) + (40 - 1)(4.26) + (111 - 1)(4.30) = 1{,}154$

ANOVA table

Source	Degrees of Freedom	Sum of Squares	Mean Squares	F
Treatments	$k - 1 = 3$	SST =21.71	$\frac{SST}{k-1} = \frac{21.71}{3} = 7.24$	$\frac{MST}{MSE} = \frac{7.24}{3.97} = 1.82$
Error	$n - k = 291$	SSE = 1,154	$\frac{SSE}{n-k} = \frac{1{,}154}{291} = 3.97$	

F = 1.82, p-value = .1428. There is not enough evidence to infer that education differs between the four groups of cereal buyers.

d Using the F-tests and the descriptive statistics we see that the mean ages and mean household incomes are in ascending order. For example, Sugar Smacks buyers are younger and earn less than the buyers of the other three cereals. Cheerio purchasers are older and earn the most.

15.20 $H_0: \mu_1 = \mu_2 = \mu_3$

H_1: At least two means differ.

Rejection region: $F > F_{\alpha,k-1,n-k} = F_{.05,2,232} \approx 3.07$

Grand mean = 19.50

$SST = \sum n_j(\bar{x}_j - \bar{\bar{x}})^2 = 61(18.54 - 19.50)^2 + 83(19.34 - 19.50)^2 + 91(20.29 - 19.50)^2 = 114.5$

$SSE = \sum (n_j - 1)s_j^2 = (61 - 1)(177.95) + (83 - 1)(171.42) + (91 - 1)(297.50) = 51{,}508$

ANOVA table

Source	Degrees of Freedom	Sum of Squares	Mean Squares	F
Treatments	$k - 1 = 2$	SST = 114.5	$\frac{SST}{k-1} = \frac{114.5}{2} = 57.3$	$\frac{MST}{MSE} = \frac{57.3}{222.0} = .26$
Error	$n - k = 232$	SSE = 51,508	$\frac{SSE}{n-k} = \frac{51{,}508}{232} = 222.0$	

F = .26, p-value = .7730. There is not enough evidence of a difference between the three segments.

15.22 ANOVA Table

Source	Degrees of Freedom	Sum of Squares	Mean Squares	F
Treatments	4	1,500	375.0	16.50
Blocks	11	1,000	90.91	4.00
Error	44	1,000	22.73	
Total	59	3,500		

a Rejection region: $F > F_{\alpha,k-1,n-k-b+1} = F_{.01,4,44} \approx 3.83$

F = 16.50, p-value = 0. There is enough evidence to conclude that the treatment means differ.

b Rejection region: $F > F_{\alpha,b-1,n-k-b+1} = F_{.01,11,44} \approx 2.80$

Conclusion: F = 4.00, p-value = .0005. There is enough evidence to conclude that the block means differ.

15.24 Rejection region: $F > F_{\alpha,k-1,n-k-b+1} = F_{05,2,14} = 3.74$

a ANOVA Table

Source	Degrees of Freedom	Sum of Squares	Mean Squares	F
Treatments	2	1,500	750.0	7.00
Blocks	7	500	71.43	.67
Error	14	1,500	107.1	
Total	23	3,500		

Conclusion: F = 7.00, p-value = .0078. There is enough evidence to conclude that the treatment means differ.

b ANOVA Table

Source	Degrees of Freedom	Sum of Squares	Mean Squares	F
Treatments	2	1,500	750.0	10.50
Blocks	7	1,000	142.86	2.00
Error	14	1,000	71.43	
Total	23	3,500		

Conclusion: F = 10.50, .0016. There is enough evidence to conclude that the treatment means differ

c ANOVA Table

Source	Degrees of Freedom	Sum of Squares	Mean Squares	F
Treatments	2	1,500	750	21.00

Blocks	7	1,500	214.3	6.00
Error	14	500	35.71	
Total	23	3,500		

Conclusion: F = 21.00, p-value = .0001. There is enough evidence to conclude that the treatment means differ

d The test statistic increases.

15.26 a k = 4, b = 3, Grand mean = 5.6

SS(Total) =

$$\sum_{j=1}^{k}\sum_{i=1}^{b}(x_{ij}-\bar{\bar{x}})^2 = (6-5.6)^2+(8-5.6)^2+(7-5.6)^2+(5-5.6)^2+(5-5.6)^2+(6-5.6)^2$$

$$+(4-5.6)^2+(5-5.6)^2+(5-5.6)^2+(4-5.6)^2+(6-5.6)^2+(6-5.6)^2 = 14.9$$

$$SST = \sum_{j=1}^{k} b(\bar{x}[T]_j-\bar{\bar{x}})^2 = 3[(7-5.6)^2+(5.3-5.6)^2+(4.7-5.6)^2+(5.3-5.6)^2] = 8.9$$

$$SSB = \sum_{i=1}^{b} k(\bar{x}[B]_i-\bar{\bar{x}})^2 = 4[(4.8-5.6)^2+(6-5.6)^2+(6-5.6)^2 = 4.2$$

SSE = SS(Total) – SST – SSB = 14.9- 8.9 – 4.2 = 1.8

b SS(Total) =

$$\sum_{j=1}^{k}\sum_{i=1}^{b}(x_{ij}-\bar{\bar{x}})^2 = (6-5.6)^2+(8-5.6)^2+(7-5.6)^2+(5-5.6)^2+(5-5.6)^2+(6-5.6)^2$$

$$+(4-5.6)^2+(5-5.6)^2+(5-5.6)^2+(4-5.6)^2+(6-5.6)^2+(6\ \ 5.6)^2 = 14.9$$

$$SST = \sum_{j=1}^{k} b(\bar{x}[T]_j-\bar{\bar{x}})^2 = 3[(7-5.6)^2+(5.3-5.6)^2+(4.7-5.6)^2+(5.3-5.6)^2] = 8.9$$

SSE = SS(Total) – SST = 14.9 – 8.9 = 6.0

c The variation between all the data is the same for both designs.

d The variation between treatments is the same for both designs.

e Because the randomized block design divides the sum of squares for error in the one-way analysis of variance into two parts.

15.28 $H_0: \mu_1 = \mu_2 = \mu_3$

H_1 : At least two means differ.

Rejection region: $F > F_{\alpha,k-1,n-k-b+1} = F_{.05,2,6} = 5.14$

k = 3, b = 4, Grand mean = 2.38

$$SS(Total) = \sum_{j=1}^{k}\sum_{i=1}^{b}(x_{ij} - \bar{\bar{x}})^2 = (1.4-2.38)^2 + (3.1-2.38)^2 + (2.8-2.38)^2 + (3.4-2.38)^2$$

$$+ (1.5-2.38)^2 + (2.6-2.38)^2 + (2.1-2.38)^2 + (3.6-2.38)^2$$

$$+ (1.3-2.38)^2 + (2.4-2.38)^2 + (1.5-2.38)^2 + (2.9-2.38)^2 = 7.30$$

$$SST = \sum_{j=1}^{k} b(\bar{x}[T]_j - \bar{\bar{x}})^2 = 4[(2.68-2.38)^2 + (2.45-2.38)^2 + (2.03-2.38)^2] = .87$$

$$SSB = \sum_{i=1}^{b} k(\bar{x}[B]_i - \bar{\bar{x}})^2 = 3[(1.4-2.38)^2 + (2.7-2.38)^2 + (2.1-2.38)^2 + (3.3-2.38)^2] = 5.91$$

SSE = SS(Total) – SST – SSB = 7.30 - .87 – 5.91 = .52

ANOVA Table

Source	Degrees of Freedom	Sum of Squares	Mean Squares	F
Treatments	2	.87	.44	5.06
Blocks	3	5.91	1.97	22.64
Error	6	.52	.087	
Total	11	7.30		

F = 5.08, p-value = .0512. There is not enough evidence to conclude that there are differences between the subjects being measured.

15.30 ANOVA Table

Source	Degrees of Freedom	Sum of Squares	Mean Squares	F
Treatments	2	7,131	3,566	123.36
Blocks	19	177,465	9,340	323.16
Error	38	1,098	28.90	

a $H_0: \mu_1 = \mu_2 = \mu_3$

H_1 : At least two means differ.

Rejection region: $F > F_{\alpha,k-1,n-k-b+1} = F_{.05,2,38} \approx 3.23$

$F = 123.36$, p-value = 0. There is sufficient evidence to conclude that the three fertilizers differ with respect to crop yield.

b $F = 323.16$, p-value = 0. There is sufficient evidence to indicate that there are differences between the plots.

15.32 ANOVA Table

Source	Degrees of Freedom	Sum of Squares	Mean Squares	F
Treatments	3	4,206	1,402	21.16
Blocks	29	126,843	4,374	66.02
Error	87	5,764	66.25	

a $H_0: \mu_1 = \mu_2 = \mu_3 = \mu_4$

H_1: At least two means differ.

Rejection region: $F > F_{\alpha,k-1,n-k-b+1} = F_{01,3,87} \approx 4.13$

$F = 21.16$, p-value = 0. There is sufficient evidence to conclude that differences in completion times exist between the four forms.

b $H_0: \mu_1 = \mu_2 = \ldots = \mu_{30}$

H_1: At least two means differ.

$F = 66.02$, p-value = 0. There is sufficient evidence to indicate that there are differences between the taxpayers, which tells us that this experimental design is recommended.

15.34 ANOVA Table

Source	Degrees of Freedom	Sum of Squares	Mean Squares	F
Treatments	4	1,406	351.6	10.72
Blocks	35	7,310	208.9	6.36
Error	140	4,594	32.81	

a $H_0: \mu_1 = \mu_2 = \mu_3 = \mu_4 = \mu_5$

H_1: At least two means differ.

$F = 10.72$, p-value = 0. There is enough evidence to infer differences between medical specialties.

b $H_0: \mu_1 = \mu_2 = \ldots = \mu_{36}$

H_1: At least two means differ.

F = 6.36, p-value = 0. There is sufficient evidence to indicate that there are differences between the physicians' ages, which tells us that this experimental design is recommended.

15.36 ANOVA Table

Source	Degrees of Freedom	Sum of Squares	Mean Squares	F
Factor A	2	1,560	780	5.86
Factor B	3	2,880	960	7.18
Interaction	6	7,605	1268	9.53
Error	228	30,405	133	
Total	239	42,450		

a Rejection region: $F > F_{\alpha,a-1,n-ab} = F_{01,2,228} \approx 4.61$

F = 5.86. There is enough evidence to conclude that differences exist between the levels of factor A.

b Rejection region: $F > F_{\alpha,b-1,n-ab} = F_{01,3,228} \approx 3.78$

F = 7.18. There is enough evidence to conclude that differences exist between the levels of factor B.

c Rejection region: $F > F_{\alpha,(a-1)(b-1),n-ab} = F_{.01,6,228} \approx 2.80$

F = 9.53. There is enough evidence to conclude that factors A and B interact.

15.38

	A	B	C	D	E	F	G
23	ANOVA						
24	*Source of Variation*	*SS*	*df*	*MS*	*F*	*P-value*	*F crit*
25	Sample	5.33	1	5.33	1.23	0.2995	5.32
26	Columns	56.33	1	56.33	13.00	0.0069	5.32
27	Interaction	1.33	1	1.33	0.31	0.5943	5.32
28	Within	34.67	8	4.33			
29							
30	Total	97.67	11				

a F = .31, p-value = .5943. There is not enough evidence to conclude that factors A and B interact.

b F = 1.23, p-value = .2995. There is not enough evidence to conclude that differences exist between the levels of factor A.

c F = 13.00, p-value = .0069. There is enough evidence to conclude that differences exist between the levels of factor B.

15.40 a Factor A is the drug mixture and factor B is the schedule.

b The response variable is the improvement index.

c There are a = 4 drug mixtures and b = 2 schedules.

	A	B	C	D	E	F	G
23	ANOVA						
24	*Source of Variation*	*SS*	*df*	*MS*	*F*	*P-value*	*F crit*
25	Sample	14.40	1	14.40	0.57	0.4548	4.15
26	Columns	581.80	3	193.93	7.71	0.0005	2.90
27	Interaction	548.60	3	182.87	7.27	0.0007	2.90
28	Within	804.80	32	25.15			
29							
30	Total	1949.60	39				

d F = .57, p-value = .4548. There is not enough evidence to conclude that differences exist between the schedules.

e F = 7.71, p-value = .0005. There is sufficient evidence to conclude that differences exist between the four drug mixtures.

f F = 7.27, p-value = .0007. There is sufficient evidence to conclude that the schedules and drug mixtures interact.

15.42 a There are 12 treatments.

b There are two factors, tax form and income group.

c There are a = 4 forms and b = 3 income groups.

	A	B	C	D	E	F	G
28							
29	ANOVA						
30	*Source of Variation*	*SS*	*df*	*MS*	*F*	*P-value*	*F crit*
31	Sample	6719	2	3359.4	4.11	0.0190	3.08
32	Columns	6280	3	2093.3	2.56	0.0586	2.69
33	Interaction	5102	6	850.3	1.04	0.4030	2.18
34	Within	88217	108	816.8			
35							
36	Total	106317	119				

d F =2.56, p-value = .0586. There is not enough evidence to conclude that differences exist between the forms.

e F =4.11, p-value = .0190. There is enough evidence to conclude that differences exist between the three income groups.

f F = 1.04, p-value = .4030. There is not enough evidence to conclude that forms and income groups interact.

15.44

	A	B	C	D	E	F	G
23	ANOVA						
24	*Source of Variation*	*SS*	*df*	*MS*	*F*	*P-value*	*F crit*
25	Sample	16.04	1	16.04	14.74	0.0005	4.11
26	Columns	6.77	1	6.77	6.22	0.0173	4.11
27	Interaction	0.025	1	0.025	0.023	0.8814	4.11
28	Within	39.17	36	1.09			
29							
30	Total	62.00	39				

The p-values for machines, alloys, and interaction are .0173, .0005, and .8814, respectively. Both machines and alloys are sources of variation.

15.46

	A	B	C	D	E	F	G
29	ANOVA						
30	*Source of Variation*	*SS*	*df*	*MS*	*F*	*P-value*	*F crit*
31	Sample	211.78	2	105.89	21.04	0.0000	3.22
32	Columns	0.59	1	0.59	0.12	0.7348	4.07
33	Interaction	0.13	2	0.0640	0.0127	0.9874	3.22
34	Within	211.42	42	5.03			
35							
36	Total	423.91	47				

The p-values for methods, skills, and interaction are .7348, 0, and .9874. The only source of variation is skill level.

15.48 a $\alpha = .05$: $t_{\alpha/2,n-k} = t_{.025,20} = 2.086$

$$LSD = t_{\alpha/2,n-k}\sqrt{MSE\left(\frac{1}{n_i}+\frac{1}{n_j}\right)} = 2.086\sqrt{125\left(\frac{1}{5}+\frac{1}{5}\right)} = 14.75$$

Treatment	Means		Difference
$i = 1, j = 2$	227	205	22
$i = 1, j = 3$	227	219	8
$i = 1, j = 4$	227	248	-21
$i = 1, j = 5$	227	202	25
$i = 2, j = 3$	205	219	-14
$i = 2, j = 4$	205	248	-43
$i = 2, j = 5$	205	202	3
$i = 3, j = 4$	219	248	-29
$i = 3, j = 5$	219	202	17
$i = 4, j = 5$	248	202	46

Conclusion: The following pairs of means differ. μ_1 and μ_2, μ_1 and μ_4, μ_1 and μ_5, μ_2 and μ_4, μ_3 and μ_4, μ_3 and μ_5, and μ_4 and μ_5.

b $C = 5(4)/2 = 10, \alpha_E = .05,\ \alpha = \alpha_E / C = .005\ \ t_{\alpha/2,n-k} = t_{.0025,20} = 3.153$ (from Excel)

$$LSD = t_{\alpha/2,n-k}\sqrt{MSE\left(\frac{1}{n_i}+\frac{1}{n_j}\right)} = 3.153\sqrt{125\left(\frac{1}{5}+\frac{1}{5}\right)} = 22.30$$

Treatment	Means		Difference
$i = 1, j = 2$	227	205	22
$i = 1, j = 3$	227	219	8
$i = 1, j = 4$	227	248	-21
$i = 1, j = 5$	227	202	25
$i = 2, j = 3$	205	219	-14
$i = 2, j = 4$	205	248	-43
$i = 2, j = 5$	205	202	3
$i = 3, j = 4$	219	248	-29
$i = 3, j = 5$	219	202	17
$i = 4, j = 5$	248	202	46

Conclusion: The following pairs of means differ. μ_1 and μ_5, μ_2 and μ_4, μ_3 and μ_4, and μ_4 and μ_5.

c $q_\alpha(k, \nu) = q_{.05}(5, 20) = 4.23\ \varpi = q_\alpha(k, \nu)\sqrt{\frac{MSE}{n_g}} = 4.23\sqrt{\frac{125}{5}} = 21.15$

Treatment	Means		Difference
$i = 1, j = 2$	227	205	22
$i = 1, j = 3$	227	219	8
$i = 1, j = 4$	227	248	-21
$i = 1, j = 5$	227	202	25
$i = 2, j = 3$	205	219	-14
$i = 2, j = 4$	205	248	-43
$i = 2, j = 5$	205	202	3
$i = 3, j = 4$	219	248	-29
$i = 3, j = 5$	219	202	17
$i = 4, j = 5$	248	202	46

Conclusion: The following pairs of means differ. μ_1 and μ_2, μ_1 and μ_5, μ_2 and μ_4, μ_3 and μ_4, and μ_4 and μ_5.

15.50 a $LSD = t_{\alpha/2,n-k}\sqrt{MSE\left(\frac{1}{n_i}+\frac{1}{n_j}\right)} = 1.782\sqrt{1.06\left(\frac{1}{5}+\frac{1}{5}\right)} = 1.16$

Treatment	Means		Difference
$i = 1, j = 2$	3.94	4.78	-.84
$i = 1, j = 3$	3.94	5.76	-1.82
$i = 2, j = 3$	4.78	5.76	-1.02

Means of BAs and BBAs differ.

b $C = 3(2)/2 = 3, \alpha_E = .10,\ \alpha = \alpha_E / C = .0333$: $t_{\alpha/2,n-k} = t_{.0167,12} = 2.404$ (from Excel)

$LSD = t_{\alpha/2,n-k}\sqrt{MSE\left(\frac{1}{n_i}+\frac{1}{n_j}\right)} = 2.404\sqrt{1.06\left(\frac{1}{5}+\frac{1}{5}\right)} = 1.57$

Treatment	Means		Difference
$i = 1, j = 2$	3.94	4.78	-.84
$i = 1, j = 3$	3.94	5.76	-1.82
$i = 2, j = 3$	4.78	5.76	-1.02

Means of BAs and BBAs differ.

15.52 Tukey's method: $q_{\alpha}(k, \nu) = q_{.05}(4, 116) \approx 3.68$ $\varpi = 3.68\sqrt{\frac{961}{30}} = 20.83$

LSD method: $C = 4(3)/2 = 6, \alpha_E = .05,\ \alpha = \alpha_E / C = .0083$ $t_{\alpha/2,n-k} = t_{.0042,116} = 2.686$ (from Excel)

$$LSD = t_{\alpha/2,n-k}\sqrt{MSE\left(\frac{1}{n_i}+\frac{1}{n_j}\right)} = 2.686\sqrt{961\left(\frac{1}{30}+\frac{1}{30}\right)} = 21.50$$

Treatment	Means		Difference
i = 1, j = 2	90.17	95.77	-5.60
i = 1, j = 3	90.17	106.83	-16.66
i = 1, j = 4	90.17	111.17	-21.00
i = 2, j = 3	95.77	106.83	-11.06
i = 2, j = 4	95.77	111.17	-15.40
i = 3, j = 4	106.83	111.17	-4.34

a The means of forms 1 and 4 differ.

b No means differ.

15.54 a LSD method: $C = 5(4)/2 = 10, \alpha_E = .05,\ \alpha = \alpha_E / C = .005$ $t_{\alpha/2,n-k} = t_{.0025,120} = 2.860$ (from Excel)

$$LSD = t_{\alpha/2,n-k}\sqrt{MSE\left(\frac{1}{n_i}+\frac{1}{n_j}\right)} = 2.860\sqrt{1300\left(\frac{1}{25}+\frac{1}{25}\right)} = 29.17$$

b Tukey's method: $q_{\alpha}(k, \nu) = q_{.05}(5,120) = 3.92$ $\varpi = 3.92\sqrt{\frac{1300}{25}} = 28.27$

Treatment	Means		Difference
i = 1, j = 2	164.6	185.6	-21.0
i = 1, j = 3	164.6	154.8	9.8
i = 1, j = 4	164.6	182.6	-18.0
i = 1, j = 5	164.6	178.9	-14.3
i = 2, j = 3	185.6	154.8	30.8
i = 2, j = 4	185.6	182.6	3.0
i = 2, j = 5	185.6	178.9	6.7
i = 3, j = 4	154.8	182.6	-27.8
i = 3, j = 5	154.8	178.9	-24.1
i = 4, j = 5	182.6	178.9	3.7

a The means of lacquers 2 and 3 differ

b The means of lacquers 2 and 3 differ.

15.56 Tukey's method: $q_{\alpha}(k, \nu) = q_{.05}(3,57) \approx 3.40$ $\varpi = 3.40\sqrt{\frac{2,838}{20}} = 40.50$

LSD method: $C = 3(2)/2 = 3, \alpha_E = .05, \alpha = \alpha_E / C = .0167$ $t_{\alpha/2,n-k} = t_{.0083,57} = 2.466$ (from Excel)

$$LSD = t_{\alpha/2,n-k}\sqrt{MSE\left(\frac{1}{n_i}+\frac{1}{n_j}\right)} = 2.466\sqrt{2,838\left(\frac{1}{20}+\frac{1}{20}\right)} = 41.54$$

Treatment	Means		Difference
$i = 1, j = 2$	551.5	576.8	-25.3
$i = 1, j = 3$	551.5	559.5	-8.0
$i = 2, j = 3$	576.8	559.5	17.3

a There are no differences.

b There are no differences.

15.58 $H_0: \mu_1 = \mu_2 = \mu_3 = \mu_4$

H_1: At least two means differ.

	A	B	C	D	E	F	G
31	ANOVA						
32	*Source of Variation*	*SS*	*df*	*MS*	*F*	*P-value*	*F crit*
33	Rows	43980	19	2314.72	21.58	0.0000	1.77
34	Columns	4438	3	1479.21	13.79	0.0000	2.77
35	Error	6113	57	107.25			
36							
37	Total	54530	79				

F = 13.79, p-value = 0. There is sufficient evidence to conclude that the reading speeds differ between the four typefaces. The typeface that was read the fastest should be used.

15.60a $H_0: \mu_1 = \mu_2 = \mu_3 = \mu_4$

H_1: At least two means differ.

	A	B	C	D	E	F	G
11	ANOVA						
12	*Source of Variation*	*SS*	*df*	*MS*	*F*	*P-value*	*F crit*
13	Between Groups	9.90	3	3.30	7.67	0.0001	2.70
14	Within Groups	41.33	96	0.43			
15							
16	Total	51.23	99				

F = 7.67, p-value = .0001. There is sufficient evidence to infer that differences in productivity exist between the four groups of companies.

b

	A	B	C	D	E
1	**Multiple Comparisons**				
2					
3				LSD	Omega
4	Treatment	Treatment	Difference	Alpha = 0.0083	Alpha = 0.05
5	*Extensive*	*Some*	0.534	0.500	0.483
6		*Little*	0.722	0.500	0.483
7		*No*	0.811	0.500	0.483
8	*Some*	*Little*	0.188	0.500	0.483
9		*No*	0.277	0.500	0.483
10	*Little*	*No*	0.089	0.500	0.483

Using either the Bonferroni adjustment or Tukey's method we conclude that μ_1 differs from μ_2, μ_3 and μ_4. Companies that offered extensive training have productivity levels different from the other companies.

15.62a There are 4 levels of ranks and 4 levels of faculties for a total of 16 treatments.

b

	A	B	C	D	E	F	G
23	ANOVA						
24	*Source of Variation*	*SS*	*df*	*MS*	*F*	*P-value*	*F crit*
25	Between Groups	1091.15	15	72.74	2.84	0.0019	1.83
26	Within Groups	1638.40	64	25.60			
27							
28	Total	2729.55	79				

F = 2.84, p-value = .0019. There is enough evidence to infer that at least two treatment means differ.

c Factor A (columns) is the faculty. The levels are business, engineering, arts, and science. Factor B (samples) is the rank. The levels are professor, associate professor, assistant professor, and lecturer.

	A	B	C	D	E	F	G
35	ANOVA						
36	*Source of Variation*	*SS*	*df*	*MS*	*F*	*P-value*	*F crit*
37	Sample	46.85	3	15.62	0.61	0.6109	2.75
38	Columns	344.65	3	114.88	4.49	0.0064	2.75
39	Interaction	699.65	9	77.74	3.04	0.0044	2.03
40	Within	1638.40	64	25.60			
41							
42	Total	2729.55	79				

d F =.61, p-value = .6109. There is not enough evidence to conclude that differences exist between the ranks.

e F = 4.49, p-value = .0064. There is enough evidence to conclude that differences exist between the faculties.

f F = 3.04, p-value = .0044. There is evidence to conclude that ranks and faculties interact.

15.64 $H_0: \mu_1 = \mu_2 = \mu_3$

H_1 : At least two means differ

	A	B	C	D	E	F	G
17	ANOVA						
18	*Source of Variation*	*SS*	*df*	*MS*	*F*	*P-value*	*F crit*
19	Rows	195.33	6	32.56	11.55	0.0002	3.00
20	Columns	43.52	2	21.76	7.72	0.0070	3.89
21	Error	33.81	12	2.82			
22							
23	Total	272.67	20				

F = 7.72, p-value = .0070. There is enough evidence to infer that differences in attention span exist between the three products.

15.66

	A	B	C	D	E	F	G
23	ANOVA						
24	*Source of Variation*	*SS*	*df*	*MS*	*F*	*P-value*	*F crit*
25	Sample	123553	1	123553	3.66	0.0576	3.91
26	Columns	3965110	2	1982555	58.78	0.0000	3.06
27	Interaction	30006	2	15003	0.44	0.6418	3.06
28	Within	4856578	144	33726			
29							
30	Total	8975248	149				

Age: F = 58.78, p-value = 0. There is sufficient evidence to conclude that differences in offers exist between the three age groups.

Gender: F = 3.66, p-value = .0576. There is not enough evidence to conclude that differences in offers exist between males and females

Interaction: F = .44, p-value = .6418. There is not enough evidence to conclude that age and gender interact.

15.68a $H_0: \mu_1 = \mu_2 = \mu_3$

H_1 : At least two means differ.

	A	B	C	D	E	F	G
10	ANOVA						
11	*Source of Variation*	*SS*	*df*	*MS*	*F*	*P-value*	*F crit*
12	Between Groups	1913	2	956.70	9.54	0.0002	3.10
13	Within Groups	8727	87	100.31			
14							
15	Total	10640	89				

F = 9.54, p-value = .0002. There is sufficient evidence to infer that there are differences between the three groups.

b

	A	B	C	D	E
1	**Multiple Comparisons**				
2					
3				LSD	Omega
4	Treatment	Treatment	Difference	Alpha = 0.0167	Alpha = 0.05
5	*Mozart*	*White noise*	-9.30	6.31	6.14
6		*Glass*	-10.20	6.31	6.14
7	*White noise*	*Glass*	-0.90	6.31	6.14

The mean time of the Mozart group differs from the mean times of white noise and the Glass groups.

15.70 $H_0: \mu_1 = \mu_2 = \mu_3 = \mu_4$

H_1 : At least two means differ.

	A	B	C	D	E	F	G
11	ANOVA						
12	*Source of Variation*	*SS*	*df*	*MS*	*F*	*P-value*	*F crit*
13	Between Groups	3263	3	1087.8	10.26	0.0000	2.64
14	Within Groups	29685	280	106.0			
15							
16	Total	32948	283				

F = 10.26, p-value = 0. There is enough evidence of differences between the four groups of investors.

15.72 $H_0: \mu_1 = \mu_2 = \mu_3 = \mu_4$

H_1 : At least two means differ.

	A	B	C	D	E	F	G
11	ANOVA						
12	*Source of Variation*	*SS*	*df*	*MS*	*F*	*P-value*	*F crit*
13	Between Groups	2.12	3	0.705	9.17	0.0000	2.69
14	Within Groups	7.99	104	0.0769			
15							
16	Total	10.11	107				

F = 9.17, p-value = 0. There is sufficient evidence to infer that there are differences in changes to the TSE depending on the loss the previous day.

15.74 $H_0: \mu_1 = \mu_2 = \mu_3$

H_1 : At least two means differ.

	A	B	C	D	E	F	G
1	ANOVA						
2	*Source of Variation*	*SS*	*df*	*MS*	*F*	*P-value*	*F crit*
3	Between Groups	11374	2	5687	45.49	0.0000	3.00
4	Within Groups	229170	1833	125.0			
5							
6	Total	240544	1835				

F = 45.49, p-value = 0. There is enough evidence to infer that family incomes differ between the three market segments.

15.76 $H_0: \mu_1 = \mu_2 = \mu_3 = \mu_4$

H_1 : At least two means differ.

	A	B	C	D	E	F	G
1	ANOVA						
2	*Source of Variation*	*SS*	*df*	*MS*	*F*	*P-value*	*F crit*
3	Between Groups	6636.1	3	2212.03	211.61	0.0000	2.63
4	Within Groups	3595.9	344	10.45			
5							
6	Total	10232.0	347				

F = 211.61, p-value = 0. There is enough evidence to conclude that there are differences in the age of the car between the four market segments.

Chapter 16

16.2 $H_0: p_1 = .1,\ p_2 = .2,\ p_3 = .3,\ p_4 = .2,\ p_5 = .2$

H_1: At least one p_i is not equal to its specified value.

Cell i	f_i	e_i	$(f_i - e_i)$	$(f_i - e_i)^2 / e_i$
1	12	150(.1) = 15	-3	.60
2	32	150(.2) = 30	2	.13
3	42	150(.3) = 45	-3	.20
4	36	150(.2) = 30	6	1.20
5	28	150(.2) = 30	-2	.13
Total	150	150		$\chi^2 = 2.26$

Rejection region: $\chi^2 > \chi^2_{\alpha,k-1} = \chi^2_{.01,4} = 13.2767$

$\chi^2 = 2.26$, p-value = .6868. There is not enough evidence to infer that at least one p_i is not equal to its specified value.

16.4 The χ^2 statistic decreases.

16.5 16.5 $H_0: p_1 = .3,\ p_2 = .3,\ p_3 = .2,\ p_4 = .2$

H_1: At least one p_i is not equal to its specified value.

Cell i	f_i	e_i	$(f_i - e_i)$	$(f_i - e_i)^2 / e_i$
1	76	300(.3) = 90	-14	2.18
2	100	300(.3) = 90	10	1.11
3	76	300(.2) = 60	16	4.27
4	48	300(.2) = 60	-12	2.40
Total	300	300		$\chi^2 = 9.96$

Rejection region: $\chi^2 > \chi^2_{\alpha,k-1} = \chi^2_{05,3} = 7.81473$

$\chi^2 = 9.96$, p-value = .0189. There is enough evidence to infer that at least one p_i is not equal to its specified value.

16.6 $H_0: p_1 = .3,\ p_2 = .3,\ p_3 = .2,\ p_4 = .2$

H_1 : At least one p_i is not equal to its specified value.

Cell i	f_i	e_i	$(f_i - e_i)$	$(f_i - e_i)^2 / e_i$
1	38	150(.3) = 45	-7	1.09
2	50	150(.3) = 45	5	0.56
3	38	150(.2) = 30	8	2.13
4	24	150(.2) = 30	-6	1.20
Total	150	150		$\chi^2 = 4.98$

Rejection region: $\chi^2 > \chi^2_{\alpha,k-1} = \chi^2_{.05,3} = 7.81473$

$\chi^2 = 4.98$, p-value = .1734. There is not enough evidence to infer that at least one p_i is not equal to its specified value.

16.8 $H_0: p_1 = .15,\ p_2 = .40,\ p_3 = .35,\ p_4 = .10$

H_1 : At least one p_i is not equal to its specified value.

Cell i	f_i	e_i	$(f_i - e_i)$	$(f_i - e_i)^2 / e_i$
1	41	233(.15) = 34.95	6.05	1.05
2	107	233(.40) = 93.20	13.80	2.04
3	66	233(.35) = 81.55	-15.55	2.97
4	19	233(.10) = 23.30	-4.30	0.79
Total	233	233		$\chi^2 = 6.85$

Rejection region: $\chi^2 > \chi^2_{\alpha,k-1} = \chi^2_{.05,3} = 7.81473$

$\chi^2 = 6.85$, p-value = .0769. There is not enough evidence to infer that at least one p_i is not equal to its specified value.

16.10 $H_0: p_1 = .05,\ p_2 = .25\ p_3 = .40,\ p_4 = .25\ p_5 = .05$

H_1 : At least one p_i is not equal to its specified value.

Cell i	f_i	e_i	$(f_i - e_i)$	$(f_i - e_i)^2 / e_i$
1	11	150(.05) = 7.5	3.5	1.63

2	32	150(.25) = 37.5	-5.5	0.81
3	62	150(.40) = 60.0	2.0	0.07
4	29	150(.25) = 37.5	-8.5	1.93
5	16	150(.05) = 7.5	8.5	9.63
Total	150	150		$\chi^2 = 14.07$

Rejection region: $\chi^2 > \chi^2_{\alpha,k-1} = \chi^2_{10,4} = 7.77944$

$\chi^2 = 14.07$, p-value = .0071. There is enough evidence to infer that grades are distributed differently from grades in the past.

16.12 $H_0: p_1 = .2,\ p_2 = .2\ p_3 = .2,\ p_4 = .2\ p_5 = .2$

H_1 : At least one p_i is not equal to its specified value.

Cell i	f_i	e_i	$(f_i - e_i)$	$(f_i - e_i)^2 / e_i$
1	8	25(.2) = 5.0	3.0	1.80
2	4	25(.2) = 5.0	-1.0	0.20
3	3	25(.2) = 5.0	-2.0	0.80
4	8	25(.2) = 5.0	3.0	1.80
5	2	25(.2) = 5.0	-3.0	1.80
Total	25	25		$\chi^2 = 6.40$

Rejection region: $\chi^2 > \chi^2_{\alpha,k-1} = \chi^2_{.05,4} = 9.48773$

$\chi^2 = 6.40$, p-value = .1712. There is not enough evidence to infer that the professor does not randomly distribute the correct answer over the five choices.

16.14 $H_0: p_1 = .31,\ p_2 = .51,\ p_3 = .18$

H_1 : At least one p_i is not equal to its specified value.

Cell i	f_i	e_i	$(f_i - e_i)$	$(f_i - e_i)^2 / e_i$
1	408	1200(.31) = 372	36	3.48
2	571	1200(.51) = 612	-41	2.75
3	221	1200(.18) = 216	5	0.12
Total	1200	1200		$\chi^2 = 6.35$

Rejection region: $\chi^2 > \chi^2_{\alpha,k-1} = \chi^2_{.10,2} = 4.60517$

$\chi^2 = 6.35$, p-value = .0419. There is enough evidence to infer that voter support has changed since the election.

16.16 $H_0: p_1 = .23,\ p_2 = .40,\ p_3 = .15,\ p_4 = .22$

H_1: At least one p_i is not equal to its specified value.

Cell i	f_i	e_i	$(f_i - e_i)$	$(f_i - e_i)^2 / e_i$
1	63	320(.23) = 73.6	-10.6	1.53
2	125	320(.40) = 128.0	-3.0	0.07
3	45	320(.15) = 48.0	-3.0	0.19
4	87	320(.22) = 70.4	16.6	3.91
Total	320	320		$\chi^2 = 5.70$

Rejection region: $\chi^2 > \chi^2_{\alpha,k-1} = \chi^2_{05,3} = 7.81473$

$\chi^2 = 5.70$, p-value = .1272. There is not enough evidence to infer that there has been a change in proportions.

16.18 H_0: The two variables are independent

H_1: The two variables are dependent

Cell i	f_i	e_i	$(f_i - e_i)$	$(f_i - e_i)^2 / e_i$
1	14	48(42)/188 = 21.45	-7.45	2.59
2	34	48(52)/188 = 26.55	7.45	2.09
3	28	46(42)/188 = 20.55	7.45	2.70
4	18	46(52)/188 = 25.45	-7.45	2.18
Total	94	94		$\chi^2 = 9.56$

Rejection region: $\chi^2 > \chi^2_{\alpha,(r-1)(c-1} = \chi^2_{.05,1} = 3.84146$

$\chi^2 = 9.56$, p-value = .0020. There is enough evidence to infer that the two classifications L and M are dependent.

16.20 The χ^2 statistic decreases.

16.22 H_0 : The two variables (shirt condition and shift) are independent

H_1 : The two variables are dependent

Cell i	f_i	e_i	$(f_i - e_i)$	$(f_i - e_i)^2 / e_i$
1	240	570(250)/600 = 237.5	2.5	.03
2	191	570(200)/600 = 190.0	1.0	.01
3	139	570(150)/600 = 142.5	-3.5	.09
4	10	30(250)/600 = 12.5	-2.5	.50
5	9	30(200)/600 = 10.0	-1.0	10
6	11	30(150)/600 = 7.5	3.5	1.63
Total	600	600		$\chi^2 = 2.36$

Rejection region: $\chi^2 > \chi^2_{\alpha,(r-1)(c-1} = \chi^2_{05,2} = 5.99147$

$\chi^2 = 2.36$, p-value = .3087. There is not enough evidence to infer that there are differences in quality among the three shifts.

16.24 H_0 : The two variables economic option and political affiliation) are independent

H_1 : The two variables are dependent

Cell i	f_i	e_i	$(f_i - e_i)$	$(f_i - e_i)^2 / e_i$
1	101	444(331)/1000 = 146.96	-45.96	14.376
2	282	444(557)/1000 = 233.99	48.01	9.852
3	61	444(142)/1000 = 63.05	-2.05	0.067
4	38	130(331)/1000 = 43.03	-5.03	0.588
5	67	130(557)/1000 = 68.51	-1.51	0.033
6	25	130(142)/1000 = 18.46	6.54	2.317
7	131	250(331)/1000 = 82.75	48.25	28.134
8	88	250(557)/1000 = 131.75	-43.75	14.528
9	31	250(142)/1000 = 35.50	-4.50	0.570
10	61	176(331)/1000 = 58.26	2.74	0.129
11	90	176(557)/1000 = 92.75	-2.75	0.082

12	25	176(142)/1000 = 24.99	0.01	0.000
Total	1000	1000		$\chi^2 = 70.675$

Rejection region: $\chi^2 > \chi^2_{\alpha,(r-1)(c-1} = \chi^2_{01,6} = 16.8119$

$\chi^2 = 70.675$, p-value = 0. There is sufficient evidence to infer that political affiliation affects support for economic options.

16.26 H_0 : The two variables (inducement and return) are independent

H_1 : The two variables are dependent

Cell i	f_i	e_i	$(f_i - e_i)$	$(f_i - e_i)^2 / e_i$
1	80	300(200)/1000 = 60	20	6.67
2	100	300(300)/1000 = 90	10	1.11
3	120	300(500)/1000 = 150	-30	6.00
4	120	700(200)/1000 = 140	-20	2.86
5	200	700(300)/1000 = 210	-10	0.50
6	380	700(500)/1000 = 350	30	2.57
Total	1000	1000		$\chi^2 = 19.71$

Rejection region: $\chi^2 > \chi^2_{\alpha,(r-1)(c-1} = \chi^2_{.05,2} = 5.99147$

Conclusion: $\chi^2 = 19.71$, p-value = .0001. There is sufficient evidence to infer that the return rates differ among the different inducements.

16.28 H_0 : The two variables (group and improvement) are independent

H_1 : The two variables are dependent

Cell i	f_i	e_i	$(f_i - e_i)$	$(f_i - e_i)^2 / e_i$
1	42	50(87)/150 = 29	13	5.83
2	8	50(63)/150 = 21	-13	8.05
3	32	50(87)/150 = 29	3	.28
4	18	50(63)/150 = 21	-3	.43
5	13	50(87)/150 = 29	-16	8.83
6	37	50(63)/150 = 21	16	12.19

Total	150	150		$\chi^2 = 35.61$

Rejection region: $\chi^2 > \chi^2_{\alpha,(r-1)(c-1} = \chi^2_{05,2} = 5.99147$

$\chi^2 = 35.61$, p-value = 0. There is sufficient evidence to infer there are differences between the three groups.

16.30 H_0 : The two variables (last purchase and second-last purchase) are independent

H_1 : The two variables are dependent

Cell i	f_i	e_i	$(f_i - e_i)$	$(f_i - e_i)^2 / e_i$
1	47	102(121)/513 = 24.06	22.94	21.88
2	14	102(148)/513 = 29.43	-15.43	8.09
3	27	102(148)/513 = 29.43	-2.43	.20
4	14	102(96)/513 = 19.09	-5.09	1.36
5	18	127(121)/513 = 29.96	-11.96	4.77
6	63	127(148)/513 = 36.64	26.36	18.97
7	33	127(148)/513 = 36.64	-3.64	.36
8	13	127(96)/513 = 23.77	-10.77	4.88
9	26	149(121)/513 = 35.14	-9.14	2.38
10	18	149(148)/513 = 42.99	5.01	.58
11	59	149(148)/513 = 42.99	16.01	5.97
12	16	149(96)/513 = 27.88	-11.88	5.06
13	30	135(121)/513 = 31.84	-1.84	.11
14	23	135(148)/513 = 38.95	-15.95	6.53
15	29	135(148)/513 = 38.95	-9.95	2.54
16	53	135(96)/513 = 25.26	27.74	30.45
Total	513	513		$\chi^2 = 114.12$

Rejection region: $\chi^2 > \chi^2_{\alpha,(r-1)(c-1} = \chi^2_{.05,9} = 16.9190$

Conclusion: $\chi^2 = 114.12$, p-value = 0. There is sufficient evidence to conclude that there is a relationship.

16.32 H_0 : The two variables (results and financial ties) are independent

H_1 : The two variables are dependent

Cell i	f_i	e_i	$(f_i - e_i)$	$(f_i - e_i)^2 / e_i$
1	29	30(48)/70 = 20.57	8.43	3.45
2	1	30(22)/70 = 9.43	-8.43	7.54
3	10	17(48)/70 = 11.66	-1.66	.24
4	7	17(22)/70 = 5.34	1.66	.52
5	9	23(48)/70 = 15.77	-6.77	2.91
6	14	23(22)/70 =7.23	6.77	6.34
Total	70	70		$\chi^2 = 21.00$

Rejection region: $\chi^2 > \chi^2_{\alpha,(r-1)(c-1} = \chi^2_{05,2} = 5.99147$

$\chi^2 = 21.00$, p-value = 0. There is sufficient evidence to infer that the research findings are related to whether drug companies fund the research.

16.34 H_0 : The data are normally distributed

H_1 : The data are not normally distributed

Interval	Probability	Expected Value e_i	Observed Value f_i	$f_i - e_i$	$(f_i - e_i)^2 / e_i$
$Z \le -1.5$	.0668	6.68	10	3.32	1.65
$-1.5 < Z \le -0.5$	.2417	24.17	18	-6.17	1.58
$-0.5 < Z \le 0.5$	.3829	38.29	48	9.71	2.46
$0.5 < Z \le 1.5$	.2417	24.17	16	-8.17	2.76
$Z > 1.5$	.0668	6.68	8	1.32	0.26
Total	1	100	100		$\chi^2 = 8.71$

Rejection region: $\chi^2 > \chi^2_{\alpha,k-3} = \chi^2_{05,2} = 5.99147$

$\chi^2 = 8.71$, p-value = .0128. There is enough evidence to infer that the data are not normally distributed.

16.36 H_0 : Times are normally distributed

H_1 : Times are not normally distributed.

	A	B	C	D
1	**Chi-Squared Test of Normality**			
2				
3		*Hours*		
4	Mean	7.15		
5	Standard deviation	1.65		
6	Observations	200		
7				
8	Intervals	Probability	Expected	Observed
9	(z <= -1.5)	0.0668	13.36	11
10	(-1.5 < z <= -0.5)	0.2417	48.35	55
11	(-0.5 < z <= 0.5)	0.3829	76.59	52
12	(0.5 < z <= 1.5)	0.2417	48.35	67
13	(z > 1.5)	0.0668	13.36	15
14				
15				
16	chi-squared Stat	16.6238		
17	df	2		
18	p-value	0.0002		
19	chi-squared Critical	4.6052		

$\chi^2 = 16.6238$, p-value = .0002. There is sufficient evidence to infer that the amount of time at part-time jobs is not normally distributed.

16.38 Successful firms:

H_0 : Productivity in successful firms is normally distributed

H_1 : Productivity in successful firms is not normally distributed

	A	B	C	D
1	**Chi-Squared Test of Normality**			
2				
3		*Successful*		
4	Mean	5.02		
5	Standard deviation	1.39		
6	Observations	200		
7				
8	Intervals	Probability	Expected	Observed
9	(z <= -1.5)	0.0668	13.36	12
10	(-1.5 < z <= -0.5)	0.2417	48.35	52
11	(-0.5 < z <= 0.5)	0.3829	76.59	72
12	(0.5 < z <= 1.5)	0.2417	48.35	55
13	(z > 1.5)	0.0668	13.36	9
14				
15				
16	chi-squared Stat	3.0288		
17	df	2		
18	p-value	0.2199		
19	chi-squared Critical	5.9915		

χ^2 =3.0288, p-value = .2199. There is not enough evidence to infer that productivity in successful firms is not normally distributed.

Unsuccessful firms:

H_0 : Productivity in unsuccessful firms is normally distributed

H_1 : Productivity in unsuccessful firms is not normally distributed

	A	B	C	D
1	**Chi-Squared Test of Normality**			
2				
3		*Unsuccessful*		
4	Mean	7.80		
5	Standard deviation	3.09		
6	Observations	200		
7				
8	Intervals	Probability	Expected	Observed
9	(z <= -1.5)	0.0668	13.36	12
10	(-1.5 < z <= -0.5)	0.2417	48.35	47
11	(-0.5 < z <= 0.5)	0.3829	76.59	83
12	(0.5 < z <= 1.5)	0.2417	48.35	44
13	(z > 1.5)	0.0668	13.36	14
14				
15				
16	chi-squared Stat	1.1347		
17	df	2		
18	p-value	0.567		
19	chi-squared Critical	5.9915		

$\chi^2 = 1.1347$, p-value = .5670. There is not enough evidence to infer that productivity in unsuccessful firms is not normally distributed.

16.40 H_0 : Matched pairs differences of sales are normally distributed

H_1 : Matched pairs differences of sales are not normally distributed

	A	B	C	D
1	**Chi-Squared Test of Normality**			
2				
3		*Difference*		
4	Mean	19.75		
5	Standard deviation	30.63		
6	Observations	40		
7				
8	Intervals	Probability	Expected	Observed
9	(z <= -1)	0.1587	6.35	6
10	(-1 < z <= 0)	0.3413	13.65	14
11	(0 < z <= 1)	0.3413	13.65	14
12	(z > 1)	0.1587	6.35	6
13				
14				
15				
16	chi-squared Stat	0.0553		
17	df	1		
18	p-value	0.8140		
19	chi-squared Critical	2.7055		

$\chi^2 = .0553$, p-value = .8140. There is not enough evidence to infer that matched pairs difference of sales iis not normally distributed.

16.42 $H_0: p_1 = .2,\ p_2 = .2,\ p_3 = .2,\ p_4 = .2,\ p_5 = .2$

H_1: At least one p_i is not equal to its specified value.

Cell i	f_i	e_i	$(f_i - e_i)$	$(f_i - e_i)^2 / e_i$
1	87	362(.2) = 72.4	14.6	2.94
2	62	362(.2) = 72.4	-10.4	1.49
3	71	362(.2) = 72.4	-1.4	0.03
4	68	362(.2) = 72.4	-4.4	0.27
5	74	362(.2) = 72.4	1.6	0.04
Total	362	362		$\chi^2 = 4.77$

Rejection region: $\chi^2 > \chi^2_{\alpha,k-1} = \chi^2_{.05,4} = 9.48773$

Conclusion: $\chi^2 = 4.77$, p-value = .3119. There is not enough evidence to infer that absenteeism is higher on some days of the week.

16.44 H_0 : The two variables (satisfaction and relationship) are independent

H_1 : The two variables are dependent

Cell i	f_i	e_i	$(f_i - e_i)$	$(f_i - e_i)^2 / e_i$
1	21	171(91)/447 = 34.81	-13.81	5.48
2	25	171(122)/447 = 46.67	-21.67	10.06
3	54	171(114)/447 = 43.61	10.39	2.48
4	71	171(120)/447 = 45.91	25.09	13.72
5	39	176(91)/447 = 35.83	3.17	0.28
6	49	176(122)/447 = 48.04	0.96	0.02
7	50	176(114)/447 = 44.89	5.11	0.58
8	38	176(120)/447 = 47.25	-9.25	1.81
9	31	100(91)/447 = 20.36	10.64	5 56
10	48	100(122)/447 = 27.29	20.71	15.71
11	10	100(114)/447 = 25.50	-15.50	9.42
12	11	100(120)/447 = 26.85	-15.85	9.35
Total	447	447		$\chi^2 = 74.47$

Rejection region: $\chi^2 > \chi^2_{\alpha,(r-1)(c-1} = \chi^2_{.05,6} = 12.5916$

Conclusion: $\chi^2 = 74.47$, p-value = 0. There is sufficient evidence to infer that the level of job satisfaction depends on boss/employee gender relationship.

16.46 H_0 : The two variables (method and quit) are independent

H_1 : The two variables are dependent

	A	B	C	D	E	F	G
1	**Contingency Table**						
2							
3		*Quit*					
4	*Method*		1	2	3	4	TOTAL
5		1	104	125	32	49	310
6		2	14	17	5	9	45
7		TOTAL	118	142	37	58	355
8							
9							
10		chi-squared Stat			0.5803		
11		df			3		
12		p-value			0.9009		
13		chi-squared Critical			7.8147		

$\chi^2 = .5803$, p-value = .9009. There is not enough evidence to infer that the four methods differ in their success rates.

16.48a The expected frequency is 1/49.

b $H_0: p_1 = 1/49,\ p_2 = 1/49, \ldots,\ p_{49} = 1/49$

H_1: At least one p_i is not equal to its specified value.

Number i	f_i	e_i	$(f_i - e_i)$	$(f_i - e_i)^2 / e_i$
1	5	312(1/49) = 6.37	-1.38	0.29
2	6	312(1/49) = 6.37	-0.38	0.02
3	7	312(1/49) = 6.37	0.63	0.06
.		.		
.		.		
.		.		
47	6	312(1/49) = 6.37	-0.37	0.02
48	10	312(1/49) = 6.37	3.63	2.07
49	6	312(1/49) = 6.37	-0.37	0.02
Total	312	312		$\chi^2 = 38.22$

Conclusion: $\chi^2 = 38.22$, p-value = .8427. There is not enough evidence to infer that the numbers were not generated randomly.

16.50 Binomial probabilities with n = 5 and p = .5: P(X = 0) = .0313, P(X = 1) = .1563, P(X = 2) = .3125, P(X = 3) = .3125, P(X = 4) = .1563, P(X = 5) = .0313

$H_0: p_0 = .0313, p_1 = .1563,\ p_2 = .3125,\ p_3 = .3125,\ p_4 = .1563,\ p_5 = .0313$

H_1 : At least one p_i is not equal to its specified value.

Cell i	f_i	e_i	$(f_i - e_i)$	$(f_i - e_i)^2 / e_i$
0	8	200(.0313) = 6.26	1.74	0.48
1	35	200(.1563) = 31.26	3.74	0.45
2	57	200(.3125) = 62.50	-5.50	0.48
3	69	200(.3125) = 62.50	6.50	0.68
4	28	200(.1563) = 31.26	-3.26	0.34
5	3	200(.0313) = 6.26	-3.26	1.70
Total	200	200		$\chi^2 = 4.13$

Rejection region: $\chi^2 > \chi^2_{\alpha,6-1-2} = \chi^2_{.05,3} = 7.81473$

$\chi^2 = 4.13$, p-value = .5310. There is not enough evidence to infer that at the number of boys in families with 5 children is not a binomial random variable with p =.5.

16.52 H_0 : The two variables (faculty and retire) are independent

H_1 : The two variables are dependent

	A	B	C	D	E	F	G	H
1	**Contingency Table**							
2								
3		*Retire*						
4	*Faculty*		1	2	3	4	5	TOTAL
5		1	174	51	113	42	86	466
6		2	13	7	22	7	6	55
7		TOTAL	187	58	135	49	92	521
8								
9								
10		chi-squared Stat			9.732			
11		df			4			
12		p-value			0.0452			
13		chi-squared Critical			9.4877			

$\chi^2 = 9.732$, p-value = .0452. There is enough evidence to infer that whether a professor wishes to retire is related to the faculty.

16.54 H_0 : The two variables (newspaper and subscribe) are independent

H_1 : The two variables are dependent

	A	B	C	D	E	F
1	**Contingency Table**					
2						
3		*Subscribe*				
4	*Newspaper*		1	2	3	TOTAL
5		1	90	160	85	335
6		2	32	21	12	65
7		TOTAL	122	181	97	400
8						
9						
10		chi-squared Stat			12.8731	
11		df			2	
12		p-value			0.0016	
13		chi-squared Critical			5.9915	

$\chi^2 = 12.8731$, p-value = .0016. There is enough evidence to infer that the response to subscribing to the new paper differs between the readers of the current newspapers.

16.56 H_0 : The two variables (income category and show) are independent

H_1 : The two variables are dependent

	A	B	C	D	E	F	G
1	**Contingency Table**						
2							
3		*Shows*					
4	*Income*		1	2	3	4	TOTAL
5		1	43	63	76	44	226
6		2	25	60	69	41	195
7		3	6	26	33	41	106
8		4	47	103	112	66	328
9		5	226	418	280	221	1145
10		TOTAL	347	670	570	413	2000
11							
12							
13		chi-squared Stat			58.8799		
14		df			12		
15		p-value			0		
16		chi-squared Critical			21.0261		

$\chi^2 = 58.8799$, p-value = 0. There is enough evidence to conclude that what people watch at 11:40 P.M. is related to income.

16.58 H_0 : The two variables are (type of work and segment) independent

H_1 : The two variables are dependent

	A	B	C	D	E	F
1	**Contingency Table**					
2						
3		*Segment*				
4	*Work*		1	2	3	TOTAL
5		1	157	44	217	418
6		2	219	53	264	536
7		3	256	102	524	882
8		TOTAL	632	199	1005	1836
9						
10						
11		chi-squared Stat			23.0946	
12		df			4	
13		p-value			0.0001	
14		chi-squared Critical			9.4877	

$\chi^2 = 23.0946$, p-value = .0001. There is enough evidence to infer that there are differences in employment between the three market segments.

16.60 H_0 : The two variables (breakfast and group) are independent

H_1 : The two variables are dependent

	A	B	C	D	E	F	G
1	**Contingency Table**						
2							
3		*Group*					
4	*Breakfast*		1	2	3	4	TOTAL
5		1	3	15	29	222	269
6		2	44	53	95	292	484
7		3	17	10	79	135	241
8		4	25	77	77	77	256
9		TOTAL	89	155	280	726	1250
10							
11							
12		chi-squared Stat			206.4984		
13		df			9		
14		p-value			0		
15		chi-squared Critical			16.919		

$\chi^2 = 206.4908$, p-value = 0. There is enough evidence to infer that there are differences in frequency of healthy breakfasts between the three four segments.

Chapter 17

17.2 a

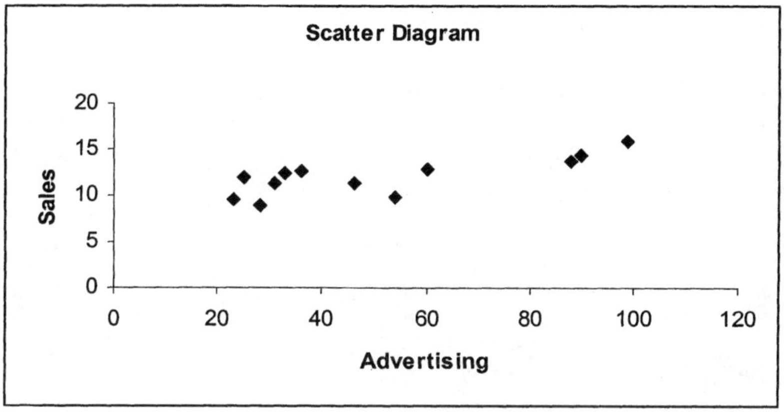

b

	x_i	y_i	x_i^2	y_i^2	x_iy_i
	23	9.6	529	92.16	220.8
	46	11.3	2,116	127.69	519.8
	60	12.8	3,600	163.84	768.0
	54	9.8	2,916	96.04	529.2
	28	8.9	784	79.21	249.2
	33	12.5	1,089	156.25	412.5
	25	12.0	625	144.00	300.0
	31	11.4	961	129.96	353.4
	36	12.6	1,296	158.76	453.6
	88	13.7	7,744	187.69	1205.6
	90	14.4	8,100	207.36	1296.0
	99	15.9	9,801	252.81	1,574.1
Total	613	144.9	39,561	1,795.77	7,882.2

$$\sum_{i=1}^{n} x_i = 613 \quad \sum_{i=1}^{n} y_i = 144.9 \quad \sum_{i=1}^{n} x_i^2 = 39,561 \quad \sum_{i=1}^{n} x_i y_i = 7,882.2$$

$$s_{xy} = \frac{1}{n-1}\left[\sum_{i=1}^{n} x_i y_i - \frac{\sum_{i=1}^{n} x_i \sum_{i=1}^{n} y_i}{n}\right] = \frac{1}{12-1}\left[7,882.2 - \frac{(613)(144.9)}{12}\right] = 43.66$$

$$s_x^2 = \frac{1}{n-1}\left[\sum_{i=1}^{n} x_i^2 - \frac{\left(\sum_{i=1}^{n} x_i\right)^2}{n}\right] = \frac{1}{12-1}\left[39{,}561 - \frac{(613)^2}{12}\right] = 749.7$$

$$b_1 = \frac{s_{xy}}{s_x^2} = \frac{43.66}{749.7} = .0582$$

$$\bar{x} = \frac{\sum x_i}{n} = \frac{613}{12} = 51.08$$

$$\bar{y} = \frac{\sum y_i}{n} = \frac{144.9}{12} = 12.08$$

$$b_0 = \bar{y} - b_1\bar{x} = 12.08 - (.0582)(51.08) = 9.107$$

The sample regression line is

$$\hat{y} = 9.107 + .0582x$$

The slope tells us that for each additional thousand dollars of advertising sales increase on average by .0582 million. The y-intercept has no practical meaning.

17.4

	x_i	y_i	x_i^2	y_i^2	x_iy_i
	42	18	1,764	324	756
	34	6	1,156	36	204
	25	0	625	0	0
	35	–1	1,225	1	–35
	37	13	1,369	169	481
	38	14	1,444	196	532
	31	7	961	49	217
	33	7	1,089	49	231
	19	–9	361	81	–171
	29	8	841	64	232
	38	8	1,444	64	304
	28	5	784	25	140
	29	3	841	9	87
	36	14	1,296	196	504
	18	–7	324	49	–126
Total	472	86	15,524	1,312	3,356

$$\sum_{i=1}^{n} x_i = 472 \quad \sum_{i=1}^{n} y_i = 86 \quad \sum_{i=1}^{n} x_i^2 = 15{,}524 \quad \sum_{i=1}^{n} x_iy_i = 3{,}356$$

$$s_{xy} = \frac{1}{n-1}\left[\sum_{i=1}^{n} x_i y_i - \frac{\sum_{i=1}^{n} x_i \sum_{i=1}^{n} y_i}{n}\right] = \frac{1}{15-1}\left[3{,}356 - \frac{(472)(86}{15}\right] = 46.42$$

$$s_x^2 = \frac{1}{n-1}\left[\sum_{i=1}^{n} x_i^2 - \frac{\left(\sum_{i=1}^{n} x_i\right)^2}{n}\right] = \frac{1}{15-1}\left[15{,}524 - \frac{(472)^2}{15}\right] = 47.98$$

$$b_1 = \frac{s_{xy}}{s_x^2} = \frac{46.42}{47.98} = .9675$$

$$\bar{x} = \frac{\sum x_i}{n} = \frac{472}{15} = 31.47$$

$$\bar{y} = \frac{\sum y_i}{n} = \frac{86}{15} = 5.73$$

$$b_0 = \bar{y} - b_1\bar{x} = 5.73 - (.9675)(31.47) = -24.72$$

The sample regression line is

$$\hat{y} = -24.72 + .9675x$$

The slope coefficient indicates that for each additional hour of television weight increases on average by .9675 pounds. The y-intercept is the point at which the regression line hits the y–axis; it has no practical meaning.

17.6 a

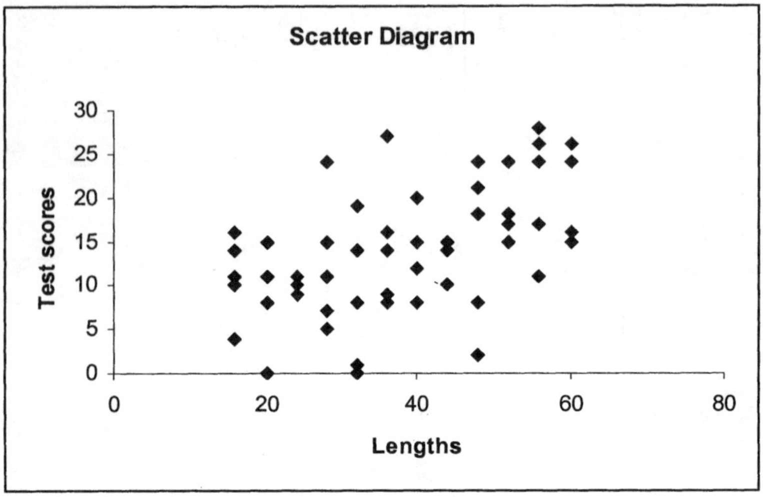

b $b_1 = \frac{s_{xy}}{s_x^2} = \frac{51.86}{193.9} = .2675$, $b_0 = \bar{y} - b_1\bar{x} = 13.80 - .2675(38.00) = 3.635$

Regression line: $\hat{y} = 3.635 + .2675x$ (Excel: $\hat{y} = 3.636 + .2675x$)

c $b_1 = .2675$; for each additional second of commercial, the memory test score increases on average by .2675. $b_0 = 3.64$ is the y-intercept.

17.8 a

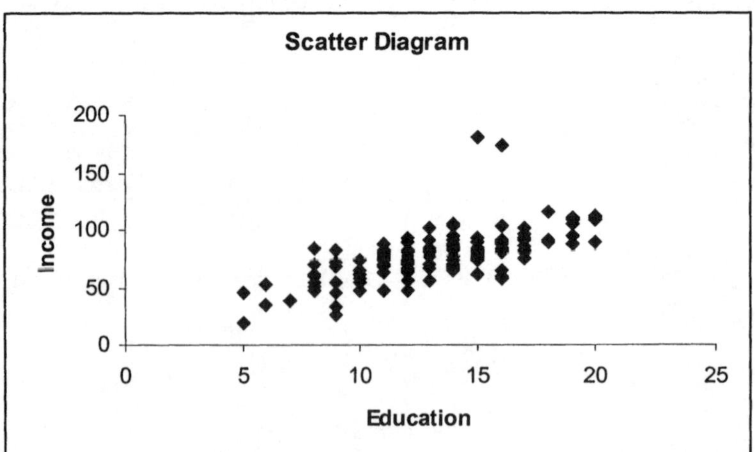

b $b_1 = \frac{s_{xy}}{s_x^2} = \frac{46.02}{11.12} = 4.138$, $b_0 = \bar{y} - b_1\bar{x} = 78.13 - 4.138(13.17) = 23.63$.

Regression line: $\hat{y} = 23.63 + 4.138x$ (Excel: $\hat{y} = 23.63 + 4.137x$)

c The slope coefficient tells us that for each additional year of education income increases on average by $4.138 thousand ($4,138). The y-intercept has no meaning.

17.10a $b_1 = \frac{s_{xy}}{s_x^2} = \frac{20.55}{108.3} = .1898$, $b_0 = \bar{y} - b_1\bar{x} = 14.43 - .1898(37.64) = 7.286$.

Regression line: $\hat{y} = 7.286 + .1898x$ (Excel: $\hat{y} = 7.287 + .1897x$)

b For each additional cigarette the number of days absent from work increases on average by .1898. The y-intercept has no meaning.

17.12a $b_1 = \frac{s_{xy}}{s_x^2} = \frac{30,945}{688.2} = 44.97$, $b_0 = \bar{y} - b_1\bar{x} = 6,465 - 44.97(53.93) = 4040$.

Regression line: $\hat{y} = 4040 + 44.97x$ (Excel: $\hat{y} = 4040 + 44.97x$)

17.14 $b_1 = \frac{s_{xy}}{s_x^2} = \frac{19.07}{56.36} = .3384$, $b_0 = \bar{y} - b_1\bar{x} = 12.13 - .3384(40.93) = -1.721$.

Regression line: $\hat{y} = -1.721 + .3384x$ (Excel: : $\hat{y} = -1.725 + .3385x$)

17.16 a $b_1 = \frac{s_{xy}}{s_x^2} = \frac{-10.78}{35.47} = -.3039$, $b_0 = \bar{y} - b_1\bar{x} = 17.20 - (-.3039)(11.33) = 20.64$.

Regression line: $\hat{y} = 20.64 - .3039x$ (Excel: $\hat{y} = 20.64 - .3038x$)

b The slope indicates that for each additional one percentage point increase in the vacancy rate rents on average decrease by $.3039. The y-intercept is 20.64.

17.18 $b_1 = \frac{s_{xy}}{s_x^2} = \frac{.8258}{16.07} = .0514$, $b_0 = \bar{y} - b_1\bar{x} = 93.89 - .0514(79.47) = 89.81$.

Regression line: $\hat{y} = 89.81 + .0514x$ (Excel: $\hat{y} = 89.81 + .0514x$)

17.20 For each number of years of education incomes are normally distributed with constant variance and a mean that is a linear function of the number of years of education.

17.22 a $s_y^2 = \frac{1}{n-1}\left[\sum_{i=1}^{n} y_i^2 - \frac{\left(\sum_{i=1}^{n} y_i\right)^2}{n}\right] = \frac{1}{12-1}\left[1{,}795.77 - \frac{(144.9)^2}{12}\right] = 4.191$

$$SSE = (n-1)\left(s_y^2 - \frac{s_{xy}^2}{s_x^2}\right) = (12-1)\left(4.191 - \frac{(43.66)^2}{749.7}\right) = 18.13$$

$s_\varepsilon = \sqrt{\frac{SSE}{n-2}} = \sqrt{\frac{18.13}{12-2}} = 1.347$ (Excel: $s_\varepsilon = 1.347$)

b $H_0: \beta_1 = 0$

$H_1: \beta_1 \neq 0$

Rejection region: $t > t_{\alpha/2,n-2} = t_{.025,10} = 2.228$ or $t < -t_{\alpha/2,n-2} = -t_{.025,10} = -2.228$

$$s_{b_1} = \frac{s_\varepsilon}{\sqrt{(n-1)s_x^2}} = \frac{1.347}{\sqrt{(12-1)(749.7)}} = .0148$$

$t = \frac{b_1 - \beta_1}{s_{b_1}} = \frac{.0582 - 0}{.0148} = 3.93$ (Excel: t = 3.93, p–value = .0028. There is enough evidence to infer a linear relationship between advertising and sales.

c $b_1 \pm t_{\alpha/2,n-2} s_{b_1} = .0582 \pm 2.228(.0148) = .0582 \pm .0330$ LCL = .0252, UCL = .0912

d $R^2 = \frac{s_{xy}^2}{s_x^2 s_y^2} = \frac{(43.66)^2}{(749.7)(4.191)} = .6067$ (Excel: $R^2 = .6066$). 60.67% of the variation in sales is explained by the variation in advertising.

e There is evidence of a linear relationship. For each additional dollar of advertising sales increase, on average by .0582.

17.24 $s_y^2 = \frac{1}{n-1}\left[\sum_{i=1}^{n} y_i^2 - \frac{\left(\sum_{i=1}^{n} y_i\right)^2}{n}\right] = \frac{1}{15-1}\left[1{,}312 - \frac{(86)^2}{15}\right] = 58.50$

$SSE = (n-1)\left(s_y^2 - \frac{s_{xy}^2}{s_x^2}\right) = (15-1)\left(58.50 - \frac{(46.42)^2}{47.98}\right) = 190.2$

$s_\varepsilon = \sqrt{\frac{SSE}{n-2}} = \sqrt{\frac{190.2}{15-2}} = 3.825$

$H_0: \beta_1 = 0$

$H_1: \beta_1 \neq 0$

Rejection region: $t > t_{\alpha/2,n-2} = t_{.025,13} = 2.160$ or $t < -t_{\alpha/2,n-2} = -t_{.025,13} = -2.160$

$s_{b_1} = \frac{s_\varepsilon}{\sqrt{(n-1)s_x^2}} = \frac{3.825}{\sqrt{(15-1)(47.98)}} = .1476$

$t = \frac{b_1 - \beta_1}{s_{b_1}} = \frac{.9675 - 0}{.1476} = 6.55$ (Excel: t = 6.55, p–value = 0.) There is enough evidence to conclude that there is a linear relationship between hours of television viewing and how overweight the child is.

17.26 a $SSE = (n-1)\left(s_y^2 - \frac{s_{xy}^2}{s_x^2}\right) = (60-1)\left(47.96 - \frac{(51.86)^2}{193.9}\right) = 2{,}011$

$s_\varepsilon = \sqrt{\frac{SSE}{n-2}} = \sqrt{\frac{2{,}011}{60-2}} = 5.888$ (Excel: $s_\varepsilon = 5.888$). Relative to the values of the dependent variable the standard error of estimate appears to be large indicating a weak linear relationship.

b $R^2 = \frac{s_{xy}^2}{s_x^2 s_y^2} = \frac{(51.86)^2}{(193.9)(47.96)} = .2892$ (Excel: $R^2 = .2893$).

c $H_0: \beta_1 = 0$

$H_1: \beta_1 \neq 0$

Rejection region: $t > t_{\alpha/2,n-2} = t_{.025,58} \approx 2.000$ or $t < -t_{\alpha/2,n-2} = -t_{.025,58} = -2.000$

$$s_{b_1} = \frac{s_\varepsilon}{\sqrt{(n-1)s_x^2}} = \frac{5.888}{\sqrt{(60-1)(193.9)}} = .0550$$

$t = \frac{b_1 - \beta_1}{s_{b_1}} = \frac{.2675 - 0}{.0550} = 4.86$ (Excel: t = 4.86, p–value = 0). There is enough evidence to infer a linear relationship between memory test scores and length of commercial.

d $b_1 \pm t_{\alpha/2,n-2} s_{b_1} = .2675 \pm 1.671(.0550) = .2675 \pm .0919$ LCL = .1756, UCL = .3594

17.28 $SSE = (n-1)\left(s_y^2 - \frac{s_{xy}^2}{s_x^2}\right) = (150-1)\left(437.9 - \frac{(46.02)^2}{11.12}\right) = 36{,}870$

$$s_\varepsilon = \sqrt{\frac{SSE}{n-2}} = \sqrt{\frac{36{,}870}{150-2}} = 15.78$$

$H_0 : \beta_1 = 0$

$H_1 : \beta_1 \neq 0$

Rejection region: $t > t_{\alpha/2,n-2} = t_{.025,148} \approx 1.977$ or $t < -t_{\alpha/2,n-2} = -t_{.025,148} = -1.977$

$$s_{b_1} = \frac{s_\varepsilon}{\sqrt{(n-1)s_x^2}} = \frac{15.78}{\sqrt{(150-1)(11.12)}} = .3877$$

$t = \frac{b_1 - \beta_1}{s_{b_1}} = \frac{4.138 - 0}{.3877} = 10.67$ (Excel: t = 10.67, p–value = 0.) There is evidence of a linear relationship between education and income.

17.30 $SSE = (n-1)\left(s_y^2 - \frac{s_{xy}^2}{s_x^2}\right) = (231-1)\left(19.80 - \frac{(20.55)^2}{108.3}\right) = 3657$

$$s_\varepsilon = \sqrt{\frac{SSE}{n-2}} = \sqrt{\frac{3657}{231-2}} = 3.996$$

$H_0 : \beta_1 = 0$

$H_1 : \beta_1 \neq 0$

Rejection region: $t > t_{\alpha/2,n-2} = t_{.025,229} \approx 1.960$ or $t < -t_{\alpha/2,n-2} = -t_{025,229} \approx -1.960$

$$s_{b_1} = \frac{s_\varepsilon}{\sqrt{(n-1)s_x^2}} = \frac{3.996}{\sqrt{(231-1)(108.3)}} = .02532$$

$t = \frac{b_1 - \beta_1}{s_{b_1}} = \frac{.1898 - 0}{.02532} = 7.50$ (Excel: t =7.49, p–value = 0.) There is evidence of a linear relationship between cigarettes smoked and the number of sick days.

17.32 $SSE = (n-1)\left(s_y^2 - \frac{s_{xy}^2}{s_x^2}\right) = (40-1)\left(11{,}918{,}489 - \frac{(30{,}945)^2}{688.2}\right) = 410{,}554{,}683$

a $s_\varepsilon = \sqrt{\frac{SSE}{n-2}} = \sqrt{\frac{410{,}554{,}683}{40-2}} = 3{,}287$ (Excel: $s_\varepsilon = 3{,}287$). There is a weak linear relationship.

b $H_0: \beta_1 = 0$

$H_1: \beta_1 \neq 0$

Rejection region: $t > t_{\alpha/2,n-2} = t_{.025,38} \approx 2.021$ or $t < -t_{\alpha/2,n-2} = -t_{.025,38} \approx -2.021$

$s_{b_1} = \frac{s_\varepsilon}{\sqrt{(n-1)s_x^2}} = \frac{3{,}287}{\sqrt{(40-1)(688.2)}} = 20.06$

$t = \frac{b_1 - \beta_1}{s_{b_1}} = \frac{44.97 - 0}{20.06} = 2.24$ (Excel: t = 2.24, p–value = .0309); evidence of a linear relationship.

c $R^2 = \frac{s_{xy}^2}{s_x^2 s_y^2} = \frac{(30{,}945)^2}{(688.2)(11{,}918{,}489)} = .1167$ (Excel: R^2 = .) 11.67% of the variation in percent damage is explained by the variation in distance to the fire station.

17.34 $SSE = (n-1)\left(s_y^2 - \frac{s_{xy}^2}{s_x^2}\right) = (140-1)\left(20.73 - \frac{(19.07)^2}{56.36}\right) = 1985$

$s_\varepsilon = \sqrt{\frac{SSE}{n-2}} = \sqrt{\frac{1{,}985}{140-2}} = 3.793$ (Excel: $s_\varepsilon = 3.792$).

$R^2 = \frac{s_{xy}^2}{s_x^2 s_y^2} = \frac{(19.07)^2}{(56.36)(20.73)} = .3113$ (Excel: $R^2 = .3114$) 31.13% of the variation in the duration of flu symptoms is explained by the variation in age.

$H_0: \beta_1 = 0$

$H_1: \beta_1 \neq 0$

Rejection region: $t > t_{\alpha/2,n-2} = t_{.025,138} \approx 1.977$ or $t < -t_{\alpha/2,n-2} = -t_{.025,138} \approx -1.977$

$$s_{b_1} = \frac{s_\varepsilon}{\sqrt{(n-1)s_x^2}} = \frac{3.793}{\sqrt{(140-1)(56.36)}} = .04285$$

$t = \frac{b_1 - \beta_1}{s_{b_1}} = \frac{.3384 - 0}{.04285} = 7.90$ (Excel: t =, p–value = 0.) There is enough evidence of a linear relationship.

17.36 $SSE = (n-1)\left(s_y^2 - \frac{s_{xy}^2}{s_x^2}\right) = (30-1)\left(11.24 - \frac{(-10.78)^2}{35.47}\right) = 230.9$

$s_\varepsilon = \sqrt{\frac{SSE}{n-2}} = \sqrt{\frac{230.9}{30-2}} = 2.872$ (Excel: $s_\varepsilon = 2.873$).

$H_0: \beta_1 = 0$

$H_1: \beta_1 \neq 0$

Rejection region: $t > t_{\alpha/2,n-2} = t_{.025,28} = 2.048$ or $t < -t_{\alpha/2,n-2} = -t_{.025,28} = -2.048$

$$s_{b_1} = \frac{s_\varepsilon}{\sqrt{(n-1)s_x^2}} = \frac{2.872}{\sqrt{(30-1)(35.47)}} = .08955$$

$t = \frac{b_1 - \beta_1}{s_{b_1}} = \frac{-.3039 - 0}{.08955} = -3.39$ (Excel: $t = -3.39$, p–value = .0021.) There is sufficient evidence to conclude that office rents and vacancy rates are linearly related.

17.38 $R^2 = \frac{s_{xy}^2}{s_x^2 s_y^2} = \frac{(.8258)^2}{(16.07)(1.283)} = .0331$ (Excel: $R^2 = .0331$) 3.31% of the variation in percentage of defectives is explained by the variation in aptitude test scores.

$SSE = (n-1)\left(s_y^2 - \frac{s_{xy}^2}{s_x^2}\right) = (45-1)\left(1.283 - \frac{(.8258)^2}{16.07}\right) = 54.58$

$s_\varepsilon = \sqrt{\frac{SSE}{n-2}} = \sqrt{\frac{54.58}{45-2}} = 1.127$ (Excel: $s_\varepsilon = 1.127$).

$H_0: \beta_1 = 0$

$H_1: \beta_1 \neq 0$

Rejection region: $t > t_{\alpha/2,n-2} = t_{025,43} \approx 2.014$ or $t < -t_{\alpha/2,n-2} = -t_{.025,43} \approx -2.014$

$$s_{b_1} = \frac{s_\varepsilon}{\sqrt{(n-1)s_x^2}} = \frac{1.127}{\sqrt{(45-1)(16.07)}} = .04238$$

$t = \frac{b_1 - \beta_1}{s_{b_1}} = \frac{.0516 - 0}{.04238} = 1.22$ (Excel: t = 1.21, p–value = .2319) There is not enough evidence to conclude that aptitude test scores and percentage of defectives are linearly related.

17.40 $H_0: \rho = 0$

$H_1: \rho \neq 0$

Rejection region: $t > t_{\alpha/2,n-2} = t_{.025,58} \approx 2.000$ or $t < -t_{\alpha/2,n-2} = -t_{025,58} = -2.000$

$$r = \frac{s_{xy}}{s_x s_y} = \frac{51.86}{\sqrt{(193.9)(47.96)}} = .5378$$

$t = r\sqrt{\frac{n-2}{1-r^2}} = (.5378)\sqrt{\frac{60-2}{1-(.5378)^2}} = 4.86$ (Excel: t = 4.86, p–value = 0) This result is identical to the one produced in Exercise 17.26.

17.42 $H_0: \rho = 0$

$H_1: \rho \neq 0$

Rejection region: $t > t_{\alpha,n-2} = t_{.05,229} \approx 1.645$

$$r = \frac{s_{xy}}{s_x s_y} = \frac{20.55}{\sqrt{(108.3)(19.80)}} = .4438$$

$t = r\sqrt{\frac{n-2}{1-r^2}} = (.4438)\sqrt{\frac{231-2}{1-(.4438)^2}} = 7.49$ (Excel: t = 7.49, p–value = 0.) There is evidence of a positive linear relationship between cigarettes smoked and the number of sick days.

17.44 Motorola's beta is 1.12, which means its stock is more volatile than the market. The coefficient of determination is .1142, which means that only 11.42% of the total risk is market related. The remaining 88.58% of the total risk is associated specifically with Motorola.

17.46 Gillette's beta is .777, which means its stock is less volatile than the market. The coefficient of determination is .1459, which means that only 14.59% of the total risk is market related. The remaining 85.41% of the total risk is associated specifically with Gillette.

17.48 Seagram's beta is 1.17, which means its stock is more volatile than the market. The coefficient of determination is .2022, which means that only 20.22% of the total risk is market related. The remaining 79.78% of the total risk is associated specifically with Seagram.

17.50 McDonalds' beta is 1.05, which means its stock is more volatile than the market. The coefficient of determination is .2772, which means that only 27.72% of the total risk is market related. The remaining 72.28% of the total risk is associated specifically with McDonalds.

17.52 Biomira's beta is 1.51, which means its stock is more volatile than the market. The coefficient of determination is .1131, which means that only 11.31% of the total risk is market related. The remaining 88.69% of the total risk is associated specifically with Biomira.

17.54 Petro Canada's beta is .539, which means its stock is less volatile than the market. The coefficient of determination is .1216, which means that only 12.16% of the total risk is market related. The remaining 87.84% of the total risk is associated specifically with Petro Canada.

17.56 National Bank's beta is .691, which means its stock is less volatile than the market. The coefficient of determination is .3199, which means that 31.99% of the total risk is market related. The remaining 68.01% of the total risk is associated specifically with National Bank.

17.58 Bombardier's beta is .709, which means its stock is less volatile than the market. The coefficient of determination is .2973, which means that only 29.73% of the total risk is market related. The remaining 70.27% of the total risk is associated specifically with Bombardier.

17.60 The stock that is least sensitive is Suncor whose beta is .326. The most sensitive is Lorus with a beta of 1.69. Suncor's R^2 is 5.75%, which means that its firm–specific risk is 94.25%. The stock with the smallest firm–specific risk is National Bank (68.01%).

17.62 $\hat{y} = b_0 + b_1 x_g = 91.07 + .0582(90) = 14.35$

Prediction interval: $\hat{y} \pm t_{\alpha/2,n-2} s_\varepsilon \sqrt{1 + \frac{1}{n} + \frac{(x_g - \bar{x})^2}{(n-1)s_x^2}}$ (where $t_{\alpha/2,n-2} = t_{.05,10} = 1.812$)

$$= 14.35 \pm 1.812(1.347)\sqrt{1 + \frac{1}{12} + \frac{(90 - 51.08)^2}{(12-1)(749.7)}} = 14.35 \pm 2.747$$

Lower prediction limit = 11.60, Upper prediction limit = 17.10 (Excel: 11.59, 17.09)

17.64 $\hat{y} = b_0 + b_1 x_g = -24.72 + .9675(30) = 4.305$

a Prediction interval: $\hat{y} \pm t_{\alpha/2,n-2} s_\varepsilon \sqrt{1 + \frac{1}{n} + \frac{(x_g - \bar{x})^2}{(n-1)s_x^2}}$ (where $t_{\alpha/2,n-2} = t_{.05,13} = 1.771$)

$$= 4.305 \pm 1.771(3.825)\sqrt{1 + \frac{1}{15} + \frac{(30 - 31.47)^2}{(15-1)(47.98)}} = 4.305 \pm 7.007$$

Lower prediction limit = –2.702, Upper prediction limit = 11.31 (Excel: –2.692, 11.32)

b Confidence interval estimate: $\hat{y} \pm t_{\alpha/2,n-2} s_\varepsilon \sqrt{\frac{1}{n} + \frac{(x_g - \bar{x})^2}{(n-1)s_x^2}}$

$$= 4.305 \pm 1.771(3.825)\sqrt{\frac{1}{15} + \frac{(30 - 31.47)^2}{(15-1)(47.98)}} = 4.305 \pm 1.791$$

LCL = 2.514, UCL = 6.096 (Excel: 2.524, 6.105)

17.66 $\hat{y} = b_0 + b_1 x_g = 3.636 + .2675(36) = 13.27$

a Prediction interval: $\hat{y} \pm t_{\alpha/2,n-2} s_\varepsilon \sqrt{1 + \frac{1}{n} + \frac{(x_g - \bar{x})^2}{(n-1)s_x^2}}$ (where $t_{\alpha/2,n-2} = t_{.025,58} \approx 2.000$)

$$= 13.27 \pm 2.000(5.888)\sqrt{1 + \frac{1}{60} + \frac{(36 - 38)^2}{(60-1)(193.9)}} = 13.27 \pm 11.88$$

Lower prediction limit =1.39, Upper prediction limit = 25.15 (Excel: 1.378, 25.15)

b Confidence interval estimate: $\hat{y} \pm t_{\alpha/2,n-2} s_\varepsilon \sqrt{\frac{1}{n} + \frac{(x_g - \bar{x})^2}{(n-1)s_x^2}}$

$$= 13.27 \pm 2.000(5.888)\sqrt{\frac{1}{60} + \frac{(36-38)^2}{(60-1)(193.9)}} = 13.27 \pm 1.536$$

LCL = 11.73, UCL = 14.81 (Excel: 11.73, 14.80)

17.68 $\hat{y} = b_0 + b_1 x_g = 23.63 + 4.138(15) = 85.70$

Confidence interval estimate: $\hat{y} \pm t_{\alpha/2,n-2} s_\varepsilon \sqrt{\frac{1}{n} + \frac{(x_g - \bar{x})^2}{(n-1)s_x^2}}$ (where $t_{\alpha/2,n-2} = t_{05,148} \approx 1.656$)

$$= 85.70 \pm 1.656(15.78)\sqrt{\frac{1}{150} + \frac{(15-13.17)^2}{(150-1)(11.12)}} = 85.70 \pm 2.436$$

LCL = 83.26, UCL = 88.14 (Excel:83.25, 88.18)

17.70 $\hat{y} = b_0 + b_1 x_g = 7.286 + .1898(30) = 12.98$

Prediction interval: $\hat{y} \pm t_{\alpha/2,n-2} s_\varepsilon \sqrt{1 + \frac{1}{n} + \frac{(x_g - \bar{x})^2}{(n-1)s_x^2}}$ (where $t_{\alpha/2,n-2} = t_{.025,229} \approx 1.960$)

$$= 12.98 \pm 1.960(3.996)\sqrt{1 + \frac{1}{231} + \frac{(30-37.64)^2}{(231-1)(108.3)}} = 12.98 \pm 7.858$$

Lower prediction limit = 5.12, Upper prediction limit = 20.84 (Excel: 5.078, 20.88)

7.72 $\hat{y} = b_0 + b_1 x_g = 4{,}040 + 44.97(50) = 6{,}289$

Confidence interval estimate: $\hat{y} \pm t_{\alpha/2,n-2} s_\varepsilon \sqrt{\frac{1}{n} + \frac{(x_g - \bar{x})^2}{(n-1)s_x^2}}$ (where $t_{\alpha/2,n-2} = t_{.025,38} \approx 2.021$)

$$= 6{,}289 \pm 2.021(3{,}287)\sqrt{\frac{1}{40} + \frac{(50-53.93)^2}{(40-1)(688.2)}} = 6{,}289 \pm 1{,}062$$

LCL = 5,227, UCL = 7,351 (Excel: LCL = 5,224, UCL = 7,352)

17.74 $\hat{y} = b_0 + b_1 x_g = -1.721 + .3384(65) = 20.28$

Confidence interval estimate: $\hat{y} \pm t_{\alpha/2,n-2} s_\varepsilon \sqrt{\frac{1}{n} + \frac{(x_g - \bar{x})^2}{(n-1)s_x^2}}$ (where $t_{\alpha/2,n-2} = t_{05,138} \approx 1.656$)

$$= 20.28 \pm 1.656(3.793)\sqrt{\frac{1}{140}+\frac{(65-40.93)^2}{(140-1)(56.36)}} = 20.28 \pm 1.789$$

LCL = 18.49, UCL = 22.07 (Excel: 18.49, 22.06)

17.76 $\hat{y} = b_0 + b_1 x_g = 20.64 - .3039(10) = 17.60$

Prediction interval: $\hat{y} \pm t_{\alpha/2,n-2} s_\varepsilon \sqrt{1+\frac{1}{n}+\frac{(x_g-\bar{x})^2}{(n-1)s_x^2}}$ (where $t_{\alpha/2,n-2} = t_{.025,28} = 2.048$)

$$= 17.60 \pm 2.048(2.872)\sqrt{1+\frac{1}{30}+\frac{(10-11.33)^2}{(30-1)(35.47)}} = 17.60 \pm 5.984$$

Lower prediction limit = 11.62 , Upper prediction limit =23.58 (Excel: 11.61, 23.59)

17.78 $\hat{y} = b_0 + b_1 x_g = 89.81 + .0514(75) = 93.64$

Confidence interval estimate: $\hat{y} \pm t_{\alpha/2,n-2} s_\varepsilon \sqrt{\frac{1}{n}+\frac{(x_g-\bar{x})^2}{(n-1)s_x^2}}$ where $t_{\alpha/2,n-2} = t_{025,43} \approx 2.014$)

$$= 93.64 \pm 2.014(1.127)\sqrt{\frac{1}{45}+\frac{(75-79.47)^2}{(45-1)(16.07)}} = 93.64 \pm .510$$

LCL = 93.13, UCL = 94.15 (Excel: 93.15, 94.17)

17.80

x_i	y_i	$\hat{y}_i = 9.107 - .0582x$	$e_i = y_i - \hat{y}_i$
23	9.6	10.45	–.85
46	11.3	11.78	–.48
60	12.8	12.60	.20
54	9.8	12.25	–2.45
28	8.9	10.74	–1.84
33	12.5	11.03	1.47
25	12.0	10.56	1.44
31	11.4	10.91	.49
36	12.6	11.20	1.40
88	13.7	14.23	–.53
90	14.4	14.35	.06
99	15.9	14.87	1.03

17.82 a & b

x_i	y_i	$\hat{y} = -24.72 + .9675x$	$e_i = y_i - \hat{y}_i$
42	18	15.92	2.09
34	6	8.18	–2.18
25	0	–.53	.53
35	–1	9.14	–10.14
37	13	11.08	1.92
38	14	12.05	1.96
31	7	5.27	1.73
33	7	7.21	–.21
19	–9	–6.34	–2.66
29	8	3.34	4.66
38	8	12.05	–4.05
28	5	2.37	2.63
29	3	3.34	–.34
36	14	10.11	3.89
18	–7	–7.31	.31

c

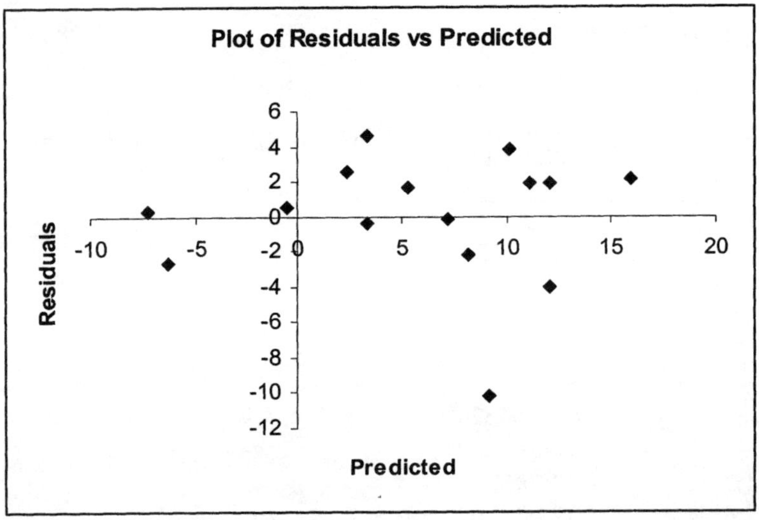

The histograms drawn below are of the standardized residuals, which make it easier to see whether the shape is extremely nonnormal. It also makes it easier to identify outliers. The shape of the resulting histogram is identical to the histogram of the residuals using the equivalent class limits.

17.84 b & c

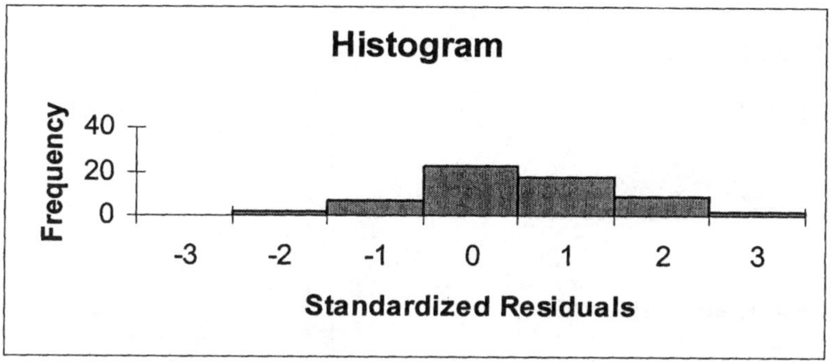

Because the histogram is approximately bell shaped the errors appear to be normally distributed.

There are two residuals whose absolute value exceeds 2.0.

d

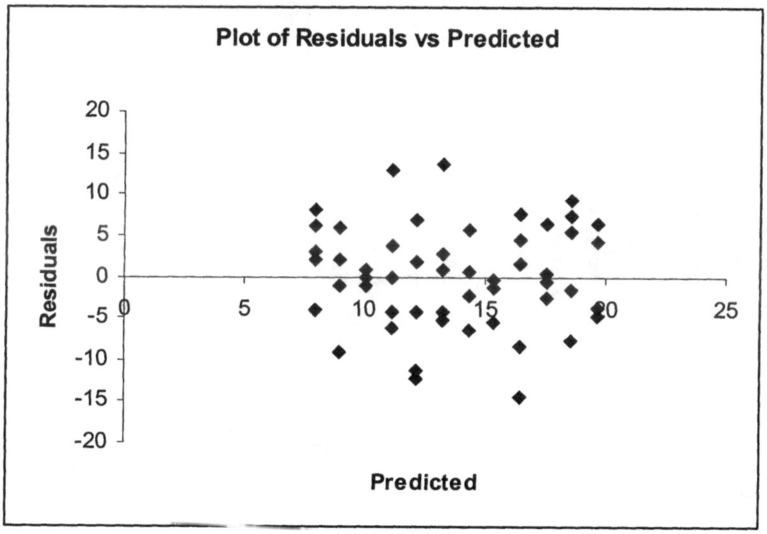

There is no indication of heteroscedasticity.

17.86

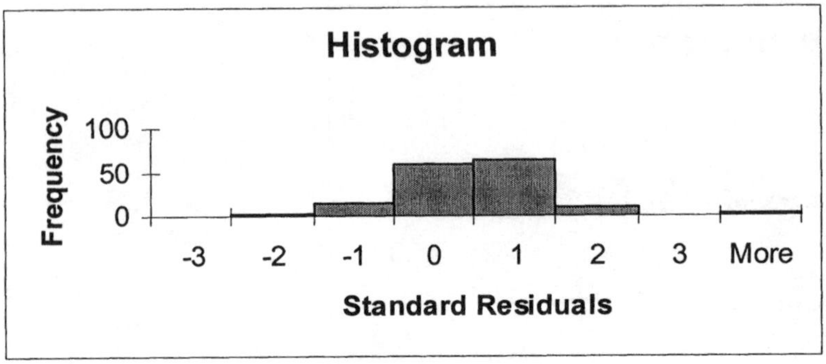

The normality requirement appears to be satisfied. There are two outliers.

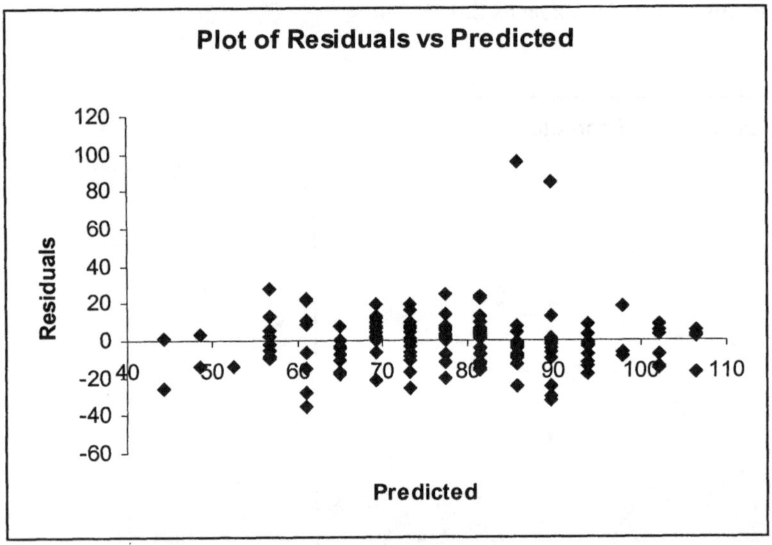

The variance of the error variable appears to be constant. The two outliers are clearly seen.

17.88

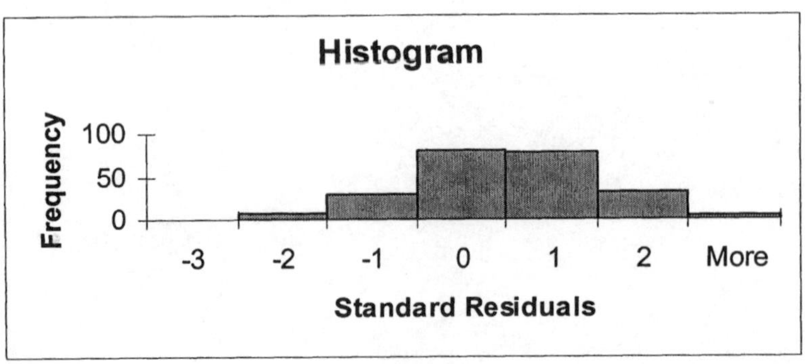

The error variable appears to be normally distributed.

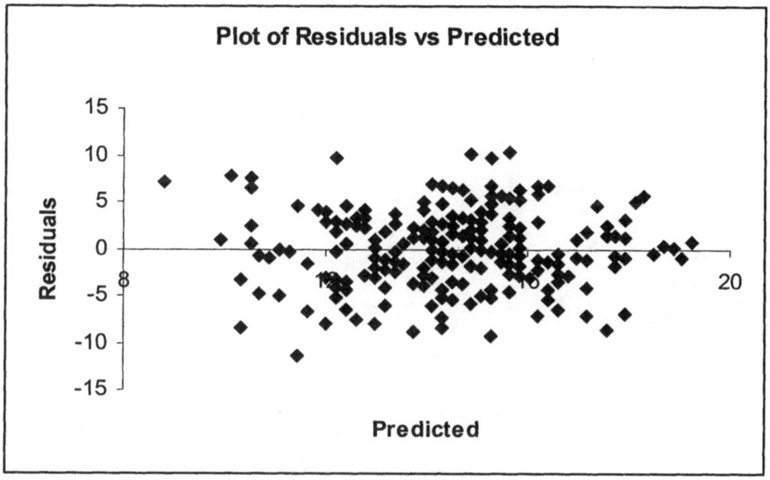

The variance of the error variable is constant.

17.90

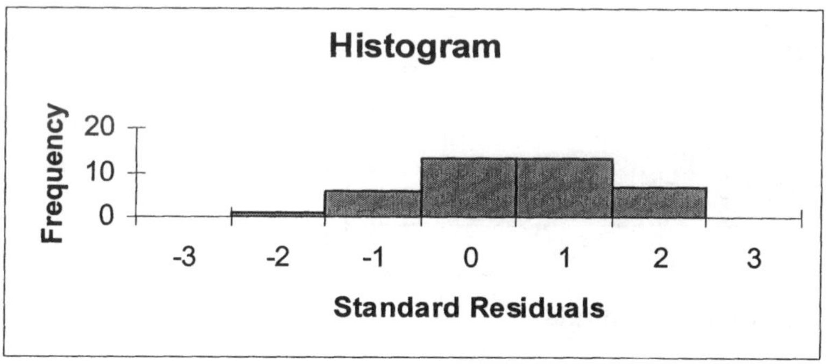

The error variable appears to be normally distributed.

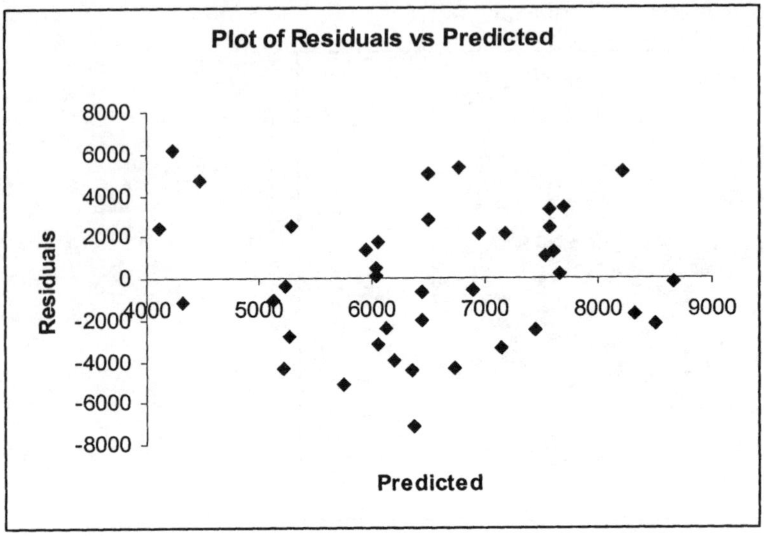

There is no clear sign of heteroscedasticity.

17.92

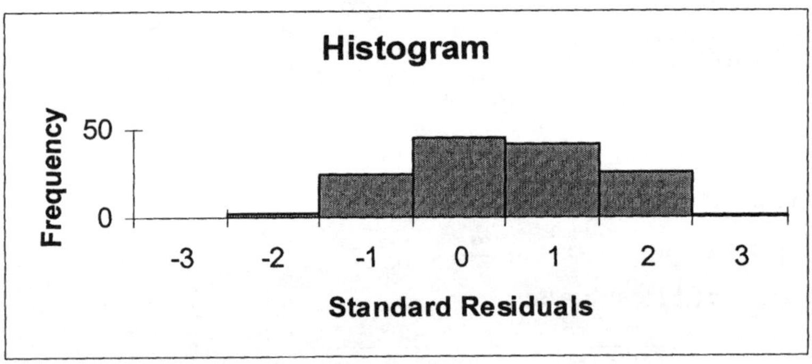

The error variable appears to be normal.

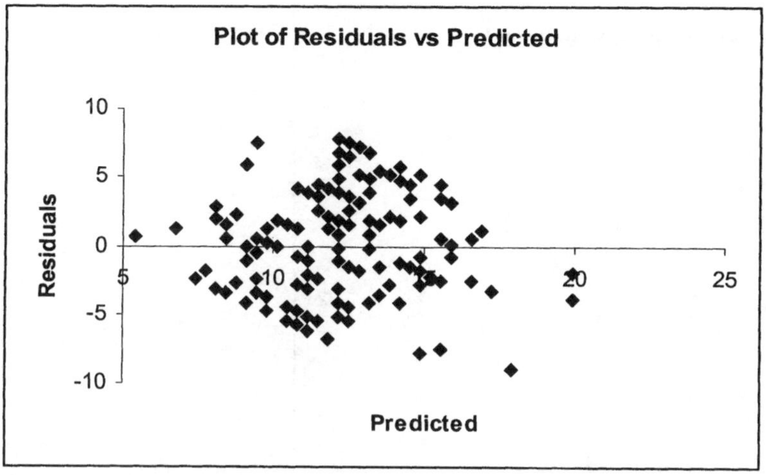

Heteroscedasticity appears to be a problem.

17.94

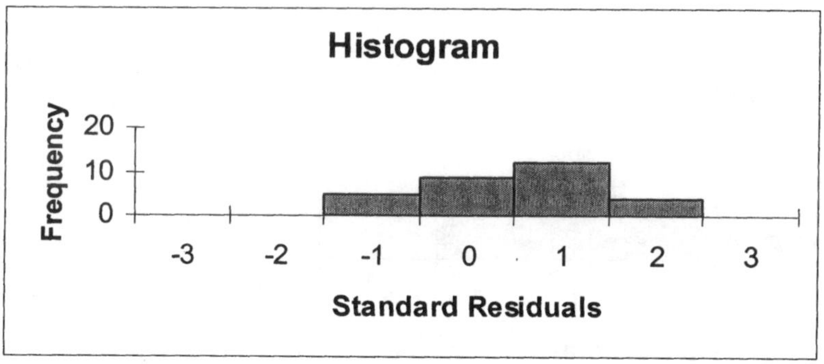

The error variable appears to be normal.

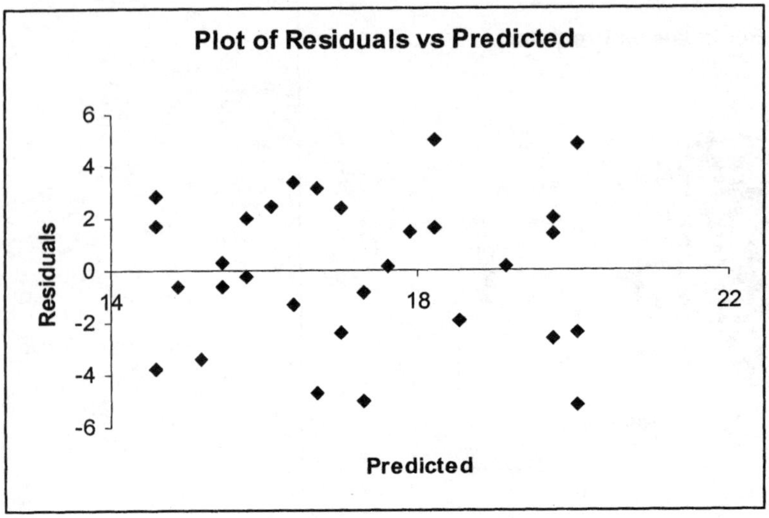

The variance of the error variable is constant.

17.96

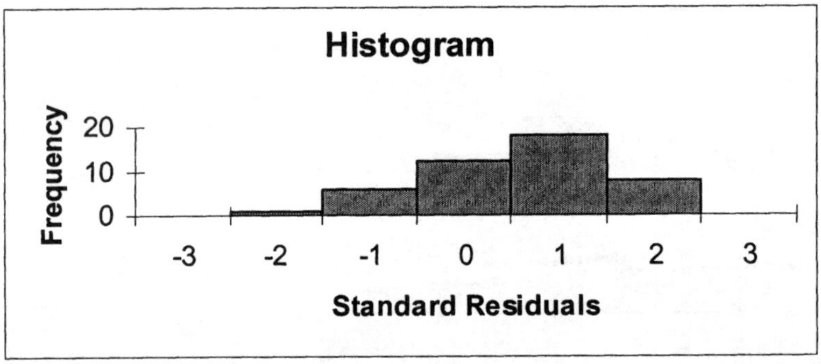

The error variable appears to be normal.

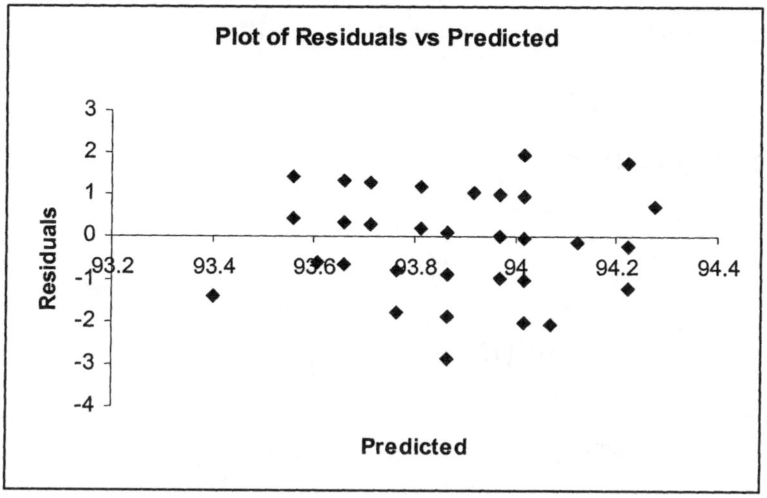

The variance of the error variable is constant.

17.98 a $b_1 = \frac{s_{xy}}{s_x^2} = \frac{936.82}{378.77} = 2.47$ $b_0 = \bar{y} - b_1\bar{x} = 395.21 - 2.47(113.35) = 115.24.$

Regression line: $\hat{y} = 115.24 + 2.47x$ (Excel: $\hat{y} = 114.85 + 2.47x$)

b $b_1 = 2.47$; for each additional month of age, repair costs increase on average by $2.47.

$b_0 = 114.85$ is the y-intercept.

c $R^2 = \frac{s_{xy}^2}{s_x^2 s_y^2} = \frac{(936.82)^2}{(378.77)(4{,}094.79)} = .5659$ (Excel: $R^2 = .5659$) 56.59% of the variation in repair costs s explained by the variation in ages.

d $SSE = (n-1)\left(s_y^2 - \frac{s_{xy}^2}{s_x^2}\right) = (20-1)\left(4{,}094.79 - \frac{(936.82)^2}{378.77}\right) = 33{,}777$

$s_\varepsilon = \sqrt{\frac{SSE}{n-2}} = \sqrt{\frac{33{,}777}{20-2}} = 43.32$ (Excel: $s_\varepsilon = 43.32$).

$H_0: \beta_1 = 0$

$H_1: \beta_1 \neq 0$

Rejection region: $t > t_{\alpha/2,n-2} = t_{025,18} = 2.101$ or $t < -t_{\alpha/2,n-2} = -t_{.025,18} = -2.101$

$s_{b_1} = \frac{s_\varepsilon}{\sqrt{(n-1)s_x^2}} = \frac{43.32}{\sqrt{(20-1)(378.77)}} = .511$

$t = \frac{b_1 - \beta_1}{s_{b_1}} = \frac{2.47 - 0}{.511}$ = 4.84 (Excel: t = 4.84, p–value = .0001. There is enough evidence to infer that repair costs and age are linearly related.

e $\hat{y} = b_0 + b_1 x_g = 115.24 + 2.47(120) = 411.64$

Prediction interval: $\hat{y} \pm t_{\alpha/2,n-2} s_\varepsilon \sqrt{1 + \frac{1}{n} + \frac{(x_g - \bar{x})^2}{(n-1)s_x^2}}$ (where $t_{\alpha/2,n-2} = t_{.025,18} = 2.101$)

$$= 411.64 \pm 2.101(43.32)\sqrt{1 + \frac{1}{20} + \frac{(120 - 113.35)^2}{(20-1)(378.77)}} = 411.64 \pm 93.54$$

Lower prediction limit = 318.1, upper prediction limit = 505.2 (Excel: 318.1, 505.2)

17.100 $H_0: \rho = 0$

$H_1: \rho \neq 0$

	A	B
1	**Correlation**	
2		
3	*CO and NO3*	
4	Pearson Coefficient of Correlation	0.8913
5	t Stat	13.62
6	df	48
7	P(T<=t) one tail	0
8	t Critical one tail	1.6772
9	P(T<=t) two tail	0
10	t Critical two tail	2.0106

r = .8913, t = 13.62, p–value = 0; there is enough evidence to infer that the belief is correct.

17.102a $H_0: \rho = 0$

$H_1: \rho \neq 0$

	A	B
1	**Correlation**	
2		
3	*Tar and Nicotine*	
4	Pearson Coefficient of Correlation	0.9766
5	t Stat	21.78
6	df	23
7	P(T<=t) one tail	0
8	t Critical one tail	1.7139
9	P(T<=t) two tail	0
10	t Critical two tail	2.0687

r = .9766, t = 21.78, p–value = 0. There is sufficient evidence to infer that levels of tar and nicotine are linearly related.

b $H_0 : \rho = 0$

$H_1 : \rho \neq 0$

	A	B
1	**Correlation**	
2		
3	*Nicotine and CO*	
4	Pearson Coefficient of Correlation	0.9259
5	t Stat	11.76
6	df	23
7	P(T<=t) one tail	0
8	t Critical one tail	1.7139
9	P(T<=t) two tail	0
10	t Critical two tail	2.0687

r = .9259, t = 11.76, p–value = 0. There is sufficient evidence to infer that levels of nicotine and carbon monoxide are linearly related.

17.104 $H_0 : \rho = 0$

$H_1 : \rho > 0$

Rejection region: $t > t_{\alpha,n-2} = t_{05,428} = 1.645$ or

$$r = \frac{s_{xy}}{s_x s_y} = \frac{255{,}877}{\sqrt{(99.11)(2{,}152{,}602{,}614)}} = .5540 \text{ (Excel: .5540)}$$

$t = r\sqrt{\frac{n-2}{1-r^2}} = (.5540)\sqrt{\frac{430-2}{1-(.5540)^2}} = 13.77$ (Excel: t = 13.77, p–value = 0). There is enough evidence of a positive linear relationship. The theory appears to be valid.

17.106 $H_0 : \rho = 0$

$H_1 : \rho \neq 0$

	A	B
1	**Correlation**	
2		
3	*Italian Index and Hong Kong Index*	
4	Pearson Coefficient of Correlation	0.1974
5	t Stat	1.52
6	df	57
7	P(T<=t) one tail	0.0669
8	t Critical one tail	1.6720
9	P(T<=t) two tail	0.1338
10	t Critical two tail	2.0025

r = .1974, t = 1.52, p–value = .1338. There is not enough evidence to infer that the returns on the indexes are linearly related.

17.108 $H_0 : \rho = 0$

$H_1 : \rho \neq 0$

	A	B
1	**Correlation**	
2		
3	*Times and Amount*	
4	Pearson Coefficient of Correlation	0.7976
5	t Stat	29.51
6	df	498
7	P(T<=t) one tail	0
8	t Critical one tail	1.6479
9	P(T<=t) two tail	0
10	t Critical two tail	1.9647

r = .7976, t = 29.51, p–value = 0. There is overwhelming evidence of a linear relationship between listening times and amounts spent on music.

Chapter 18

18.2

	A	B	C	D	E	F
1	SUMMARY OUTPUT					
2						
3	*Regression Statistics*					
4	Multiple R	0.8734				
5	R Square	0.7629				
6	Adjusted R Square	0.7453				
7	Standard Error	3.75				
8	Observations	30				
9						
10	ANOVA					
11		*df*	*SS*	*MS*	*F*	*Significance F*
12	Regression	2	1223.2	611.59	43.43	0.0000
13	Residual	27	380.2	14.08		
14	Total	29	1603.4			
15						
16		*Coefficients*	*Standard Error*	*t Stat*	*P-value*	
17	Intercept	13.01	3.53	3.69	0.0010	
18	Assignment	0.194	0.200	0.97	0.3417	
19	Midterm	1.11	0.122	9.12	0.0000	

a $\hat{y} = 13.01 + .194x_1 + 1.11x_2$

b The standard error of estimate is $s_\varepsilon = 3.75$. It is an estimate of the standard deviation of the error variable.

c The coefficient of determination is $R^2 = .7629$; 76.29% of the variation in final exam marks is explained by the model.

d $H_0: \beta_1 = \beta_2 = 0$

H_1: At least one β_i is not equal to zero

F = 43.43, p-value = 0. There is enough evidence to conclude that the model is valid.

e $b_1 = .194$; for each addition mark on assignments the final exam mark on average increases by .194 provided that the other variable remains constant.

$b_2 = 1.112$; for each addition midterm mark the final exam mark on average increases by 1.112 provided that the other variable remains constant.

f $H_0: \beta_1 = 0$

$H_1: \beta_1 \neq 0$

t = .97, p-value = .3417. There is not enough evidence to infer that assignment marks and final exam marks are linearly related.

g $H_0: \beta_2 = 0$

$H_1: \beta_2 \neq 0$

t = 9.12, p-value = 0. There is sufficient evidence to infer that midterm marks and final exam marks are linearly related.

h

	A	B	C	D
1	**Prediction Interval**			
2				
3			Final	
4				
5	Predicted value		31	
6				
7	Prediction Interval			
8	Lower limit		23	
9	Upper limit		39	
10				
11	Interval Estimate of Expected Value			
12	Lower limit		29	
13	Upper limit		33	

Pat's final exam mark is predicted to lie between 23 and 39

i Pat's predicted final grade: LCL = 12 + 14 + 23 = 49, UCL = 12 + 14 + 39 = 65

18.4a

	A	B	C	D	E	F
1	SUMMARY OUTPUT					
2						
3	*Regression Statistics*					
4	Multiple R	0.5926				
5	R Square	0.3511				
6	Adjusted R Square	0.3352				
7	Standard Error	6.99				
8	Observations	126				
9						
10	ANOVA					
11		*df*	*SS*	*MS*	*F*	*Significance F*
12	Regression	3	3228	1075.87	22.01	0.0000
13	Residual	122	5965	48.89		
14	Total	125	9192			
15						
16		*Coefficients*	*Standard Error*	*t Stat*	*P-value*	
17	Intercept	-1.97	9.55	-0.21	0.8369	
18	Minor HR	0.666	0.087	7.64	0.0000	
19	Age	0.136	0.524	0.26	0.7961	
20	Years Pro	1.18	0.671	1.75	0.0819	

b $b_1 = .666$; for each additional minor league home run the number of major league home runs increases on average by .666 provided that the other variables remain constant.

$b_2 = .136$; for each additional year of age the number of major league home runs increases on average by .14 provided that the other variables remain constant.

$b_3 = 1.18$; for each additional year as a professional the number of major league home runs increases on average by 1.18 provided that the other variables remain constant.

c $s_\varepsilon = 6.99$ and $R^2 = .3511$; The model's fit is not very good.

d $H_0: \beta_1 = \beta_2 = \beta_3 = 0$

H_1: At least one β_i is not equal to zero

F = 22.01, p-value = 0. There is enough evidence to conclude that the model is valid.

e $H_0: \beta_i = 0$

$H_1: \beta_i \neq 0$

Minor league home runs: t = 7.64, p-value = 0

Age: t = .26, p-value = .7961

Years professional: t = 1.75, p-value = .0819

At the 5% significance level only the number of minor league home runs is linearly related to the number of major league home runs.

f

	A	B	C	D
1	**Prediction Interval**			
2				
3			Major HR	
4				
5	Predicted value		24.31	
6				
7	Prediction Interval			
8	Lower limit		9.86	
9	Upper limit		38.76	
10				
11	Interval Estimate of Expected Value			
12	Lower limit		20.16	
13	Upper limit		28.45	

We predict that the player will hit between 9.86 (rounded to 10) and 38.76 (rounded to 39) home runs.

g

	A	B	C	D
1	**Prediction Interval**			
2				
3			Major HR	
4				
5	Predicted value		19.56	
6				
7	Prediction Interval			
8	Lower limit		4.88	
9	Upper limit		34.25	
10				
11	Interval Estimate of Expected Value			
12	Lower limit		14.66	
13	Upper limit		24.47	

It is estimated that the average player will hit between 14.66 and 24.47 home runs

18.6

	A	B	C	D	E	F
1	SUMMARY OUTPUT					
2						
3	*Regression Statistics*					
4	Multiple R	0.5369				
5	R Square	0.2882				
6	Adjusted R Square	0.2660				
7	Standard Error	2.0302				
8	Observations	100				
9						
10	ANOVA					
11		*df*	*SS*	*MS*	*F*	*Significance F*
12	Regression	3	160.23	53.41	12.96	0.0000
13	Residual	96	395.70	4.12		
14	Total	99	555.93			
15						
16		*Coefficients*	*Standard Error*	*t Stat*	*P-value*	
17	Intercept	0.721	1.87	0.39	0.7006	
18	HS GPA	0.611	0.101	6.06	0.0000	
19	SAT	0.00135	0.00144	0.94	0.3485	
20	Activities	0.0462	0.0641	0.72	0.4720	

b The coefficient of determination is $R^2 = .2882$; 28.82% of the variation in university GPAs is explained by the model.

c $H_0 : \beta_1 = \beta_2 = \beta_3 = 0$

H_1 : At least one β_i is not equal to zero

F = 12.96, p-value = 0. There is enough evidence to conclude that the model is valid.

d $b_1 = .611$; for each additional point of high school GPA university GPA increases on average by .611 provided that the other variables remain constant.

$b_2 = .00135$; for each additional point of SAT university GPA increases on average by .00135 provided that the other variables remain constant.

$b_3 = .0462$; for each additional hour of activities university GPA increases on average by .0462 provided that the other variables remain constant.

e

	A	B	C	D
1	**Prediction Interval**			
2				
3			Univ GPA	
4				
5	Predicted value		8.55	
6				
7	Prediction Interval			
8	Lower limit		4.45	
9	Upper limit		12.65	
10				
11	Interval Estimate of Expected Value			
12	Lower limit		7.79	
13	Upper limit		9.31	

We predict that the student's GPA will fall between 4.45 and 12.00 (12 is the maximum).

f

	A	B	C	D
1	**Prediction Interval**			
2				
3			Univ GPA	
4				
5	Predicted value		7.56	
6				
7	Prediction Interval			
8	Lower limit		4.12	
9	Upper limit		10.99	
10				
11	Interval Estimate of Expected Value			
12	Lower limit		6.90	
13	Upper limit		8.22	

The mean GPA is estimated to lie between 6.90 and 8.22.

18.8

	A	B	C	D	E	F
1	SUMMARY OUTPUT					
2						
3	*Regression Statistics*					
4	Multiple R	0.8415				
5	R Square	0.7081				
6	Adjusted R Square	0.7021				
7	Standard Error	213.7				
8	Observations	100				
9						
10	ANOVA					
11		*df*	*SS*	*MS*	*F*	*Significance F*
12	Regression	2	10,744,454	5,372,227	117.6	0.0000
13	Residual	97	4,429,664	45,667		
14	Total	99	15,174,118			
15						
16		*Coefficients*	*Standard Error*	*t Stat*	*P-value*	
17	Intercept	576.8	514.0	1.12	0.2646	
18	Space	90.61	6.48	13.99	0.0000	
19	Water	9.66	2.41	4.00	0.0001	

a The regression equation is $\hat{y} = 576.8 + 90.61x_1 + 9.66x_2$

b The coefficient of determination is $R^2 = .7081$; 70.81% of the variation in electricity consumption is explained by the model. The model fits reasonably well.

c $H_0 : \beta_1 = \beta_2 = 0$

H_1 : At least one β_i is not equal to zero

F = 117.6, p-value = 0. There is enough evidence to conclude that the model is valid.

d & e

	A	B	C	D
1	**Prediction Interval**			
2				
3			Consumption	
4				
5	Predicted value		8175	
6				
7	Prediction Interval			
8	Lower limit		7748	
9	Upper limit		8601	
10				
11	Interval Estimate of Expected Value			
12	Lower limit		8127	
13	Upper limit		8222	

e We predict that the house will consume between 7748 and 8601 units of electricity.

f We estimate that the average house will consume between 8127 and 8222 units of electricity.

18.10a

	A	B	C	D	E	F
1	SUMMARY OUTPUT					
2						
3	*Regression Statistics*					
4	Multiple R	0.8608				
5	R Square	0.7411				
6	Adjusted R Square	0.7301				
7	Standard Error	2.66				
8	Observations	100				
9						
10	ANOVA					
11		*df*	*SS*	*MS*	*F*	*Significance F*
12	Regression	4	1930	482.38	67.97	0.0000
13	Residual	95	674	7.10		
14	Total	99	2604			
15						
16		*Coefficients*	*Standard Error*	*t Stat*	*P-value*	
17	Intercept	3.24	5.42	0.60	0.5512	
18	Mother	0.451	0.0545	8.27	0.0000	
19	Father	0.411	0.0498	8.26	0.0000	
20	Gmothers	0.0166	0.0661	0.25	0.8028	
21	Gfathers	0.0869	0.0657	1.32	0.1890	

b $H_0: \beta_1 = \beta_2 = \beta_3 = 0$

H_1: At least one β_i is not equal to zero

F = 67.97, p-value = 0. There is enough evidence to conclude that the model is valid.

c $b_1 = .451$; for each one year increase in the mother's age the customer's age increases on average by .451 provided the other variables are constant (which may not be possible because of the multicollinearity).

$b_2 = .411$; for each one year increase in the father's age the customer's age increases on average by .411 provided the other variables are constant.

$b_3 = .0166$; for each one year increase in the grandmothers' mean age the customer's age increases on average by .0166 provided the other variables are constant.

$b_4 = .0869$; for each one year increase in the grandfathers' mean age the customer's age increases on average by .0869 provided the other variables are constant.

$H_0 : \beta_i = 0$

$H_1 : \beta_i \neq 0$

Mothers: t = 8.27, p-value = 0

Fathers: t = 8.26, p-value = 0

Grandmothers: t = .25, p-value .8028

Grandfathers: t = 1.32, p-value = .1890

The ages of mothers and fathers are linearly related to the ages of their children. The other two variables are not.

d

	A	B	C	D
1	**Prediction Interval**			
2				
3			Longvity	
4				
5	Predicted value		71.43	
6				
7	Prediction Interval			
8	Lower limit		65.54	
9	Upper limit		77.31	
10				
11	Interval Estimate of Expected Value			
12	Lower limit		68.85	
13	Upper limit		74.00	

The man is predicted to live to an age between 65.54 and 77.31

g

	A	B	C	D
1	**Prediction Interval**			
2				
3			Longvity	
4				
5	Predicted value		71.71	
6				
7	Prediction Interval			
8	Lower limit		65.65	
9	Upper limit		77.77	
10				
11	Interval Estimate of Expected Value			
12	Lower limit		68.75	
13	Upper limit		74.66	

The mean longevity is estimated to fall between 68.75 and 74.66.

18.12

	A	B	C	D	E	F
1	SUMMARY OUTPUT					
2						
3	*Regression Statistics*					
4	Multiple R	0.8984				
5	R Square	0.8072				
6	Adjusted R Square	0.7990				
7	Standard Error	7.07				
8	Observations	50				
9						
10	ANOVA					
11		*df*	*SS*	*MS*	*F*	*Significance F*
12	Regression	2	9,832	4,916	98.37	0.0000
13	Residual	47	2,349	49.97		
14	Total	49	12,181			
15						
16		*Coefficients*	*Standard Error*	*t Stat*	*P-value*	
17	Intercept	-28.43	6.89	-4.13	0.0001	
18	Boxes	0.604	0.0557	10.85	0.0000	
19	Weight	0.374	0.0847	4.42	0.0001	

a $\hat{y} = -28.43 + .604x_1 + .374x_2$

b $s_\varepsilon = 7.07$ and $R^2 = .8072$; the model fits well.

c $b_1 = .604$; for each one additional box, the amount of time to unload increases on average by .604 minutes provided the weight is constant.

$b_2 = .374$; for each additional hundred pounds the amount of time to unload increases on average by .374 minutes provided the number of boxes is constant.

$$H_0: \beta_i = 0$$

$$H_1: \beta_i \neq 0$$

Boxes: t = 10.85, p-value = 0

Weight: t = 4.42, p-value = .0001

Both variables are linearly related to time to unload.

d & e

	A	B	C	D
1	**Prediction Interval**			
2				
3			Time	
4				
5	Predicted value		50.70	
6				
7	Prediction Interval			
8	Lower limit		35.16	
9	Upper limit		66.24	
10				
11	Interval Estimate of Expected Value			
12	Lower limit		44.43	
13	Upper limit		56.96	

d It is predicted that the truck will be unloaded in a time between 35.16 and 66.24 minutes.

e The mean time to unload the trucks is estimated to lie between 44.43 and 56.96 minutes.

18.14 a

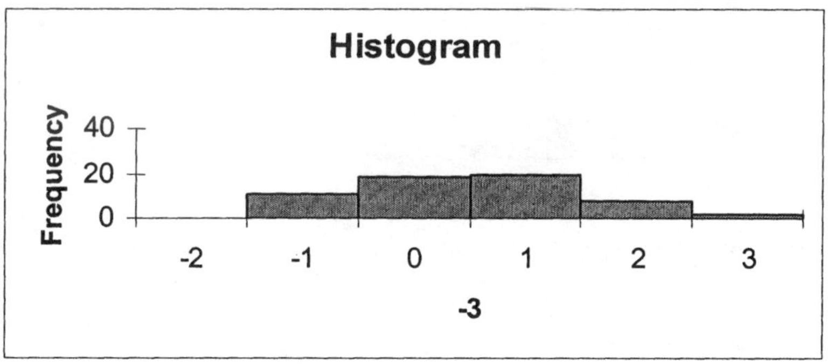

The normality requirement is satisfied.

b

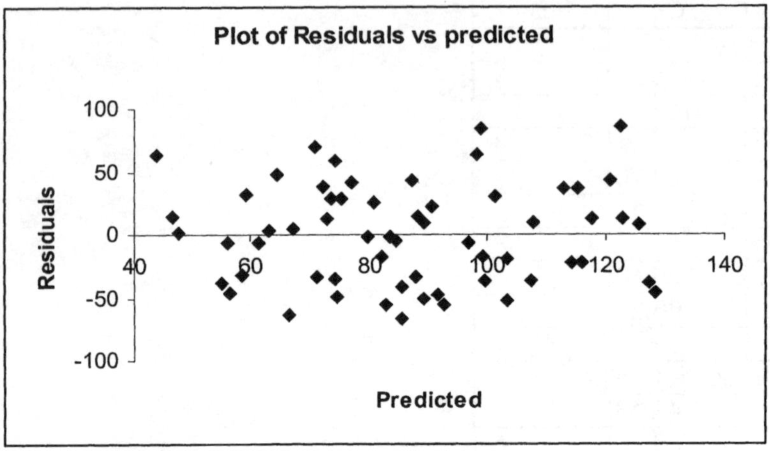

The variance of the error variable appears to be constant.

18.16b

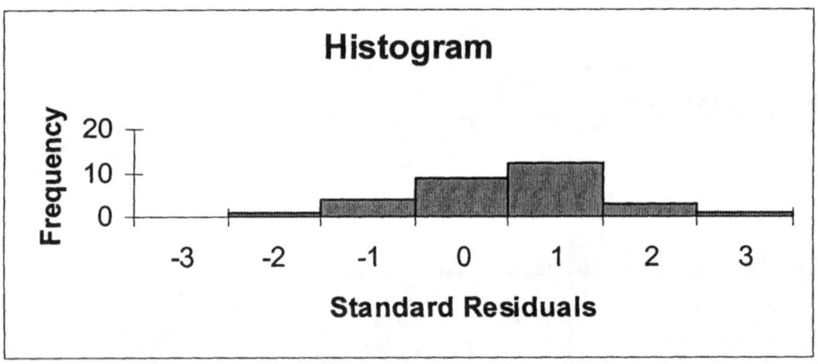

The normality requirement has not been violated.

c

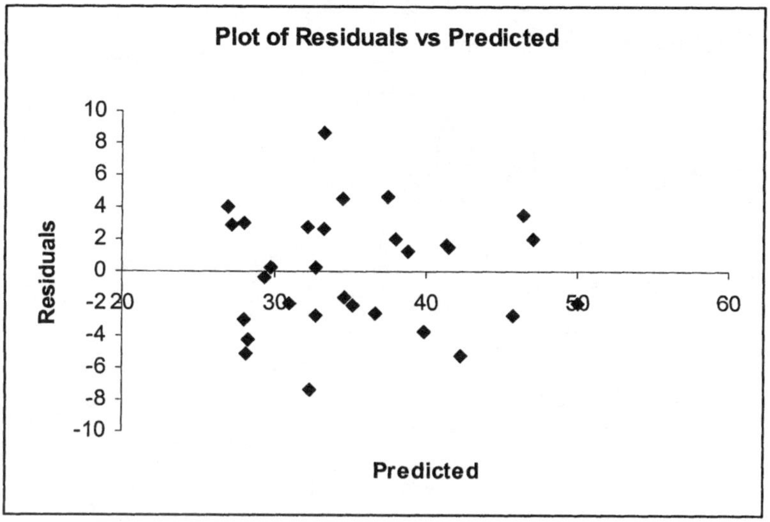

The variance of the error variable appears to be constant.

d

	A	B	C
1		*Assignment*	*Midterm*
2	Assignment	1	
3	Midterm	0.1037	1

The lack of multicollinearity means that the t–tests were valid.

18.18a

	A	B	C	D
1		*Minor HR*	*Age*	*Years Pro*
2	Minor HR	1		
3	Age	0.0354	1	
4	Years Pro	-0.0392	0.7355	1

Age and years as a professional are highly correlated. The correlations of the other combinations are small.

b The t–tests may not be valid.

18.20

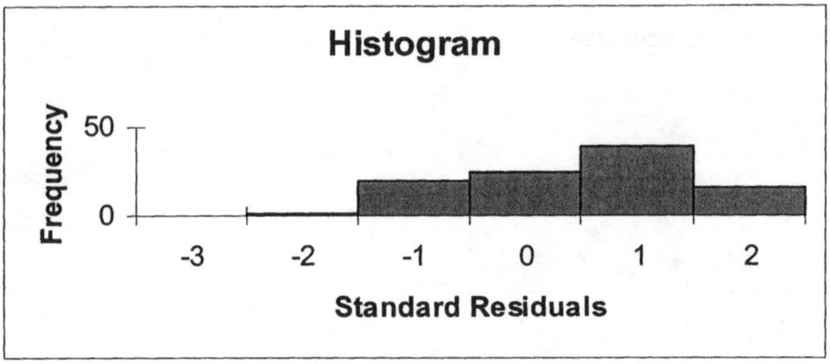

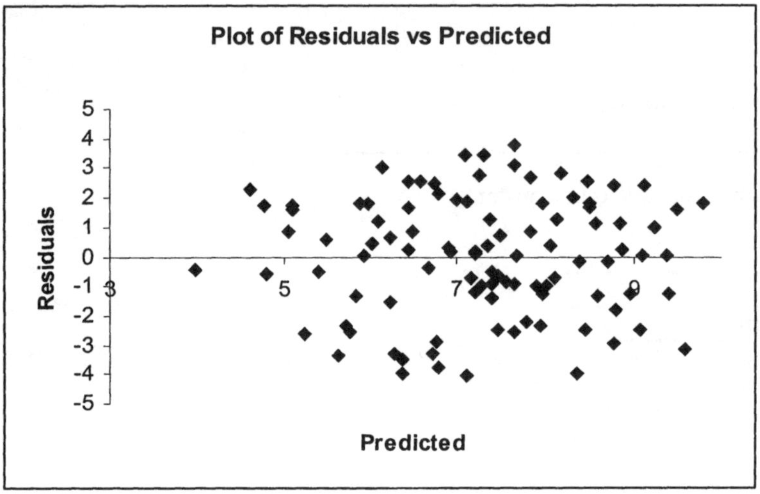

The error variable is approximately normally distributed and the variance is constant.

18.22

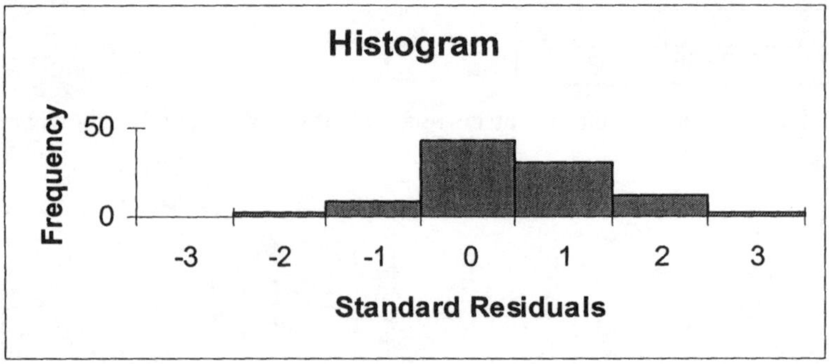

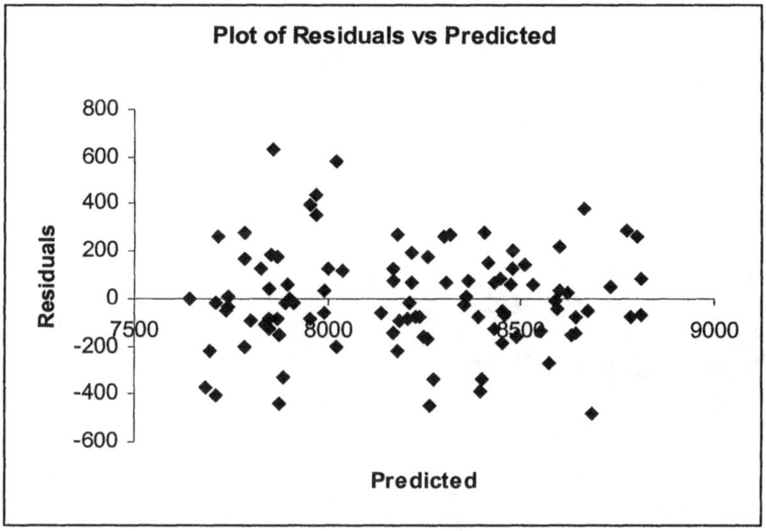

The requirements are satisfied.

18.24a

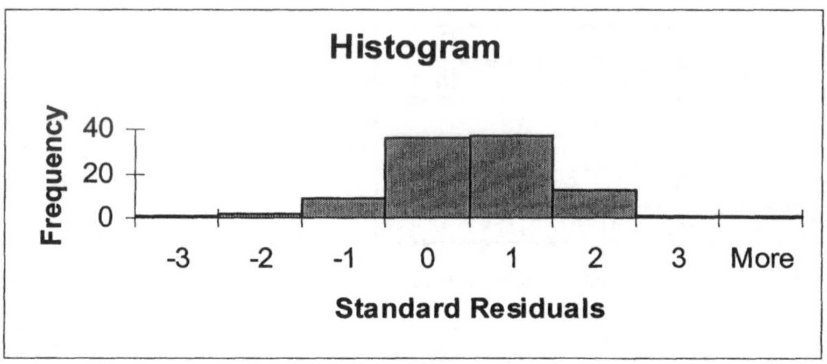

The normality requirement is satisfied.

b

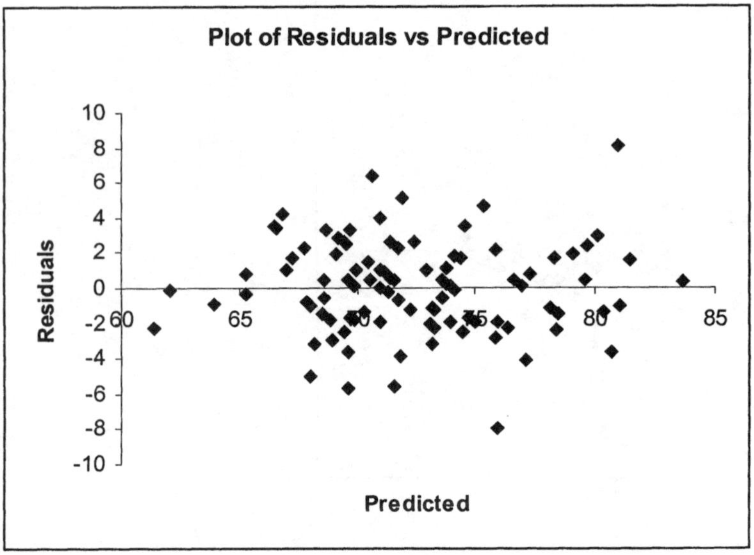

The variance of the error variable is constant.

c

	A	B	C	D	E
1		*Mother*	*Father*	*Gmothers*	*Gfathers*
2	Mother	1			
3	Father	0.2766	1		
4	Gmothers	0.4343	0.2409	1	
5	Gfathers	0.3910	0.3752	-0.0077	1

The correlations are large enough to cause problems with the t–tests.

18.26

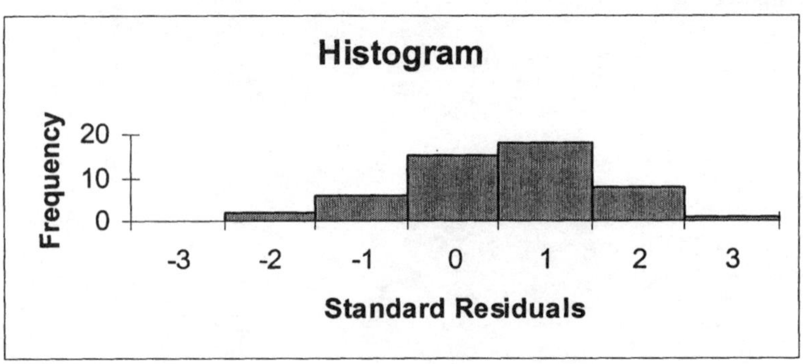

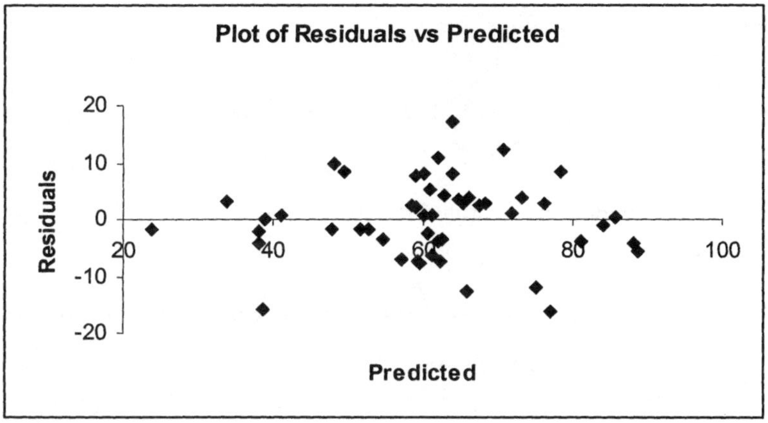

c The error variable appears to be normally distributed. The variance of the errors appears to be constant.

18.28

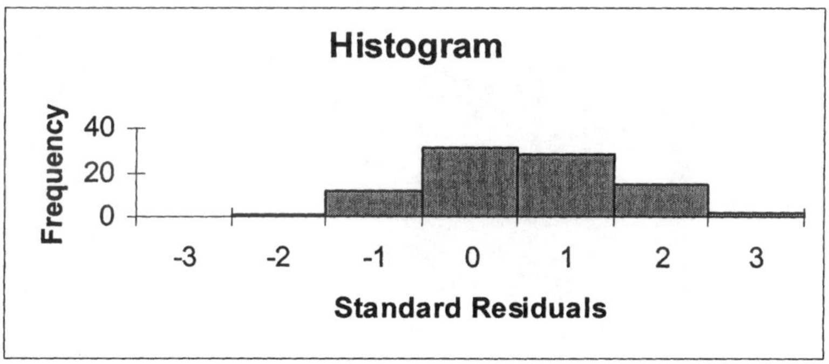

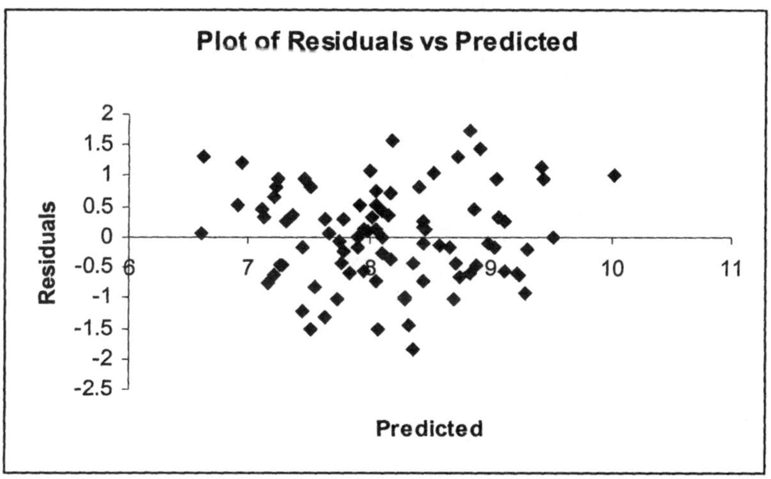

The requirements are satisfied.

18.30 $d_L = 1.16$, $d_U = 1.59$, $4 - d_U = 2.84$, $4 - d_L = 2.41$. The test is inconclusive.

18.32 $d_L = 1.46$, $d_U = 1.63$. There is evidence of positive first-order autocorrelation.

18.34 $4 - d_U = 4 - 1.73 = 2.27$, $4 - d_L = 4 - 1.19 = 2.81$. There is no evidence of negative first-order autocorrelation.

18.36 a The regression equation is $\hat{y} = 2260 + .423x$

b

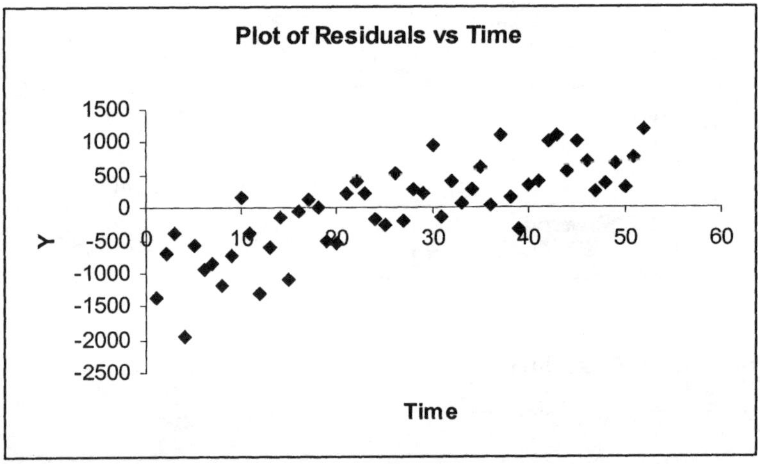

There appears to be a strong autocorrelation.

c

	A	B	C
1	**Durbin-Watson Statistic**		
2			
3	d = 0.7859		

$d_L \approx 1.50$, $d_U \approx 1.59$, $4 - d_U \approx 2.41$, $4 - d_L \approx \approx 2.50$. There is evidence of first-order autocorrelation.

d The model is $y = \beta_0 + \beta_1 x + \beta_2 t + \varepsilon$

The regression equation is $\hat{y} = 446.2 + 1.10x + 38.92t$

e

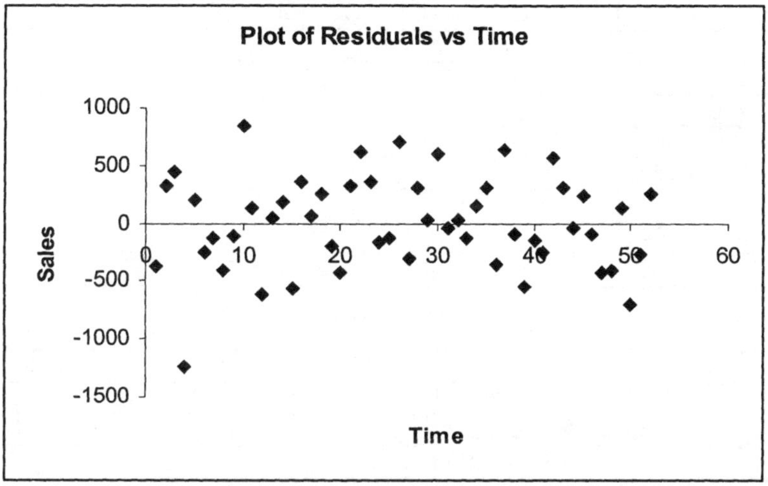

	A	B	C
1	Durbin-Watson Statistic		
2			
3	d = 2.2631		

There is no evidence of autocorrelation.

First model: $s_\varepsilon = 709.7$ and $R^2 = .0146$. Second model: $s_\varepsilon = 413.7$ and $R^2 = .6718$.

The second model fits better.

18.38

	A	B	C
1	Durbin-Watson Statistic		
2			
3	d = 2.2003		

$d = 2.2003$; $d_L = 1.30$, $d_U = 1.46$, $4 - d_U = 2.70$, $4 - d_L = 2.54$. There is no evidence of first order autocorrelation.

18.40

	A	B	C	D	E	F
1	SUMMARY OUTPUT					
2						
3	*Regression Statistics*					
4	Multiple R	0.6882				
5	R Square	0.4736				
6	Adjusted R Square	0.4134				
7	Standard Error	2,644				
8	Observations	40				
9						
10	ANOVA					
11		*df*	*SS*	*MS*	*F*	*Significance F*
12	Regression	4	220,130,124	55,032,531	7.87	0.0001
13	Residual	35	244,690,939	6,991,170		
14	Total	39	464,821,063			
15						
16		*Coefficients*	*Standard Error*	*t Stat*	*P-value*	
17	Intercept	1,433	2,093	0.68	0.4980	
18	Size	-14.55	20.70	-0.70	0.4866	
19	Apartments	113.0	24.01	4.70	0.0000	
20	Age	-50.10	98.81	-0.51	0.6153	
21	Floors	-223.8	171.1	-1.31	0.1994	

b $H_0: \beta_1 = \beta_2 = \beta_3 = \beta_4 = 0$

H_1: At least one β_i is not equal to zero

F = 7.87, p-value = .0001. There is enough evidence to conclude that the model is valid.

The regression equation for Exercise 17.12 is $\hat{y} = 4040 + 44.97x$. The addition of the new variables changes the coefficients of the regression line in Exercise 17.12.

18.42a

	A	B	C	D	E	F
1	SUMMARY OUTPUT					
2						
3	*Regression Statistics*					
4	Multiple R	0.6447				
5	R Square	0.4157				
6	Adjusted R Square	0.3724				
7	Standard Error	57.29				
8	Observations	30				
9						
10	ANOVA					
11		*df*	*SS*	*MS*	*F*	*Significance F*
12	Regression	2	63,043	31,521	9.60	0.0007
13	Residual	27	88,626	3,282		
14	Total	29	151,669			
15						
16		*Coefficients*	*Standard Error*	*t Stat*	*P-value*	
17	Intercept	194.8	32.58	5.98	0.0000	
18	Fetilizer	0.123	0.0740	1.66	0.1088	
19	Water	0.0248	0.0061	4.06	0.0004	

For each additional unit of fertilizer crop yield increases on average by .123 (holding the amount of water constant).

For each additional unit of water crop yield increases on average by .0248 (holding the fertilizer constant).

b $H_0: \beta_1 = 0$

$H_1: \beta_1 \neq 0$

t =1.66, p-value = .1088. There is not enough evidence to conclude that there is a linear relationship between crop yield and amount of fertilizer.

c $H_0: \beta_2 = 0$

$H_1: \beta_2 \neq 0$

t =4.06, p-value = .0004. There is enough evidence to conclude that there is a linear relationship between crop yield and amount of water.

d $s_\varepsilon = 57.29$ and $R^2 = .4157$; the model fits moderately well.

e

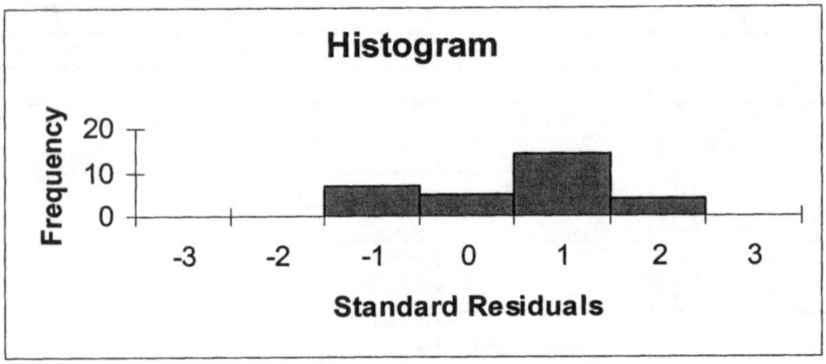

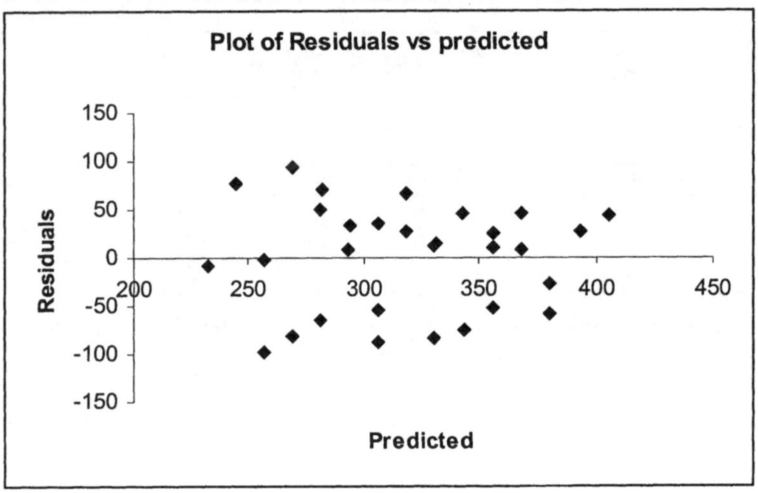

There appears to be problems with both requirements.

f

	A	B	C	D
1	**Prediction Interval**			
2				
3			Yield	
4				
5	Predicted value		232.0	
6				
7	Prediction Interval			
8	Lower limit		104.7	
9	Upper limit		359.2	
10				
11	Interval Estimate of Expected Value			
12	Lower limit		183.3	
13	Upper limit		280.6	

We predict that the crop yield will fall between 104.7 and 359.2.

Chapter 19

19.2 a

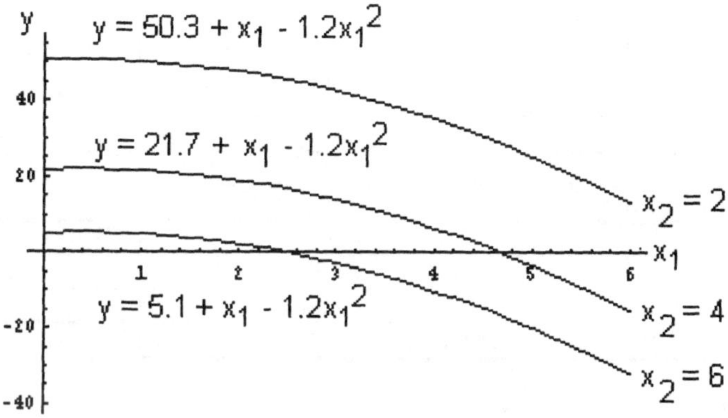

b

19.4a First–order model: a Demand = $\beta_0 + \beta_1$ Price+ ε

Second–order model: a Demand = $\beta_0 + \beta_1$ Price + β_2 Price ^{2} + ε

First–order model:

	A	B	C	D	E	F
1	SUMMARY OUTPUT					
2						
3	*Regression Statistics*					
4	Multiple R	0.9249				
5	R Square	0.8553				
6	Adjusted R Square	0.8473				
7	Standard Error	13.29				
8	Observations	20				
9						
10	ANOVA					
11		*df*	*SS*	*MS*	*F*	*Significance F*
12	Regression	1	18,798	18,798	106.44	0.0000
13	Residual	18	3,179	176.6		
14	Total	19	21,977			
15						
16		*Coefficients*	*Standard Error*	*t Stat*	*P-value*	
17	Intercept	453.6	15.18	29.87	0.0000	
18	Price	-68.91	6.68	-10.32	0.0000	

Second–order model:

	A	B	C	D	E	F
1	SUMMARY OUTPUT					
2						
3	*Regression Statistics*					
4	Multiple R	0.9862				
5	R Square	0.9726				
6	Adjusted R Square	0.9693				
7	Standard Error	5.96				
8	Observations	20				
9						
10	ANOVA					
11		*df*	*SS*	*MS*	*F*	*Significance F*
12	Regression	2	21,374	10,687	301.15	0.0000
13	Residual	17	603	35.49		
14	Total	19	21,977			
15						
16		*Coefficients*	*Standard Error*	*t Stat*	*P-value*	
17	Intercept	766.9	37.40	20.50	0.0000	
18	Price	-359.1	34.19	-10.50	0.0000	
19	Price-sq	64.55	7.58	8.52	0.0000	

c The second order model fits better because its standard error of estimate is 5.96, whereas that of the first–order models is 13.29

d $\hat{y}$.= 766.9 –359.1(2.95) + 64.55$(2.95)^2$ = 269.3

19.6a MBA GPA= $\beta_0 + \beta_1$ UnderGPA + β_2GMAT + β_3 Work + β_4 UnderGPA$\times$GMAT + ε

b

	A	B	C	D	E	F
1	SUMMARY OUTPUT					
2						
3	*Regression Statistics*					
4	Multiple R	0.6836				
5	R Square	0.4674				
6	Adjusted R Square	0.4420				
7	Standard Error	0.790				
8	Observations	89				
9						
10	ANOVA					
11		*df*	*SS*	*MS*	*F*	*Significance F*
12	Regression	4	45.97	11.49	18.43	0.0000
13	Residual	84	52.40	0.62		
14	Total	88	98.37			
15						
16		*Coefficients*	*Standard Error*	*t Stat*	*P-value*	
17	Intercept	-11.11	14.97	-0.74	0.4601	
18	UnderGPA	1.19	1.46	0.82	0.4159	
19	GMAT	0.0311	0.0255	1.22	0.2265	
20	Work	0.0956	0.0312	3.06	0.0030	
21	UGPA-GMAT	-0.0019	0.0025	-0.78	0.4392	

F = 18.43, p-value = 0; $s_\varepsilon = .790$ and $R^2 = .4674$. The model is valid, but the fit is relatively poor.

c MBA example $s_\varepsilon = .788$ and $R^2 = .4635$. There is little difference between the fits of the two models.

19.8a

	A	B	C	D	E	F
1	SUMMARY OUTPUT					
2						
3	*Regression Statistics*					
4	Multiple R	0.9255				
5	R Square	0.8566				
6	Adjusted R Square	0.8362				
7	Standard Error	5.20				
8	Observations	25				
9						
10	ANOVA					
11		*df*	*SS*	*MS*	*F*	*Significance F*
12	Regression	3	3398.7	1132.9	41.83	0.0000
13	Residual	21	568.8	27.08		
14	Total	24	3967.4			
15						
16		*Coefficients*	*Standard Error*	*t Stat*	*P-value*	
17	Intercept	260.7	162.3	1.61	0.1230	
18	Temperature	-3.32	2.09	-1.59	0.1270	
19	Currency	-164.3	667.1	-0.25	0.8078	
20	Temp-Curr	3.64	8.54	0.43	0.6741	

b

	A	B	C	D	E	F
1	SUMMARY OUTPUT					
2						
3	*Regression Statistics*					
4	Multiple R	0.9312				
5	R Square	0.8671				
6	Adjusted R Square	0.8322				
7	Standard Error	5.27				
8	Observations	25				
9						
10	ANOVA					
11		*df*	*SS*	*MS*	*F*	*Significance F*
12	Regression	5	3440.3	688.1	24.80	0.0000
13	Residual	19	527.1	27.74		
14	Total	24	3967.4			
15						
16		*Coefficients*	*Standard Error*	*t Stat*	*P-value*	
17	Intercept	274.8	283.8	0.97	0.3449	
18	Temperature	-1.72	6.88	-0.25	0.8053	
19	Currency	-828.6	888.5	-0.93	0.3627	
20	Temp-sq	-0.0024	0.0475	-0.05	0.9608	
21	Curr-sq	2054.0	1718.5	1.20	0.2467	
22	Temp-Curr	-0.870	10.57	-0.08	0.9353	

c Both models fit equally well. The standard errors of estimate and coefficients of determination are quite similar.

19.10a Yield = $\beta_0 + \beta_1$ Pressure + β_2 Temperature + β_3 Pressure^2

$+ \beta_4$ Temperature^2 + β_5 Pressure Temperature + ε

b

	A	B	C	D	E	F
1	SUMMARY OUTPUT					
2						
3	*Regression Statistics*					
4	Multiple R	0.8290				
5	R Square	0.6872				
6	Adjusted R Square	0.6661				
7	Standard Error	512				
8	Observations	80				
9						
10	ANOVA					
11		*df*	*SS*	*MS*	*F*	*Significance F*
12	Regression	5	42,657,846	8,531,569	32.52	0.0000
13	Residual	74	19,413,277	262,342		
14	Total	79	62,071,123			
15						
16		*Coefficients*	*Standard Error*	*t Stat*	*P-value*	
17	Intercept	74462	7526	9.89	0.0000	
18	Pressure	14.40	5.92	2.43	0.0174	
19	Temperature	-613.3	59.95	-10.23	0.0000	
20	Press-sq	-0.0159	0.0032	-5.04	0.0000	
21	Temp-sq	1.23	0.12	9.86	0.0000	
22	Press-temp	0.0381	0.0174	2.19	0.0316	

c $s_\varepsilon = 512$ and $R^2 = .6872$. The model's fit is good.

19.12 a $I_1 = 1$ if Catholic

$I_1 = 0$ otherwise

$I_2 = 1$ if Protestant

$I_2 = 0$ otherwise

b $I_1 = 1$ if 8:00 A.M. to 4:00 P.M.

$I_1 = 0$ otherwise

$I_2 = 1$ if 4:00 P.M. to midnight

$I_2 = 0$ otherwise

c $I_1 = 1$ if Jack Jones

$I_1 = 0$ otherwise

$I_2 = 1$ if Mary Brown

$I_2 = 0$ otherwise

$I_3 = 1$ if George Fosse

$I_3 = 0$ otherwise

19.14a

	A	B	C	D
1	**Prediction Interval**			
2				
3			MBA GPA	
4				
5	Predicted value		10.11	
6				
7	Prediction Interval			
8	Lower limit		8.55	
9	Upper limit		11.67	
10				
11	Interval Estimate of Expected Value			
12	Lower limit		9.53	
13	Upper limit		10.68	

Prediction: MBA GPA will lie between 8.55 and 11.67

b

	A	B	C	D
1	**Prediction Interval**			
2				
3			MBA GPA	
4				
5	Predicted value		9.73	
6				
7	Prediction Interval			
8	Lower limit		8.15	
9	Upper limit		11.31	
10				
11	Interval Estimate of Expected Value			
12	Lower limit		9.10	
13	Upper limit		10.36	

Prediction: MBA GPA will lie between 8.15 and 11.31

19.16a

	A	B	C	D	E	F
1	SUMMARY OUTPUT					
2						
3	*Regression Statistics*					
4	Multiple R	0.8368				
5	R Square	0.7002				
6	Adjusted R Square	0.6659				
7	Standard Error	810.8				
8	Observations	40				
9						
10	ANOVA					
11		*df*	*SS*	*MS*	*F*	*Significance F*
12	Regression	4	53,729,535	13,432,384	20.43	0.0000
13	Residual	35	23,007,438	657,355		
14	Total	39	76,736,973			
15						
16		*Coefficients*	*Standard Error*	*t Stat*	*P-value*	
17	Intercept	3490	469.2	7.44	0.0000	
18	Yest Att	0.369	0.078	4.73	0.0000	
19	I1	1623	492.5	3.30	0.0023	
20	I2	733.5	394.4	1.86	0.0713	
21	I3	-765.5	484.7	-1.58	0.1232	

b $H_0: \beta_1 = \beta_2 = \beta_3 = \beta_4 = 0$

H_1 : At least on β_i is not equal to 0

F = 20.43, p-value = 0. There is enough evidence to infer that the model is valid.

c $H_0: \beta_i = 0$

$H_1: \beta_i \neq 0$

I_2 : t = 1.86, p-value = .0713

I_3 : t = −1.58, p-value = .1232

Weather is not a factor in attendance.

d $H_0: \beta_2 = 0$

$H_1: \beta_2 > 0$

t = 3.30, p-value = .0023/2 = .0012. There is sufficient evidence to infer that weekend attendance is larger than weekday attendance.

19.18a

	A	B	C	D	E	F
1	SUMMARY OUTPUT					
2						
3	*Regression Statistics*					
4	Multiple R	0.5602				
5	R Square	0.3138				
6	Adjusted R Square	0.2897				
7	Standard Error	5.84				
8	Observations	60				
9						
10	ANOVA					
11		*df*	*SS*	*MS*	*F*	*Significance F*
12	Regression	2	887.9	443.95	13.03	0.0000
13	Residual	57	1941.7	34.06		
14	Total	59	2829.6			
15						
16		*Coefficients*	*Standard Error*	*t Stat*	*P-value*	
17	Intercept	7.02	3.24	2.17	0.0344	
18	Length	0.250	0.056	4.46	0.0000	
19	Type	-1.35	0.947	-1.43	0.1589	

b $H_0 : \beta_2 = 0$

$H_1 : \beta_2 \neq 0$

$t = -1.43$, p-value = .1589. There is not enough evidence to infer that the type of commercial affects memory test scores.

c Let

$I_1 = 1$ if humorous

$I_1 = 0$ otherwise

$I_2 = 1$ if musical

$I_2 = 0$ otherwise

	A	B	C	D	E	F
1	SUMMARY OUTPUT					
2						
3	*Regression Statistics*					
4	Multiple R	0.6231				
5	R Square	0.3882				
6	Adjusted R Square	0.3554				
7	Standard Error	5.56				
8	Observations	60				
9						
10	ANOVA					
11		*df*	*SS*	*MS*	*F*	*Significance F*
12	Regression	3	1099	366.17	11.85	0.0000
13	Residual	56	1731	30.91		
14	Total	59	2830			
15						
16		*Coefficients*	*Standard Error*	*t Stat*	*P-value*	
17	Intercept	2.53	2.15	1.18	0.2445	
18	Length	0.223	0.054	4.10	0.0001	
19	I1	2.91	1.81	1.61	0.1130	
20	I2	5.50	1.83	3.01	0.0039	

d $H_0: \beta_i = 0$

$H_1: \beta_i \neq 0$

I1: t = 1.61, p-value = .1130

I2: t = 3.01, p-value = .0039

There is enough evidence to infer that there is a difference in memory test scores between watchers of humorous and serious commercials.

e The variable type of commercial in parts (a) and (b) is nominal. It is usually meaningless to conduct a regression analysis with such variables without converting them to indicator variables.

19.20a Let

$I_1 = 1$ if no scorecard

$I_1 = 0$ otherwise

$I_2 = 1$ if scorecard overturned more than 10% of the time

$I_2 = 0$ otherwise

b

	A	B	C	D	E	F
1	SUMMARY OUTPUT					
2						
3	*Regression Statistics*					
4	Multiple R	0.7299				
5	R Square	0.5327				
6	Adjusted R Square	0.5181				
7	Standard Error	4.20				
8	Observations	100				
9						
10	ANOVA					
11		*df*	*SS*	*MS*	*F*	*Significance F*
12	Regression	3	1933	644.46	36.48	0.0000
13	Residual	96	1696	17.67		
14	Total	99	3629			
15						
16		*Coefficients*	*Standard Error*	*t Stat*	*P-value*	
17	Intercept	4.65	2.06	2.26	0.0260	
18	Loan Size	0.00012	0.00015	0.83	0.4084	
19	I1	4.08	1.14	3.57	0.0006	
20	I2	10.18	1.01	10.08	0.0000	

c $s_\varepsilon = 4.20$ and $R^2 = .5327$. The model's fit is mediocre.

d

	A	B	C	D	E
1		*Pct Bad*	*Loan Size*	*I1*	*I2*
2	Pct Bad	1			
3	Loan Size	0.1099	1		
4	I1	-0.1653	-0.0346	1	
5	I2	0.6835	0.0737	-0.5471	1

There is a high correlation between I_1 and I_2 that may distort the t–tests.

e $b_1 = .00012$; in this sample for each additional dollar lent the default rate increases by .00012 provided the other variables remain the same.

$b_2 = 4.08$; In this sample banks that don't use scorecards on average have default rates 4.08 percentage points higher than banks that overturn their scorecards less than 10% of the time.

$b_3 = 10.18$; In this sample banks that overturn their scorecards more than 10% of the time on average have default rates 10.18 percentage points higher than banks that overturn their scorecards less than 10% of the time.

f

	A	B	C	D
1	**Prediction Interval**			
2				
3			Pct Bad	
4				
5	Predicted value		9.94	
6				
7	Prediction Interval			
8	Lower limit		1.39	
9	Upper limit		18.49	
10				
11	Interval Estimate of Expected Value			
12	Lower limit		8.08	
13	Upper limit		11.81	

We predict that the bank's default rate will fall between 1.39 and 18.49%.

19.22a

	A	B	C	D	E	F
1	SUMMARY OUTPUT					
2						
3	*Regression Statistics*					
4	Multiple R	0.5125				
5	R Square	0.2626				
6	Adjusted R Square	0.2234				
7	Standard Error	5866				
8	Observations	100				
9						
10	ANOVA					
11		*df*	*SS*	*MS*	*F*	*Significance F*
12	Regression	5	1,151,889,624	230,377,925	6.70	0.0000
13	Residual	94	3,234,297,164	34,407,417		
14	Total	99	4,386,186,788			
15						
16		*Coefficients*	*Standard Error*	*t Stat*	*P-value*	
17	Intercept	30,523	2,358	12.95	0.0000	
18	Pct PT	-108.9	77.58	-1.40	0.1635	
19	Pct U	63.95	33.86	1.89	0.0620	
20	Av Shift	2591	1,287	2.01	0.0470	
21	UM Rel	-3714	1,347	-2.76	0.0070	
22	Absent	-1260	221.5	-5.69	0.0000	

b $H_0 : \beta_4 = 0$

$H_1 : \beta_4 \neq 0$

t = 2.01, p-value = .0470. There is enough evidence to infer that the availability of shiftwork affects absenteeism.

c $H_0 : \beta_5 = 0$

$H_1 : \beta_5 \neq 0$

t = –2.76, p-value =.0070. There is enough evidence to infer that in organizations where the union–management relationship is good absenteeism is lower.

19.24

	A	B	C	D	E	F
1	SUMMARY OUTPUT					
2						
3	*Regression Statistics*					
4	Multiple R	0.8311				
5	R Square	0.6907				
6	Adjusted R Square	0.5670				
7	Standard Error	1.86				
8	Observations	8				
9						
10	ANOVA					
11		*df*	*SS*	*MS*	*F*	*Significance F*
12	Regression	2	38.47	19.24	5.58	0.0532
13	Residual	5	17.23	3.45		
14	Total	7	55.70			
15						
16		*Coefficients*	*Standard Error*	*t Stat*	*P-value*	
17	Intercept	2.01	4.02	0.50	0.6385	
18	Score	3.25	1.00	3.25	0.0227	
19	Gender	-0.039	1.35	-0.03	0.9782	

In this case male–dominated jobs are paid on average $.039 (3.9 cents) *less* than female–dominated jobs after adjusting for the value of each job.

19.26 The strength of this approach lies in regression analysis. This statistical technique allows us to determine whether gender is a factor in determining salaries. However, the conclusion is very much dependent upon the subjective assignment of weights. Change the value of the weights and a totally different conclusion is achieved.

19.28 $\ln(\hat{y}) = -2.15 + .00847x_1 + .00214x_2 + .00539x_3 + .00989x_4 - .0288x_5$

$= -2.15 + .00847(0) + .00214(200) + .00539(25) + .00989(50) - .0288(0) = -1.0928$

$\hat{y} = e^{\ln(\hat{y})} = e^{-1.0928} = .3353$

$$\text{Probability of heart attack} = \frac{\hat{y}}{\hat{y}+1} = \frac{.3353}{.3353+1} = .2511$$

19.30 $\ln(\hat{y}) = -2.15 + .00847x_1 + .00214x_2 + .00539x_3 + .00989x_4 - .0288x_5$

$$= -2.15 + .00847(20) + .00214(200) + .00539(0) + .00989(50) - .0288(0) = -1.0581$$

$\hat{y} = e^{\ln(\hat{y})} = e^{-1.0581} = .3471$

$$\text{Probability of heart attack} = \frac{\hat{y}}{\hat{y}+1} = \frac{.3471}{.3471+1} = .2577$$

19.32 $\ln(\hat{y}) = .1524 + .0281x_1 + .0223x_2 + .0152x_3 + .0114x_4$

Applicant 1: $\ln(\hat{y}) = .1524 + .0281(37) + .0223(55) + .0152(6) + .0114(5) = 2.5668$

$\hat{y} = e^{\ln(\hat{y})} = e^{2.5668} = 13.0241$

$$\text{Probability of repaying loan} = \frac{\hat{y}}{\hat{y}+1} = \frac{13.0241}{13.0241+1} = .9287$$

Applicant 2: $\ln(\hat{y}) = .1524 + .0281(58) + .0223(78) + .0152(3) + .0114(12) = 3.7040$

$\hat{y} = e^{\ln(\hat{y})} = e^{3.7040} = 40.6094$

$$\text{Probability of repaying loan} = \frac{\hat{y}}{\hat{y}+1} = \frac{40.6094}{40.6094+1} = .9760$$

Applicant 3: $\ln(\hat{y}) = .1524 + .0281(47) + .0223(39) + .0152(12) + .0114(10) = 2.6392$

$\hat{y} = e^{\ln(\hat{y})} = e^{2.6392} = 14.0020$

$$\text{Probability of repaying loan} = \frac{\hat{y}}{\hat{y}+1} = \frac{14.0020}{14.0020+1} = .9333$$

For each applicant the probability of repaying the loan increased.

19.34 $\ln(\hat{y}) = 5.8687 - 5.1546x_1 - .3725x_2 - .3213x_3$

$$= 5.8687 - 5.1546(.25) - .3725(3) - .3213(1) = 3.1413$$

$$\hat{y} = e^{\ln(\hat{y})} = e^{3\ 1413} = 23.1328$$

$$\text{Probability of repaying the loan} = \frac{\hat{y}}{\hat{y}+1} = \frac{23.1328}{23.1328+1} = .9586$$

19.36 $\ln(\hat{y}) = 6.1889 - .6462x_1 - .0009254x_2 - .8721x_3$

$$= 6.1889 - .6462(4) - .0009254(1{,}855) - .8721(1) = 1.0154$$

$$\hat{y} = e^{\ln(\hat{y})} = e^{1\ 0154} = 2.7604$$

$$\text{Probability of repaying loan} = \frac{\hat{y}}{\hat{y}+1} = \frac{2.7604}{2.7604+1} = .7341$$

19.38a

	I	J	K	L	M	N	O
1	**Results of stepwise regression**						
2							
3	**Step 1 - Entering variable: GMAT**						
4							
5	Summary measures						
6		Multiple R	0.6365				
7		R-Square	0.4052				
8		Adj R-Square	0.3984				
9		StErr of Est	0.8201				
10							
11	ANOVA Table						
12		Source	df	SS	MS	F	p-value
13		Explained	1	39.8580	39.8580	59.2645	0.0000
14		Unexplained	87	58.5113	0.6725		
15							
16	Regression coefficients						
17			Coefficient	Std Err	t-value	p-value	
18		Constant	1.7991	0.8304	2.1667	0.0330	
19		GMAT	0.0111	0.0014	7.6983	0.0000	
20							
21	**Step 2 - Entering variable: I_2**						
22							
23	Summary measures			Change	% Change		
24		Multiple R	0.6837	0.0471	%7.4		
25		R-Square	0.4674	0.0622	%15.4		
26		Adj R-Square	0.4550	0.0567	%14.2		
27		StErr of Est	0.7805	-0.0396	-%4.8		
28							
29	ANOVA Table						
30		Source	df	SS	MS	F	p-value
31		Explained	2	45.9787	22.9894	37.7375	0.0000
32		Unexplained	86	52.3905	0.6092		
33							
34	Regression coefficients						
35			Coefficient	Std Err	t-value	p-value	
36		Constant	0.8175	0.8488	0.9630	0.3382	
37		GMAT	0.0125	0.0014	8.6786	0.0000	
38		I_2	0.7046	0.2223	3.1698	0.0021	
39							
40	**Step 3 - Entering variable: Work**						
41							
42	Summary measures			Change	% Change		
43		Multiple R	0.7341	0.0504	%7.4		
44		R-Square	0.5389	0.0715	%15.3		
45		Adj R-Square	0.5226	0.0676	%14.8		
46		StErr of Est	0.7305	-0.0500	-%6.4		
47							
48	ANOVA Table						
49		Source	df	SS	MS	F	p-value
50		Explained	3	53.0079	17.6693	33.1095	0.0000
51		Unexplained	85	45.3613	0.5337		
52							
53	Regression coefficients						
54			Coefficient	Std Err	t-value	p-value	
55		Constant	-0.0629	0.8307	-0.0757	0.9398	
56		GMAT	0.0129	0.0014	9.5336	0.0000	
57		I_2	0.7891	0.2094	3.7690	0.0003	
58		Work	0.1047	0.0288	3.6293	0.0005	

b The stepwise regression equation includes the independent variables that are significantly related to the dependent variable. It does not include the variables undergraduate GPA, I_1, and I_3.

19.40a

	H	I	J	K	L	M	N
1	**Results of stepwise regression**						
2							
3	**Step 1 - Entering variable: Absent**						
4							
5	Summary measures						
6		Multiple R	0.3989				
7		R-Square	0.1591				
8		Adj R-Square	0.1505				
9		StErr of Est	6134.7729				
10							
11	ANOVA Table						
12		Source	df	SS	MS	F	p-value
13		Explained	1	697913636.0400	697913636.0400	18.5441	0.0000
14		Unexplained	98	3688273152.0000	37635440.3265		
15							
16	Regression coefficients						
17			Coefficient	Std Err	t-value	p-value	
18		Constant	28516.9941	1298.6729	21.9586	0.0000	
19		Absent	-790.9393	183.6711	-4.3063	0.0000	
20							
21	**Step 2 - Entering variable: UM_Rel**						
22							
23	Summary measures			Change	% Change		
24		Multiple R	0.4509	0.0520	%13.0		
25		R-Square	0.2033	0.0442	%27.8		
26		Adj R-Square	0.1869	0.0363	%24.1		
27		StErr of Est	6002.1040	-132.6689	-%2.2		
28							
29	ANOVA Table						
30		Source	df	SS	MS	F	p-value
31		Explained	2	891737380.0400	445868690.0200	12.3766	0.0000
32		Unexplained	97	3494449408.0000	36025251.6289		
33							
34	Regression coefficients						
35			Coefficient	Std Err	t-value	p-value	
36		Constant	31636.3125	1850.1073	17.0997	0.0000	
37		Absent	-967.8824	195.2204	-4.9579	0.0000	
38		UM_Rel	-3150.9519	1358.4437	-2.3195	0.0225	

b In the stepwise regression equation only the number of days absent and union–management relations were statistically significant.

c The three variables that were not statistically significant and one that was borderline were excluded by the stepwise regression process.

19.42a Mileage = $\beta_0 + \beta_1$ Speed $+ \beta_2$ Speed^2 + ε

b

	A	B	C	D	E	F
1	SUMMARY OUTPUT					
2						
3	*Regression Statistics*					
4	Multiple R	0.8428				
5	R Square	0.7102				
6	Adjusted R Square	0.6979				
7	Standard Error	3.86				
8	Observations	50				
9						
10	ANOVA					
11		*df*	*SS*	*MS*	*F*	*Significance F*
12	Regression	2	1719.9	859.94	57.60	0.0000
13	Residual	47	701.64	14.93		
14	Total	49	2421.5			
15						
16		*Coefficients*	*Standard Error*	*t Stat*	*P-value*	
17	Intercept	9.34	1.71	5.47	0.0000	
18	Speed	0.802	0.077	10.39	0.0000	
19	Speed-sq	-0.0079	0.00073	-10.73	0.0000	

c $s_\varepsilon = 3.86$ and $R^2 = .7102$. The model fits moderately well.

19.44a

	A	B	C	D	E	F
1	SUMMARY OUTPUT					
2						
3	*Regression Statistics*					
4	Multiple R	0.8668				
5	R Square	0.7514				
6	Adjusted R Square	0.7284				
7	Standard Error	1.27				
8	Observations	60				
9						
10	ANOVA					
11		*df*	*SS*	*MS*	*F*	*Significance F*
12	Regression	5	262.95	52.59	32.65	0.0000
13	Residual	54	86.99	1.61		
14	Total	59	349.93			
15						
16		*Coefficients*	*Standard Error*	*t Stat*	*P-value*	
17	Intercept	404.5	327.0	1.24	0.2214	
18	Cars	-66.57	6.54	-10.19	0.0000	
19	Speed	-2.35	10.54	-0.22	0.8246	
20	Cars-sq	0.107	0.097	1.10	0.2741	
21	Speed-sq	-0.070	0.085	-0.82	0.4180	
22	Cars-Speed	1.08	0.096	11.21	0.0000	

b F = 32.65, p-value = 0. There is enough evidence to infer that the model is valid.

19.46

	A	B	C	D	E	F
1	SUMMARY OUTPUT					
2						
3	*Regression Statistics*					
4	Multiple R	0.9347				
5	R Square	0.8736				
6	Adjusted R Square	0.8654				
7	Standard Error	0.0183				
8	Observations	50				
9						
10	ANOVA					
11		*df*	*SS*	*MS*	*F*	*Significance F*
12	Regression	3	0.107	0.0355	106.01	0.0000
13	Residual	46	0.0154	0.00034		
14	Total	49	0.122			
15						
16		*Coefficients*	*Standard Error*	*t Stat*	*P-value*	
17	Intercept	0.357	0.0592	6.03	0.0000	
18	BA	-0.401	0.236	-1.70	0.0964	
19	ERA	0.0764	0.00478	15.98	0.0000	
20	Fired	-0.0509	0.00591	-8.61	0.0000	

b $H_0 : \beta_3 = 0$

$H_1 : \beta_3 < 0$

$t = -8.61$, p-value = 0. There is enough evidence to infer that a team that fires its manager within 12 months wins less frequently than other teams.

19.48a Depletion = $\beta_0 + \beta_1$ Temperature $+ \beta_2$ PH–level $+ \beta_3$ PH–level^2 + $\beta_4 I_4 + \beta_5 I_5 + \varepsilon$

where

$I_1 = 1$ if mainly cloudy

$I_1 = 0$ otherwise

$I_2 = 1$ if sunny

$I_2 = 0$ otherwise

b

	A	B	C	D	E	F
1	SUMMARY OUTPUT					
2						
3	*Regression Statistics*					
4	Multiple R	0.8085				
5	R Square	0.6537				
6	Adjusted R Square	0.6452				
7	Standard Error	4.14				
8	Observations	210				
9						
10	ANOVA					
11		*df*	*SS*	*MS*	*F*	*Significance F*
12	Regression	5	6596	1319	77.00	0.0000
13	Residual	204	3495	17.13		
14	Total	209	10091			
15						
16		*Coefficients*	*Standard Error*	*t Stat*	*P-value*	
17	Intercept	1003	55.12	18.19	0.0000	
18	Temperature	0.194	0.029	6.78	0.0000	
19	PH Level	-265.6	14.75	-18.01	0.0000	
20	PH-sq	17.76	0.983	18.07	0.0000	
21	I1	-1.07	0.700	-1.53	0.1282	
22	I2	1.16	0.700	1.65	0.0997	

c $H_0: \beta_1 = \beta_2 = \beta_3 = \beta_4 = \beta_5 = 0$

$H_1:$ At least on β_i is not equal to 0

F = 77.00, p-value = 0. There is enough evidence to infer that the model is valid.

d $H_0: \beta_1 = 0$

$H_1: \beta_1 > 0$

t = 6.78, p-value = 0. There is enough evidence to infer that higher temperatures deplete chlorine more quickly.

e $H_0: \beta_3 = 0$

$H_1: \beta_3 > 0$

t = 18.07, p-value = 0. There is enough evidence to infer that there is a quadratic relationship between chlorine depletion and PH level.

f $H_0: \beta_i = 0$

$H_1: \beta_i \neq 0$

I_1: t = –1.53, p-value = .1282. There is not enough evidence to infer that chlorine depletion differs between mainly cloudy days and partly sunny days.

I_2 : t = 1.65, p-value = .0997. There is not enough evidence to infer that chlorine depletion differs between sunny days and partly sunny days.

Weather is not a factor in chlorine depletion.

Chapter 20

20.2 Time series	Moving average
48	
41	
37	(48 +41+37+32+36)/5 = 38.8
32	(41+37+32+36+31)/5 = 35.4
36	(37+32+36+31+43)/5 = 35.8
31	(32+36+31+43+52)/5 = 38.8
43	(36+31+43+52+60)/5 = 44.4
52	(31+43+52+60+48)/5 = 46.8
60	(43+52+60+48+41)/5 = 48.8
48	(52+60+48+41+30)/5 = 46.2
41	
30	

20.4 Time series	Moving average
16	
22	(16+22+19)/3 = 19.00
19	(22+19+24)/3 = 21.67
24	(19+24+30)/3 = 24.33
30	(24+30+26)/3 = 26.67
26	(30+26+24)/3 = 26.67
24	(26+24+29)/3 = 26.33
29	(24+29+21)/3 = 24.67
21	(29+21+23)/3 = 24.33
23	(21+23+19)/3 = 21.00
19	(23+19+15)/3 = 19.00
15	

20.6

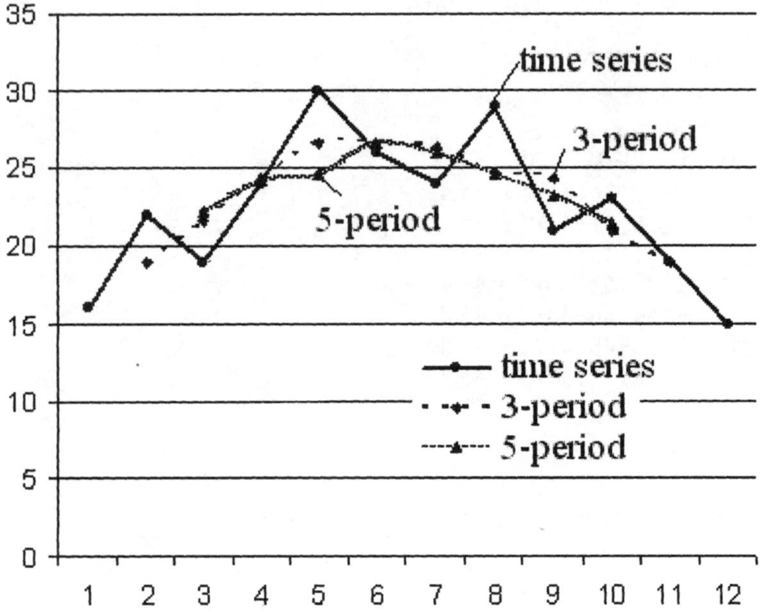

20.8 Time series	Exponentially smoothed time series
12	12
18	.8(18) +. 2(12) = 16.80
16	.8(16) +. 2(16.80) = 16.16
24	.8(24) +. 2(16.16) = 22.43
17	.8(17) +. 2(22.43) = 18.09
16	.8(16) +. 2(18.09) = 16.42
25	.8(25) +. 2(16.42) = 23.28
21	.8(21) +. 2(23.28) = 21.46
23	.8(23) + .2(21.46) = 22.69
14	.8(14) + .2(22.69) = 15.74

20.10 Time series	Exponentially smoothed time series
38	38
43	.1(43) +. 9(38) = 38.50
42	.1(42) +. 9(38.50) = 38.85
45	.1(45) +. 9(38.85) = 39.47
46	.1(46) +. 9(39.47) = 40.12
48	.1(48) +. 9(40.12) = 40.91
50	.1(50) +. 9(40.91) = 41.82
49	.1(49) +. 9(41.82) = 42.53
46	.1(46) + .9(42.53) = 42.88
45	.1(45) + .9(42.88) = 43.09

20.12 There is a trend component.

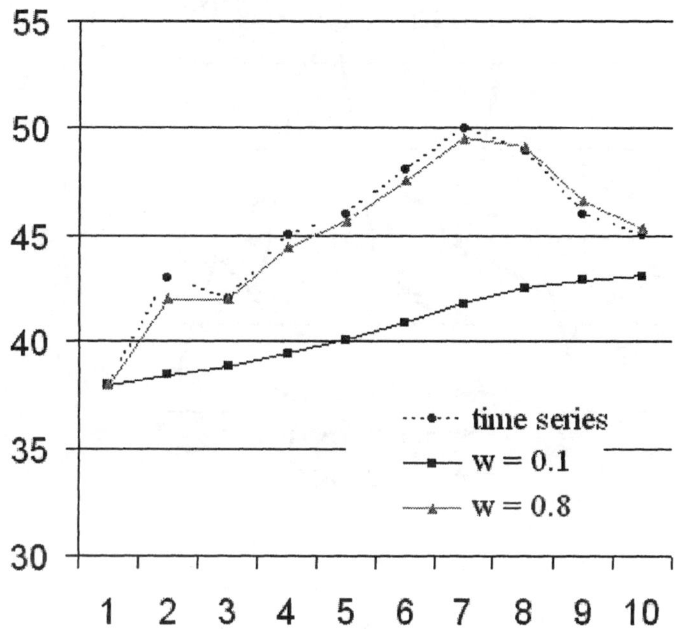

20.13 & 20.14

Sales	3-Day moving average	5-Day moving average
43		
45	(43+45+22)/3 = 36.67	
22	(45+22+25)/3 = 30.67	(43+45+22+25+31)/5 = 33.2
25	(22+25+31)/3 = 26.00	(45+22+25+31+51)/5 = 34.8
31	(25+31+51)/3 = 35.67	(22+25+31+51+41)/5 = 34.0
51	(31+51+41)/3 = 41.00	(25+31+51+41+37)/5 = 37.0
41	(51+41+37)/3 = 43.00	(31+51+41+37+22)/5 = 36.4
37	(41+37+22)/3 = 33.33	(51+41+37+22+25)/5 = 35.2
22	(37+22+25)/3 = 28.00	(41+37+22+25+40)/5 = 33.0
25	(22+25+40)/3 = 29.00	(37+22+25+40+57)/5 = 36.2
40	(25+40+57)/3 = 40.67	(22+25+40+57+30)/5 = 34.8
57	(40+57+30)/3 = 42.33	(25+40+57+30+33)/5 = 37.0
30	(57+30+33)/3 = 40.00	(40+57+30+33+37)/5 = 39.4
33	(30+33+37)/3 = 33.33	(57+30+33+37+64)/5 = 44.2
37	(33+37+64)/3 = 44.67	(30+33+37+64+58)/5 = 44.4
64	(37+64+58)/3 = 53.00	(33+37+64+58+33)/5 = 45.0
58	(64+58+33)/3 = 51.67	(37+64+58+33+38)/5 = 46.0
33	(58+33+38)/3 = 43.00	(64+58+33+38+25)/5 = 43.6
38	(33+38+25)/3 = 32.00	
25		

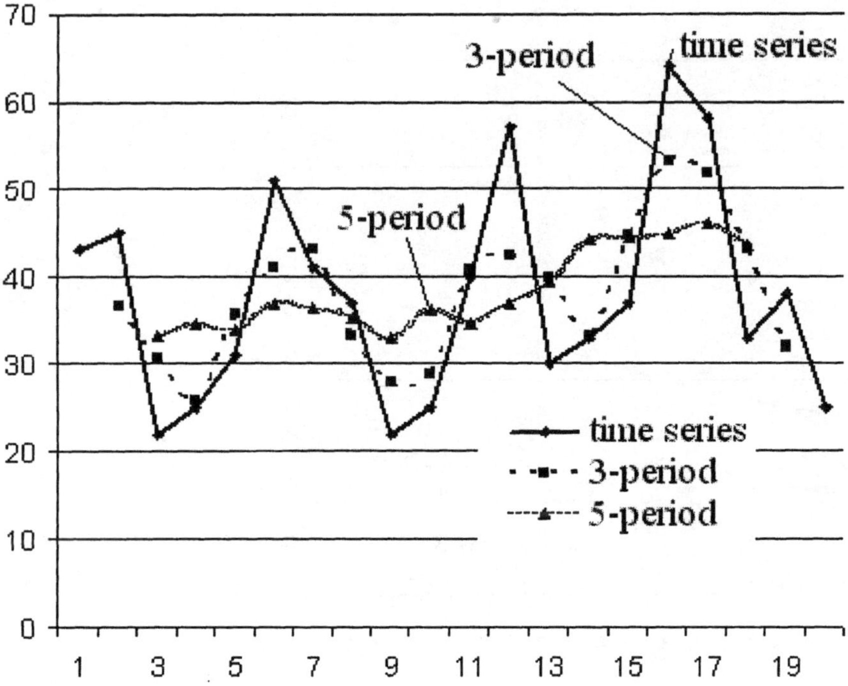

c There appears to be a seasonal (weekly) pattern.

20.16 & 20.17

Sales	Exponentially smoothed w = .4	Exponentially smoothed w = .8
18	18	18
22	.4(22)+.6(18) = 19.60	.8(22)+.2(18) = 21.20
27	.4(27)+.6(19.6) = 22.56	.8(27)+.2(21.2) = 25.84
31	.4(31)+.6(22.56) = 25.94	.8(31)+.2(25.84) = 29.97
33	.4(33)+.6(25.94) = 28.76	.8(33)+.2(29.97) = 32.39
20	.4(20)+.6(28.76) = 25.26	.8(20)+.2(32.39) = 22.48
38	.4(38)+.6(25.26) = 30.35	.8(38)+.2(22.48) = 34.90
26	.4(26)+.6(30.35) = 28.61	.8(26)+.2(34.90) = 27.78
25	.4(25)+.6(28.61) = 27.17	.8(25)+.2(27.78) = 25.56
36	.4(36)+.6(27.17) = 30.70	.8(36)+.2(25.56) = 33.91
44	.4(44)+.6(30.70) = 36.02	.8(44)+.2(33.91) = 41.98
29	.4(29)+.6(36.02) = 33.21	.8(29)+.2(41.98) = 31.60
41	.4(41)+.6(33.21) = 36.33	.8(41)+.2(31.60) = 39.12
33	.4(33)+.6(36.33) = 35.00	.8(33)+.2(39.12) = 34.22
52	.4(52)+.6(35.00) = 41.80	.8(52)+.2(34.22) = 48.44
45	.4(45)+.6(41.80) = 43.08	.8(45)+.2(48.44) = 45.69

20.16 b

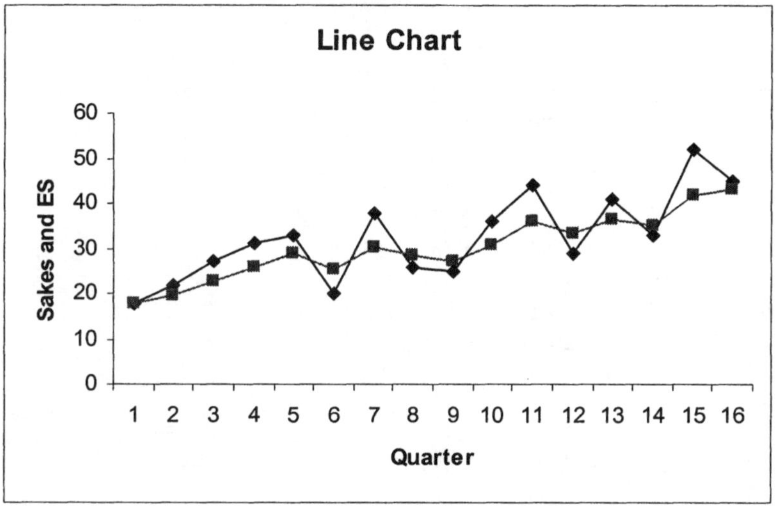

20.18

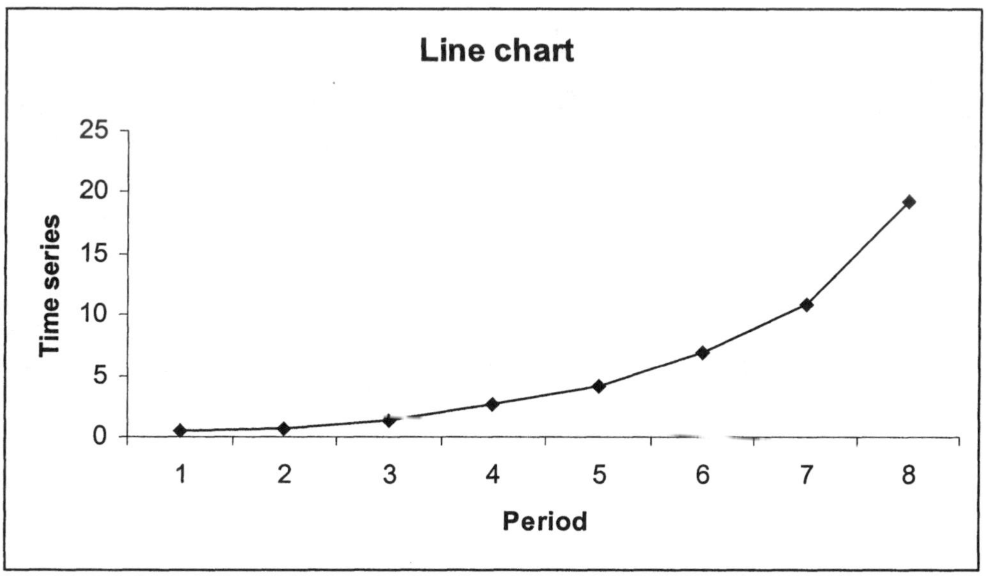

The quadratic model would appear to be the best model.

20.20

$\hat{y} = -4.96 + 2.38t$ $(R^2 = .81)$

$\hat{y} = 3.14 - 2.48t + .54t^2$ $(R^2 = .98)$

The quadratic trend line fits better.

20.22

Week	Day	Period	y	ŷ	y / ŷ
1	1	1	12	17.2	.699
	2	2	18	17.5	1.027
	3	3	16	17.9	.894
	4	4	25	18.3	1.369
	5	5	31	18.6	1.664
2	1	6	11	19.0	.579
	2	7	17	19.4	.878
	3	8	19	19.7	.963
	4	9	24	20.1	1.194
	5	10	27	20.5	1.320
3	1	11	14	20.8	.672
	2	12	16	21.2	.755
	3	13	16	21.6	.742
	4	14	28	21.9	1.277
	5	15	25	22.3	1.122
4	1	16	17	22.7	.750
	2	17	21	23.0	.912
	3	18	20	23.4	.855
	4	19	24	23.8	1.101
	5	20	32	24.1	1.327

Week	Monday	Tuesday	Wednesday	Thursday	Friday	Total
1	.699	1.027	.894	1.369	1.664	
2	.579	.878	.963	1.194	1.320	
3	.672	.755	.742	1.277	1.122	
4	.750	.912	.855	1.010	1.327	
Average	.675	.893	.864	1.213	1.358	5.003
Seasonal Index	.675	.892	.864	1.212	1.357	5.000

20.24

Week	Day	Period	y	ŷ	y / ŷ
1	1	1	12	17.2	.699
	2	2	18	17.5	1.027
	3	3	16	17.9	.894
	4	4	25	18.3	1.369
	5	5	31	18.6	1.664

2	1	6	11	19.0	.579
	2	7	17	19.4	.878
	3	8	19	19.7	.963
	4	9	24	20.1	1.194
	5	10	27	20.5	1.320
3	1	11	14	20.8	.672
	2	12	16	21.2	.755
	3	13	16	21.6	.742
	4	14	28	21.9	1.277
	5	15	25	22.3	1.122
4	1	16	17	22.7	.750
	2	17	21	23.0	.912
	3	18	20	23.4	.855
	4	19	24	23.8	1.101
	5	20	32	24.1	1.327

Week	Monday	Tuesday	Wednesday	Thursday	Friday	Total
1	.699	1.027	.894	1.369	1.664	
2	.579	.878	.963	1.194	1.320	
3	.672	.755	.742	1.277	1.122	
4	.750	.912	.855	1.010	1.327	
Average	.675	.893	.864	1.213	1.358	5.003
Seasonal Index	.675	.892	.864	1.212	1.357	5.000

20.26a

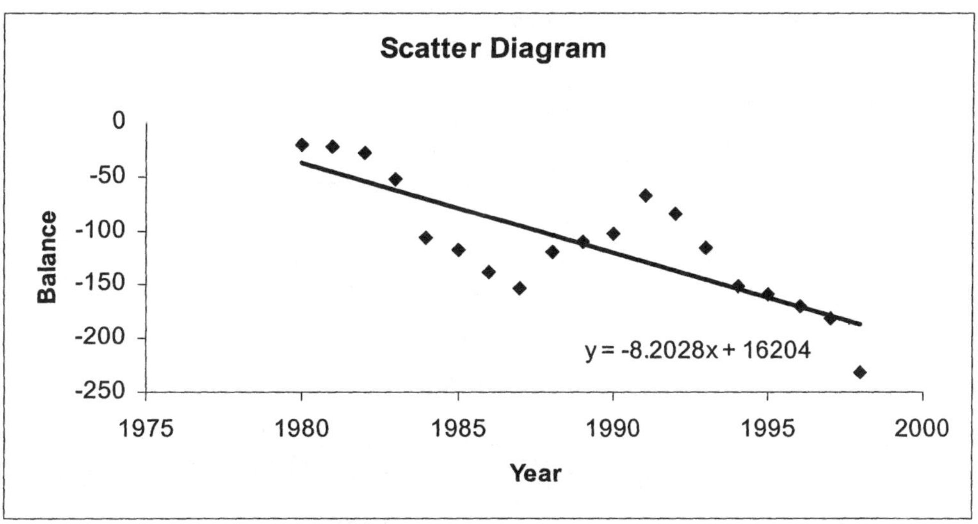

b $\hat{y} = 16{,}204 - 8.20\text{Year}$

20.28

Regression line: $\hat{y} = 145 + 1.66\,t$

Week	Day	Period	y	$\hat{y} = 145 + 1.66t$	$y / \hat{y}$
1	1	1	240	146.66	1.636
	2	2	85	148.32	.573
	3	3	93	149.98	.620
	4	4	106	151.64	.699
	5	5	125	153.3	.815
	6	6	188	154.96	1.213
	7	7	314	156.62	2.005
2	1	8	221	158.28	1.396
	2	9	80	159.94	.500
	3	10	75	161.6	.464
	4	11	12	163.26	.741
	5	12	110	164.92	.667
	6	13	202	166.58	1.213
	7	14	386	168.24	2.294
3	1	15	235	169.9	1.383
	2	16	86	171.56	.501
	3	17	74	173.22	.427
	4	18	100	174.88	.572
	5	19	117	176.54	.663
	6	20	205	178.20	1.150
	7	21	402	179.86	2.235
4	1	22	219	181.52	1.206
	2	23	91	183.18	.497
	3	24	102	184.84	.552
	4	25	89	186.50	.477
	5	26	105	188.16	.558
	6	27	192	189.82	1.011
	7	28	377	191.48	1.969

Week	1	2	3	4	5	6	7	Total
1	1.636	.573	.620	.699	.815	1.213	2.005	
2	1.396	.500	.464	.741	.667	1.213	2.294	
3	1.383	.501	.427	.572	.663	1.150	2.235	
4	1.206	.497	.552	.477	.558	1.011	1.969	
Average	1.405	.518	.516	.657	.676	1.187	2.126	7.085
Seasonal index	1.404	.517	.515	.621	.675	1.145	2.123	7.000

20.30

$$\text{MAD} = \frac{|166-173| + |179-186| + |195-192| + |214-211| + |220-223|}{5}$$

$$= \frac{7+7+3+3+3}{5} = \frac{23}{5} = 4.60$$

$$\text{SSE} = (166-173)^2 + (179-186)^2 + (195-192)^2 + (214-211)^2 + (220-223)^2$$

$$= 49 + 49 + 9 + 9 + 9 = 125$$

20.32

$$\text{MAD} = \frac{|57-63| + |60-72| + |70-86| + |75-71| + |70-60|}{5}$$

$$= \frac{6+12+16+4+10}{5} = \frac{48}{5} = 9.6$$

$$\text{SSE} = (57-63)^2 + (60-72)^2 + (70-86)^2 + (75-71)^2 + (70-60)^2 = 36 + 144 + 256 + 16 + 100 = 552$$

20.34

Quarter	t	$\hat{y} = 150 + 3t$	Seasonal Index	Forecast
1	41	273	7	191.1
2	42	276	1.2	331.2
3	43	279	1.5	418.5
4	44	282	.6	169.2

20.36 $\hat{y}_t = 625 - 1.3_{y_{t-1}} = 625 - 1.3(65) = 540.5$

20.38 $F_{17} = F_{18} = F_{19} = F_{20} = S_{16} = 43.08$

20.40

Quarter	t	$\hat{y} = 47.7 - 1.06t$	Seasonal Index	Forecast
1	21	25.44	1.207	30.71
2	22	24.38	.959	23.38
3	23	23.32	.972	22.67
4	24	22.26	.863	19.21

20.42a $\hat{y}_{2002} = 10{,}797 + .299y_{2001} = 10{,}797 + .299(15{,}873) = 15{,}543$

b $F_{2002} = S_{2001} = 15{,}297$

20.44

Quarter	t	$\hat{y} = 143 + 7.42t$	Seasonal index	Forecast
1	25	328.50	1.063	349.20
2	26	335.92	.962	323.16
3	27	343.34	.927	318.28
4	28	350.76	1.048	367.60

20.46

Quarter	t	$\hat{y} = 90.4 + 2.02t$	Seasonal index	Forecast
1	17	124.74	1.094	136.47
2	18	126.76	.958	121.44
3	19	128.78	.688	88.60
4	20	130.80	1.260	164.81

20.48 The only component appears to be seasonality.

20.50

	A	B
1	**Seasonal Indexes**	
2		
3	**Season**	**Index**
4	1	0.646
5	2	1.045
6	3	1.405
7	4	0.904

Chapter 21

21.2 H_0 : The two population locations are the same

H_1 : The location of population 1 is to the right of the location of population 2

Rejection region: $z > z_{\alpha} = z_{.01} = 2.33$

$$E(T) = \frac{n_1(n_1 + n_2 + 1)}{2} = \frac{30(30 + 40 + 1)}{2} = 1{,}065$$

$$\sigma_T = \sqrt{\frac{n_1 n_2 (n_1 + n_2 + 1)}{12}} = \sqrt{\frac{(30)(40)(30 + 40 + 1)}{12}} = 84.26$$

a $z = \frac{T - E(T)}{\sigma_T} = \frac{1{,}205 - 1{,}065}{84.26} = 1.66$, p-value $P(Z > 1.66) = .5 - .4515 = .0485$. There is not enough evidence to infer that the location of population 1 is to the right of the location of population 2.

b $z = \frac{T - E(T)}{\sigma_T} = \frac{1{,}065 - 1{,}065}{84.26} = 0$, p-value $= P(Z > 0) = .5$. There is not enough evidence to infer that the location of population 1 is to the right of the location of population 2.

c The value of the test statistic decreases and the p-value increases.

21.4 H_0 : The two population locations are the same

H_1 : The location of population 1 is different from the location of population 2

Rejection region: $T \geq T_U = 127$ or $T \leq T_L = 83$

Sample 1	Rank	Sample 2	Rank
15	4.0	8	2.0
7	1.0	27	18.0
22	14.0	17	7.0
20	.5	25	16.0
32	20.0	20	11.5
18	9.5	16	5.0
26	17.0	21	13.0
17	7.0	17	7.0
23	15.0	10	3.0
30	19.0	18	9.5
	$T_1 = 118$		$T_2 = 92$

There is not enough evidence to infer that the location of population 1 is different from the location of population 2.

21.6 H_0 : The two population locations are the same

H_1 : The location of population 1 is different from the location of population 2

	A	B	C	D	E
1	**Wilcoxon Rank Sum Test**				
2					
3			Rank Sum	Observations	
4	*Business*		4004	40	
5	*Economy*		8086	115	
6	z Stat		3.6149		
7	P(Z<=z) one-tail		0.0002		
8	z Critical one-tail		1.6449		
9	P(Z<=z) two-tail		0.0004		
10	z Critical two-tail		1.96		

a z = 3.61, p-value = .0004. There is enough evidence to infer that the business and economy class differ in their degree of satisfaction.

b The printout is identical to that of part a.

c All codes that preserve the order produce the same results.

21.8 H_0 : The two population locations are the same

H_1 : The location of population 1 is to the right of the location of population 2

Rejection region: $z > z_{\alpha} = z_{05} = 1.645$

$$E(T) = \frac{n_1(n_1 + n_2 + 1)}{2} = \frac{82(82 + 75 + 1)}{2} = 6478$$

$$\sigma_T = \sqrt{\frac{n_1 n_2 (n_1 + n_2 + 1)}{12}} = \sqrt{\frac{(82)(75)(82 + 75 + 1)}{12}} = 284.6$$

$z = \frac{T - E(T)}{\sigma_T} = \frac{6{,}807 - 6{,}478}{284.6} = 1.16$, p-value $P(Z > 1.16) = .5 - .3770 = .1230$. There is not enough evidence to infer that members of the Mathematics department rate nonparametric techniques as more important than do members of other departments.

21.10 H_0 : The two population locations are the same

H_1 : The location of population 1 is to the left of the location of population 2

Rejection region: $z < -z_{\alpha} = -z_{.05} = -1.645$

$$E(T) = \frac{n_1(n_1+n_2+1)}{2} = \frac{125(125+125+1)}{2} = 15{,}687.5$$

$$\sigma_T = \sqrt{\frac{n_1 n_2(n_1+n_2+1)}{12}} = \sqrt{\frac{(125)(125)(125+125+1)}{12}} = 571.7$$

$z = \frac{T - E(T)}{\sigma_T} = \frac{14{,}873 - 15{,}687.5}{571.7} = -1.42$, p-value $P(Z < -1.42) = .5 - .4222 = .0778$. There is not enough evidence to infer that women are doing less housework today than last year.

21.12 H_0: The two population locations are the same

H_1: The location of population 1 is different from the location of population 2

Rejection region: $z < -z_{\alpha/2} = -z_{.025} = -1.96$ or $z > z_{\alpha/2} = z_{.025} = 1.96$

$$E(T) = \frac{n_1(n_1+n_2+1)}{2} = \frac{50(50+50+1)}{2} = 2525$$

$$\sigma_T = \sqrt{\frac{n_1 n_2(n_1+n_2+1)}{12}} = \sqrt{\frac{(50)(50)(50+50+1)}{12}} = 145.1$$

$z = \frac{T - E(T)}{\sigma_T} = \frac{2810 - 2525}{145.1} = 1.964$, p-value = $2P(Z > 1.964)$, which is slightly less than $2P(Z > 1.96) = 2(.5 - .4750) = .05$. There is enough evidence to infer that men and women experience different levels of stomach upset.

21.14 H_0: The two population locations are the same

H_1: The location of population 1 is to the right of the location of population 2

Rejection region: $z > z_\alpha = z_{.05} = 1.645$

$$E(T) = \frac{n_1(n_1+n_2+1)}{2} = \frac{20(20+20+1)}{2} = 410,$$

$$\sigma_T = \sqrt{\frac{n_1 n_2(n_1+n_2+1)}{12}} = \sqrt{\frac{(20)(20)(20+20+1)}{12}} = 37.0$$

$z = \frac{T - E(T)}{\sigma_T} = \frac{439.5 - 410}{37.0} = .80$, p-value = $P(Z > .80) = .5 - .2881 = .2119$. There is not enough evidence to infer that women perceive another woman wearing a size 6 dress as more professional than one wearing a size 14 dress.

21.16 H_0 : The two population locations are the same

H_1 : The location of population 1 is different from the location of population 2

Rejection region: $z < -z_{\alpha/2} = -z_{.025} = -1.96$ or $z > z_{\alpha/2} = z_{.025} = 1.96$

$$E(T) = \frac{n_1(n_1 + n_2 + 1)}{2} = \frac{182(182 + 163 + 1)}{2} = 31{,}486$$

$$\sigma_T = \sqrt{\frac{n_1 n_2 (n_1 + n_2 + 1)}{12}} = \sqrt{\frac{(182)(163)(182 + 163 + 1)}{12}} = 924.9$$

$z = \frac{T - E(T)}{\sigma_T} = \frac{32{,}225.5 - 31{,}486}{924.9} = .80$, p-value = 2P(Z > .80) = 2(.5 – .2881) = .4238. There is not enough evidence to infer that the night and day shifts rate the service differently.

21.18 H_0 : The two population locations are the same

H_1 : The location of population 1 is to the left of the location of population 2

Rejection region: $z < -z_{\alpha} = -z_{10} = -1.28$

$z = \frac{x - .5n}{.5\sqrt{n}} = \frac{28 - .5(69)}{.5\sqrt{69}} = -1.57$, p-value = P(Z < –1.57) = .5 – .4418 = .0582. There is enough evidence to infer that the location of population 1 is to the left of the location of population 2.

21.20 H_0 : The two population locations are the same

H_1 : The location of population 1 is to the right of the location of population 2

Pair	A	B	Sign of Difference
1	5	3	+
2	3	2	+
3	4	4	0
4	2	3	–
5	3	3	0
6	4	1	+
7	3	3	0
8	5	4	+
9	4	2	+
10	3	5	–
11	4	1	+
12	5	2	+
13	4	2	+
14	5	3	+
15	3	2	+
16	2	2	0

Rejection region: $z > z_\alpha = z_{.05} = 1.645$

$x = 10$, $n = 12$, $z = \frac{x - .5n}{.5\sqrt{n}} = \frac{10 - .5(12)}{.5\sqrt{12}} = 2.31$, p-value = $P(Z > 2.31) = .5 - .4896 = .0104$

There is enough evidence to infer that the population 1 is located to the right of population 2.

21.22 H_0 : The two population locations are the same

H_1 : The location of population 1 is to the right of the location of population 2

Rejection region: $z > z_\alpha = z_{01} = 2.33$

$$E(T) = \frac{n(n+1)}{4} = \frac{108(109)}{4} = 2943\ ;\ \sigma_T = \sqrt{\frac{n(n+1)(2n+1)}{24}} = \sqrt{\frac{108(109)(217)}{24}} = 326.25$$

$z = \frac{T - E(T)}{\sigma_T} = \frac{3457 - 2943}{326.25} = 1.58$, p-value = $P(Z > 1.58) = .5 - .4429 = .0571$. There is not enough evidence to conclude that population 1 is located to the right of the location of population 2.

21.24 H_0 : The two population locations are the same

H_1 : The location of population 1 is different from the location of population 2

Rejection region: $T \ge T_U = 39$ or $T \le T_L = 6$

Pair	Sample 1	Sample 2	Difference	|Difference|	Ranks	
1	18.2	18.2	0	0		
2	14.1	14.1	0	0		
3	24.5	23.6	.9	.9	6.5	
4	11.9	12.1	−.2	.2		2
5	9.5	9.5	0	0		
6	12.1	11.3	.8	.8	5	
7	10.9	9.7	1.2	1.2	8	
8	16.7	17.6	−.9	.9		6.5
9	19.6	19.4	.2	.2	2	
10	8.4	8.1	.3	.3	4	
11	21.7	21.9	−.2	.2		2
12	23.4	21.6	1.8	1.8	9	
					$T^+ = 34.5$	$T^- = 10.5$

T = 34.5. There is not enough evidence to conclude that the population locations differ.

21.26 $H_0 : H_0$: The two population locations are the same

H_1 : The location of population 1 is to the right of the location of population 2

	A	B	C	D	E
1	**Sign Test**				
2					
3	Difference			*Brand A - Brand B*	
4					
5	Positive Differences			21	
6	Negative Differences			15	
7	Zero Differences			14	
8	z Stat			1.00	
9	P(Z<=z) one-tail			0.1587	
10	z Critical one-tail			1.6449	
11	P(Z<=z) two-tail			0.3174	
12	z Critical two-tail			1.96	

a z = 1.00, p-value = .1587. There is no evidence to infer that Brand A is preferred.

b The printout is identical to that of part a.

c All codes that preserve the order produce the same results.

21.28 H_0 : The two population locations are the same

H_1 : The location of population 1 is different from the location of population 2

	A	B	C	D	E
1	**Sign Test**				
2					
3	Difference			*Sample 1 - Sample 2*	
4					
5	Positive Differences			51	
6	Negative Differences			74	
7	Zero Differences			0	
8	z Stat			-2.06	
9	P(Z<=z) one-tail			0.0198	
10	z Critical one-tail			1.6449	
11	P(Z<=z) two-tail			0.0396	
12	z Critical two-tail			1.96	

z = –2.06, p-value = .0396. There is enough evidence to infer that the population locations differ.

b

	A	B	C	D	E
1	**Wilcoxon Signed Rank Sum Test**				
2					
3	Difference		*Sample 1 - Sample 2*		
4					
5	T+		3726.5		
6	T-		4148.5		
7	Observations (for test)		125		
8	z Stat		-0.52		
9	P(Z<=z) one-tail		0.3016		
10	z Critical one-tail		1.6449		
11	P(Z<=z) two-tail		0.6032		
12	z Critical two-tail		1.96		

z = –.52, p-value = .6032. There is not enough evidence to infer that the population locations differ.

c The sign test ignores the magnitudes of the paired differences whereas the Wilcoxon signed rank sum test does not.

b

	A	B	C	D
1	**Wilcoxon Signed Rank Sum Test**			
2				
3	Difference		*Sample 1 - Sample 2*	
4				
5	T+		304	
6	T-		872	
7	Observations (for test)		48	
8	z Stat		-2.91	
9	P(Z<=z) one-tail		0.0018	
10	z Critical one-tail		1.6449	
11	P(Z<=z) two-tail		0.0036	
12	z Critical two-tail		1.96	

z = –2.91, p-value = .0036. There is enough evidence to conclude that the population locations differ.

c The sign test ignores the magnitudes of the paired differences whereas the Wilcoxon signed rank sum test does not.

21.30 H_0 : The two population locations are the same

H_1 : The location of population 1 is to the left of the location of population 2

Rejection region: $z < -z_{\alpha} = -z_{.05} = -1.645$

$$E(T) = \frac{n(n+1)}{4} = \frac{72(72+1)}{4} = 1314\,;\ \sigma_T = \sqrt{\frac{n(n+1)(2n+1)}{24}} = \sqrt{\frac{72(72+1)(2[72]+1)}{24}} = 178.2$$

$z = \frac{T - E(T)}{\sigma_T} = \frac{378.5 - 1314}{178.2} = -5.25$, p-value = P(Z < –5.25) = 0. There is enough evidence to infer that the drug is effective.

21.32 H_0 : The two population locations are the same

H_1 : The location of population 1 is to the right of the location of population 2

Rejection region: $z > z_\alpha = z_{.05} = 1.645$

$z = \frac{x - .5n}{.5\sqrt{n}} = \frac{60 - .5(98)}{.5\sqrt{98}} = 2.22$, p-value = P(Z > 2.22) = .5 – .4868= .0132. There is enough evidence to conclude that concern about a gasoline shortage exceeded concern about an electricity shortage.

21.34 H_0 : The two population locations are the same

H_1 : The location of population 1 is to the left of the location of population 2

Rejection region: $z < -z_\alpha = -z_{05} = -1.645$

$$E(T) = \frac{n(n+1)}{4} = \frac{26(26+1)}{4} = 175.5\,;\ \sigma_T = \sqrt{\frac{n(n+1)(2n+1)}{24}} = \sqrt{\frac{26(26+1)(2[26]+1)}{24}} = 39.4$$

$z = \frac{T - E(T)}{\sigma_T} = \frac{111 - 175.5}{39.4} = -1.64$, p-value = P(z < –1.64) = .5 – .4495 = .0505. There is not enough evidence to infer that the swimming department has higher gross sales.

21.36 H_0 : The two population locations are the same

H_1 : The location of population 1 is to the left of the location of population 2

Rejection region: $z < -z_\alpha = -z_{01} = -2.33$

$z = \frac{x - .5n}{.5\sqrt{n}} = \frac{5 - .5(20)}{.5\sqrt{20}} = -2.24$, p-value = P(Z < –2.24) = .5 – .4875 = .0125. There is not enough evidence to conclude that children feel less pain.

21.38 H_0 : The two population locations are the same

H_1 : The location of population 1 is to the right of the location of population 2

Rejection region: $z > z_{\alpha} = z_{.05} = 1.645$

$z = \frac{x - .5n}{.5\sqrt{n}} = \frac{32 - .5(53)}{.5\sqrt{53}} = 1.51$, p-value = P(Z > 1.51) = .5 – .4345 = .0655. There is not enough evidence to infer that preference should be given to students for high school 1.

21.40 H_0 : The locations of all 3 populations are the same.

H_1 : At least two population locations differ.

Rejection region: $H > \chi^2_{\alpha,k-1} = \chi^2_{.05,2} = 5.99147$

$$H = \left[\frac{12}{n(n+1)}\sum\frac{T_j^2}{n_j}\right] - 3(n+1) = \left[\frac{12}{88(88+1)}\left(\frac{984^2}{23} + \frac{1502^2}{36} + \frac{1430^2}{29}\right)\right] - 3(88+1) = 1.56$$

There is not enough evidence to conclude that the population locations differ.

21.42 H_0 : The locations of all 3 populations are the same.

H_1 : At least two population locations differ.

Rejection region: $H > \chi^2_{\alpha,k-1} = \chi^2_{10,2} = 4.60517$

$$H = \left[\frac{12}{n(n+1)}\sum\frac{T_j^2}{n_j}\right] - 3(n+1) = \left[\frac{12}{143(143+1)}\left(\frac{3741^2}{47} + \frac{1610^2}{29} + \frac{4945^2}{67}\right)\right] - 3(143+1) = 6.30.$$

There is enough evidence to conclude that the population locations differ.

21.44 H_0 : The locations of all 3 populations are the same.

H_1 : At least two population locations differ.

Rejection region: $H > \chi^2_{\alpha,k-1} = \chi^2_{05,2} = 5.99147$

1	Rank	2	Rank	3	Rank
25	10.5	19	2	27	12
15	1	21	4	25	10.5
20	3	23	8.5	22	6
22	6	22	6	29	15
23	8.5	28	13.5	28	13.5
$T_1 = 29$		$T_2 = 34$		$T_3 = 57$	

$$H = \left[\frac{12}{n(n+1)}\sum\frac{T_j^2}{n_j}\right] - 3(n+1) = \left[\frac{12}{15(15+1)}\left(\frac{29^2}{5}+\frac{34^2}{5}+\frac{57^2}{5}\right)\right] - 3(15+1) = 4.46, \text{ p-value} = .1075.$$

There is not enough evidence to conclude that at least two population locations differ.

21.46 H_0 : The locations of all 4 populations are the same.

H_1 : At least two population locations differ.

	A	B	C	D
1	**Kruskal-Wallis Test**			
2				
3	Group	Rank Sum	Observations	
4	*Printer 1*	4889.5	50	
5	*Printer 2*	5350	50	
6	*Printer 3*	4864.5	50	
7	*Printer 4*	4996	50	
8				
9	H Stat		0.899	
10	df		3	
11	p-value		0.8257	
12	chi-squared Critical		7.8147	

a H = .899, p-value = .8257. There is not enough evidence to conclude that differences exist between the ratings of the four printings.

b The printout is identical to that of part a.

c All codes that preserve the order produce the same results.

21.48 H_0 : The locations of all 3 populations are the same.

H_1 : At least two population locations differ.

Rejection region: $H > \chi^2_{\alpha,k-1} = \chi^2_{.05,2} = 5.99147$

$$H = \left[\frac{12}{n(n+1)}\sum_{j=1}^{k}\frac{T_j^2}{n_j}\right] - 3(n+1) = \frac{12}{75(75+1)}\left(\frac{767.5^2}{25}+\frac{917^2}{25}+\frac{1165^2}{25}\right) - 3(75+1) = 6.81, \text{ p-value}$$

= .0333. There is enough evidence to infer that there are differences in student satisfaction between the teaching methods.

21.50 H_0 : The locations of all 4 populations are the same.

H_1 : At least two population locations differ.

Rejection region: $H > \chi^2_{\alpha,k-1} = \chi^2_{05,3} = 7.81473$

$$H = \left[\frac{12}{n(n+1)}\sum_{j=1}^{k}\frac{T_j^2}{n_j}\right] - 3(n+1) = \frac{12}{132(132+1)}\left(\frac{2195^2}{33}+\frac{1650.5^2}{34}+\frac{2830^2}{34}+\frac{2102.5^2}{31}\right) - 3(132+1)$$

= 14.04, p-value = .0029. There is enough evidence to conclude that there are differences in grading standards between the four high schools.

21.52 H_0 : The locations of all 3 populations are the same.

H_1 : At least two population locations differ.

Rejection region: $H > \chi^2_{\alpha,k-1} = \chi^2_{.05,2} = 5.99147$

$$H = \left[\frac{12}{n(n+1)}\sum_{j=1}^{k}\frac{T_j^2}{n_j}\right] - 3(n+1) = \frac{12}{90(90+1)}\left(\frac{1565^2}{30}+\frac{1358.5^2}{30}+\frac{1171.5^2}{30}\right) - 3(90+1) = 3.78,$$

p-value = .1507. There is not enough evidence to infer that Democrat's ratings of their chances changed over the 3–month period.

21.54 H_0 : The locations of all 4 populations are the same.

H_1 : At least two population locations differ.

Rejection region: $H > \chi^2_{\alpha,k-1} = \chi^2_{05,3} = 7.81473$

$$H = \left[\frac{12}{n(n+1)}\sum_{j=1}^{k}\frac{T_j^2}{n_j}\right] - 3(n+1)$$

$$= \frac{12}{428(428+1)}\left(\frac{28{,}304^2}{123}+\frac{21{,}285^2}{109}+\frac{21{,}796^2}{102}+\frac{20{,}421^2}{94}\right) - 3(428+1) = 4.64,$$

p-value = .1999. There is not enough evidence to infer that there are differences in support between the four levels of students.

21.56 H_0 : The locations of all 4 populations are the same.

H_1 : At least two population locations differ.

Rejection region: $F_r > \chi^2_{\alpha,k-1} = \chi^2_{10,3} = 6.25139$

	Treatment							
Block	1	Rank	2	Rank	3	Rank	4	Rank
1	10	2	12	3	15	4	9	1
2	8	2	10	3	11	4	6	1
3	13	2	14	3	16	4	11	1
4	9	1.5	9	1.5	12	3	13	4
5	7	1	8	2	14	4	10	3
		$T_1 = 8.5$		$T_2 = 12.5$		$T_3 = 19$		$T_4 = 10$

$$F_r = \left[\frac{12}{b(k)(k+1)}\sum_{j=1}^{k} T_j^2\right] - 3b(k+1) = \left[\frac{12}{(5)(4)(5)}(8.5^2 + 12.5^2 + 19^2 + 10^2\right] - 3(5)(5) = 7.74,$$

p-value = .0517. There is enough evidence to infer that at least two population locations differ.

21.58 H_0 : The locations of all 4 populations are the same.

H_1 : At least two population locations differ.

Rejection region: $F_r > \chi^2_{\alpha,k-1} = \chi^2_{.05,3} = 7.81473$

	Orange Juice Brand							
Judge	1	Rank	2	Rank	3	Rank	4	Rank
1	3	1.5	5	4	4	3	3	1.5
2	2	1	3	2	5	4	4	3
3	4	3	4	3	3	1	4	3
4	3	2	4	3	5	4	2	1
5	2	1	4	3.5	4	3.5	3	2
6	4	2	5	3.5	5	3.5	3	1
7	3	1.5	3	1.5	4	3.5	4	3.5
8	2	1	3	3	3	3	3	3
9	4	2.5	3	1	5	4	4	2.5
10	2	1	4	3	5	4	3	2
		$T_1 = 16.5$		$T_2 = 27.5$		$T_3 = 33.5$		$T_4 = 22.5$

$$F_r = \left[\frac{12}{b(k)(k+1)}\sum_{j=1}^{k} T_j^2\right] - 3b(k+1) = \left[\frac{12}{(10)(4)(5)}(16.5^2 + 27.5^2 + 33.5^2 + 22.5^2\right] - 3(10)(5) = 9.42,$$

p-value = .0242. There is enough evidence to infer that differences in sensory perception exist between the four brands of orange juice.

21.60 H_0 : The locations of all 4 populations are the same.

H_1 : At least two population locations differ.

	A	B	C
1	**Friedman Test**		
2			
3	Group		Rank Sum
4	*Brand A*		65
5	*Brand B*		65
6	*Brand C*		85
7	*Brand D*		85
8			
9	Fr Stat		8.00
10	df		3
11	p-value		0.0460
12	chi-squared Critical		7.8147

a $F_r = 8.00$, p-value = .0460. There is enough evidence to infer that differences exist between the ratings of the four brands of coffee.

b Printout is identical to that of part a.

c Different codes produce identical results provided the codes are in order.

21.62 H_0 : The locations of all 3 populations are the same.

H_1 : At least two population locations differ.

Rejection region: $F_r > \chi^2_{\alpha,k-1} = \chi^2_{.05,2} = 5.99147$

$$F_r = \left[\frac{12}{b(k)(k+1)}\sum_{j=1}^{k} T_j^2\right] - 3b(k+1) = \left[\frac{12}{(20)(3)(4)}(33^2 + 39.5^2 + 47.5^2\right] - 3(20)(4) = 5.28,$$

p-value = .0715. There is not enough evidence to infer that there are differences in the ratings of the three recipes.

21.64 H_0 : The locations of all 3 populations are the same.

H_1 : At least two population locations differ.

Rejection region: $F_r > \chi^2_{\alpha,k-1} = \chi^2_{.05,2} = 5.99147$

$$F_r = \left[\frac{12}{b(k)(k+1)}\sum_{j=1}^{k} T_j^2\right] - 3b(k+1) = \left[\frac{12}{(12)(3)(4)}(28.5^2 + 22.5^2 + 21^2\right] - 3(12)(4) = 2.63,$$

p-value = .2691. There is not enough evidence to infer that there are differences in delivery times between the three couriers.

21.66 Rejection region: $z < -z_{\alpha/2} = -z_{.025} = -1.96$ or $z > z_{\alpha/2} = z_{.025} = 1.96$

$z = r_S\sqrt{n-1} = (.23)\sqrt{50-1} = 1.61$, p-value = 2P(Z > 1.61) = 2(.5 – .4463) = .1074 There is not enough evidence to reject the null hypothesis.

21.68

Mathematics	a	Economics	b	a^2	b^2	ab
4	5.5	5	6.5	30.25	42.25	35.75
2	3	2	1.5	9	2.25	4.5
5	7	3	4	49	16	28
4	5.5	5	6.5	30.25	42.25	35.75
2	3	3	4	9	16	12
2	3	3	4	9	16	12
1	1	2	1.5	1	2.25	1.5
Totals	28		28	137.5	137.0	129.5

$$\sum_{i=1}^{n} a_i = 28 \quad \sum_{i=1}^{n} b_i = 28 \quad \sum_{i=1}^{n} a_i^2 = 137.5 \quad \sum_{i=1}^{n} b_i^2 = 137.0 \quad \sum_{i=1}^{n} a_i b_i = 129.5$$

$$s_{ab} = \frac{1}{n-1}\left[\sum_{i=1}^{n} a_i b_i - \frac{\sum_{i=1}^{n} a_i \sum_{i=1}^{n} b_i}{n}\right] = \frac{1}{7-1}\left[129.5 - \frac{(28)(28}{7}\right] = 2.917$$

$$s_a^2 = \frac{1}{n-1}\left[\sum_{i=1}^{n} a_i^2 - \frac{\left(\sum_{i=1}^{n} a_i\right)^2}{n}\right] = \frac{1}{7-1}\left[137.5 - \frac{(28)^2}{7}\right] = 4.250,\ s_a = \sqrt{s_a^2} = \sqrt{4.250} = 2.062$$

$$s_b^2 = \frac{1}{n-1}\left[\sum_{i=1}^{n} b_i^2 - \frac{\left(\sum_{i=1}^{n} b_i\right)^2}{n}\right] = \frac{1}{7-1}\left[137.0 - \frac{(28)^2}{7}\right] = 4.167,\ s_b = \sqrt{s_b^2} = \sqrt{4.167} = 2.041$$

$$r_S = \frac{s_{ab}}{s_b s_b} = \frac{2.917}{(2.062)(2.041)} = .6931$$

$H_0: \rho_S = 0$

$H_1: \rho_S \neq 0$

Rejection region: $r_S > .786$ or $r_S < -.786$

There is not enough evidence to infer a relationship between the grades in the two courses.

21.70

Stock 1	a	Stock 2	b	a^2	b^2	ab
−7	4.5	6	8.5	20.25	72.25	38.25
−4	6.5	6	8.5	42.25	72.25	55.25
−7	4.5	−4	2	20.25	4	9
−3	8	9	12.5	64	156.25	100
2	10.5	3	5	110.25	25	52.5
−10	2.5	−3	3.5	6.25	12.25	8.75
−10	2.5	7	10.5	6.25	110.25	26.25
5	12	−3	3.5	144	12.25	42
1	9	4	6	81	36	54
−4	6.5	7	10.5	42.25	110.25	68.25
2	10.5	9	12.5	110.25	156.25	131.25
6	13	5	7	169	49	91
−13	1	−7	1	1	1	1
Totals	91		91	817	817	677.5

$$\sum_{i=1}^{n} a_i = 91 \quad \sum_{i=1}^{n} b_i = 91 \quad \sum_{i=1}^{n} a_i^2 = 817 \sum_{i=1}^{n} b_i^2 = 817 \sum_{i=1}^{n} a_i b_i = 677.5$$

$$s_{ab} = \frac{1}{n-1}\left[\sum_{i=1}^{n} a_i b_i - \frac{\sum_{i=1}^{n} a_i \sum_{i=1}^{n} b_i}{n}\right] = \frac{1}{13-1}\left[677.5 - \frac{(91)(91}{13}\right] = 3.375$$

$$s_a^2 = \frac{1}{n-1}\left[\sum_{i=1}^{n} a_i^2 - \frac{\left(\sum_{i=1}^{n} a_i\right)^2}{n}\right] = \frac{1}{13-1}\left[817 - \frac{(91)^2}{13}\right] = 15.00,\ s_a = \sqrt{s_a^2} = \sqrt{15.00} = 3.873$$

$$s_b^2 = \frac{1}{n-1}\left[\sum_{i=1}^{n} b_i^2 - \frac{\left(\sum_{i=1}^{n} b_i\right)^2}{n}\right] = \frac{1}{13-1}\left[817 - \frac{(91)^2}{13}\right] = 15.00,\ s_b = \sqrt{s_b^2} = \sqrt{15.00} = 3.873$$

$$r_S = \frac{s_{ab}}{s_b s_b} = \frac{3.375}{(3.873)(3.873)} = .2250$$

$$H_0: \rho_S = 0$$

$$H_1: \rho_S \neq 0$$

Rejection region: $r_S > .566$ or $r_S < -.566$

There is not enough evidence to infer a relationship between the two stock returns.

21.72 $H_0: \rho_S = 0$

$H_1: \rho_S \neq 0$

	A	B	C	D
1	**Spearman Rank Correlation**			
2				
3	*Price and Odometer*			
4	Spearman Rank Correlation			-0.0201
5	z Stat			-0.20
6	P(Z<=z) one tail			0.4206
7	z Critical one tail			1.6449
8	P(Z<=z) two tail			0.8412
9	z Critical two tail			1.96

$z = -.20$, p-value = .8412. There is not enough evidence to infer that odometer reading and price are related.

21.74 $H_0 : \rho_S = 0$

$H_1 : \rho_S > 0$

	A	B	C	D
1	**Spearman Rank Correlation**			
2				
3	*Age and Heartburn*			
4	Spearman Rank Correlation			0.0302
5	z Stat			0.54
6	P(Z<=z) one tail			0.2931
7	z Critical one tail			1.6449
8	P(Z<=z) two tail			0.5862
9	z Critical two tail			1.96

z = .54, p-value = .2931. There is not enough evidence to conclude that age and severity of heartburn are positively related.

21.76 $H_0 : \rho_S = 0$

$H_1 : \rho_S > 0$

	A	B	C	D
1	**Spearman Rank Correlation**			
2				
3	*Floor and Price*			
4	Spearman Rank Correlation			0.553
5	z Stat			3.87
6	P(Z<=z) one tail			0.0001
7	z Critical one tail			1.6449
8	P(Z<=z) two tail			0.0002
9	z Critical two tail			1.96

z = 3.87, p-value = .0001. There is sufficient evidence to conclude that price and floor number are positively related.

21.78 $H_0: \rho_S = 0$

$H_1: \rho_S > 0$

	A	B	C	D
1	**Spearman Rank Correlation**			
2				
3	*Wager and Enjoyment*			
4	Spearman Rank Correlation			0.3912
5	z Stat			5.52
6	P(Z<=z) one tail			0
7	z Critical one tail			1.6449
8	P(Z<=z) two tail			0
9	z Critical two tail			1.96

z = 5.52, p-value = 0. There is enough evidence to infer that the greater the wager the more enjoyable the game is.

21.80 H_0 : The two population locations are the same

H_1 : The location of population 1 is different from the location of population 2

	A	B	C	D	E
1	**Wilcoxon Rank Sum Test**				
2					
3			Rank Sum	Observations	
4	*Section 1*		15297.5	113	
5	*Section 2*		14592.5	131	
6	z Stat		2.65		
7	P(Z<=z) one-tail		0.0041		
8	z Critical one-tail		1.6449		
9	P(Z<=z) two-tail		0.0082		
10	z Critical two-tail		1.96		

z = 2.65, p-value = .0082. There is enough evidence to infer that the two teaching methods differ

21.82 H_0 : The locations of all 4 populations are the same.

H_1 : At least two population locations differ.

	A	B	C
1	**Friedman Test**		
2			
3	Group		Rank Sum
4	*Typeface 1*		50.5
5	*Typeface 2*		38
6	*Typeface 3*		66
7	*Typeface 4*		45.5
8			
9	Fr Stat		12.615
10	df		3
11	p-value		0.0055
12	chi-squared Critical		7.8147

$F_r = 12.615$, p-value = .0055. There is enough evidence to conclude that there are differences between typefaces.

21.84 H_0 : The two population locations are the same

H_1 : The location of population 1 is to the left of the location of population 2

	A	B	C	D
1	**Wilcoxon Signed Rank Sum Test**			
2				
3	Difference		*Drug A - Drug B*	
4				
5	T+		36	
6	T-		342	
7	Observations (for test)		27	
8	z Stat		-3.68	
9	P(Z<=z) one-tail		0.0001	
10	z Critical one-tail		1.6449	
11	P(Z<=z) two-tail		0.0002	
12	z Critical two-tail		1.96	

$z = -3.68$, p-value = .0001. There is enough evidence to conclude that drug B is more effective.

21.86 H_0 : The two population locations are the same

H_1 : The location of population 1 is to the right of the location of population 2

	A	B	C	D	E
1	**Wilcoxon Rank Sum Test**				
2					
3			Rank Sum	Observations	
4	*New Material*		2747	50	
5	*Old Material*		2303	50	
6	z Stat		1.53		
7	P(Z<=z) one-tail		0.063		
8	z Critical one-tail		1.6449		
9	P(Z<=z) two-tail		0.126		
10	z Critical two-tail		1.96		

z = 1.53, p-value = .0630. There is not enough evidence to conclude that the new material takes longer to burst into flames.

21.88 H_0 : The two population locations are the same

H_1 : The location of population 1 is different from the location of population 2

	A	B	C	D	E	F
1	**Sign Test**					
2						
3	Difference			*Commercial 1 - Commercial 2*		
4						
5	Positive Differences			15		
6	Negative Differences			21		
7	Zero Differences			24		
8	z Stat			-1.00		
9	P(Z<=z) one-tail			0.1587		
10	z Critical one-tail			1.6449		
11	P(Z<=z) two-tail			0.3174		
12	z Critical two-tail			1.96		

z = –1.00, p-value = .3174. There is not enough evidence to infer differences in believability between the two commercials.

21.90 H_0 : The two population locations are the same

H_1 : The location of population 1 is to the left of the location of population 2

	A	B	C	D	E
1	**Wilcoxon Rank Sum Test**				
2					
3			Rank Sum	Observations	
4	*This Year*		37525.5	200	
5	*10 Years Ago*		42674.5	200	
6	z Stat		-2.23		
7	P(Z<=z) one-tail		0.013		
8	z Critical one-tail		1.6449		
9	P(Z<=z) two-tail		0.026		
10	z Critical two-tail		1.96		

$z = -2.23$, p-value = .0130. There is enough evidence to infer that people perceive newspapers as doing a better job 10 years ago than today.

21.92 H_0 : The two population locations are the same

H_1 : The location of population 1 is different from the location of population 2

	A	B	C	D	E
1	**Wilcoxon Rank Sum Test**				
2					
3			Rank Sum	Observations	
4	*Males*		10336.5	100	
5	*Females*		9763.5	100	
6	z Stat		0.70		
7	P(Z<=z) one-tail		0.24		
8	z Critical one-tail		1.6449		
9	P(Z<=z) two-tail		0.484		
10	z Critical two-tall		1.96		

$z = .70$, p-value = .4840. There is not enough evidence to conclude that businesswomen and business men differ in the number of business trips taken per year.

21.94 H_0 : The two population locations are the same

H_1 : The location of population 1 is to the right of the location of population 2

	A	B	C	D	E
1	**Wilcoxon Rank Sum Test**				
2					
3			Rank Sum	Observations	
4	*2 Years Ago*		10786.5	100	
5	*ThisYear*		9313.5	100	
6	z Stat		1.80		
7	P(Z<=z) one-tail		0.036		
8	z Critical one-tail		1.6449		
9	P(Z<=z) two-tail		0.072		
10	z Critical two-tail		1.96		

z = 1.80, p-value = .0360. There is enough evidence to indicate that the citizens of Stratford should be concerned.

21.96a H_0 : The two population locations are the same

H_1 : The location of population 1 is to the right of the location of population 2

	A	B	C	D	E	F	G
1	**Sign Test**						
2							
3	Difference			*Female Professor - Male Professor*			
4							
5	Positive Differences			45			
6	Negative Differences			7			
7	Zero Differences			48			
8	z Stat			5.27			
9	P(Z<=z) one-tail			0			
10	z Critical one-tail			1.6449			
11	P(Z<=z) two-tail			0			
12	z Critical two-tail			1.96			

z = 5.27, p-value = 0. There is enough evidence to infer that female students rate female professors higher than they rate male professors.

b H_0 : The two population locations are the same

H_1 : The location of population 1 is to the left of the location of population 2

	A	B	C	D	E	F	G
1	**Sign Test**						
2							
3	Difference			*Female Professor - Male Professor*			
4							
5	Positive Differences			21			
6	Negative Differences			31			
7	Zero Differences			48			
8	z Stat			-1.39			
9	P(Z<=z) one-tail			0.0828			
10	z Critical one-tail			1.6449			
11	P(Z<=z) two-tail			0.1656			
12	z Critical two-tail			1.96			

z = –1.39, p-value = .0828. There is not enough evidence to infer that male students rate male professors higher than they rate female professors.

21.98 H_0 : The two population locations are the same

H_1 : The location of population 1 is to the right of the location of population 2

	A	B	C	D	E
1	**Wilcoxon Rank Sum Test**				
2					
3			Rank Sum	Observations	
4	*Telecommuters*		10934.5	100	
5	*Office*		9165.5	100	
6	z Stat		2.16		
7	P(Z<=z) one-tail		0.0153		
8	z Critical one-tail		1.6449		
9	P(Z<=z) two-tail		0.0306		
10	z Critical two-tail		1.96		

z = 2.16, p-value = .0153. There is enough evidence to conclude that telecommuters are more satisfied with their jobs.

21.100 H_0 : The two population locations are the same

H_1 : The location of population 1 is to the left of the location of population 2

	A	B	C	D	E
1	**Wilcoxon Rank Sum Test**				
2					
3			Rank Sum	Observations	
4	*3 Hours Before*		22553.5	180	
5	*Closing*		42426.5	180	
6	z Stat		-10.06		
7	P(Z<=z) one-tail		0		
8	z Critical one-tail		1.6449		
9	P(Z<=z) two-tail		0		
10	z Critical two-tail		1.96		

$z = -10.06$, p-value = 0. There is enough evidence to conclude that alcohol impairs judgment.

Chapter 22

22.4a Chance variation represents the variation in student achievement caused by differences in preparation, motivation, and ability.

b Special variation represents variation due to

22.6 $ARL = \frac{1}{.0124} = 81$

22.8 $ARL = \frac{1}{.0456} = 22$

22.10a From Beta-mean spreadsheet, $\beta = .6604$

b Probability $= .6604^8 = .0362$

22.12 Number of units = Production × ARL = 50(385) = 19,250

22.14 $P = 1 - \beta = 1 - .8133 = .1867$; $ARL = \frac{1}{P} = \frac{1}{.1867} = 5.36$

22.16 Number of units = Production × ARL = 2000(385) = 770,000

22.18 $P = 1 - \beta = 1 - .7389 = .2611$; $ARL = \frac{1}{P} = \frac{1}{.2611} = 3.83$

22.20a From Beta-mean spreadsheet, $\beta = .3660$

b Probability $= .3660^4 = .0179$

22.22 Sampling 10 units per half hour means that on average we will produce 770,000 units before erroneously concluding that the process is out of control when it isn't. Sampling 20 units per hour doubles this figure. Sampling 10 units per half hour means that when the process goes out of control, the probability of not detecting a shift of .75 standard deviations is .7389 and we will produce on average 3.83 × 2000 = 7660 units until the chart indicates a problem. Sampling 20 units per hour decreases the probability of not detecting the shift to .3660 and decreases the average number of units produced when the process is out of control to 4000 × 1.58 = 6320.

22.24 Centerline = $\bar{\bar{x}}$ = 181.1

Lower control limit = $\bar{x} - \frac{3S}{\sqrt{n}} = 181.1 - 3\left(\frac{11.0}{\sqrt{9}}\right) = 170.1$

Upper control limit = $\bar{x} + \frac{3S}{\sqrt{n}} = 181.1 + 3\left(\frac{11.0}{\sqrt{9}}\right) = 192.1$

Zone boundaries: 170.10, 173.77, 177.73, 181.10, 184.77, 188.43, 192.10

22.26a S Chart

	A	B	C	D
1	**Statistical Process Control**			
2				
3			*Data*	
4	Upper control limit		10.0885	
5	Centerline		4.452	
6	Lower control limit		0	

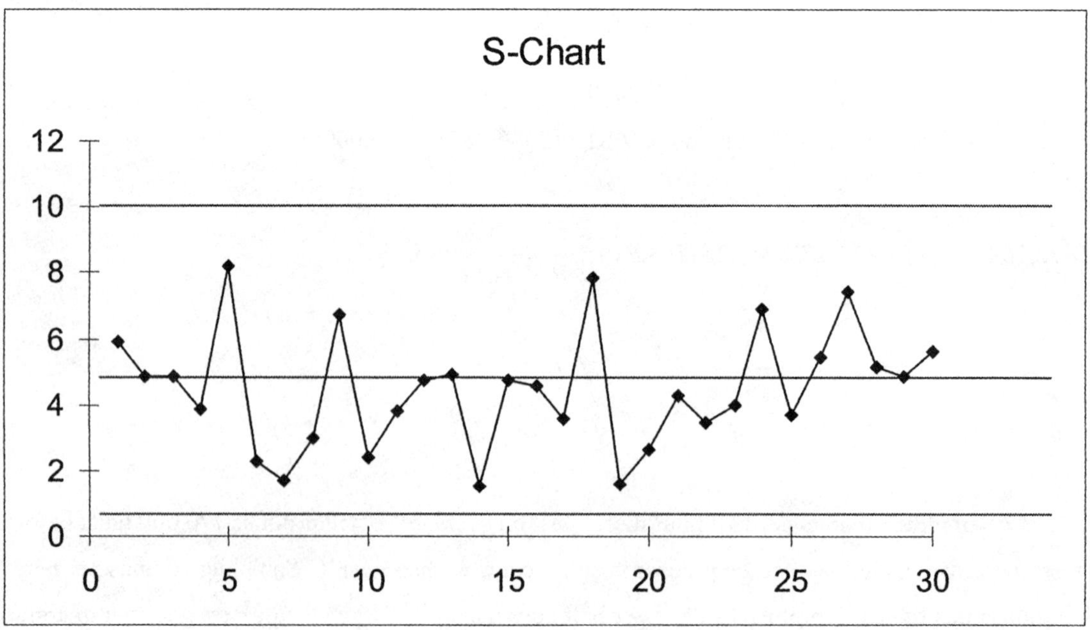

$\bar{x}$ Chart

	A	B	C	D
1	**Statistical Process Control**			
2				
3			*Data*	
4	Upper control limit		19.9668	
5	Centerline		12.7386	
6	Lower control limit		5.5103	
7	Pattern Test #2 Failed at Points: 29			
8	Pattern Test #6 Failed at Points: 29, 30			

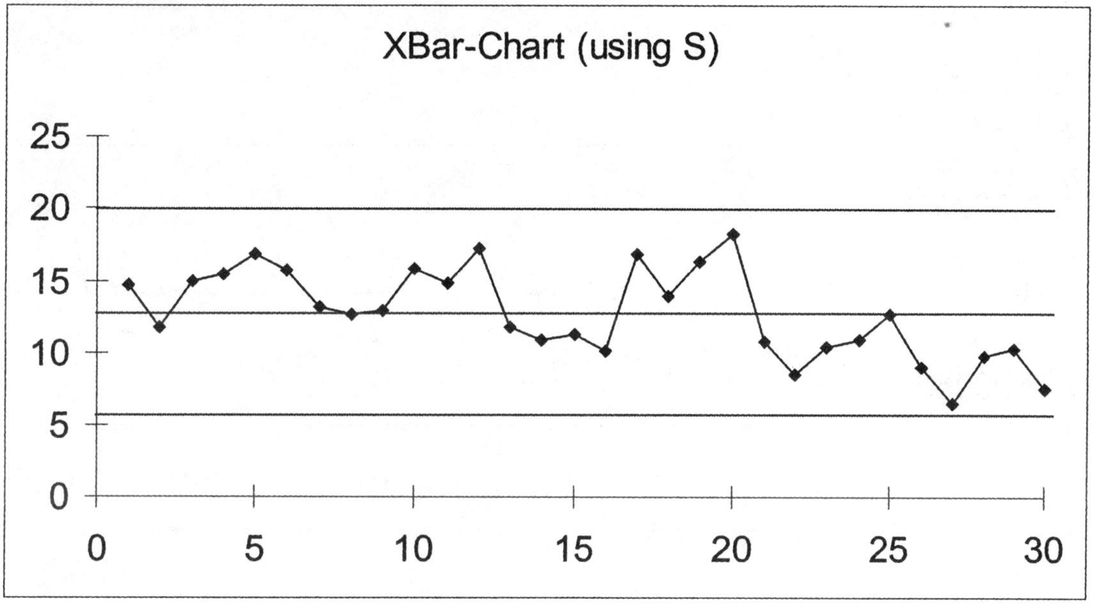

c The process is out of control at samples 29 and 30.

d A level shift occurred.

22.28

	A	B	C
1	**Statistical Process Control**		
2			
3			*AEU*
4	Upper control limit		0.0031
5	Centerline		0.0015
6	Lower control limit		0

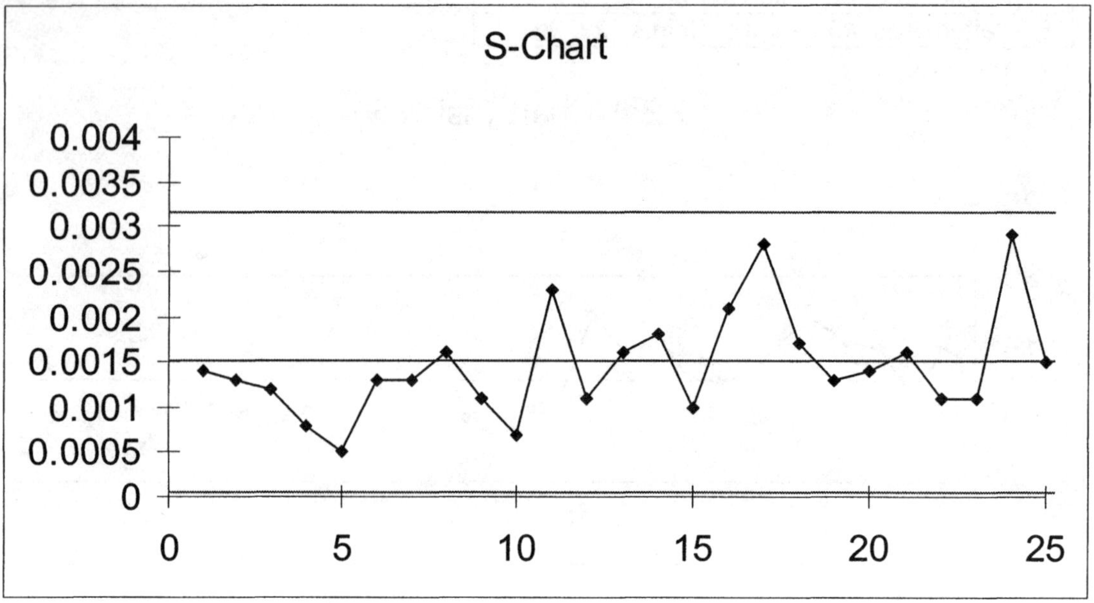

	A	B	C
1	**Statistical Process Control**		
2			
3			*AEU*
4	Upper control limit		0.4408
5	Centerline		0.4387
6	Lower control limit		0.4366

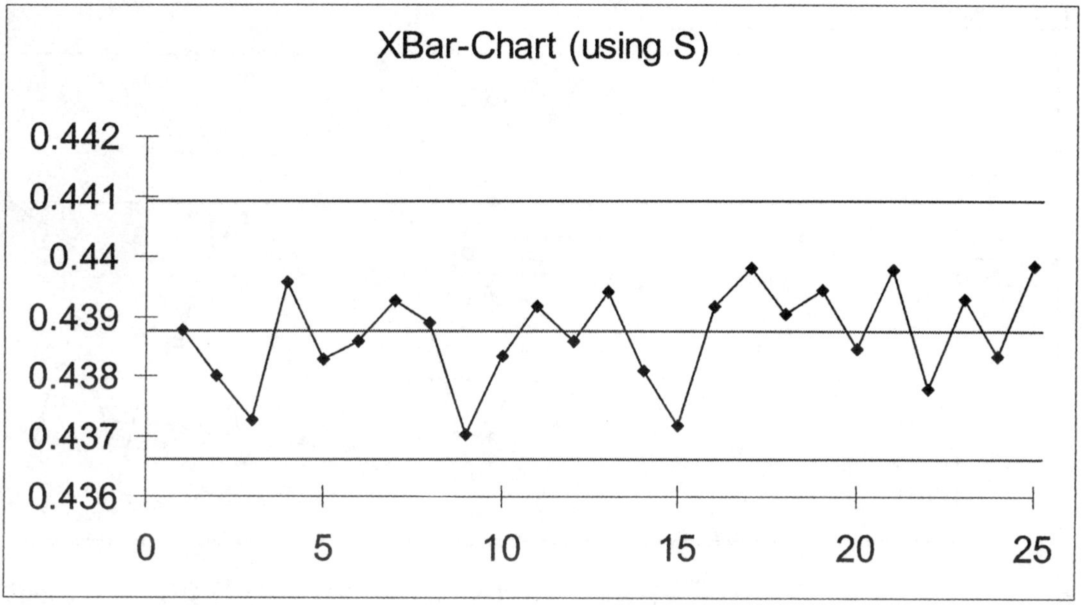

The process is under control.

22.30

	A	B	C
1	**Statistical Process Control**		
2			
3			*Volume*
4	Upper control limit		1.8995
5	Centerline		0.9093
6	Lower control limit		0

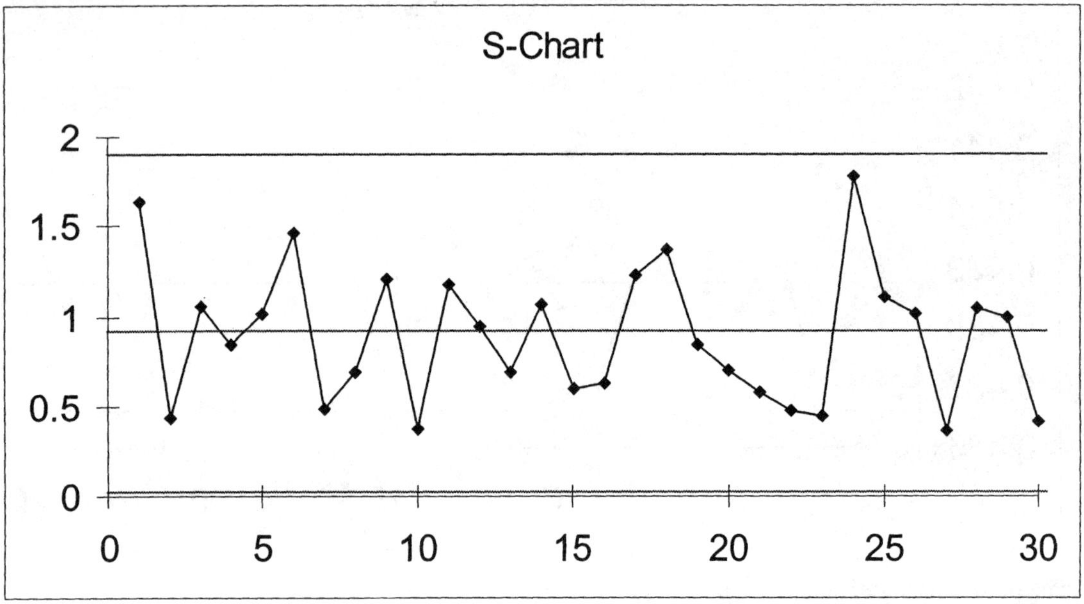

	A	B	C
1	**Statistical Process Control**		
2			
3			*Volume*
4	Upper control limit		1.3871
5	Centerline		0.092
6	Lower control limit		-1.2031

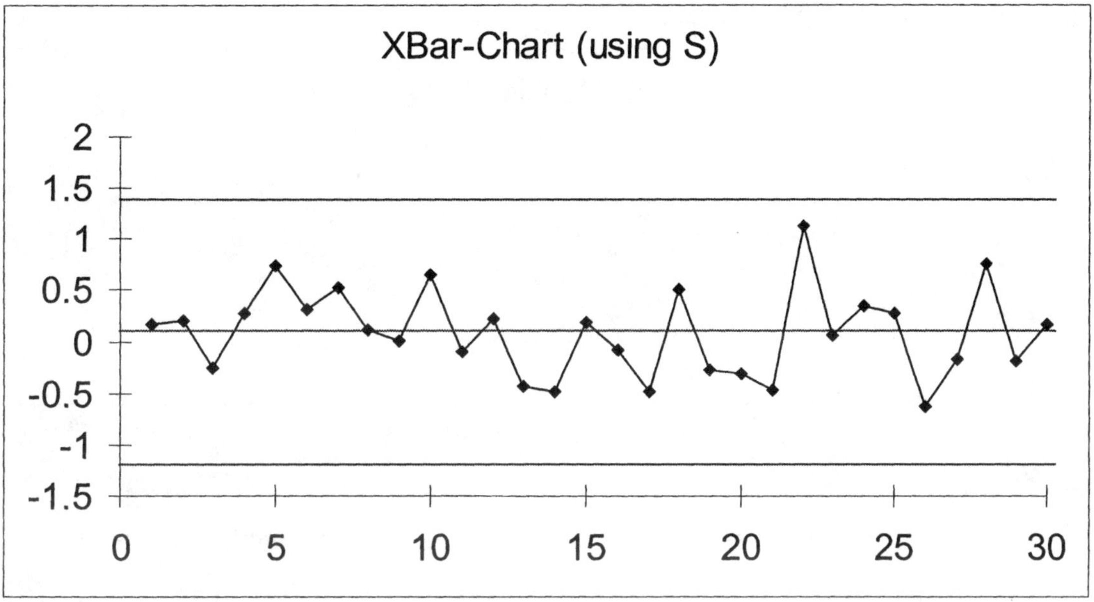

The process is under control.

22.32

	A	B	C
1	**Statistical Process Control**		
2			
3			*Headrest*
4	Upper control limit		2.3313
5	Centerline		0.9078
6	Lower control limit		0

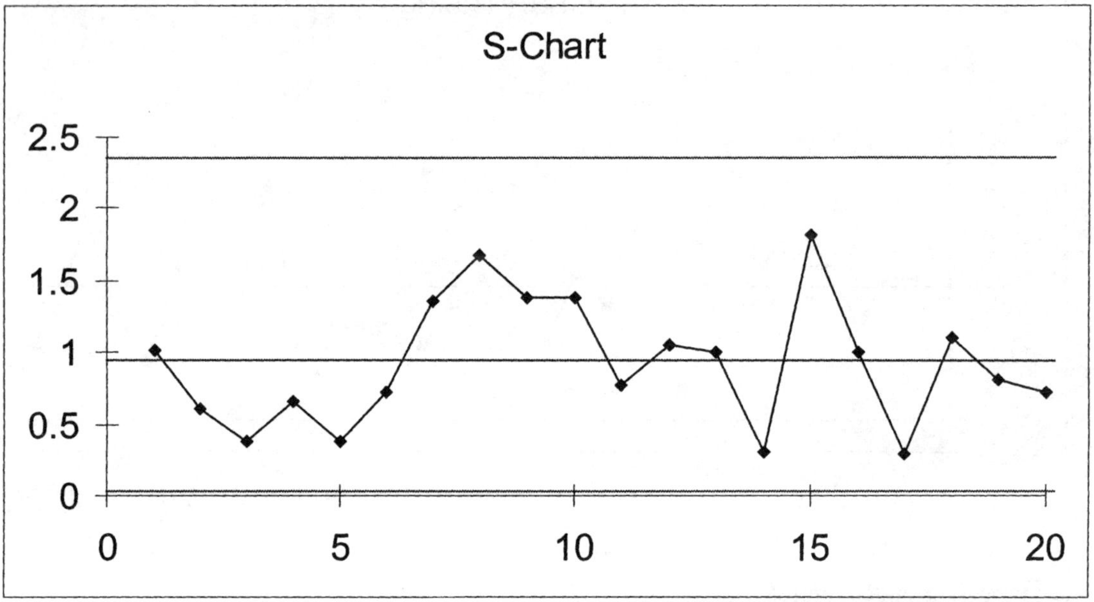

	A	B	C	D
1	**Statistical Process Control**			
2				
3			*Headrest*	
4	Upper control limit		241.3248	
5	Centerline		239.5617	
6	Lower control limit		237.7986	
7	Pattern Test #1 Failed at Points:			19, 20
8	Pattern Test #5 Failed at Points:			20

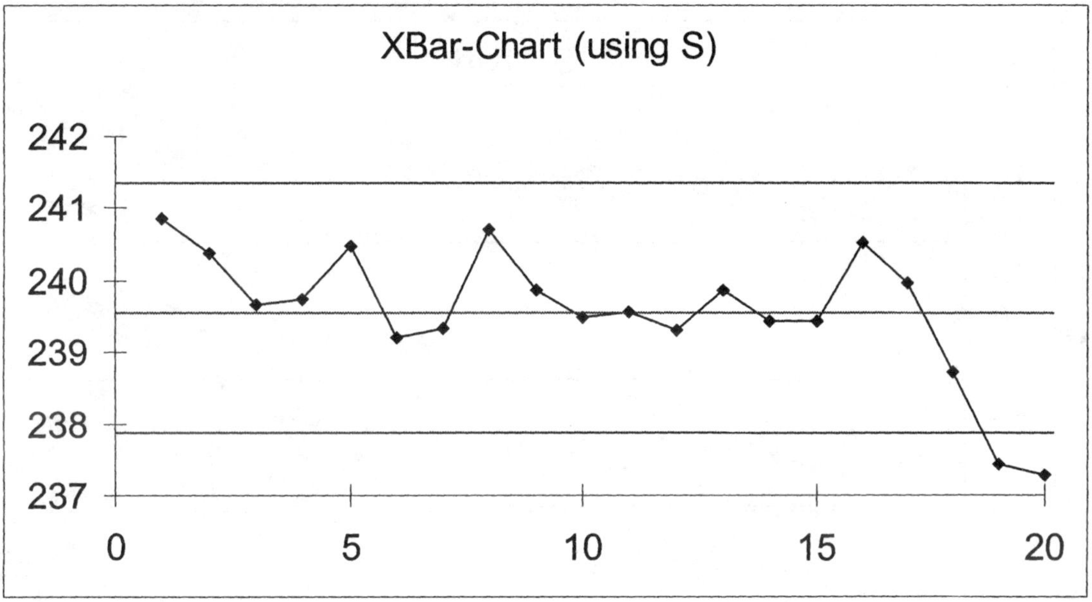

a The process is out of control.

b The process is out of control at sample 19.

c The width became too small.

22.34

	A	B	C	D
1	**Statistical Process Control**			
2				
3			*Seats*	
4	Upper control limit		11.1809	
5	Centerline		5.3523	
6	Lower control limit		0	
7	Pattern Test #1 Failed at Points:			23, 24

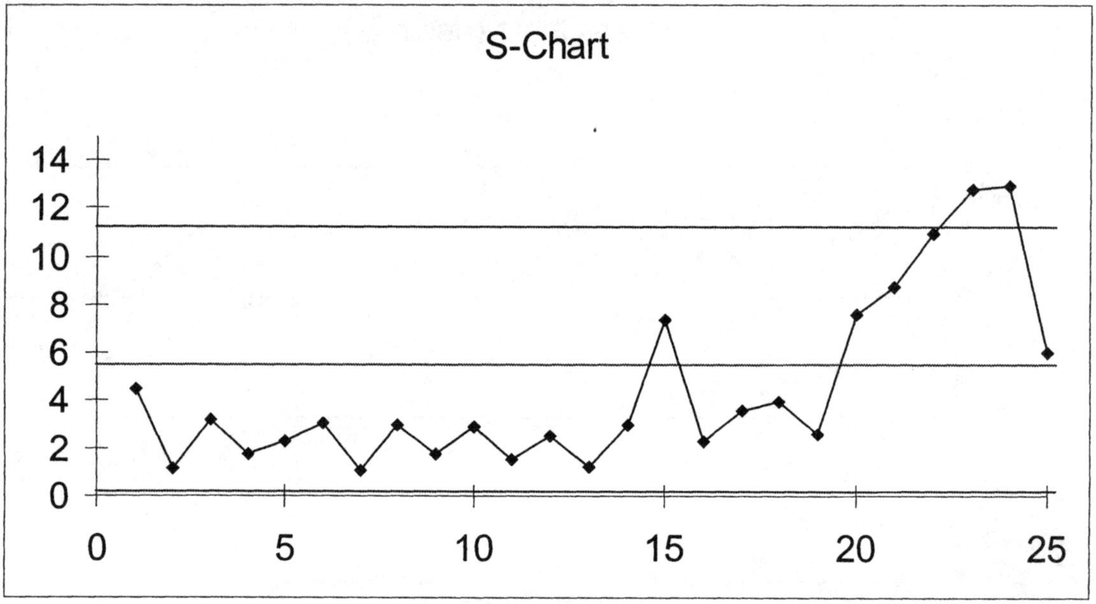

The process is out of control at sample 23. It is not necessary to draw the $\overline{x}$ chart.

22.36 $S = \dfrac{\text{Upper control limit} - \text{Centerline}}{3} = \dfrac{4.9873 - 4.9841}{3} = .00107$

$$CPL = \frac{\overline{\overline{x}} - LSL}{3S} = \frac{4.9841 - 4.981}{3(.00107)} = .97$$

$$CPU = \frac{USL - \overline{\overline{x}}}{3S} = \frac{4.987 - 4.9841}{3(.00107)} = .90$$

$$C_{pk} = \text{Min}(CPL, CPU) = .90$$

22.38

	A	B	C
1	**Statistical Process Control**		
2			
3			*Bottles*
4	Upper control limit		69.6821
5	Centerline		33.3567
6	Lower control limit		0

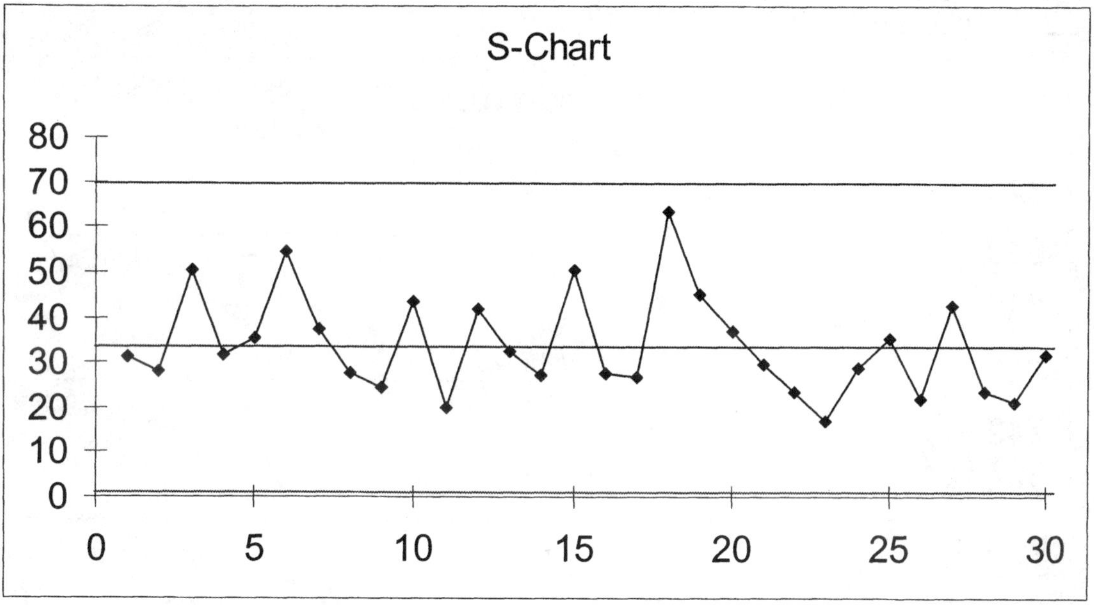

	A	B	C	D
1	**Statistical Process Control**			
2				
3			*Bottles*	
4	Upper control limit		803.9376	
5	Centerline		756.4267	
6	Lower control limit		708.9157	
7	Pattern Test #1 Failed at Points:			30
8	Pattern Test #5 Failed at Points:			29, 30
9	Pattern Test #6 Failed at Points:			30

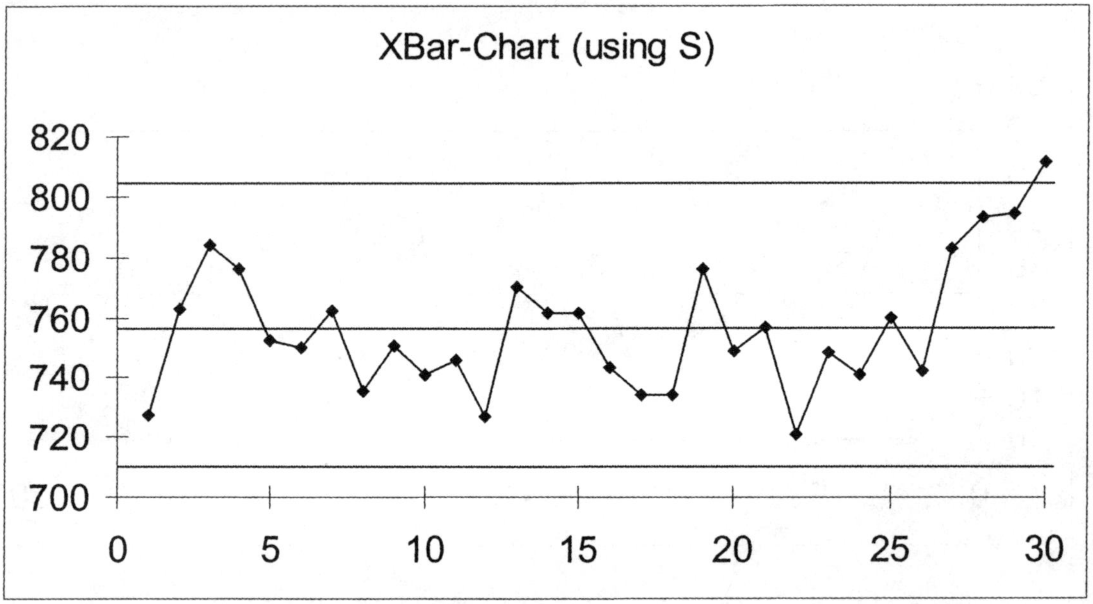

The process went out of control at sample 29.

22.40

	A	B	C
1	**Statistical Process Control**		
2			
3			*Pipes*
4	Upper control limit		0.0956
5	Centerline		0.0372
6	Lower control limit		0

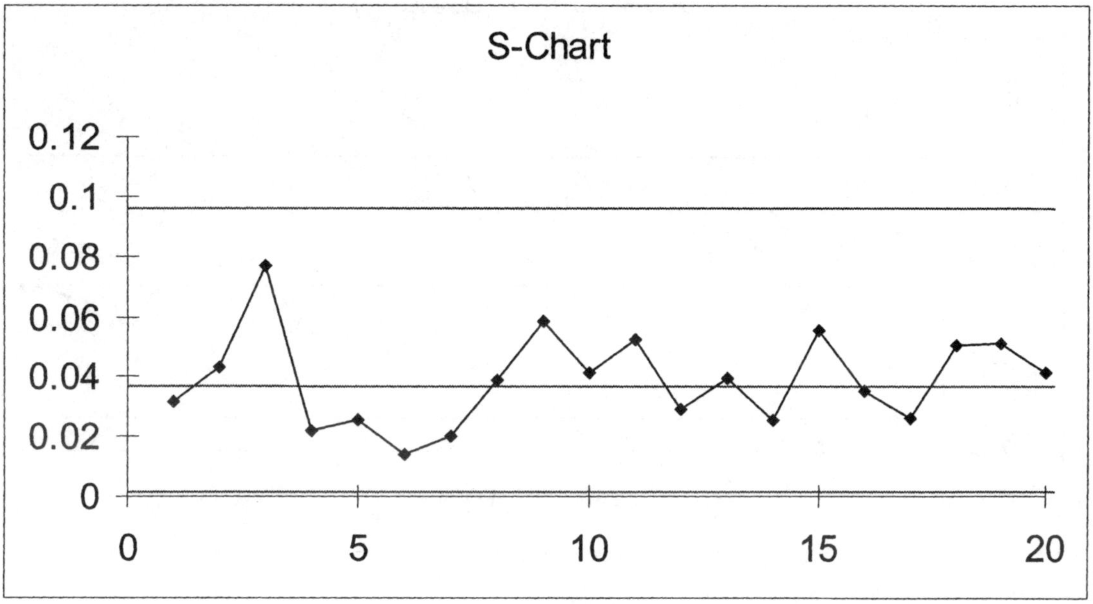

	A	B	C
1	**Statistical Process Control**		
2			
3			*Pipes*
4	Upper control limit		3.0615
5	Centerline		2.9892
6	Lower control limit		2.9168

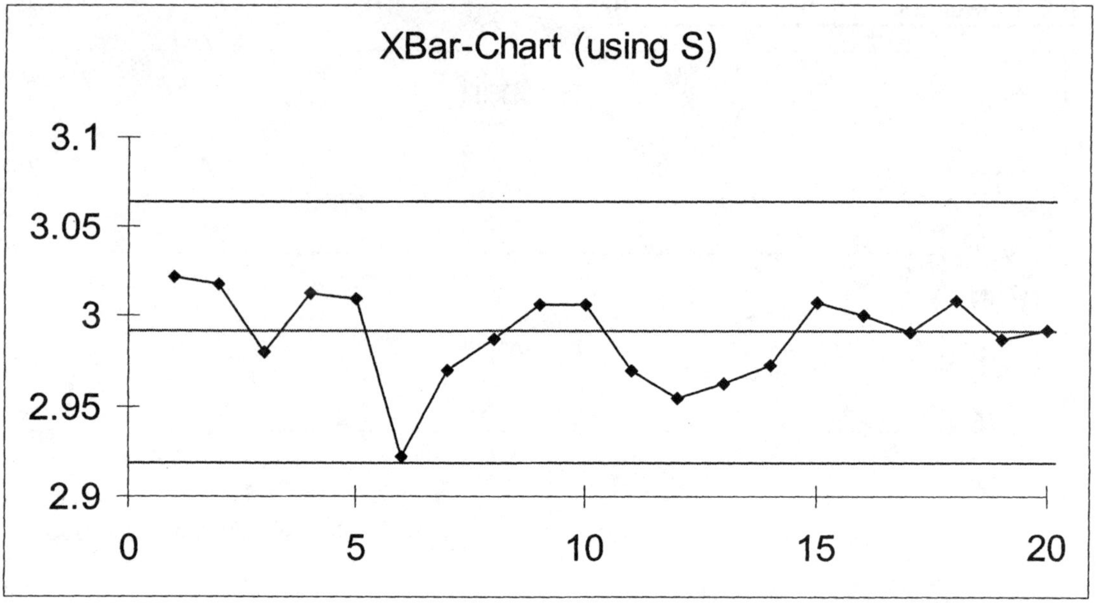

The process is under control.

$$22.42\ S = \frac{\text{Upper control limit} - \text{Centerline}}{3} = \frac{1504.572 - 1496.952}{3} = 2.54$$

$$\text{CPL} = \frac{\overline{\overline{x}} - \text{LSL}}{3S} = \frac{1496.952 - 1494.5}{3(2.54)} = .32$$

$$\text{CPU} = \frac{\text{USL} - \overline{\overline{x}}}{3S} = \frac{1497.5 - 1496.952}{3(2.54)} = .07$$

$$C_{pk} = \text{Min}(\text{CPL}, \text{CPU}) = .07$$

The value of the index is low because the statistics used to calculate the control limits and centerline were taken when the process was out of control.

22.44 Centerline = $\overline{p} = .0324$

Lower control limit = $\overline{p} - 3\sqrt{\frac{\overline{p}(1-\overline{p})}{n}} = .0324 - 3\sqrt{\frac{(.0324)(1-.0324)}{200}} = -.00516\ (=0)$

Upper control limit = $\overline{p} + 3\sqrt{\frac{\overline{p}(1-\overline{p})}{n}} = .0324 + 3\sqrt{\frac{(.0324)(1-.0324)}{200}} = .06996$

	A	B	C	D
1	**Statistical Process Control**			
2				
3			*Copiers*	
4	Upper control limit		0.07	
5	Centerline		0.0324	
6	Lower control limit		0	
7	Pattern Test #1 Failed at Points: 25			

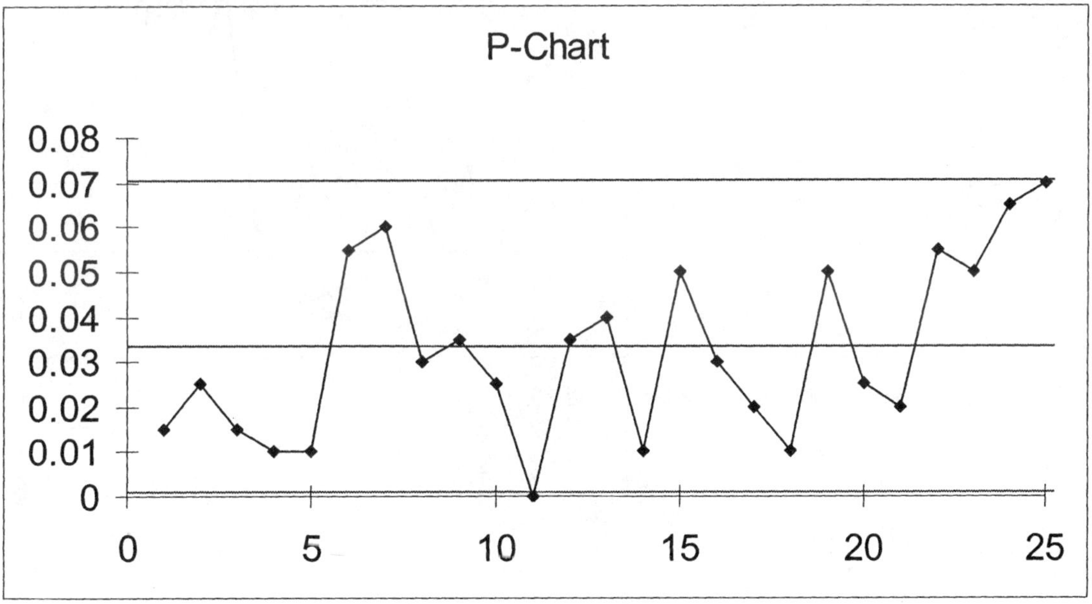

The process is out of control at sample 25.

22.46 Centerline = $\overline{p} = .0383$

Lower control limit = $\overline{p} - 3\sqrt{\frac{\overline{p}(1-\overline{p})}{n}} = .0383 - 3\sqrt{\frac{(.0383)(1-.0383)}{100}} = -.0193\ (=0)$

Upper control limit = $\overline{p} + 3\sqrt{\frac{\overline{p}(1-\overline{p})}{n}} = .0383 + 3\sqrt{\frac{(.0383)(1-.0383)}{100}} = .0959$

	A	B	C	D
1	**Statistical Process Control**			
2				
3			*Telephones*	
4	Upper control limit		0.0097	
5	Centerline		0.0038	
6	Lower control limit		0	
7	Pattern Test #1 Failed at Points:			25, 30

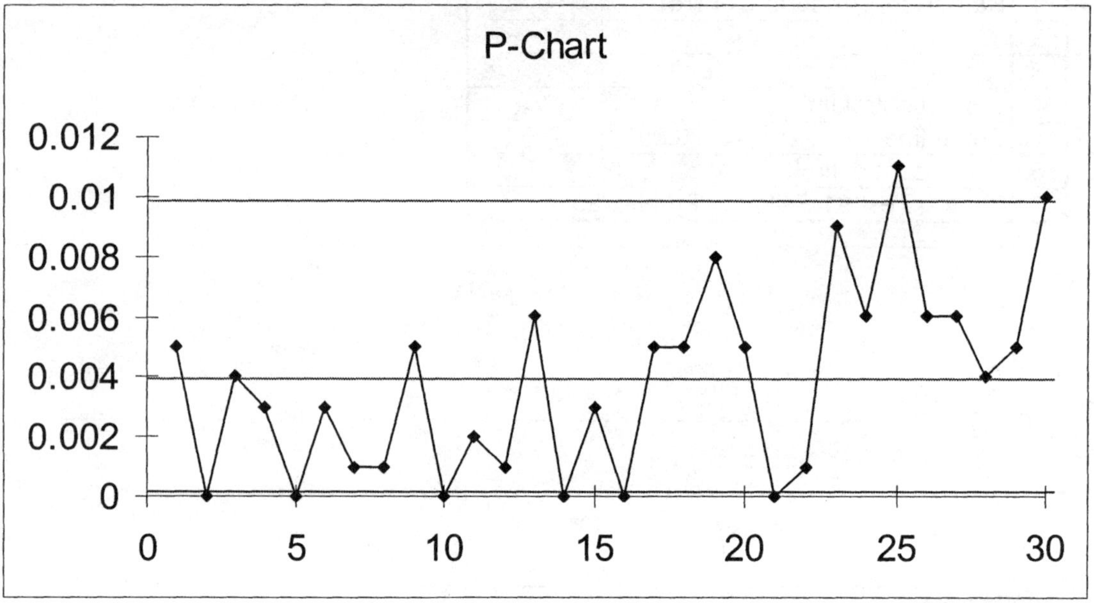

The process is out of control at samples 25 and 30.

22.48

	A	B	C	D	E
1	**Statistical Process Control**				
2					
3			*Batteries*		
4	Upper control limit		0.047		
5	Centerline		0.0257		
6	Lower control limit		0.0045		
7	Pattern Test #1 Failed at Points:			28, 29, 30	

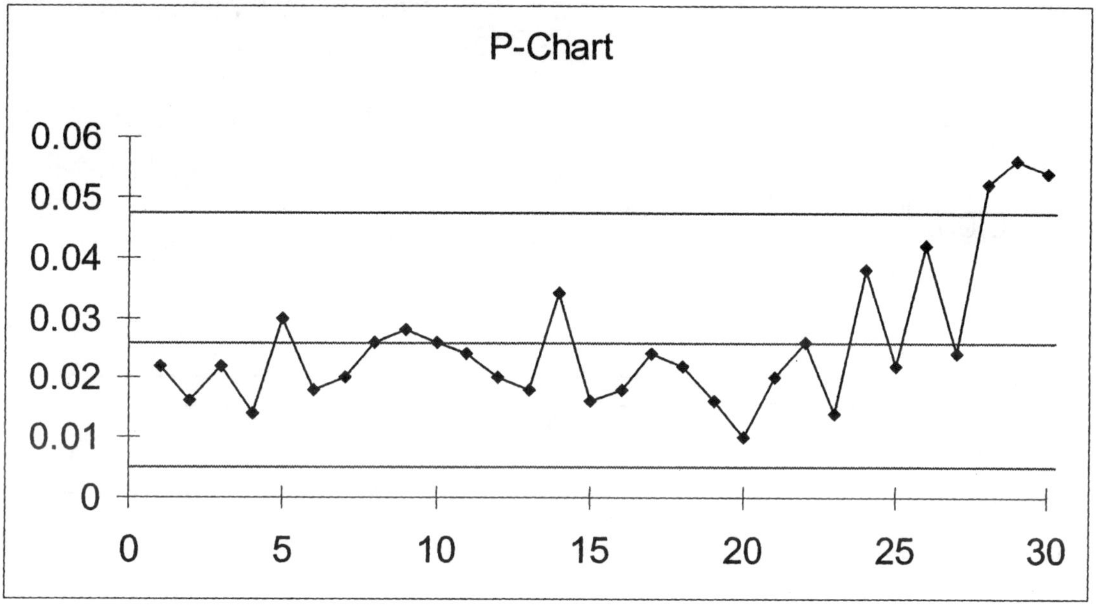

The process is out of control at sample 28.

22.50

	A	B	C	D
1	**Statistical Process Control**			
2				
3			*Scanners*	
4	Upper control limit		0.0275	
5	Centerline		0.0126	
6	Lower control limit		0	
7	Pattern Test #1 Failed at Points: 24			

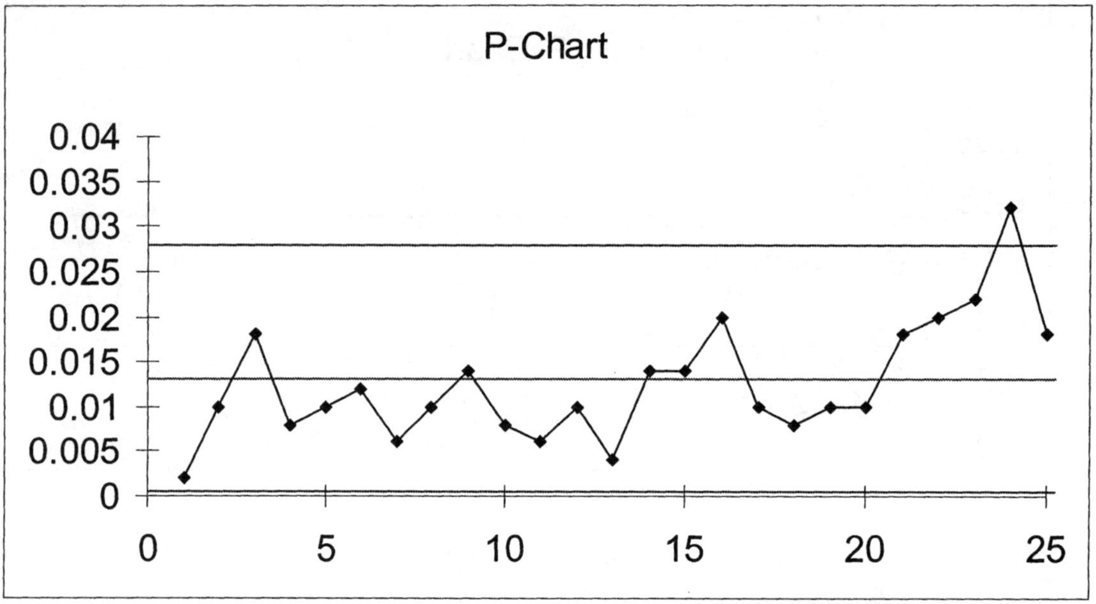

The process is out of control at sample 24.

Chapter 23

23.2

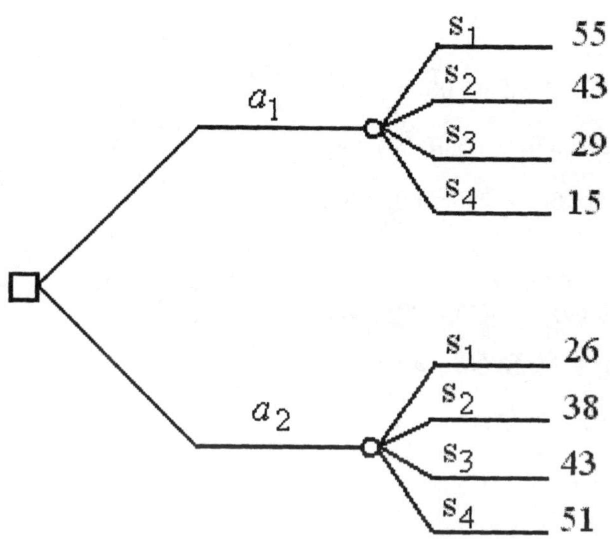

23.4

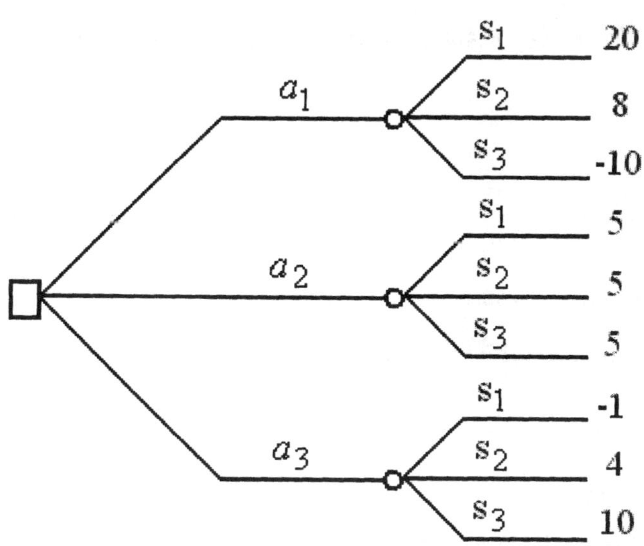

23.6 $EOL(a_1) = .2(0) + .6(0) + .2(20) = 4.0$

$EOL(a_2) = .2(15) + .6(3) + .2(5) = 5.8$

$EOL(a_3) = .2(21) + .6(4) + .2(0) = 6.6$

The EOL decision is a_1.

23.8a $EMV(a_0) = 0$

$EMV(a_1) = .25(-3.00) + .25(5.00) + .25(5.00) + .25(5.00) = 3.00$

$EMV(a_2) = .25(-6.00) + .25(2.00) + .25(10.00) + .25(10.00) = 4.00$

$EMV(a_3) = .25(-9.00) + .25(-1.00) + .25(7.00) + .25(15.00) = 3.00$

EMV decision is a_2 (bake 2 cakes)

b $EOL(a_0) = .25(0) + .25(5.00) + .25(10.00) + .25(15.00) = 7.50$

$EOL(a_1) = .25(3.00) + .25(0) + .25(5.00) + .25(10.00) = 4.50$

$EOL(a_2) = .25(6.00) + .25(3.00) + .25(0) + .25(5.00) = 3.50$

$EOL(a_2) = .25(9.00) + .25(6.00) + .25(3.00) + .25(0) = 4.50$

EOL decision is a_2 (bake 2 cakes)

23.10 $EMV(a_1) = -40{,}000$

$EMV(a_2) = .05(0) + .15(-18{,}000) + .30(-36{,}000) + .40(-54{,}000) + .10(-72{,}000) = -42{,}300$

EMV decision is a_1

23.12

$EMV(a_{100}) = 200$

$EMV(a_{200}) = .20(0) + .25(300) + .40(600) + .15(600) = 405$

$EMV(a_{300}) = .20(-150) + .25(150) + .40(450) + .15(750) = 300$

EMV decision is order 200 shirts.

23.14a EMV(Small) = .15(-220) + .55(-330) + .30(-440) = -346.5

EMV(Medium) = .15(-300) + .55(-320) + .30(-390) = -338.0

EMV(Large) = .15(-350) + .55(-350) + .30(-350) =-350.0

EMV decision: build a medium size plant; EMV*= -338.0

b Opportunity Loss Table

	Small	Medium	Large
Low	0	80	130
Moderate	10	0	30
High	90	40	0

c EOL(Small) = .15(0) + .55(10) + .30(90) = 32.5

EOL(Medium) = .15(80) + .55(0) + .30(40) = 24.0

EOL(Large) = .15(130) + .55(30) + .30(0) = 36.0

EOL decision: build a medium size plant

23.16 Payoff Table

Market share	Produce	Don't produce
5%	-28 million	0
10%	2 million	0
15%	8 million	0

EMV(produce) = .15(-28 million) + .45(2 million) + .40 (8 million) = -.1 million

EMV (don't produce) = 0

EMV decision: don't produce

23.18 Opportunity Loss Table

	a_1	a_2	a_3
s_1	50	0	35
s_2	110	40	0
s_3	0	100	135
s_4	0	130	120

$EOL(a_1) = .10(50) + .25(110) + .50(0) + .15(0) = 32.5$

$EOL(a_2) = .10(0) + .25(40) + .50(100) + .15(130) = 79.5$

$EOL(a_3) = .10(35) + .25(0) + .50(135) + .15(120) = 89$

EOL* = 32.5

23.20 a EPPI = .75(65) + .25(110) = 76.25

$EMV(a_1) = .75(65) + .25(70) = 66.25$

$EMV(a_2) = .75(20) + .25(110) = 42.5$

$EMV(a_3) = .75(45) + .25(80) = 53.75$

$EMV(a_4) = .75(30) + .25(95) = 46.25$

EVPI = EPPI – EMV* = 76.25 – 66.25 = 10

b EPPI = .95(65) + .05(110) = 67.25

$EMV(a_1) = .95(65) + .05(70) = 65.25$

$EMV(a_2) = .95(20) + .05(110) = 24.5$

$EMV(a_3) = .95(45) + .05(80) = 46.75$

$EMV(a_4) = .95(30) + .05(95) = 33.25$

EVPI = EPPI – EMV* = 67.25 – 65.25 = 2

23.22 Posterior Probabilities for I_1

s_j	$P(s_j)$	$P(I_1 \mid s_j)$	$P(s_j \text{ and } I_1)$	$P(s_j \mid I_1)$
s_1	.25	.40	(.25)(.40) = .10	.12/.20 = .500
s_2	.40	.25	(.40)(.25) = .10	.10/.20 = .500
s_3	.35	0	(.35)(0) = .0	0/.20 = 0
			$P(I_1) = .20$	

Posterior Probabilities for I_2

s_j	$P(s_j)$	$P(I_2 \mid s_j)$	$P(s_j \text{ and } I_2)$	$P(s_j \mid I_2)$
s_1	.25	.30	(.25)(.30) = .075	.075/.28 = .268
s_2	.40	.25	(.40)(.25) = .10	.10/.28 = .357
s_3	.35	30	(.35)(.30) = .105	.105/.28 = .375
			$P(I_2) = .28$	

Posterior Probabilities for I_3

s_j	$P(s_j)$	$P(I_3 \mid s_j)$	$P(s_j \text{ and } I_3)$	$P(s_j \mid I_3)$
s_1	.25	.20	(.25)(.20) = .05	.05/.29 = .172
s_2	.40	.25	(.40)(.25) = .10	.10/.29 = .345
s_3	.35	.40	(.35)(.40) = .14	.14/.29 = .483
			$P(I_3) = .29$	

Posterior Probabilities for I_4

s_j	$P(s_j)$	$P(I_4 \mid s_j)$	$P(s_j \text{ and } I_4)$	$P(s_j \mid I_4)$
s_1	.25	.10	(.25)(.10) = .025	.025/.23 = .109
s_2	.40	.25	(.40)(.25) = .10	.10/.23 = .435
s_3	.35	.30	(.35)(.30) = .105	.105/.23 = .456
			$P(I_4) = .23$	

23.24a Prior probabilities: $EMV(a_1) = .5(10) + .5(22) = 16$

$EMV(a_2) = .5(18) + .5(19) = 18.5$

$EMV(a_3) = .5(23) + .5(15) = 19$

$EMV^* = 19$

I_1: $EMV(a_1) = .951(10) + .049(22) = 10.588$

$EMV(a_2) = .951(18) + .049(19) = 18.049$

$EMV(a_3) = .951(23) + .049(15) = 22.608$

Optimal act: a_3

I_2 : $EMV(a_1) = .021(10) + .979(22) = 21.748$

$EMV(a_2) = .021(18) + .979(19) = 18.979$

$EMV(a_3) = .021(23) + .979(15) = 15.168$

Optimal act: a_1

b $EMV` = .515(22.608) + .485(21.748) = 22.191$

$EVSI = EMV` - EMV^* = 22.191 – 19 = 3.191$

23.26 Prior probabilities: $EMV(a_1) = .5(60) + .4(90) + .1(150) = 81$

$EMV(a_2) = 90$

$EMV^* = 90$

Posterior Probabilities for I_1

s_j	$P(s_j)$	$P(I_1 \mid s_j)$	$P(s_j \text{ and } I_1)$	$P(s_j \mid I_1)$
s_1	.5	.7	(.5)(.7) = .35	.35/.57 = .614
s_2	.4	.5	(.4)(.5) = .20	.20/.57 = .351
s_3	.1	.2	(.1)(.2) = .02	.02/.57 = .035
			$P(I_1) = .57$	

Posterior Probabilities for I_2

s_j	$P(s_j)$	$P(I_2 \mid s_j)$	$P(s_j \text{ and } I_2)$	$P(s_j \mid I_2)$
s_1	.5	.3	(.5)(.3) = .15	.15/.43 = .349
s_2	.4	.5	(.4)(.5) = .20	.20/.43 = .465
s_3	.1	.8	(.1)(.8) = .08	.08/.43 = .186
			$P(I_1) = .43$	

I_1: $EMV(a_1) = .614(60) + .351(90) + .035(150) = 73.68$

$EMV(a_2) = 90$

I_1: $EMV(a_1) = .349(60) + .465(90) + .186(150) = 90.69$

$EMV(a_2) = 90$

EMV\` = .57(90) + .43(90.69) = 90.30

EVSI = EMV\` - EMV* = 90.30 – 90 = .30

23.28 As the prior probabilities become more diverse EVSI decreases.

23.30 EMV* = 0

EPPI = .15(0) + .45(2 million) + .40(8 million) = 4.1 million

EVPI = EPPI – EMV* = 4.1 million – 0 = 4.1 million

23.32a Payoff Table

Market share	Switch	Don't switch
5%	5(100,000) – 700,000 = -200,000	285,000
10%	10(100,000) – 700,000 = 300,000	285,000
20%	20(100,000)-700,000 = 1,300,000	285,000

b EMV(switch) = .4(-200,000) + .4(300,000) + .2(1,300,000) = 300,000

EMV(don't switch) = 285,000

Optimal act: switch (EMV* = 300,000)

c EPPI = .4(285,000) + .4(300,000) + .2(1,300,000) = 494,000

EVPI = EPPI – EMV* = 494,000 – 300,000= 194,000

23.34 Likelihood probabilities (binomial probabilities)

$P(I \mid s_1) = P(x = 12, n= 100 \mid p = .05) = .0028$

$P(I \mid s_2) = P(x = 12, n= 100 \mid p = .10) = .0988$

$P(I \mid s_3) = P(x = 12, n= 100 \mid p = .20) = .0128$

$P(I \mid s_4) = P(x = 12, n= 100 \mid p = .30) = .000013$

Posterior Probabilities

s_j	$P(s_j)$	$P(I \mid s_j)$	$P(s_j \text{ and } I)$	$P(s_j \mid I)$
s_1	. 5	.0028	(.5)(.0028) = .0014	.0014/.0323 = .0433
s_2	.3	.0988	(.3)(.0988) = .0296	.0296/.0323 = .9164
s_3	.1	.0128	(.1)(.0128) = .0013	.0013/.0323 = .0402
s_4	.1	.000013	(.1)(.000013) = .000001	.000001/.0323 = .000031
			P(I) = .0323	

EMV(proceed) = .0433(-30,000) + .9164(-5,000) + .0402(45,000) + .000031(95,000) = -4,069

EMV (don't proceed = 0

EMV decision: don't proceed

23.36

I_0 = neither person supports format change

I_1 = one person supports format change

I_2 = both people support format change

Likelihood probabilities $P(I_i \mid s_j)$

	I_0	I_1	I_2
5%	.9025	.0950	.0025
10%	.81	.18	.01
20%	.64	.32	.04

Posterior Probabilities for I_0

s_j	$P(s_j)$	$P(I_0 \mid s_j)$	$P(s_j \text{ and } I_0)$	$P(s_j \mid I_0)$
s_1	.4	.9025	(.4)(.9025) = .361	.361/.813 = .444
s_2	.4	.81	(.4)(.81) = .324	.324/.813 = .399
s_3	.2	.64	(.2)(.64) = .128	.128/.813 = .157
			$P(I_0)$ = .813	

Posterior Probabilities for I_1

s_j	$P(s_j)$	$P(I_1 \mid s_j)$	$P(s_j \text{ and } I_1)$	$P(s_j \mid I_1)$
s_1	.4	.0950	(.4)(.0950) = .038	.038/.174 = .218
s_2	.4	.18	(.4)(.18) = .072	.072/.174 = .414
s_3	.2	.32	(.2)(.32) = .064	.064/.174 = .368
			$P(I_1)$ = .174	

Posterior Probabilities for I_3

s_j	$P(s_j)$	$P(I_2 \mid s_j)$	$P(s_j \text{ and } I_2)$	$P(s_j \mid I_2)$
s_1	.4	.0025	(.4)(.0025) = .001	.001/.013 = .077
s_2	.4	.01	(.4)(.01) = .004	.004/.013 = .308
s_3	.2	.04	(.2)(.04) = .008	.008/.013 = .615
			$P(I_2)$ = .013	

I_1: EMV(switch) = .444(-200,000) + .399(300,000) + .157(1,300,000) = 235,000

EMV(don't switch) = 285,000

Optimal act: don't switch

I_2: EMV(switch) = .218(-200,000) + .414(300,000) + .368(1,300,000) = 559,000

EMV(don't switch) = 285,000

Optimal act: switch

I_3: EMV(switch) = .077(-200,000) + .308(300,000) + .615(1,300,000) = 876,500

EMV(don't switch) = 285,000

Optimal act: switch

EMV\` = .813(285,000) + .174(546,000) + .013(876,500) = 338,104

EVSI = EMV\` - EMV* = 338,104 – 300,000 = 38,104

23.38a Payoff Table

Demand	Battery 1	Battery 2	Battery 3
50,000	20(50,000)-900,000	23(50,000)-1,150,000	25(50,000)-1,400,000
	= 100,000	=0	=-150,000
100,000	20(100,000)-900,000	23(100,000)-1,150,000	25(100,000)-1,400,000
	=1,100,000	=1,150,000	=1,100,000
150,000	20(150,000)-900,000	23(150,000)-1,150,000	25(150,000)-1,400,000
	=2,100,000	=2,300,000	=2,350,000

b Opportunity Loss table

Demand	Battery 1	Battery 2	Batter3
50,000	0	100,000	250,000
100,000	50,000	0	50,000
150,000	250,000	50,000	9

c EMV(Battery 1) = .3(100,000) + .3(1,100,000) + .4(2,100,000) = 1,200,000

EMV(Battery 2) = .3(0) + .3(1,150,000) + .4(2,300,000) = 1,265,000

EMV(Battery 3) = .3(-150,000) + .3(1,100,000) + .4(2,350,000) = 1,225,000

EMV decision: Battery 2

d EOL(Battery 2) = .3(100,000) + .3(0) + .4(50,000) = 50,000

EVP = EOL* = 50,000

23.40

I_0 = person does not believe the ad

I_1 = person believes the ad

Likelihood probabilities $P(I_i \mid s_j)$

	I_0	I_1
30%	.70	.30
31%	.69	.31
32%	.68	.32
33%	.67	.33
34%	.66	.34

Posterior Probabilities for I_0

s_j	$P(s_j)$	$P(I_0 \mid s_j)$	$P(s_j \text{ and } I_0)$	$P(s_j \mid I_0)$
s_1	.1	.70	(.1)(.70) = .070	.070/.674 = .104
s_2	.1	.69	(.1)(.69) = .069	.069/.674 = .102
s_3	.2	.68	(.2)(.68) = .136	.136/.674 = .202
s_4	.3	.67	(.3)(.67) = .201	.201/.674 = .298
s_5	.3	.66	(.3)(.66) = .198	.198/.674 = .294
			$P(I_0)$ = .674	

Posterior Probabilities for I_1

s_j	$P(s_j)$	$P(I_1 \mid s_j)$	$P(s_j \text{ and } I_1)$	$P(s_j \mid I_1)$
s_1	.1	.30	(.1)(.30) = .030	.030/.326 = .092
s_2	.1	.31	(.1)(.31) = .031	.031/.326 = .095
s_3	.2	.32	(.2)(.32) = .064	.064/.326 = .196
s_4	.3	.33	(.3)(.33) = .099	.099/.326 = .304
s_5	.3	.34	(.3)(.34) = .102	.102/.326 = .313
			$P(I_1)$ = .326	

I_0: EMV(Change ad) = .104(-258,000) + .102(-158,000) + .202(-58,000) + .298(42,000) + .294(142,000) = -400

EMV (don't change) = 0.

Optimal decision: don't change ad

I_1: EMV(Change ad) = .092(-258,000) + .095(-158,000) + .196(-58,000) + .304(42,000) + .313(142,000) = 7,100

EMV (don't change) = 0.

Optimal decision: change ad

EMV` = .674(0) + .326(7,100) = 2,315

EVSI = EMV` - EMV* = 2,315 – 2,000 = 315

23.42

EMV(25 telephones) = 50,000

EMV(50 telephones) = .50(30,000) + .25(60,000) + .25(60,000) = 45,000

EMV(100 telephones) = .50(20,000) + .25(40,000) + .25(80,000) = 40,000

Optimal decision: 25 telephones (EMV* = 50,000)

I_1 = small number of calls

I_2 = medium number of calls

I_3 = large number of calls

Likelihood probabilities (Poisson distribution)

	I_1	I_2	I_3
$\mu = 5$	$P(X < 8 \mid \mu = 5)$	$P(8 \le X < 17 \mid \mu = 5)$	$P(X \ge 17 \mid \mu = 5)$
	= .8667	= .1334	= 0
$\mu = 10$	$P(X < 8 \mid \mu = 10)$	$P(8 \le X < 17 \mid \mu = 10)$	$P(X \ge 17 \mid \mu = 10)$
	= .2202	= .7527	= .0270
$\mu = 15$	$P(X < 8 \mid \mu = 15)$	$P(8 \le X < 17 \mid \mu = 15)$	$P(X \ge 17 \mid \mu = 15)$
	= .0180	= .6461	= .3359

Posterior Probabilities for I_1

s_j	$P(s_j)$	$P(I_1 \mid s_j)$	$P(s_j \text{ and } I_1)$	$P(s_j \mid I_1)$
s_1	.50	.8667	(.50)(.8667) = .4333	.4333/.4929 = .8792
s_2	.25	.2202	(.25)(.2202) = .0551	.0551/.4929 = .1117
s_3	.25	.0180	(.25)(.0180) = .0045	.0045/.4929 = .0091
			$P(I_1)$ = .4929	

Posterior Probabilities for I_2

s_j	$P(s_j)$	$P(I_2 \mid s_j)$	$P(s_j \text{ and } I_2)$	$P(s_j \mid I_2)$
s_1	.50	.1334	(.50)(.1334) = .0667	.0667/.4164 = .1601
s_2	.25	.7527	(.25)(.7527) = .1882	.1882/.4164 = .4519
s_3	.25	.6461	(.25)(.6461) = .1615	.1615/.4164 = .3879
			$P(I_2)$ = .4164	

Posterior Probabilities for I_3

s_j	$P(s_j)$	$P(I_3 \mid s_j)$	$P(s_j \text{ and } I_3)$	$P(s_j \mid I_3)$
s_1	.50	.0	(.50)(0) = 0	0/.0907 = 0
s_2	.25	.0270	(.25)(.0270) = .0068	.0068/.0907 = .0745
s_3	.25	.3359	(.25)(.3359) = .0840	.0840/.0907 = .9254
			$P(I_3)$ = .0907	

I_1: EMV(25 telephones) = 50,000

EMV(50 telephones) = .8792(30,000) + .1117(60,000) + .0091(60,000) = 33,624

EMV(100 telephones) = .8792(20,000) + .1117(40,000) + .0091(80,000) = 22,780

Optimal act: 25 telephones

I_2: EMV(25 telephones) = 50,000

EMV(50 telephones) = .1601(30,000) + .4519(60,000) + .3879(60,000) = 55,191

EMV(100 telephones) = .1601(20,000) + .4519(40,000) + .38791(80,000) = 52,310

Optimal act: 50 telephones

I_3: EMV(25 telephones) = 50,000

EMV(50 telephones) = 0(30,000) + .0745(60,000) + .9254(60,000) = 60,000

EMV(100 telephones) = 0(20,000) + .0745(40,000) + .9254(80,000) = 77,012

Optimal act: 100 telephones

EMV` = .4929(50,000) + .4164(55,191) + .0907(77,012) = 54,612

EVSI = EMV` - EMV* = 54,612 – 50,000 = 4,612

Because the value is greater than the cost ($4,000) Max should not sample. If he sees a small number of calls install 25 telephones. If there is a medium number install 50 telephones. If there is a large number of calls, install 100 telephones.

23.44 EMV(Release in North America) = .5(33 million) + .3(12 million) + .2(-15 million) = 17.1 million

EMV(European distributor) = 12 million

Optimal decision: Release in North America

Posterior Probabilities for I_1 (Rave review)

s_j	$P(s_j)$	$P(I_1 \mid s_j)$	$P(s_j \text{ and } I_1)$	$P(s_j \mid I_1)$
s_1	.5	.8	(.5)(.8) = .40	.40/.63 = .635
s_2	.3	.5	(.3)(.5) = .15	.15/.63 = .238
s_3	.2	.4	(.2)(.4) = .08	.08/.63 = .127
			$P(I_1)$ = .63	

EMV(Release in North America) = .635(33 million) + .238(12 million) + .127(-15 million) =21.9 million

EMV(European distributor) = 12 million

Optimal decision: Release in North America

Posterior Probabilities for I_2 (lukewarm response)

s_j	$P(s_j)$	$P(I_2 \mid s_j)$	$P(s_j \text{ and } I_2)$	$P(s_j \mid I_2)$
s_1	.5	.1	(.5)(.1) = .05	.05/.20 = .25
s_2	.3	.3	(.3)(.3) = .09	.09/.20 = .45
s_3	.2	.3	(.2)(.3) = .06	.06/.20 = .30
			$P(I_2)$ = .20	

EMV(Release in North America) = .25(33 million) + .45(12 million) + .30(-15 million) = 9.2 million

EMV(European distributor) = 12 million

Optimal decision: Sell to European distributor

Posterior Probabilities for I_3 (poor response)

s_j	$P(s_j)$	$P(I_3 \mid s_j)$	$P(s_j \text{ and } I_3)$	$P(s_j \mid I_3)$
s_1	.5	.1	(.5)(.1) = .05	.05/.17 = .294
s_2	.3	.2	(.3)(.2) = .06	.06/.17 = .353
s_3	.2	.3	(.2)(.3) = .06	.06/.17 = .353
			(I_3) = .17	

EMV(Release in North America) = .294(33 million) + .353(12 million) + .353(-15 million) = 8.6 million

EMV(European distributor) = 12 million

Optimal decision: Sell to European distributor.

EMV` = .63(21.9 million) + .20(12 million) + .17(12 million) = 18.2 million

EVSI = EMV` - EMV* = 18.2 million – 17.1 million = 1.1 million

Because EVSI is greater than the sampling cost (100,000) the studio executives should show the movie to a random sample of North Americans. If the response is a rave review release the movie in North America. If not sell it to Europe.

CHAPTER 24

24.2 z-test of p

$H_0: p = .5$

$H_1: p \neq .5$

$$z = \frac{\hat{p} - p}{\sqrt{\frac{p(1-p)}{n}}}$$

	A	B	C	D
1	**z-Test of a Proportion**			
2				
3	**Sample proportion**	0.88	**z Stat**	**3.15**
4	**Sample size**	17	**P(Z<=z) one-tail**	**0.0008**
5	**Hypothesized proportion**	0.5	**z Critical one-tail**	**1.6449**
6	**Alpha**	0.05	**P(Z<=z) two-tail**	**0.0016**
7			**z Critical two-tail**	**1.9600**

z = 3.15, p-value = .0016. There is overwhelming evidence to conclude that the new technology affects the sex of the baby.

24.4 t-test of μ_D

$H_0: \mu_D = 0$

$H_1: \mu_D < 0$

$$t = \frac{\bar{x}_D - \mu_D}{s_D / \sqrt{n_D}}$$

	A	B	C
1	t-Test: Paired Two Sample for Means		
2			
3		*Prior*	*After*
4	Mean	24.91	26.24
5	Variance	48.65	87.88
6	Observations	100	100
7	Pearson Correlation	0.79	
8	Hypothesized Mean Difference	0	
9	df	99	
10	t Stat	-2.29	
11	P(T<=t) one-tail	0.0121	
12	t Critical one-tail	1.6604	
13	P(T<=t) two-tail	0.0242	
14	t Critical two-tail	1.9842	

t = –2.29, p-value = .0121. There is enough evidence to conclude that company should proceed to stage 2.

24.6 a t-estimator of μ

t-Estimate: Mean			
			Overdue
Mean			7.0875
Standard Deviation			6.9682
LCL			6.4026
UCL			7.7724

b LCL = 50,000($.25)(6.4026) = $80,033

UCL = 50,000($.25)(7.7724) = $97,155

It does appear that not all fines are collected.

24.8 Chi-squared test of a contingency table

H_0 : The two variables are independent

H_1 : The two variables are dependent

$$\chi^2 = \sum_{i=1}^{6} \frac{(f_i - e_i)^2}{e_i}$$

	A	B	C	D	E
1	**Contingency Table**				
2					
3		*Age Category*			
4	*Alcohol*		1	2	TOTAL
5		1	87	325	412
6		2	44	297	341
7		3	87	214	301
8		TOTAL	218	836	1054
9					
10					
11		chi-squared Stat			25.0273
12		df			2
13		p-value			0
14		chi-squared Critical			5.9915

$\chi^2 = 25.0273$, p-value = 0. There is overwhelming evidence to infer that differences exist among the age categories with respect to alcohol use.

24.10 z-test of $p_1 - p_2$ (case 2)

$$H_0: p_1 - p_2 = -.15$$

$$H_1: p_1 - p_2 < -.15$$

$$z = \frac{(\hat{p}_1 - \hat{p}_2) - (p_1 - p_2)}{\sqrt{\frac{\hat{p}_1(1-\hat{p}_1)}{n_1} + \frac{\hat{p}_2(1-\hat{p}_2)}{n_2}}}$$

	A	B	C
1	**z-Test: Two Proportions**		
2			
3		*Comm 1*	*Comm 2*
4	Sample Proportions	0.268	0.486
5	Observations	500	500
6	Hypothesized Difference	-0.15	
7	z Stat	-2.28	
8	P(Z<=z) one tail	0.0114	
9	z Critical one-tail	1.6449	
10	P(Z<=z) two-tail	0.0228	
11	z Critical two-tail	1.9600	

$z = -2.28$, p-value = .0114. There is evidence to indicate that the second commercial is viable.

24.12 Analysis of variance, single-factor independent samples design

$H_0 : \mu_1 = \mu_2 = \mu_3$

H_1 : At least two means differ

F = MST/MSE

	A	B	C	D	E	F	G
10	ANOVA						
11	*Source of Variation*	*SS*	*df*	*MS*	*F*	*P-value*	*F crit*
12	Between Groups	3.34	2	1.67	0.17	0.8425	3.09
13	Within Groups	971.59	100	9.72			
14							
15	Total	974.93	102				

F = .17, p-value = .8425. There is not enough evidence to conclude that there are differences in reduction of low-density cholesterol between the three groups.

24.14 Multiple regression, test of coefficients

$$t = \frac{b_i - \beta_i}{s_{b_i}}$$

The ordinary multiple regression model fit quite well. The coefficient of determination is .7042 and the p-value of the F-test is 0. However, no independent variable is linearly related to salary. This is a clear sign of multicollinearity. Stepwise regression was used with the outcome shown below.

The only independent variables that are linearly related to salary are assists in 1992-93 and goals in 1992-93. It appears that players' salaries are most strongly related to the number of goals and the number of assists in the previous season.

	M	N	O	P	Q	R	S
1	**Results of stepwise regression**						
2							
3	**Step 1 - Entering variable: Ast92_93**						
4							
5	Summary measures						
6		Multiple R	0.7725				
7		R-Square	0.5967				
8		Adj R-Square	0.5883				
9		StErr of Est	380046.1250				
10							
11	ANOVA Table						
12		Source	df	SS	MS	F	p-value
13		Explained	1	10258242603399.2000	10258242603399.2000	71.0232	0.0000
14		Unexplained	48	6932882522112.0000	144435052544.0000		
15							
16	Regression coefficients						
17			Coefficient	Std Err	t-value	p-value	
18		Constant	38325.8711	82112.9297	0.4667	0.6428	
19		Ast92_93	25746.7754	3055.0806	8.4275	0.0000	
20							
21	**Step 2 - Entering variable: Goal92_93**						
22							
23	Summary measures			Change	% Change		
24		Multiple R	0.8086	0.0361	%4.7		
25		R-Square	0.6538	0.0571	%9.6		
26		Adj R-Square	0.6390	0.0507	%8.6		
27		StErr of Est	355859.9375	-24186.1875	-%6.4		
28							
29	ANOVA Table						
30		Source	df	SS	MS	F	p-value
31		Explained	2	11239219530119.2000	5619609765059.6100	44.3760	0.0000
32		Unexplained	47	5951905595392.0000	126636289263.6600		
33							
34	Regression coefficients						
35			Coefficient	Std Err	t-value	p-value	
36		Constant	65924.4297	77524.0313	0.8504	0.3994	
37		Ast92_93	14124.2783	5061.7593	2.7904	0.0076	
38		Goal92_93	18523.1426	6655.2490	2.7832	0.0077	

24.16 Analysis of variance, single-factor independent samples design

$H_0 : \mu_1 = \mu_2 = \mu_3$

H_1 : At least two means differ

F = MST/MSE

	A	B	C	D	E	F	G
10	ANOVA						
11	*Source of Variation*	*SS*	*df*	*MS*	*F*	*P-value*	*F crit*
12	Between Groups	91.43	2	45.72	1.09	0.3441	3.16
13	Within Groups	2397.5	57	42.06			
14							
15	Total	2488.9	59				

F = 1.09, p-value = .3441. There is no evidence to infer that sales of cigarettes differ according to placement.

24.18 t-test of μ

$$H_0: \mu = 480$$

$$H_1: \mu < 480$$

$$t = \frac{\bar{x} - \mu}{s / \sqrt{n}}$$

	A	B	C	D
1	**t-Test: Mean**			
2				
3				*Complaints*
4	Mean			460.53
5	Standard Deviation			81.10
6	Hypothesized Mean			480
7	df			29
8	t Stat			-1.31
9	P(T<=t) one-tail			0.0994
10	t Critical one-tail			1.6991
11	P(T<=t) two-tail			0.1988
12	t Critical two-tail			2.0452

t = –1.31, p-value = .0994. There is little evidence to conclude that the seminars should be instituted.

24.20 t-tests of μ_D

a $$H_0: \mu_D = 40$$

$$H_1: \mu_D > 40$$

$$t = \frac{\bar{x}_D - \mu_D}{s_D / \sqrt{n_D}}$$

	A	B	C
1	t-Test: Paired Two Sample for Means		
2			
3		*SAT after*	*SAT before*
4	Mean	1235	1162
5	Variance	37970	28844
6	Observations	40	40
7	Pearson Correlation	0.94	
8	Hypothesized Mean Difference	40	
9	df	39	
10	t Stat	2.98	
11	P(T<=t) one-tail	0.0024	
12	t Critical one-tail	1.6849	
13	P(T<=t) two-tail	0.0049	
14	t Critical two-tail	2.0227	

t = 2.98, p-value = .0024. There is enough evidence to conclude that the ETS claim is false.

b $H_0 : \mu_D = 110$

$H_1 : \mu_D < 110$

$$t = \frac{\bar{x}_D - \mu_D}{s_D / \sqrt{n_D}}$$

	A	B	C
1	t-Test: Paired Two Sample for Means		
2			
3		*SAT after*	*SAT before*
4	Mean	1235	1162
5	Variance	37970	28844
6	Observations	40	40
7	Pearson Correlation	0.94	
8	Hypothesized Mean Difference	110	
9	df	39	
10	t Stat	-3.39	
11	P(T<=t) one-tail	0.0008	
12	t Critical one-tail	1.6849	
13	P(T<=t) two-tail	0.0016	
14	t Critical two-tail	2.0227	

t = –3.39, p-value = .0008. There is enough evidence to conclude that the Kaplan claim is also false.

24.22 a t-test of μ

$$H_0: \mu = 0$$

$$H_1: \mu > 0$$

$$t = \frac{\overline{x} - \mu}{s / \sqrt{n}}$$

	A	B	C	D
1	**t-Test: Mean**			
2				
3				*Decrease*
4	Mean			24.73
5	Standard Deviation			17.92
6	Hypothesized Mean			0
7	df			222
8	t Stat			20.61
9	P(T<=t) one-tail			0
10	t Critical one-tail			1.6517
11	P(T<=t) two-tail			0
12	t Critical two-tail			1.9707

t = 20.61, p-value = 0. There is overwhelming evidence to infer that there is a decrease in metabolism when children watch television.

b Wilcoxon rank sum test

H_0: The two population locations are the same.

H_1: The location of population 1 is to the right of the location of population 2.

$$z = \frac{T - E(T)}{\sigma_T}$$

	A	B	C	D
1	**Wilcoxon Rank Sum Test**			
2				
3			Rank Sum	Observations
4	*Obese*		5750	41
5	*Non-obese*		19226	182
6	z Stat		3.10	
7	P(Z<=z) one-tail		0.0010	
8	z Critical one-tail		1.6449	
9	P(Z<=z) two-tail		0.0020	
10	z Critical two-tail		1.9600	

z = 3.10, p-value = .0010. There is enough evidence to conclude that the decrease in metabolism is greater among obese children.

24.24 Two-factor analysis of variance

F = MS(AB)/MSE

F = MS(A)/MSE

F = MS(B)/MSE

	A	B	C	D	E	F	G
29	ANOVA						
30	*Source of Variation*	*SS*	*df*	*MS*	*F*	*P-value*	*F crit*
31	Sample	427.61	2	213.81	39.97	0.0000	3.06
32	Columns	20.17	1	20.17	3.77	0.0541	3.91
33	Interaction	17.77	2	8.89	1.66	0.1935	3.06
34	Within	770.32	144	5.35			
35							
36	Total	1235.87	149				

Test for gender: F = 3.77, p-value = .0541. There is not enough evidence of a difference between men and women.

Test for fitness: F = 39.97, p-value = 0. There is overwhelming evidence of differences among the three levels of fitness.

Test for interaction: F = 1.66, p-value = .1935. There is no evidence of interaction.

24.26 Multiple regression t-tests of the coefficients

$$H_0: \beta_i = 0$$

$$H_1: \beta_i \neq 0$$

$$t = \frac{b_i - \beta_i}{s_{b_i}}$$

	A	B	C	D	E
16		*Coefficients*	*Standard Error*	*t Stat*	*P-value*
17	Intercept	1.01	1.39	0.72	0.4704
18	Dexterity	-0.059	0.150	-0.39	0.6953
19	Detail	-0.177	0.16	-1.11	0.2708
20	Teamwork	0.182	0.16	1.16	0.2485
21	Math	0.065	0.16	0.40	0.6874
22	ProbSolve	1.00	0.16	6.27	0.0000
23	Tech	1.78	0.16	11.24	0.0000

Only problem-solving skill (p-value = 0) and technical knowledge (p-value = 0) are linearly related to quality.

24.28 a Equal-variances t-test of $\mu_1 - \mu_2$

$$H_0: (\mu_1 - \mu_2) = 0$$

$$H_1: (\mu_1 - \mu_2) < 0$$

$$t = \frac{(\bar{x}_1 - \bar{x}_2) - (\mu_1 - \mu_2)}{\sqrt{s_p^2\left(\frac{1}{n_1} + \frac{1}{n_2}\right)}}$$

	A	B	C
1	t-Test: Two-Sample Assuming Equal Variances		
2			
3		*4 or more*	*Less*
4	Mean	6.00	7.40
5	Variance	5.62	8.61
6	Observations	100	100
7	Pooled Variance	7.11	
8	Hypothesized Mean Difference	0	
9	df	198	
10	t Stat	-3.71	
11	P(T<=t) one-tail	0.0001	
12	t Critical one-tail	1.6526	
13	P(T<=t) two-tail	0.0003	
14	t Critical two-tail	1.9720	

$t = -3.71$, p-value = .0001. There is enough evidence to infer that children who wash their hands four or more times per day have less sick days due to cold and flu.

b Wilcoxon rank sum test

H_0: The two population locations are the same.

H_1: The location of population 1 is to the left of the location of population 2.

$$z = \frac{T - E(T)}{\sigma_T}$$

	A	B	C	D
1	**Wilcoxon Rank Sum Test**			
2				
3			Rank Sum	Observations
4	*4 or more*		7584	100
5	*Less*		12516	100
6	z Stat		-6.03	
7	P(Z<=z) one-tail		0	
8	z Critical one-tail		1.6449	
9	P(Z<=z) two-tail		0	
10	z Critical two-tail		1.9600	

z = –6.03, p-value = 0. There is enough evidence to infer that children who wash their hands four or more times per day have less sick days due to stomach illness.

24.30 Equal-variances t-test of $\mu_1 - \mu_2$

$$H_0: (\mu_1 - \mu_2) = 0$$

$$H_1: (\mu_1 - \mu_2) < 0$$

$$t = \frac{(\bar{x}_1 - \bar{x}_2) - (\mu_1 - \mu_2)}{\sqrt{s_p^2\left(\frac{1}{n_1} + \frac{1}{n_2}\right)}}$$

	A	B	C
1	t-Test: Two-Sample Assuming Equal Variances		
2			
3		*Activity*	*Usual*
4	Mean	57.06	87.28
5	Variance	296.18	215.42
6	Observations	67	67
7	Pooled Variance	255.80	
8	Hypothesized Mean Difference	0.00	
9	df	132	
10	t Stat	-10.94	
11	P(T<=t) one-tail	0.0000	
12	t Critical one-tail	1.6565	
13	P(T<=t) two-tail	0.0000	
14	t Critical two-tail	1.9781	

t = –10.94, p-value = 0. There is enough evidence to indicate to infer that graded activity is effective.

24.32 a Chi-squared test of a contingency table

H_0 : The two variables are independent

H_1 : The two variables are dependent

$$\chi^2 = \sum_{i=1}^{24} \frac{(f_i - e_i)^2}{e_i}$$

	A	B	C	D	E	F	G
1	**Contingency Table**						
2							
3		*Source*					
4	*Heartburn*		1	2	3	4	TOTAL
5		1	60	23	13	25	121
6		2	65	19	14	28	126
7		3	73	26	9	24	132
8		4	67	11	10	7	95
9		5	57	16	9	14	96
10		6	47	21	10	10	88
11		TOTAL	369	116	65	108	658
12							
13							
14		chi-squared Stat			22.358		
15		df			15		
16		p-value			0.0988		
17		chi-squared Critical			24.9958		

$\chi^2 = 22.358$, p-value = .0988. There is not enough evidence to infer that there is a relationship between adults' source of news and his or her heartburn condition.

b Chi-squared test of a contingency table

H_0 : The two variables are independent

H_1 : The two variables are dependent

$$\chi^2 = \sum_{i=1}^{4} \frac{(f_i - e_i)^2}{e_i}$$

	A	B	C	D	E	F	G
1	**Contingency Table**						
2							
3		*Source*					
4	*Heartburn*		1	2	3	4	TOTAL
5		1	198	68	36	77	379
6		2	171	48	29	31	279
7		TOTAL	369	116	65	108	658
8							
9							
10		chi-squared Stat			10.8227		
11		df			3		
12		p-value			0.0127		
13		chi-squared Critical			7.8147		

$\chi^2 = 10.8227$, p-value = .0127. There is enough evidence to infer that there is a difference in heartburn condition between adults over 50 who watch network news and those who don't.

c z-test of $p_1 - p_2$ (case 1). (Success = 4)

$$H_0: (p_1 - p_2) = 0$$

$$H_1: (p_1 - p_2) > 0$$

$$z = \frac{(\hat{p}_1 - \hat{p}_2)}{\sqrt{\hat{p}(1-\hat{p})\left(\frac{1}{n_1} + \frac{1}{n_2}\right)}}$$

	A	B	C	D
1	**z-Test: Two Proportions**			
2				
3			*Network*	*Other*
4	Sample Proportions		0.2032	0.1111
5	Observations		379	279
6	Hypothesized Difference		0	
7	z Stat		3.15	
8	P(Z<=z) one tail		0.0008	
9	z Critical one-tail		1.6449	
10	P(Z<=z) two-tail		0.0016	
11	z Critical two-tail		1.9600	

z = 3.15, p-value = .0008. There is enough evidence to conclude that adults over 50 who watch network news are more likely to suffer from heartburn and take a prescription pill than those who do not watch network news.

24.34a Chi-squared goodness-of-fit test

$H_0: p_2 = 1/36,\ p_3 = 2/36, \ldots,\ p_{12} = 1/36$

H_1 : At least one p_i is not equal to its specified value

$$\chi^2 = \sum \frac{(f_i - e_i)^2}{e_i}$$

	A	B	C	D
1	Total	Actual	Probability	Expected
2	2	37	0.0278	27.78
3	3	59	0.0556	55.56
4	4	77	0.0833	83.33
5	5	120	0.1111	111.11
6	6	134	0.1389	138.89
7	7	161	0.1667	166.67
8	8	144	0.1389	138.89
9	9	117	0.1111	111.11
10	10	67	0.0833	83.33
11	11	52	0.0556	55.56
12	12	32	0.0278	27.78
13			p-value	0.4943

p-value = .4943. There is no evidence to indicate that the dice are not fairly balanced.

b z-test of p

$H_0: p = 1/6$

$H_1: p < 1/6$

$$z = \frac{\hat{p} - p}{\sqrt{\frac{p(1-p)}{n}}}$$

	A	B	C	D
1	**z-Test: Proportion**			
2				
3				*Dice = 7*
4	Sample Proportion			0.161
5	Observations			1000
6	Hypothesized Proportion			0.1667
7	z Stat			-0.48
8	P(Z<=z) one-tail			0.3143
9	z Critical one-tail			1.6449
10	P(Z<=z) two-tail			0.6286
11	z Critical two-tail			1.9600

$z = -.48$, p-value = .3143. There is no evidence to infer that the dice are set up so that the probability of 7 is less than 6/36.

24.36 Question 1: Equal-variances t-test of $\mu_1 - \mu_2$

$$H_0: (\mu_1 - \mu_2) = 0$$

$$H_1: (\mu_1 - \mu_2) < 0$$

$$t = \frac{(\bar{x}_1 - \bar{x}_2) - (\mu_1 - \mu_2)}{\sqrt{s_p^2\left(\frac{1}{n_1} + \frac{1}{n_2}\right)}}$$

	A	B	C
1	t-Test: Two-Sample Assuming Equal Variances		
2			
3		*US Days*	*Canada Days*
4	Mean	26.98	29.44
5	Variance	55.90	56.82
6	Observations	300	300
7	Pooled Variance	56.36	
8	Hypothesized Mean Difference	0	
9	df	598	
10	t Stat	-4.00	
11	P(T<=t) one-tail	0.0000	
12	t Critical one-tail	1.6474	
13	P(T<=t) two-tail	0.0001	
14	t Critical two-tail	1.9639	

$t = -4.00$, p-value = 0. There is enough evidence to indicate that recovery is faster in the United States.

Question 2: z-tests of $p_1 - p_2$ (case 1)

$$H_0: (p_1 - p_2) = 0$$

$$H_1: (p_1 - p_2) < 0$$

$$z = \frac{(\hat{p}_1 - \hat{p}_2)}{\sqrt{\hat{p}(1-\hat{p})\left(\frac{1}{n_1} + \frac{1}{n_2}\right)}}$$

	A	B	C	D
1	**z-Test: Two Proportions**			
2				
3			*U.S.*	*Canada*
4	Sample Proportions		0.6267	0.6867
5	Observations		300	300
6	Hypothesized Difference		0	
7	z Stat		-1.55	
8	P(Z<=z) one tail		0.0609	
9	z Critical one-tail		1.6449	
10	P(Z<=z) two-tail		0.1218	
11	z Critical two-tail		1.9600	

z = –1.55, p-value = .0609. There is not enough evidence to infer that recovery is faster in the United States.

6 months after heart attack:

	A	B	C	D
1	**z-Test: Two Proportions**			
2				
3			*U.S.*	*Canada*
4	Sample Proportions		0.1867	0.1733
5	Observations		300	300
6	Hypothesized Difference		0	
7	z Stat		0.43	
8	P(Z<=z) one tail		0.3354	
9	z Critical one-tail		1.6449	
10	P(Z<=z) two-tail		0.6708	
11	z Critical two-tail		1.9600	

z = .43, p-value = 1 - .3354 = .6646. There is no evidence to infer that recovery is faster in the United States.

12 months after heart attack

	A	B	C	D
1	**z-Test: Two Proportions**			
2				
3			*U.S.*	*Canada*
4	Sample Proportions		0.1167	0.1100
5	Observations		300	300
6	Hypothesized Difference		0	
7	z Stat		0.26	
8	P(Z<=z) one tail		0.3984	
9	z Critical one-tail		1.6449	
10	P(Z<=z) two-tail		0.7968	
11	z Critical two-tail		1.9600	

z = .26, p-value = 1 – .3984 = .6016. There is no evidence to infer that recovery is faster in the United States.

24.38 b Two-factor analysis of variance

F=MS(AB)/MSE

F = MS(A)/MSE

F = MS(B)/MSE

Product C

	A	B	C	D	E	F	G
23	ANOVA						
24	*Source of Variation*	*SS*	*df*	*MS*	*F*	*P-value*	*F crit*
25	Sample	425.07	1	425.07	14.06	0.0004	4.02
26	Columns	223.05	2	111.53	3.69	0.0315	3.17
27	Interaction	62.48	2	31.24	1.03	0.3628	3.17
28	Within	1632.94	54	30.24			
29							
30	Total	2343.54	59				

Test for flow: F = 3.69, p-value = .0315. There is evidence to infer that there are differences in yield among the three flows.

Test for temperature: F = 14.06, p-value = .0004. There is evidence to infer that there are differences in yield between the two temperatures

Test for interaction: F = 1.03, p-value = .3628. There is no evidence of interaction.

Product Y

	A	B	C	D	E	F	G
23	ANOVA						
24	*Source of Variation*	*SS*	*df*	*MS*	*F*	*P-value*	*F crit*
25	Sample	405.08	1	405.08	32.05	0.0000	4.02
26	Columns	1714.94	2	857.47	67.85	0.0000	3.17
27	Interaction	354.63	2	177.32	14.03	0.0000	3.17
28	Within	682.49	54	12.64			
29							
30	Total	3157.14	59				

Test for flow: F = 67.85, p-value = 0. There is evidence to infer that there are differences in yield among the three flows.

Test for temperature: F = 32.05, p-value = 0. There is evidence to infer that there are differences in yield between the two temperatures

Test for interaction: F = 14.03, p-value = 0. There is enough evidence to conclude that temperature and flow interact to affect product yield.

24.40 One-way analysis of variance

$H_0: \mu_1 = \mu_2 = \mu_3$

H_1 : At least two means differ

F = MST/MSE

	A	B	C	D	E	F	G
10	ANOVA						
11	*Source of Variation*	*SS*	*df*	*MS*	*F*	*P-value*	*F crit*
12	Between Groups	595.6	2	297.81	34.35	0.0000	3.06
13	Within Groups	1144.5	132	8.67			
14							
15	Total	1740.1	134				

F = 34.35, p-value = 0. There is enough evidence to conclude that the type of music affects test results.

24.42 a Wilcoxon rank sum test

H_0 : The two population locations are the same.

H_1 :The location of population 1 is different from the location of population 2.

$$z = \frac{T - E(T)}{\sigma_T}$$

	A	B	C	D
1	**Wilcoxon Rank Sum Test**			
2				
3			Rank Sum	Observations
4	*Adults*		4248	60
5	*Students*		3012	60
6	z Stat		3.24	
7	P(Z<=z) one-tail		0.0006	
8	z Critical one-tail		1.6449	
9	P(Z<=z) two-tail		0.0012	
10	z Critical two-tail		1.9600	

z = 3.24, p-value = .0012. There is overwhelming evidence of a difference between the two groups.

b Students are poor surrogates for adults in marketing studies.

24.44 Case 24.1: Wilcoxon rank sum test

H_0 : The two population locations are the same.

H_1 : The location of population 1 is to the left of the location of population 2.

$$z = \frac{T - E(T)}{\sigma_T}$$

	A	B	C	D
1	**Wilcoxon Rank Sum Test**			
2				
3			Rank Sum	Observations
4	*W Rate*		64365.5	101
5	*M Rate*		490565.5	952
6	z Stat		3.83	
7	P(Z<=z) one-tail		0.0001	
8	z Critical one-tail		1.6449	
9	P(Z<=z) two-tail		0.0002	
10	z Critical two-tail		1.9600	

z = 3.83, p-value = .0001. There is enough evidence to conclude that women pay higher rates of interest than men.

Case 24.2 Relationship between interest rates and sales: Spearman rank correlation coefficient test

$H_0 : \rho_S = 0$

$H_1 : \rho_S \neq 0$

$z = r_S \sqrt{n-1}$

	A	B	C	D
1	**Spearman Rank Correlation**			
2				
3	*Rates and Sales*			
4	Spearman Rank Correlation			-0.2629
5	z Stat			-8.53
6	P(Z<=z) one tail			0
7	z Critical one tail			1.6449
8	P(Z<=z) two tail			0
9	z Critical two tail			1.9600

$z = -8.53$, p-value = 0. There is overwhelming evidence to infer that interest rates and sales are linearly related.

Relationship between interest rates and ages: Spearman rank correlation coefficient test

$$H_0: \rho_S = 0$$

$$H_1: \rho_S \neq 0$$

$$z = r_S \sqrt{n-2}$$

	A	B	C	D
1	**Spearman Rank Correlation**			
2				
3	*Rates and Age*			
4	Spearman Rank Correlation			-0.1853
5	z Stat			-6.01
6	P(Z<=z) one tail			0
7	z Critical one tail			1.6449
8	P(Z<=z) two tail			0
9	z Critical two tail			1.9600

$z = -6.01$, p-value = 0. There is overwhelming evidence to infer that interest rates and age of business are linearly related.

Difference between sales: Wilcoxon rank sum test

H_0: The two population locations are the same.

H_1: The location of population 1 is to the left of the location of population 2.

$$z = \frac{T - E(T)}{\sigma_T}$$

	A	B	C	D
1	**Wilcoxon Rank Sum Test**			
2				
3			Rank Sum	Observations
4	*W Sales*		12285	101
5	*M Sales*		542646	952
6	z Stat		-14.09	
7	P(Z<=z) one-tail		0	
8	z Critical one-tail		1.6449	
9	P(Z<=z) two-tail		0	
10	z Critical two-tail		1.9600	

z = –14.09, p-value = 0. There is sufficient evidence to conclude that businesses owned by women have lower sales than businesses owned by men.

Difference between ages: Wilcoxon rank sum test

H_0 : The two population locations are the same.

H_1 : The location of population 1 is to the left of the location of population 2.

$$z = \frac{T - E(T)}{\sigma_T}$$

	A	B	C	D
1	**Wilcoxon Rank Sum Test**			
2				
3			Rank Sum	Observations
4	*W Age*		35034.5	101
5	*M Age*		519896.5	952
6	z Stat		-6.26	
7	P(Z<=z) one-tail		0	
8	z Critical one-tail		1.6449	
9	P(Z<=z) two-tail		0	
10	z Critical two-tail		1.9600	

z = –6.26, p-value = 0. There is sufficient evidence to conclude that businesses owned by men are older than businesses owned by women.

Interest rates among the 3 types of businesses: Kruskal Wallis test

H_0 : The locations of all 3 populations are the same

H_1 : At least two population locations differ

$$H = \left[\frac{12}{n(n+1)}\sum\frac{T_j^2}{n_j}\right] - 3(n+1)$$

	A	B	C
1	**Kruskal-Wallis Test**		
2			
3	Group	Rank Sum	Observations
4	*Bus 1*	111554	193
5	*Bus 2*	42305.5	86
6	*Bus 3*	401071.5	774
7			
8	H Stat		7.22
9	df		2
10	p-value		0.0270
11	chi-squared Critical		5.9915

H = 7.22, p-value = .0270. There is enough evidence to conclude that there are differences in interest rates among the three types of business.